# A Practical Approach to Content Area Reading

**Richard P. Santeusanio, Ed.D.**

**Director of Reading and Special Services**
**Danvers Public Schools**

**Addison–Wesley Publishing Company**
**Reading, Massachusetts · Menlo Park, California · London**
**Amsterdam · Don Mills, Ontario · Sydney**

**Library of Congress Cataloging in Publication Data**

Santeusanio, Richard P., 1942–
  A practical approach to content area reading.

  Includes bibliographies and index.
  1. Reading (Secondary)   2. Developmental reading.
I. Title.
LB1632.S33          428.4'3'0712          82–6740
ISBN 0–201–07407–9

ISBN 0–201–07407–9
ABCDEFGHIJ–HA–898765432

*To my parents, Romeo and Louise*

. . . *for all the times I should have*
*appreciated them,*
*thanked them,*
*hugged them*
*but didn't.*

*All those times when I forgot to,*
*neglected to,*
*meant to,*
*but for whatever reason*
*didn't.**

\* Adapted from Bette Green, *Get on out of here, Philip Hall* (New York: Dial Press, 1981).

# Preface

The popular press and the professional literature have reported conflicting opinions on the reading ability of today's students. While the question of whether students read better or worse today than they did fifty years ago will be debated continually, most people will agree that a large number of students have difficulty applying reading and study skills to the content areas.

## Reading Programs: The Problems and a Solution

Even though many school systems have tried to improve the quality of their reading programs by adding reading laboratories to their middle, junior, and senior high schools, some students continue to have problems reading complex secondary textbooks. Why is this so? One reason relates to the methods and materials used in secondary reading classes. Too many reading teachers approach the teaching of reading as a subject rather than as a process that applies to *all* subjects. Their instructional materials often include the ubiquitous reading kits and workbooks, individualized learning centers and packets, and fancy, expensive reading machines. Academic textbooks or trade books are rarely seen in the reading lab, though these are the very works the school wishes the students were able to read.

Another explanation lies with the content area teachers, some of whom resist teaching reading in their academic disciplines. Yet paradoxically many of these same teachers do not realize they are addressing themselves to reading skills when, for example, the English instructor teaches the "parts of the plot" and the social studies teacher helps students with the construction of time lines. These teachers must be made aware of the skills they already possess and be given the training and support to refine their skills.

The solution to the problem, therefore, is to train or retrain both reading teachers and content area teachers to teach the reading skills adolescents need in order to master the content areas. Thus, to some extent, endorsement is given to the cliché that "every teacher is a teacher of reading." Reading teachers must bring real textbooks to their reading classes and use them as the basis of reading improvement exercises. They must lay aside kits and special materials that foster the notion that reading is a separate content area. Content area teachers, on the other hand, must bring appropriate reading skills into their teaching of content. They must analyze their reading assignments, determine the reading skills students need to comprehend the assignments, and make a deliberate attempt to integrate the teaching of those skills with the teaching of their subject matter.

## Objectives of the Text

The purpose of this book, then, is to provide preservice and in-service reading and content area teachers with specific, practical, and effective techniques for incorporating the teaching of reading with the various academic disciplines. The techniques are based on a definition of reading that stresses the interaction of writers and readers. Writers begin with their ideas, which are then put into writing or, stated differently, translated to the written medium. The readers' task is to translate the written medium back to the thoughts or ideas and to react to the ideas.

The techniques suggested in this book are designed to assist teachers with their responsibility for helping students reconstruct and evaluate the ideas authors have put into print. Readers of this text, however, should not expect just a cookbook of reading recipes. All topics, techniques, and models suggested are accompanied with some theory and rationale as well as related research.

## Outline of the Text

Most chapters in the book begin with a brief, fictionalized, school-related situation that is germane to the topic(s) to be covered in the chapter. The situation typically reaches a climax or turning point and ends. Readers should then study the information contained in the chapter. Doing so will help readers understand more fully the concise resolution or outcome at the end of the chapter.

Chapter 1, "Teaching Reading in the Secondary Schools," begins with a review of elementary reading programs and continues with a discussion of the reading process and a rationale for middle and secondary content area reading programs. Chapter 2, "Developing Readiness for Reading Assignments," introduces readers to several procedures for preparing students for reading assignments. These are techniques teachers can use *before* students tackle the textbook chapters.

The next three chapters deal with the organization of written communication, including patterns such as main idea, data, sequence, cause/effect, and persuasive. Each of these chapters contains a review of literature and research relative to the pattern; reproductions from middle and secondary textbooks that exemplify the pattern; practical techniques for teaching the pattern; and specific models that help students apply the skills to the secondary content areas of English, science, social studies, business education and, when applicable, mathematics and real life functional or survival reading areas. Interlinear comments are included in these models to highlight their virtues or uniqueness.

Chapter 6, "Developing Self-Directed Study Techniques," demonstrates how the comprehension patterns and skills interrelate with study skills such as SQ3R and note taking. Most of the information contained in the comprehension and study skills chapters provides teachers with suggestions for activities students can complete *during* their reading and *after* their reading assignment has been completed.

The topic of Chapter 7, "Identifying Student Needs," appears toward the end of the text because the author feels teachers must understand the basic components of reading and study skills before diagnosing them. This section includes a discussion of achievement tests, individual reading inventories, group reading inventories, and cloze tests. The chapter also contains a section on learning styles, an area of considerable concern and interest to many educators.

Chapter 8, "Applying Readability Formulas," reviews the advantages and disadvantages of techniques designed to determine the reading level of textbooks. Chapter 9, "Accommodating Students with Special Needs," reviews ways of identifying learning-disabled and gifted children and procedures for differentiating instruction for them.

Chapter 10, the final chapter, concisely reviews the basic strategies teachers can use to help students master material contained in reading assignments. The chapter also describes the ways content area reading programs are organized in different school systems.

In summary, this book presents a workable program for the interaction of reading and content area teachers. My experiences have demonstrated that if practical, easily applied techniques are presented to reading and content teachers, the techniques will be used—to the benefit, it is hoped, of many middle and high school students.

## Acknowledgments

I wish to acknowledge those who assisted in the development of this book. First, the support, suggestions, and friendship of editor Brian Walker helped to make this project an enjoyable one. My thanks go to editor Linda Fisher for directing final phases of the book's publication. I am indebted to John Savage and Dixie Lee Spiegel for their careful, critical reading of and cogent suggestions for the manuscript. Appreciation is extended to the students and teachers in the Danvers, Massachusetts, School System for contributing to my understanding of the various facets of content area reading programs. I wish to thank my supervisors and the Danvers School Committee for giving me the opportunity to implement many of the ideas contained in this book.

Special thanks go to Alphonse Tatarunis, for his assistance with the preparation of Chapter 10, and to the following people for sharing their ideas with me on organizing content area reading programs: Pamela Mason, Catherine Earhart, Rose Feinberg, Patricia Avolio, Dorothy Ryan, Ellen Stoppe-Gorsey, Karen J. McNall, Elaine Rosen, Vida Gavin, Elinor Reynolds, Barbara Conley, Lynn Fletcher, Barbara Hunt, and Shirley Harwood. I wish to acknowledge Cynthia Homer, Kathy Amico, Harry Christensen, and Morris Shapiro for reviewing and offering their suggestions on portions of the text. I also wish to thank those who helped to type the manuscript, Judy Kuell and Kay Cappola. Last, but not least, I am greatly indebted to my wife, Joan, and our children, David and Christine, who once again gave me their time and love.

Marblehead, Mass.                                                            RPS
September 1982

# Contents

# Chapter 4.  Recognizing Sequence and Cause/Effect

# Chapter 5.  Evaluating Persuasive Techniques

# Chapter 9.  Accommodating Students with Special Needs     337

# Chapter 10.  Summing Up                                     367

# Index                                                       377

# Chapter 1

# Teaching Reading
# in the Secondary
# School

# Pleading His Case, Part I

"Remember," said Superintendent of Schools Dr. Charles Goring, "you need three school committee votes besides my support to get your new reading specialist."

"I know," replied Reading Director Fred Sears. "When are the school committee budget hearings?"

"Some time next month. I'll try to let you know a week ahead of time. We're going to have trouble with Gordon Harvey and Mrs. Lazarus. They are adamant about keeping the budget down. I don't think we have to worry about Langley and Slevin. They usually go along with me. I'm never sure about Page; he's always on the fence."

It was only three weeks later when Fred parked his car in the high school parking lot and headed for the principal's conference room, where the school committee's budget hearings were being held. Fred was scheduled to present his case for adding to his reading staff of eight. He was a little early, so he reviewed his notes while he waited to be called into the meeting. Fred was a bit nervous; he disliked making these presentations and the fact that Dr. Goring didn't call him into the meeting until 8:30 didn't help matters.

As Goring escorted Fred to the conference room, he whispered with a smile, "Give 'em hell, Fred." Fred felt a bit reassured.

"We are sorry, Mr. Sears, for keeping you waiting. But you know how these meetings can be. I presume you know all the members of the committee. As chairperson of the committee, I'll try to keep your portion of the budget hearing down to no more than fifteen minutes."

"That's fine, Mrs. Langley."

"Now we see here," continued Mrs. Langley, "you have a request for an additional reading specialist at the secondary level. Mr. Sears, could you go over your rationale for making the request?"

"I'd be happy to," answered Sears. Fred then told the committee that he wanted to add to the staff a reading specialist who would provide direct instruction in content area classrooms rather than only in the reading laboratory.

"There are two advantages to this," he said. "First, students learn reading skills and subject matter simultaneously. Therefore the application of reading skills to the content areas is not left to chance. Second, the reading department will be able to serve more students, because students who ordinarily are not enrolled in remedial reading, but who still have trouble applying skills to content areas, would get assistance.

"Another positive aspect of the program in content area reading instruction is that classroom teachers are provided with in-service training without having to attend classes after school. For example, the techniques utilized by the reading specialists are often adopted by the classroom teachers, who employ the techniques in their content classes. In summary, adding a new reading specialist will allow us to implement a program in content area reading that will enable our students to become more efficient readers of their textbooks."

At this point some members of the school committee expressed their opinions on the request. Then chairperson Langley asked, "Does anybody in the audience have any questions or comments? Yes, I see Mrs. St. Charles has her hand up."

"I just want to say that my son Michael, who I think is a good reader, brings his science book home every night and struggles with that book. I try to help him, but I never had books like that when I was in school. At least they wrote them back in those days, I hate to say how long ago, so that we could understand them. I'd really like to see somebody help my Michael. I'm all for this new teacher."

"Thank you, Mrs. St. Charles. Anybody else? Ah yes, Mr. Ryan."

"I'm all for education, you know. But the budget already is too high. When's it all going to end? Every year we're adding more teachers and new programs that cost so much money—like that fancy elementary science program that looks like kids are playing games all the time. Let's start cutting back instead of adding!"

"Thank you for your comments," said Mrs. Langley. "Unless anybody else has anything to say, let's vote on this request. I'd like Mr. Sears to summarize his position on this for us."

"We feel," began Sears, "that we want to assist students with reading all types of textbooks: science, social studies, literature, etcetera. At the secondary level textbooks become increasingly difficult for our students to read. Even some of our best readers have trouble with these books. The language is complex, the concepts are new, and the reading assignments are longer. It's not that our students have serious reading problems. It's just that, like learning any skill, say swimming, students need to have further practice and reinforcement, and we want to provide that for our students."

"That reminds me," interrupted school board member Harvey, "Dr. Goring, do we really need to continue that expensive swimming program at the high school?"

(continued)

## Pleading His Case, Part I (concluded)

Chairman Langley reminded Harvey that this was not the time to discuss swimming programs and asked for a vote. "All those in favor of adding a reading specialist to the staff, say yay; those not in favor, say nay."

The mixed responses resulted in a cacophony, so Mrs. Langley asked for a roll call.

At the end of the chapter you will find out whether or not the school committee voted to approve the hiring of a new high school reading specialist.

# In the Beginning . . . the Skills

By the time students advance to the middle and secondary grades, they have had a wide variety of reading experiences. Some began reading very early, even before entering school. Others were delayed in their progress, sometimes beginning formal reading instruction as late as grade 2. However, most students entering the secondary grades have had reasonable success in learning how to read (Farr, Fay, and Negley, 1978; Micklos, 1980, 1982).

How did these children learn how to read? Kindergarten and first grade teachers gave children a good start by getting students "ready for reading"; that is, a program was developed to prepare children for formalized reading instruction. This program included development in some reading-related skills, abilities, and understandings, such as visually discriminating letters, auditorily discriminating letter sounds, developing an interest in reading, developing language concepts, practicing left-to-right orientation, and so on. Once these *readiness skills* were developed, children began their formal reading program.

The children typically were exposed to basic skills in their formal reading program. In the primary grades major emphasis was placed on word identification skills, particularly in the areas of phonics and sight vocabulary. When providing instruction in *phonics,* teachers taught the children that certain letters represent certain sounds. They were taught, for example, that the letter *a* usually represents the sound of ă as in *cat* or ā as in *cake.* Less frequently it represents the sound of *uh* as in *want.* In cases where the usual sounds of the letters could not be used to identify a word, the word was taught as a *sight word,* such as the words *said* and *would.*

Teachers also taught words that very commonly appear in print as sight words, such as *it, so,* and *before.* The teachers used techniques such as the use of context clues, structural analysis (learning word roots, compound words, contractions, affixes, plurals, and inflectional endings), or the dictionary to assist children in recognizing these sight words instantly.

During these primary grades the children also received instruction in comprehension and study skills, but these skills were emphasized to a greater extent during the intermediate grades. Most children were exposed to instruction in comprehension skills that stressed literal recall, interpretation, and critical reasoning. Their study skills lessons probably included skills such as using book parts, locating reference material, and developing flexible reading rates.

# In the Beginning . . . the Approaches

## Basal Readers

Most children learned their basic reading skills through the use of basal readers, reading materials that are sequenced in levels of difficulty from kindergarten through grade 6 or as high as grade 8. Heathington summarized the major components of the basal reading system.

> *Student's text.* Softcover books are often used in beginning instruction; hardcover books are introduced during first grade.

> *Teacher's edition.* Often spiral bound, the manual contains reduced pupil pages, comprehensive teaching plans, and teacher resource or reference sections.

> *Student's workbook.* Consumable workbooks are designed to parallel and supplement the lessons in the text by providing independent practice activities.

> *Teacher's edition of workbook.* This reproduction of the pupil's workbook contains answers often marked in a contrasting color to facilitate checking.

> *Duplicating masters.* These sheets provide independent activities to reinforce and enrich the skills program. The teacher's edition of these masters contains a reproduction of the pages with answers marked.

> *Picture or word cards.* These cards are used to introduce, reinforce, and review vocabulary presented in the student text.

> *Pocket chart.* The pocket chart is a holder designed to facilitate the use of picture and word cards.

> *Placement tests.* Such tests—often in the form of informal reading inventories that assess word recognition, oral and silent reading, and comprehension—are used to place pupils at the appropriate instructional level.

*Mastery tests.* Used to assess a pupil's mastery of the skills developed in a particular unit or level, these tests pinpoint skill areas in which children need additional help. (Heathington, 1980, pp. 257–258)

Children usually found themselves in one of three groups, the top, middle, or bottom. Teachers typically instructed each group by using the directed reading activity (DRA), which consists of four steps: introducing vocabulary or concepts, silent reading for the purpose of finding out certain information from the story, skill-building exercises, and supplemental enrichment activities.

The new vocabulary words or concepts typically were presented in sentences on the chalkboard or on an overhead. Teachers encouraged the students to use the context of the sentences to pronounce and comprehend the words. The teacher then tried to create an interest in the story (the teacher's guide typically includes suggestions for motivating the children's reading) by relating it to the lives of the children and raising questions for the students to answer, such as, "Why do you think Sarah wanted to leave home?"

After completing the guided silent reading, the students discussed the story and were given the opportunity to orally read their favorite parts of the selection or sections that verified their answers to questions. Some teachers reviewed the story with their children by having each child take a turn reading a section (round robin reading). This latter practice has been criticized by most reading educators as serving no useful purpose.

After students completed their silent reading, discussion of the story, and some oral reading, they usually worked on skill-building exercises that were sometimes teacher-directed and usually reinforced through workbooks or study books. Phonics, comprehension, and, less often, study skills were emphasized in these exercises.

Finally, students may have had the opportunity to complete some supplementary activities designed to "enrich" the lesson. These supplementary activities consisted of reading related paperbacks, viewing filmstrips, listening to records or tapes, or integrating the reading lesson with other language arts activities such as spelling and creative writing.

The basal readers dominate the elementary classroom. It is the rare student who learned how to read without them.

# Language Experience Approach

Some children may have had their basal reading instruction supplemented with the *language experience approach*, which emphasizes the interrelationship of the communication skills of reading, writing, listening, and speaking. For beginning readers the teacher transcribed into print the language of the children. This material was then used for teaching reading.

This approach basically involved having the teacher record stories dictated by the whole class, a small group, or an individual. Once the dictated story was completed, it was read by the teacher. The teacher and students then read the story in unison. The children practiced reading the story for some time. As children learned words, they developed "word banks," which served as a record of the words they had learned or recognized by sight. As word banks grew and when children showed a readiness for writing, they engaged in writing activities that reflected their own choice of words, ideas, order, spelling, and pronunciation.

When and if students were exposed to the language experience approach, their teachers were integrating the teaching of phonics, context clues, and comprehension. Their teacher was probably very well organized as she planned and carried out these lessons without the benefit of a teacher's manual. Stauffer's (1980) book, *The Language Experience Approach to the Teaching of Reading*, provides a complete description of this approach.

## Individualized Reading

*Individualized reading* is based on the principles of seeking, self-selection, and pacing. Students who were taught by this method had an opportunity to draw on their own needs, experiences, and interests ("seeking") in selecting their own books to read ("self-selection"). These books were the students' basic reading materials, which they read at their own rate ("pacing").

Students had frequent, private individual conferences with their teacher, who assessed their needs and took steps to improve their reading performance. The teacher discussed the contents of the book with the child and, when necessary, taught or reinforced a skill. Both the teacher and the students kept records of books the students had read. The children were given the opportunity to share with classmates and report on the books they had read.

Students with common needs were frequently grouped together. They may have worked on a skill together, such as "main idea," completed projects together, or planned ways of sharing their reading. While students exposed to this approach did not necessarily score higher on achievement tests than those taught by other approaches, they may have developed a greater interest in reading (Veatch, 1978).

# In the Present . . .
## the Process

Once children complete the elementary grades, have they learned all the skills necessary for successfully reading secondary textbooks? Perhaps Goethe (1833) answered the question best over a century ago when he said, "The dear people do not know how long it takes to learn to read. I have been at it all my life and I cannot say I have reached the goal.''

Reading is an enormously complex process, and the skills that contribute to that process must be refined and extended as children advance to the secondary grades. Perhaps this is an appropriate point to explain some of the complexities of the reading process.

Reading is an active thinking process involving the interaction of readers and writers. The major task of readers is to reconstruct the ideas of people who have put their ideas into writing. Readers must try to understand what was going on in the heads of authors when they put their thoughts and ideas into writing. In interpreting the writing of authors, the readers also use what is in *their* heads. That is, the topic discussed activates what they already know about it, and this background knowledge in turn influences the quality of their comprehension or their ability to reconstruct the authors' ideas. (The meshing of ''new'' information contained in texts with related ''old'' information that students already have about the ''new'' topic is called *schema theory*. This theory is discussed further in Chapter 2.)

Tierney and Lazansky (1980) believe a successful interaction or reasonable communication will take place if both readers and writers live up to their ''contractual agreement.'' The writers' contract states that they will try to predict the intentions and background experiences of the readers of their books. They should strive to be informative, sincere, relevant, and clear. They should have respect for their readers by trying to project their readers' goals, beliefs, background knowledge, and purposes for reading their books. Britton stated it differently when he said, ''The writer . . . having in mind the reader addressed, must try to envisage the initial preoccupations with which that reader will approach the task, since these preoccupations provide the context into which a text is filled'' (Britton, 1978, p. 20). Tierney and Lazansky further wrote, ''An author, accountable in one sense to a selected audience of readers and in another sense to a message deemed worth their consideration, will do greater justice to that message, if the needs of readers are attended'' (Tierney and Lazansky, 1980, p. 5).

Readers, too, have their contractual obligations. Recognizing that writers communicate for certain purposes and to certain audiences, readers have a responsibility to decide for what and for whom a specific text is intended and whether or not their own purpose and experiential background fits with a specific text. They should make every effort to make accurate interpretations of a text and not to lose the message of the author. Further, ''It is the responsibility of a reader to employ those strategies which are sensitive to the purposes for which the text was designed and selected to be read'' (Tierney and Lazansky, 1980, p. 11). While readers should evaluate what they read, they should not unjustifiably criticize an author.

The essence of both readers' and writers' contracts is that they both must strive to construct meaning. When writers translate their thoughts into writing, they must select appropriate words, choose the correct organizational patterns, and employ whatever techniques they can in order to convey their intended meaning. Yet while authors may have intended to convey a particular message,

> readers bring to a text idiosyncratic perspectives which, at least in part, account for the degree to which their interpretations are in consonance with the author's intended message. It is most likely, then, that readers will include in their accounts of text not only that which is specified in a text, but also that which is not stated. (Tierney and Lazansky, 1980, p. 7)

This phenomenon was observed when college students enrolled in a reading improvement course met writers of the college newspaper for the purpose of discussing the writers' articles (Santeusanio, 1967). Both the students and the writers were surprised at the variety of interpretations expressed on materials that appeared to be rather literal and straightforward. One reason for the variety of interpretations had to be the "idiosyncratic perspectives" of the different readers. If we accept the notion that readers' distinctive views and unique experiences allow them to bring meaning to the written page that is not literally stated in the text, we may have to consider a greater variety of interpretations of text than we have in the past. Such may especially be the case in the field of literature. But as Armbruster (1980) warns, some types of expository writing, like that in science, call for a more restrictive interpretation of text, and a limited range of interpretations, maybe only one, is desirable.

Writers, then, provide the clues to meaning. They use words to express their thoughts or they translate their thoughts into writing. The readers, when translating the writing back into thoughts, must respond to the clues provided by the writers.

Thorndike noted that responding to these clues is like solving a mathematics problem.

> It consists in selecting the right elements of the situation and putting them together in the right relations, and also with the right amount of weight or influence or force for each. The mind is assailed, as it were, by every word in the paragraph. It must select, repress, soften, emphasize, correlate, and organize, all under the influence of the right mental set or purpose or demand. (Thorndike, 1917, p. 329)

Thorndike's idea that responding to written paragraph clues is influenced by the reader's purpose is a significant aspect of the writer/reader interaction. Declaring purposes is also an important component of what Stauffer (1969) calls the "reading-thinking process." By declaring purposes for reading, a reader must seek a solution to a problem of "perplexity" that has been set up. Stauffer also feels that "the nature of purposes to be achieved fixes the answers being sought and regulates the rate and scope of the reading-thinking process" (Stauffer, 1969, p. 12).

In the final anaysis writers and readers must work together. When they meet halfway, there is successful communication. The reader/writer interaction is ideal. However, as Schallert and Vaughan note, it is more likely that

> what the author meant to say was not perfectly represented in what actually was said, due partly to the limitations of written language and partly to the imperfect nature of anyone's ability to represent one's own cognitions. Likewise, what meaning the reader constructs, reflects the interaction of his or her own cognitions, affect and volitions, and as such represents what he or she *thinks* the author said. Of course there will be mismatches; of course there will be times when an author has not chosen words, images, or structures of ideas wisely for a particular reader, and times when the reader ignores or misperceives important clues given by the author. To the extent to which the balance can be equalized, however, communication of a sort will occur. Where we once worried about measuring the accuracy of a reader's comprehension, we now face the task of evaluating the effectiveness of communication. Responsibility for comprehension no longer rests with just the reader, but becomes the author's as well. (Schallert and Vaughan, 1979, p. 51)

[*Note:* "*Cognition* includes thought and belief, understanding, imagining, remembering, knowing how and knowing that. *Affect* includes sensations, feelings, emotions, moods, frames of mind. *Volition* includes desires, motives, decisions, intentions, trying, behavior traits" (Estes, 1979, p. 5).]

In other words, these ideas should be considered as the writer ponders his or her obligations:

- I've got to be informative.
- I've got to say something relevant and say it clearly.
- I've got to keep my audience in mind as I write this.
- I've got to consider my readers' background and their purpose for reading my writing.

And these ideas should be considered as the reader ponders his or her obligations:

- I've got to try to make an accurate interpretation of this material.
- I've got to use reading skills that are appropriate for this text.
- Is this book suitable for me? Do I have the background for this material?
- I should evaluate this material, but try to remain objective.

# In the Present . . . the Programs

This book's practical approach to the application of various reading and study skills to content areas is based on the premise that comprehension is indeed a responsibility of both the reader and the writer, both of whom have certain tasks in the communication process. When one realizes that written forms of communication become more complex as children enter the secondary grades, the need to provide continued reading instruction in these grades becomes more obvious. Is such instruction provided? If so, who provides it and how appropriate and effective is it?

## Number and Nature of Secondary Reading Programs

According to Hill (1979), three out of four school districts in some regions he surveyed had some type of secondary reading program, with programs reported less frequently in rural areas. In a recent survey of New England states approximately 81% of its respondents said they had a planned secondary program in reading development (Sager, 1980). But even though the majority of secondary school systems had instituted reading programs at the secondary level, most of the programs are judged by Sager to be inadequate, for the following reasons.

1. Programs are overwhelmingly remedial in nature.
2. There is a lack of coordination between classroom and reading clinic procedures.
3. There is practically no monitoring of student skill development in reading from the elementary grades to secondary grades or from grade level to grade level within the high school.
4. Content area teachers have little training in reading.
5. There is little involvement of content area teachers in the teaching of reading.
6. Virtually none of the schools surveyed have been able to implement a comprehensive or whole-school approach to reading at the secondary school level. (Sager, 1980, p. 9)

These inadequacies were explained by the fact that administrators, teachers, reading personnel, and members of the community do not share a common definition of reading, a definition that, according to Sager, should reflect a position similar to that expressed in this text. That is, reading should be a process of gaining meaning from the written page, a process that is dependent on the interaction between the reader and writer.

## Common Approaches

In the reports of both Hill and Sager, three common approaches to teaching reading at the secondary level are mentioned: developmental, remedial, and content area.

*Developmental programs* are for students who are reading slightly below, at, or even above grade level. The purpose of these programs is to extend and refine those skills taught to children in the elementary grades. The courses are taught by trained reading specialists or members of the English department. Often the English teachers have very little professional training in the teaching of reading.

*Remedial programs* are for poor readers. These programs are more prevalent than developmental reading programs. The purpose of these programs is to remediate gaps that students have in their basic reading skills. The courses are usually taught by trained reading specialists.

*Content area reading programs,* in which subject matter teachers and reading specialists assist students with the reading and study skills needed to master content, are offered least frequently (Hill, 1979). It is hoped that this situation will improve as more preservice and in-service teachers receive training in reading. An increasing number of states are requiring teachers to complete a secondary reading course for certification. Many colleges, regardless of state certification requirements, are requiring a course in secondary reading for students in their secondary education programs. In-service secondary content area teachers are requesting training in reading instruction. For example, when various communities involved in the Massachusetts Right to Read Effort conducted their Needs Assessments Surveys, in-service training in content area reading was a top priority for almost all communities.

With all this increased attention on secondary and content area reading, perhaps more content teachers will begin to integrate the teaching of reading and study skills with the teaching of content. But when content area teachers do so, the approach they use varies from the approach used by reading teachers involved in the direct teaching of reading in developmental and remedial reading courses, as we will see next.

## Developmental/Remedial Approach Versus Content Area Approach

The object of direct reading instruction in secondary developmental and remedial reading courses is to teach reading and study skills, such as expressing the main idea, drawing conclusions, and outlining. From test results or from informal observations, teachers select a skill or combination of skills on which to focus instruction. They then motivate their students and lead them through instructional activities designed to give students an understanding of the skill. Students are usually directed to practice the skill on teacher-made work sheets or, most likely, on commercially prepared booklets or instructional kits. When teachers are satisfied that students have learned the skill, they begin to teach different skills. Reading teachers often assume that students will be able to apply to the various content areas the skills they have learned in reading class. Unfortunately, experience and research demonstrate that many students do not successfully transfer the skills to their textbooks (Carney, 1977). Students can perform on exercises when specifically directed to in reading class, but they do not use these skills spontaneously when working independently in their content area textbooks.

Conversely, the object of content area reading instruction is to teach reading and study skills that will help to illuminate the concepts, ideas, and factual information contained in subject matter textbooks. Teachers involved in content area reading are usually the subject matter specialists. When they decide on their content-related objectives, they motivate their students and design learning activities designed to assist students in attaining the objectives. Learning activities may include lectures, simulations, films, and tape recordings. Typically one important learning activity is to ask students to gain information through the reading of textbook chapters or other supplementary materials. At this point content area teachers analyze their teaching assignments and select the reading skill or skills (process) that students must utilize in order to comprehend the reading material. Students may have to read, for example, for cause/effect relationships, the sequence of events, or factual information. At this point teachers prepare questions, guides, vocabulary exercises, or other appropriate materials to assist the students with their reading assignment. Unfortunately, some teachers do not have the professional training to complete this last step. Such teachers therefore do not provide the direct assistance that would help students to read the assignment. When teachers are satisfied that their students have attained the content-related objectives, they move on to new ones.

The steps involved in the direct teaching of reading are contrasted with those involved in content area teaching of reading in Fig. 1.1. In these models, a slight variation of those presented by Riley (1979), step 4 illustrates the point at which both reading specialists and content area teachers can use textbooks to teach reading.

## Teacher Attitudes Toward Content Area Reading

The suggestions contained in this book can help both reading specialists and content area teachers feel more comfortable with the concept of teaching reading in the content areas. But how do they really feel about this concept? No

## Figure 1.1 Content Area Reading Instruction Models for Reading Specialist and Content Teacher

| Step | Reading Specialist | Content Teacher |
|---|---|---|
| 1 | Establish reading skill objective (e.g., "Students use their understanding of cause/effect relations to comprehend reading assignments.") | Establish content objective (e.g., "Students recognize that experience with literature may be a means of developing self-understanding and personal values.") |
| 2 | Present reading lesson (e.g., demonstrate simple cause/effect relationships; point out signal words such as *consequently* and *because*) | Present learning activities (e.g., components of short story explained, nature of conflict discussed, meaning of values discussed) |
| 3 | Provide practice material (e.g., skill work sheets) | Provide reading assignment (e.g., "A Game of Catch," by Richard Wilbur) |
| 4 | Students apply skill to content area (e.g., students use skill of cause/effect in literature, social studies, science, etc.) | Teacher designs materials to assist students with reading assignment (e.g., cause/effect reading guide) |

studies on the attitudes of reading specialists have been completed, although some observers have noted a reluctance on the part of reading specialists to use textbooks in teaching reading (Readence, Baldwin, and Dishner, 1980).

Several studies have been completed on the attitudes of content area teachers. The more recent research, fortunately, indicates that content area teachers are more willing now than they were in the past to incorporate the teaching of reading with the teaching of subject matter. For example, after Jackson analyzed the data from questionnaires completed by 68 content teachers from four states, he concluded: "Secondary teachers have accepted the responsibility of teaching reading and understand that their students can benefit from reading instruction," (Jackson, 1979, p. 232). He drew this conclusion because nearly three-quarters of the respondents felt that content teachers could be reading teachers and more than two-thirds felt that they were indeed teachers of reading. Another encouraging statistic was that three-quarters were willing to take a course in teaching reading.

An additional aspect of Jackson's survey that augurs well for content area reading instruction is that a majority of the teachers surveyed were emphasizing reading skills in their teaching. When Edwards (1979) interviewed teachers who had completed the Smith-Otto Attitude Inventory (1969), she too found that content teachers were aware of and were utilizing reading techniques in their classrooms. Both Steig (1980) and Welle (1981) found that college students who completed a secondary reading course experienced a positive change in attitude toward teaching reading in the content area. O'Rourke (1980) reported that teachers in Nebraska who either had preservice or in-service training in content area reading had a significantly more positive attitude toward teaching reading in the content areas than those that did not receive similar training. These data suggest a definite positive change from the negative attitude of content area teachers toward reading instruction previously reported as long ago as 1969 (Karlin, 1969) and as recently as 1977 (Jackson, Stallard, and Steinruck, 1977).

## Summary

The majority of students entering the middle and secondary grades have developed their reading skills reasonably well. In the elementary grades they were taught basic skills such as phonics, comprehension, and study skills by teachers who primarily used a basal reader approach to teaching reading. This type of instruction may have been augmented or entirely replaced by the language experience or individualized reading approach.

However, students in the secondary grades are confronted with complex textbooks, new concepts, and longer reading assignments. Often they have little or no prior knowledge of the topics contained in these textbooks, thus making it difficult for them to reconstruct the ideas writers have put into print.

Recognizing the increased intellectual demands placed on secondary students, school systems are beginning to institute formal secondary reading programs, including remedial, developmental, and content area reading programs. The quality of these programs is improving as more reading specialists and content area teachers use regular textbooks to teach students reading and study skills.

This textbook includes many suggestions that teachers can use to help their students achieve the goal of becoming independent, critical readers and learners who are able to reconstruct, with a reasonably high degree of accuracy, the ideas presented in print by writers. Many students and adults are not capable of doing this in all content areas. Some have difficulty in achieving it in only a few areas. Thus it is imperative that content area teachers and reading specialists work hand in hand to help students accomplish this goal in as many content areas as possible.

## Pleading His Case, Part II

Fred Sears is anxiously sitting in the audience waiting to hear the school committee's roll call vote. Three affirmative votes will mean a new secondary reading specialist will be added to his high school staff. Chairperson Langley began the roll call. "Mr. Harvey."
"No."
"Mrs. Lazarus."
"No."
"Mr. Page."
"Yes."
"Mr. Slevin."
"Yes."
"And I vote in the affirmative. Good luck with your program Mr. Sears."

# Bibliography

Armbruster, Bonnie B. "A Teacher's Response." In *The Rights and Responsibilities of Readers and Writers: A Contractual Agreement,* Reading Education Report no. 15, edited by Robert J. Tierney and Jill Lazansky. Urbana: Center for the Study of Reading, University of Illinois, 1980.

Britton, J. "The Composing Process and the Functions of Writing." In *Research on Composing: Points of Departure,* edited by Charles R. Cooper and Lee Odell. Urbana, Ill.: National Council of Teachers of English, 1978.

Carney, John. "Content-Integrated Reading Instruction." In *Research in Reading in the Content Areas, the Third Report,* edited by Harold L. Herber and Richard Vacca. Syracuse University Reading and Language Arts Center, 1977.

Edwards, Patricia A. "Have Attitude Surveys About Reading Been Fair to the Secondary Teacher?" *Journal of Reading* 23(1979):21–24.

Estes, Thomas H. "Congruence in Philosophy and Pedagogy of Reading." In *Research on Reading in Secondary Schools,* Monograph no. 4, edited by Joseph L. Vaughan and Patricia L. Anders. Tucson: University of Arizona, 1979.

Farr, Roger, Leo Fay, and Harold Negley. *Then and Now: Reading Achievement in Indiana (1944–1945 and 1976).* Bloomington: Indiana Unversity, 1978.

Geothe, Johann Wolfgang. *Aus Meinem Leben, Dichtung and Wahrheit,* part II, 1833.

Heathington, Betty S. "Basal Readers." In *Teaching Reading,* edited by J. Estill Alexander. Boston: Little, Brown, 1980.

Hill, Walter R. *Secondary School Reading: Process, Program, Procedure.* Boston: Allyn & Bacon, 1979.

Jackson, James E. "Reading in the Secondary School: A Survey of Teachers." *Journal of Reading* 23(1979):229–232.

Jackson, James E., Cathy Stallard, and Yvonne Steinruck. "Secondary Teachers' Perception of Teaching Reading." Paper presented at the Illinois State Reading Conference, March 1977, at Charlston, Illinois.

Karlin, Robert. "What Does Research in Reading Reveal About Reading and the High School Student?" In *What We Know About High School Reading,* Research Bulletin of the National Conference on Research in English, edited by M. Agnella Gunn. Urbana, Ill.: National Council of Teachers of English, 1969.

Micklos, John J., Jr. "The Facts, Please, About Reading Achievement in American Schools." *Journal of Reading* 24(1980):41–45.

―――. "A Look at Reading Achievement in the United States." *Journal of Reading* 25(1982):760–762.

National Assessment of Educational Progress. *Literature Objectives.* Denver: 1975.

O'Rourke, William J. "Research on the Attitude of Secondary Teachers Toward Teaching Reading in Content Classrooms." *Journal of Reading* 23(1980):337–339.

Readence, John E., R. Scott Baldwin, and Ernest K. Dishner. "Establishing Content Reading Programs in Secondary Schools." *Journal of Reading* 23(1980):522–526.

Riley, James O. "Defining Content Reading Area Reading Instruction." *Reading World* 19(1979):129–134.

Sager, Carol. *Secondary Reading Practices in New England.* Wakefield, R.I.: New England Reading Association, 1980.

Santeusanio, Richard P. "RAMA: A Supplement to the Traditional College Reading Program." *Journal of Reading* 11(1967):133–136.

Schallert, Diane L., and Sherry C. Vaughan. "Author and Reader: The Communication Connection." In *Research on Reading in Secondary Schools,* Monograph no. 4, edited by Joseph L. Vaughan, Jr., and Patricia L. Anders. Tucson: University of Arizona, 1979.

Smith, Richard J., and Wayne Otto. "Changing Teacher Attitudes Toward Teaching Reading in the Content Areas." *Journal of Reading* 12(1969):299–304.

Stauffer, Russell G. *Teaching Reading as A Thinking Process.* New York: Harper & Row, 1969.

―――. *The Language Experience Approach to Teaching Reading.* 2nd ed. New York: Harper & Row, 1980.

Steig, Janet. "Attitudes of Preservice Secondary Teachers Towards Reading in the Content Areas." In *Research on Reading in Secondary Schools,* Monograph no. 5, edited by Joseph L. Vaughan, Jr., and Patricia L. Anders. Tucson: University of Arizona, 1980.

Thorndike, Edward L. "Reading as Reasoning: A Study of Mistakes in Paragraph Reading." *Journal of Educatonal Psychology* 8(June 1917).

Tierney, Robert J., and Jill Lazansky. *The Rights and Responsibilities of Readers and Writers: A Contractual Agreement,* Reading Education Report no. 15. Urbana: Center for the Study of Reading, University of Illinois, 1980.

Veatch, Jeannette. *Reading in the Elementary School.* 2nd ed. New York: Wiley, 1978.

Welle, Dorothy Weston. "Effects of a Required Reading Methods Course on Attitudes of Secondary Education Majors—A Three-Year Study." *Journal of Reading* 25(1981):134–136.

# Chapter 2

# Developing

# Readiness

# for Reading

# Assignments

## A Trip to Mexico, Part I

Dr. Smith, professor of reading education, began her college class in her usual manner by reviewing the main points of her last class lecture and by giving students an opportunity to ask questions about the topics covered. When she answered the last questions, her students expected her to introduce the next subject on their course syllabus. Instead Dr. Smith said, "Let's plan a trip to Mexico. I love planning trips, even if I never end up going on them. Let's do some brainstorming. Think about what we already know about Mexico and what we still would like to find out before going there. Just call out whatever comes to mind."

"I'd like to know something about the culture and customs of the people," said one student.

"Good beginning. It would be helpful for us to know, for example, that Mexicans take to strangers quite readily. And we can't forget the good old siesta at one or two o'clock in the afternoon. What else?"

"The Mexicans are quite courteous," offered another student. "But don't count on their paying much attention to time. I think the only thing that starts on time in Mexico is a bullfight!"

"And don't forget that religion is an important part of the country," said another student. "Mexico is almost totally Roman Catholic and the church is a very important part of the Mexicans' lives, especially for women."

"How about its politics?" asked Dr. Smith.

## Introduction

One way to assist students in their quest to interact successfully with textbook authors is to provide them with prereading readiness activities. Readiness has been defined as "those capacities or characteristics necessary for relatively easy acquisition of basic reading abilities in a particular program" (Otto, Rude, and Spiegel, 1979, p. 83). This definition of readiness refers to readiness for beginning elementary reading programs. However, with a slight change in wording it becomes a very appropriate definition of readiness for reading secondary content materials. *Readiness* for reading assignments in middle and secondary content subjects is defined as those capacities or characteristics necessary for the successful acquisition of information and ideas contained in a reading as-

"It's a democracy," answered another student. "The party that is consistently in power is the Partido Revolucionario Institucional. We just covered this in my history course."

"OK. You'd probably also want to know about the folklore of Mexico—its fiestas, special days like *posada,* the folk music and dances, the colorful costumes, its famous crafts, and the food."

"I'll tell you about the food!" exclaimed a student. "It's fiery and fancy, but good if you can find the right restaurant. You would also do well to drink only from bottles."

"Does anybody know what sports are popular there besides bull-fighting?" asked a student.

"You can find a little jai alai and soccer there," replied a classmate.

"What else would you like to know about Mexico before taking your trip?" asked Dr. Smith.

"I would like some historical background."

"And I'd want to know where to see the famous pyramids and shrines."

"Don't forget to put the University of Mexico on your list."

"I heard you shouldn't miss the silver shops in Taxco."

"Forget the silver shops. I'm joining the jet set in Acapulco."

"Fine," said Dr. Smith. "You've got people to see and places to go. You might want to brush up on your Spanish, too."

"You have a question, Judy?"

"Yes. This is fun, but what's it all got to do with reading?"

At the end of the chapter you will find the answer to Judy's question.

signment. The major instructional implication of this definition is that before teachers make reading assignments, they should analyze both the assignment and capacities of the students. For the assignment teachers should determine what roadblocks exist that could lead the reader astray. Are the ideas organized well? Is the vocabulary difficult? Are the visual aids easy to understand?

The teacher must also consider the capacities and characteristics of the students. What prior experiences and knowledge should they have had in order to understand the reading assignment? Can they relate to the topic? How much background information will the teacher have to provide? Recent research indicates that when teachers provide background information on the topic of their reading assignment, students' comprehension of the reading assignment improves significantly (Stevens, 1982).

When thinking about readiness for content reading assignments, then, teachers must consider both the nature of the reading assignment and the nature of the student. Techniques for finding out about the nature of students or their "capacities or characteristics" are discussed in Chapter 7. This chapter is concerned with the nature of the reading assignment and, once it is established, how teachers can develop strategies that will help students with the "acquisition of information and ideas contained in [the] reading assignment."

## Schema Theory

Planning and organizing activities to increase middle and high school students' readiness for reading assignments can bridge the gap between what students already know and what they should learn from a new reading assignment. Recently psychologists have shown great interest in the importance of readers' background and how it affects their ability to comprehend new material (Anderson, 1977; Rumelhart and Ortony, 1977; Schallert, 1980; Spiro, 1977). This concern with how human knowledge is structured and used is called *schema theory*. In its broadest sense schema theory holds that the readers' existing knowledge and experiences directly influence the content and form of new knowledge.

This point was nicely illustrated by Anderson and his colleagues (1976), who presented 60 subjects (30 male college students enrolled in a weight-lifting class and 30 female college students enrolled in an educational psychology course designed specifically for music education majors) with two ambiguous passages that could be interpreted in at least two different ways. The first passage could be interpreted as a description of a prison break or a wrestling match. The second could be interpreted as a description of a card game or a rehearsal for a performance by a woodwind ensemble.

After analyzing students' multiple-choice tests answers, written themes, and oral discussions, the researchers found a clear, significant relationship between the students' background and their interpretations of the passages. The weight lifters interpreted the passages as having to do with wrestling and a card game, while the music students interpreted the passages as having to do with a prison break and a rehearsal. For example, sentences such as "The lock that held him was strong, but he thought he could break it. He knew, however, that his timing would have to be perfect" conjured up a wrestling scene in the minds of the wrestlers, while it conjured up a prison scene in the minds of the music students.

In a similar study Reynolds and his colleagues (1981) investigated the effect of "cultural schemata" on the reading comprehension of black and white eighth-graders. These adolescents read a passage describing an exchange of good-natured insults or "kidding" that took place in a school cafeteria. Such an exchange is often referred to as a "sounding" and is found predominantly in the black community. Some of the lines from the passage included such soundings as "You so ugly that when the doctor delivered you he slapped your face" and "At least my daddy ain't no girl scout." When the researchers analyzed the results of their study, they discovered that the black subjects had a tendency to interpret the passage as being about sounding or good-natured kidding, whereas the white subjects tended to interpret it as being about physical aggression. In both studies, then, the readers' background determined how they reconstructed the author's ideas.

Although schema theory is receiving a great deal of attention in educational and psychological circles, the theorists have offered little guidelines on how the teacher can solve the problem of achieving an appropriate match between the vast differences that exist in the knowledge and background of students and the textbooks available for instruction. Further, few have presented ways of designing materials and organizing instruction to accommodate the wide range of schemata that exist in the classroom.

## Prereading Plan

One educator who has attempted to address these problems is Judith A. Langer (1981). She developed a three-step procedure known as PReP (prereading plan), which is used before teachers assign textbook reading to their classes. First the teacher introduces the class or a small group to a key word, phrase, or picture related to the text. This step is done to stimulate group discussion. Then the teacher tells the students the topic (e.g., "cities") that will be covered in their reading. At this point the three phases of PReP are covered.

Phase one is *initial association with the concept;* the teacher says, "Tell anything that comes to mind when you hear the word . . . (e.g., cities)." The teacher writes student responses on the board.

Phase two is *reflections on initial associations;* the teacher asks, "What made you think of . . . (the response given by the students)." This phase helps students to become aware of their network of associations, listen and interact with other students, and weigh, reject, accept, revise, and integrate their ideas.

Phase three is *reformulation of knowledge;* the teacher asks, "From our discussion and before we read the text, have you any new ideas about . . . (e.g., cities)?" Student responses are usually more refined than they were in phase one because they have had an opportunity to probe their memories and elaborate on their prior knowledge.

According to Langer, the teacher can determine how much prior knowledge students have with respect to the topic under consideration. Those who appear to have little prior knowledge would have to receive some direct instruction on concepts relevant to the assigned topic.

Schema theory in general and specific activities like PReP may be, as Barr suggests, "of considerable value in sensitizing teachers to the importance of reader background knowledge, the function of conceptual structures in organizing information, and the active nature of the comprehension process'' (Barr, 1980, p. 14).

This chapter presents several ways teachers can increase students' readiness for reading assignments, including presenting vocabulary reviews, writing advanced organizers, previewing books and chapters, and writing and sharing instructional objectives. Teachers should not use *all* these readiness activities prior to asking students to read a new reading assignment. After examining each approach, teachers can decide which methods best suit their teaching style, the nature of the reading assignment, and the needs and learning styles of their students.

## Vocabulary Previews

A readiness-for-reading practice familiar to most teachers is previewing and reinforcing the new, difficult, or unusual vocabulary contained in a reading assignment. The importance of vocabulary was illustrated by George Orwell in *1984*. Big Brother was able to control the thoughts of the citizens by teaching them the small vocabulary "Newspeak" and disbanding the larger vocabulary of current English, "Oldspeak." Because the citizens' vocabulary did not contain words like *freedom, rebellion,* or *tyranny,* they had no idea of what these concepts meant. Without these concepts the public had no way of even imagining a rebellion against Big Brother's dictatorship.

Like Big Brother's victims, students who do not possess an understanding of certain vocabulary contained in a reading assignment have limits placed on their opportunity to learn and react to the information contained in the text. Words are like tools in a tool chest; the more tools students have, the more jobs they can do and the more easily they can accomplish them. Students who have an understanding of pertinent vocabulary will be more ready to interact with the variety of ideas that different authors have to offer.

## Denotation and Connotation

Imprecise knowledge of the meaning of a word may be as bad as having no knowledge of the meaning of the word. Having only a rough idea of the meaning of a word is similar to being color-blind; one can distinguish the general shape (basic meaning) but one cannot appreciate the subtle beauties of the colors (shades of meanings). This difference relates to the distinction between the denotation of a word and the connotation of a word.

The *denotation* or literal meaning is the general shared agreement about what a word means. However, one word may have several denotations. The noun *root,* for example, can mean very different things to people in different disciplines. To the biologist it may mean "the underground part of a seed plant body that functions as an organ of absorption, aeration, and food storage or as a means of anchorage and support"; to the anatomist, "the part of the tooth in the socket," "the enlarged basal part of a hair in the skin," or "the proximal end of a nerve"; to the mathematician, "a quantity taken an indicated number of times as an equal factor"; to the etymologist, "the simple element inferred as the basis from which a word is derived by phonetic change or extension"; and to the musician, "the lowest tone of a chord in normal position." In the schema study discussed earlier, the word *lock* had different denotations to two different groups of students.

A word may also function as various parts of speech. The word *set,* for example, is defined and illustrated through 23 pages of the *Oxford English Dictionary* as a noun, verb, and adjective. For a more concise illustration of this variety of uses of a word, examine the word *well* in the following sentence.

*Well,* it's *well* that the water in the *well* does *well* up so *well.*

*Well* is used as an interjection, an adjective, a noun, a verb, and an adverb.

A word may also have several different, even contradictory *connotations,* depending on the context in which it is used. Connotations are the images and feelings a word suggests. The denotations of the word *church* might be "a building used for public worship." However, one person might think of High Mass in an ancient cathedral; another might picture a gospel meeting in a storefront; another might be reminded of the hypocrisy of organized religion; while another might feel association of security and mystical escape.

The only way students can be absolutely sure of the denotations of a word is to look it up in the dictionary. Many dictionaries will also give cross-references to other words and distinguish the connotations of the various synonyms. To get a good idea of the connotative possibilities of a word, however, students really must encounter the word many times in the works of good writers.

## Importance of Vocabulary

Given the obvious importance of vocabulary, it behooves teachers to preview the difficult, essential vocabulary that is contained in the reading selections they assign. The necessity for previewing potentially problematic vocabulary becomes clear when the following ideas are considered.

1.  Research demonstrates that comprehension of reading material depends heavily on knowledge of vocabulary (Anderson and Freebody, 1979; Davis, 1968; Spearitt, 1972; Thorndike, 1973). Subject matter word knowledge correlates highly with academic success.

2.  Students, especially poor readers, are intimidated by the sight of unfamiliar words. Most often they skip over new terms rather than take the time to decipher

the meaning of them. Unless the definition of an unfamiliar term appears immediately after the first appearance of the word in the text or on teacher-made word sheets, the students ignore the "stopper" word and forge ahead. Unfortunately, these words often crucially affect the meaning of the passage. Without a firm understanding of a key term, students can easily lose the gist of the passage and quickly become confused, lost, and discouraged. In a science laboratory experiment or a vocational education exercise, the misunderstanding of an important term could have extremely serious repercussions.

## Influence of Context

Perhaps the most treacherous words are those that a student has met before but in a new context have a different meaning. Students who run across the word *allotrope* for the first time know that they have come upon a new word. However, if the same students run across *mole, lake,* and *flux* (all of which have special meanings in chemistry), they may assume they know the meanings of the word. As a result, they may end up by completely misunderstanding the passage and not being able to figure out why they are having trouble.

Consider how the meanings of the following words change when they appear in the context of different content areas.

English:    foot, meter, object, case, mood, notice, perfect.
Social studies:    period, ticket, cabinet, bill, trust, left, race.
Mathematics:    sign, base, point, root, power, mean.

## Selection of Words

The words teachers select from a reading assignment to review with students must be chosen carefully. Herber (1978) suggests four criteria for selection: key concepts, relative value, students' background, and facilitation of independence.

Because teachers cannot possibly review every word that might be troublesome to students, they must select the ones that will contribute most to their students' understanding of the reading assignments or, as Herber says, select those that are most crucial to their content objectives.

If teachers come up with a lengthy list, they will have to narrow it down by judging the relative value of the words. Should the list continue to be unmanageable, they should try to eliminate those they suspect students already know (students' background). Is the list still too long? If it is, Herber thinks words should be selected that lend themselves to the teaching of skills such as context clues and affixes. When these words are pretaught by the teacher, the students also learn skills that can lead to independence in word identification.

Once vocabulary words have been identified, teachers can use some of the following activities to teach them to students.

# Teacher-Directed Approach:
# Context Clues

Teachers can provide direct instruction on context clues when the context in which the words appear in text offers clues to their understanding. Teachers can "lift" the words from the reading selection. The sentence containing the word and possibly the preceding and following sentences can be mimeographed, placed on an overhead transparency, or written on the board. Students are encouraged to figure out the meaning of the word by reading around it and trying to think of a meaning that logically fits there. When students do this activity, they are using *context clues*. Guarino (1960) demonstrated that when students receive direct instruction in using context clues, their ability to use the skill improved, leading to greater independence in identifying difficult words.

Some of the common context clues, which were validated by Ames (1966), are the following:

- *Previous contact* or *experience clue* in which readers draw on their experiences.

    She *piqued* him by refusing his invitation.

- *Contrast clue* in which the context helps the reader to figure out the meaning by comparing the word with its opposite.

    Unlike the well-mannered David, Richard was rather *uncouth*.

- *Synonym clue* in which the sentence contains a synonym or near synonym.

    The young child was excited by the *bustlings* and activities of the large gathering at the park.

- *Summary clue* in which a sentence or sentences following or preceding the word summarize it.

    Mary is a student who is interested in intellectual inquiry as well as research. She has a curious, creative mind. Mary is believed by many to be *inquisitive*. (Lapp and Flood, 1978, p. 261)

- *Direct definition clue* in which the writer simply provides a definition of the word.

    *Folkways* are informal customs regarding the correct way to behave.

- *Example clue* in which the writer provides an example of the word.

    Sean was most *industrious*. For example, he works hard at school, holds a part-time job, is vice-president of his class, and helps a lot around the house.

The following dialogue illustrates how one teacher helped students to use context clues.

**Teacher:  We have learned the various types of context clues that can be used to figure out words that are new to us. Let's see if we can use these clues as we review some words that we will meet in the first chapter of *Ragtime*. On the handout I have given to you, you will see our first sentence with the new word underlined. It reads: "Father's income was derived from the manufacture of flags and *buntings* and other accoutrements of patriotism." From the context of the sentence, what is a bunting probably like?**

*Student:  It's probably like a flag.*

**Teacher:  Yes, indeed. It's a kind of flag decorated in the colors of the flag of a nation. Let's look at the next one: "One read between the lines of journals and the *gazettes*." Have any of you seen the word *gazette* before?**

*Student:  Yes, I know a newspaper called* The Gazette, *so it must be a newspaper.*

**Teacher:  Fine. The word comes from the Italian *gazetta* and it also means "official journal." How about the next one: "His escapes were mystifying because he never damaged . . . what he escaped from. The screen was pulled away and there he stood . . . beside the *inviolate* container." If Houdini never damaged what he escaped from, then *inviolate* describes what kind of a container?**

*Student:  It probably was an undamaged container.*

**Teacher:  Good, and the next one: "In the meantime, the entire household *girded* for his departure. His gear had to be packed, arrangements had to be made for his absence from business and a thousand other details had to be seen to." How can we tell what *girded* means?**

*Student:  The following sentence tells all the kinds of things that were done to help him get ready, so it must mean to get ready.*

## Teacher-Directed Approach: Structural Analysis

Some words can be identified by breaking them into parts. Teachers may want to help students learn how to structurally analyze the parts of such words. *Structural analysis* involves dividing words into usable parts (syllables, roots, prefixes, suffixes, and common endings). When the word is divided, each division is given its appropriate sound and the parts are blended. This process assists students in learning both the pronunciation and meaning of words. A knowledge of word parts can help students to pronounce and understand many words. For example, the longest word in *Webster's Third New International Dictionary* is

pneumono • ultra • micro • scopic • silico • volcano • coni • osis

Smith (1981) offers an analysis of this unusual word. Sharing this analysis with students can sensitize them to the value of analyzing word parts.

| | |
|---:|:---|
| pneumono: | pertaining to the lungs, as in *pneumonia* |
| ultra: | beyond, as in *ultra*violet rays |
| micro: | small, as in *microscope* |
| scopic: | from the root of Greek verb *skope*in, to view or look at |
| silico: | from the element *silicon*, found in quartz, flint, and sand |
| volcano: | the meaning of this is obvious |
| coni: | the principal root, from a Greek word for dust |
| osis: | a suffix indicating illness, as trichin*osis* |

Putting them all together, one gets an *inflammation* of the *lungs,* which comes from breathing *very tiny particles* of *silicate* and *volcano dust.* (Smith, 1981, p. 32)

After sharing this most unusual example with students, teachers can move on to a lesson that relates to words contained in a particular reading assignment they plan to give. For example, a psychology teacher who plans to assign a chapter on personality characteristics could concentrate on the word root *vert,* which means "to turn." The teacher could then show how certain prefixes added to *vert* result in a list of words that are germane to the assigned chapter (*introvert, extravert, pervert*). The meanings of the prefixes can also be discussed. Then students can discover the meanings of the relevant words when the prefixes are added to the root *vert.* To reinforce students' understanding of the root *vert* (and, to some extent, the meanings of the preview words), the teacher could ask students to supply *vert* words with which they are familiar (*convertible, revert, convert*).

Figure 2.1 illustrates a teacher-prepared worksheet designed to emphasize prefixes in a vocabulary preview lesson.

## Student-Directed Approaches

The aforementioned procedures for previewing vocabulary are usually conducted under the direction of the teacher. An alternative approach is to put the responsibility for learning the important text-related vocabulary on the shoulders

# Figure 2.1 Teacher-Prepared Work Sheet on Prefixes

▶ The meaning of a word can be changed by the addition of a prefix such as <u>im-</u>, <u>in-</u>, <u>dis-</u>, <u>con-</u>, <u>re-</u> and <u>pre-</u>. The following excerpts from *The Outsiders* include words using these prefixes. Underline each of these words. Following each sentence are the meanings of the prefix and the root to which it has been added. In the space below the sentence, write a definition of the word in your own words.

1. She gave him an <u>incredulous</u> look; and then she threw her Coke in his face. (Prefix: not　Root: to believe)

2. His face <u>contracted</u> in agony, and sweat streamed down his face. (Prefix: together　Root: to draw)

3. The dream stopped <u>recurring</u> so often, but it happened enough for Darry to take me to a doctor. (Prefix: back　Root: to run)

4. The Socs even fought coldly and practically and <u>impersonally</u>. (Prefix: not　Root: personal)

5. On the fifth day I had . . . . smoked two packs of Camels, and as Johnny had <u>predicted</u>, got sick. (Prefix: before　Root: to tell)

6. He liked fights, blondes, and for some <u>unfathomable</u> reason, school. (Prefix: not　Root: to understand)

7. Right then he meant one thing: <u>contact</u> with the outside world. (Prefix: with　Root: touch)

8. "You just keeled over from smoke <u>inhalation</u> and a little shock." (Prefix: in　Root: to breathe)

9. My teeth chattered <u>unceasingly</u> and I couldn't stop them. (Prefix: not　Root: to stop)

10. She was a little woman with straight black hair and big black eyes like Johnny's. But that was as far as the <u>resemblance</u> went. (Prefix: again　Root: the same)

11. It's a pack. A snarling, <u>distrustful</u>, bickering pack like the Socs in their social clubs. (Prefix: not　Root: to trust)

12. I was too tired to tell myself I was being mean and <u>unreasonable</u>. (Prefix: not　Root: to reason)

13. Darry was the <u>unofficial</u> leader, since he kept his head best. (Prefix: not　Root: to authorize)

14. Soda fought for fun, Steve for hatred, Darry for pride, and Two-Bit for <u>conformity</u>. (Prefix: with　Root: to form)

From Gwendolyn Kerr, *Novel Ideas: The Outsiders* (Littleton, Mass.: Sundance-Publishers & Distributors of Educational Materials, 1980). Reprinted by permission.

## Figure 2.2  Multimeaning Work Sheet

| Word | Predicted Meaning | After Reading | Clue Words |
|------|-------------------|---------------|------------|
| Bill | Tells you how much you paid for something | A proposed law | Congress, committee, amended |
| Cell | The smallest unit of life | ✓ | Minimum, organism |

of the students. This approach is preferred by Kaplan and Tuchman (1980), who suggest the following strategies.

1. After previewing a chapter (see pp. 48–50), students predict words that they feel will be included in the selection. These words are listed on the board, and after they read the selection, students confirm whether they in fact found the words in the reading. Teachers may have to use probing questions to get students to contribute (e.g., "This chapter is about environment; what does that remind you of?").

2. An important concept (e.g., "freedom") from an assigned reading is written on the board. Students are told to write down in 2 minutes as many words as they can that relate to the concept. (This task activates the schema they have for the concept.) Students share their words in groups and finally write a paragraph using the words.

3. Students can complete a multimeaning work sheet (see Fig. 2.2) that contains four columns. The first column contains the multimeaning word. The students first write their predicted meanings in column 2 without seeing the word in context. After reading paragraphs containing the defined words, they write a new definition in column 3. If the definition is no different from their predicted meaning (column 2), the students simply place a check in column 3. Column 4 is used to write in clue words that help students determine the new meaning of the word or confirm their original meaning.

## Reinforcement Activities

Teachers may want to reinforce and review some words they have previewed with students. To do so, they can use wordslips and a variety of gamelike reinforcement exercises.

## Figure 2.3  Wordslip Format

New word _____

Pronunciation _____

Sentence in which you found it used _____
_____

Meaning _____

Your example of its use _____
_____

## Wordslips

Wordslips can be completed on 3 × 5 index cards or on ditto sheets. (By using the format outlined in Fig. 2.3, teachers can run off one 8½ × 11 sheet that will make two or three of these wordslips.)

The teacher should first guide students through the process of completing wordslips before asking them to complete them independently. Students are directed to the page and paragraph number of the words to be previewed. The class tries to identify the meaning of the word from context or from possible root, prefix, and suffix clues. Comparisons with similar words are used to determine pronunciation. If these techniques fail, students can be guided in the use of the dictionary.

As the teacher or student volunteer offers information to be filled in on the wordslips, members of the class copy it on their individual vocabulary slips. Students should be encouraged to transcribe pronunciation in the system that they can best understand. Accent and spelling pitfalls should be noted. Eventually students complete these wordslips independently, either in class or as a homework assignment.

Students should keep the vocabulary slips from each lesson, alphabetized with the wordslips from other lessons. They can write the new word on the back of the card or slip and then use the card or slip as a flash card. At the end of the semester students should have their own file card vocabulary glossary to the textbook. Figure 2.4 illustrates a typical example of a wordslip.

## Word Games

Students enjoy the gamelike vocabulary reinforcement exercises. After words have been introduced to students, they can be reinforced with exercises such as crossword puzzles, categorizing and matching exercises, and analogies. Stu-

# Figure 2.4 Vocabulary Slip for Mathematics

VOCABULARY SLIP

New Word *Reflexive*

Pronunciation *ri flex' siv*

Sentence in Which You Found It Used *The reflexive property states that any number is equal to itself.*

Meaning *To give back image of*

Your Example of Its Use *My camera's twin lens gives it reflexive powers.*

dents can complete these reinforcement activities either before or after completing reading assignments. Several examples of reinforcement activities teachers can use follow.

### Example 1   Mathematics: Polygons with Four Sides

*Directions:* The following questions are about four-sided figures. There are three parts to each question. At least one part is given. Fill in the other(s).

| Figure | Word | Definition |
| --- | --- | --- |
| 1. | Quadrilateral | A polygon with four sides |
| 2. | | A quadrilateral with only one pair of parallel sides |
| 3. | Parallelogram | |
| 4. | | |
| 5. | | A rectangle with four sides of equal length |

## Example 2    Mathematics: A Famous Geometrician[1]

This well-known Greek was born in Syracuse (287 B.C.) and was educated in Alexandria. He composed important works on plane and solid geometry, arithmetic, and mechanics. He discovered the principle of the lever and invented the hydraulic screw. One day while bathing he discovered the law of hydrostatics, which is named after him. It seems that as he was stepping into his bath, he noticed the displaced water overflowing. He was so excited that he rushed unclothed through the streets of Athens shouting, "Eureka!" ("I have found it!") What was his name?

1. Answer all the definitions you can. (The first one has been done for you.)
2. Transfer the letters of the words to the solution blanks below according to the matching numbers.

---

| Definitions | Words |
|---|---|
| A closed geometric figure with three sides | T R I A N G L E<br>1 2 3 4 5 6 7 8 |
| A closed geometric figure with eight sides | —  —  —  —  —  —  —<br>9 10 11 12 13 14 15 |
| A quadrilateral with two pairs of parallel sides | —  —  —  —  —  —  —  —  —  —  —  —  —<br>16 17 18 19 20 21 22 23 24 25 26 27 28 |
| An angle with perpendicular rays | —  —  —  —  —<br>29 30 31 32 33 |
| A quadrilateral with only one pair of parallel sides | —  —  —  —  —  —  —  —  —<br>34 35 36 37 38 39 40 41 42 |
| A rectangle with sides of equal length | —  —  —  —  —  —<br>43 44 45 46 47 48 |

**Solution**

A  R  __  __  I  __  E  __  __  __
4  2  10  32  3  28  8  42  22  43

---

1. This word game was prepared by Joan Smith.

## Example 3    Mathematics: Matching Columns

*Directions:* Select from the answer column on the left the word which best answers each of the statements at the right. Put the number of the word in the proper space in the magic-square answer box. If your answers are correct, they will form a magic square.

| Answer | | Statement |
|---|---|---|
| 1. Circle | A. | A line that is neither horizontal nor vertical |
| 2. Octagon | B. | An angle with perpendicular rays |
| 3. Right angle | C. | A closed geometric figure with six sides |
| 4. Trapezoid | D. | A closed geometric figure with eight sides |
| 5. Hexagon | E. | A quadrilateral with only one pair of parallel sides |
| 6. Square | F. | Two points and all the points between them |
| 7. Oblique line | G. | A rectangle with sides of equal length |
| 8. Parallelogram | H. | A quadrilateral with two pairs of parallel sides |
| 9. Line segment | I. | A plane figure bounded by a curved line, every point of which is equally distant from the center |

| A | B | C |
|---|---|---|
| D | E | F |
| G | H | I |

## Example 4    Literature: The *Light in the Forest* Crossword Puzzle

Figure 2.5 shows a word game developed for a literature class.

# Figure 2.5  A Word Game for Literature Classes

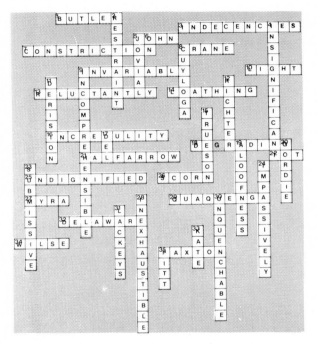

**Across**

1. True Son's white family name
3. Terrible acts; not decent
5. True Son's white name
7. Tightening, as in one's throat
8. Little _____ ; Indian boy killed by Uncle Wilse
9. Not changing
10. A word in the title
13. Not willingly
14. A strong dislike
16. Surprised disbelief
18. The whites made _____ comments about the Indians.
21. True Son's cousin
22. What Johnny was when he was kidnapped
25. Not worthy of honor
26. Hateful rejection
27. John's mother
29. True Son's mother
32. An Indian tribe
34. John's uncle
35. The _____ Boys who killed Indians

**Down**

2. Holding back
4. Not important
5. Cheerful; joking
6. Be _____ time
8. Quaquenga's husband
9. Impossible to understand
11. Being critical; making fun of
12. The author's name
15. The main character
17. A soldier and translator
19. An attitude of unconcern
20. John's brother
23. Giving in; tame
24. Without emotion
28. Never used up
30. Impossible to put out or satisfy
31. Servants
33. Aunt
35. A fort in Pennsylvania

From Donald Gallo and Maxine Glassman, *Novel Ideas: The Light in the Forest* (Littleton, Mass.: Sundance-Publishers & Distributors of Educational Materials, 1980), Activity Sheet 18. Reprinted by permission.

## Example 5    Business: Word Hunt

*Directions:* Find the words to the definitions below. The hidden words in the box appear forward, backward, up, down, or diagonally. Find each word and circle it.

```
E  E  S  K  J  S  B  O  Q  O  N  X  X
D  O  C  R  D  N  E  D  I  V  I  D  V
I  J  U  H  O  L  M  N  K  L  M  S  T
R  S  I  O  H  T  B  O  L  K  R  S  U
E  G  N  N  T  G  I  A  M  N  I  E  Q
L  H  O  O  O  A  F  D  Z  O  J  I  P
L  M  B  R  I  E  T  P  U  Y  D  R  C
O  A  B  A  C  T  Q  I  X  A  E  A  F
R  A  Z  R  D  R  A  W  O  X  O  R  G
T  W  A  I  V  E  S  V  P  N  P  E  H
P  Y  S  U  T  S  R  Q  O  X  S  N  C
M  P  X  M  U  T  V  D  Z  N  R  I  T
O  Q  R  W  L  U  V  C  A  B  N  T  B
C  S  U  O  N  I  M  U  L  O  V  I  A
O  J  U  D  I  C  I  O  U  S  L  Y  S
```

1. Those who examine accounts for accuracy.
2. Bids or prices offered.
3. Wisely.
4. Money paid to a person in appreciation.
5. Detailed plans for a trip.
6. New developments.
7. An accountant in charge of financial control.
8. Profit declared in a business.
9. Having great bulk.
10. Disperse with.

## Example 6    Humanities: The Last *A*
### Exercise

*Directions:* Read each definition below. Then write the word in the space that corresponds to the number of the definition. The last letter *a* is provided for each word.

1.         — — — — <u>A</u>
2. — — — — — — <u>A</u>
3.     — — — — — <u>A</u>
4.     — — — — <u>A</u>
5.         — — — <u>A</u>

1. Refers to one's thoughts, words and actions.
2. The flow of dying and rebirth.
3. The release from the cycle of rebirth.
4. Duty.
5. Mistaken belief that material things are real.

## Example 7    Humanities: Word
### Association

*Directions:* Examine the words listed under each concept. If the word or words are closely associated with the concept, place a plus sign next to it. If the word or words are not associated with the concept, place a minus sign next to it.

| **Karma** | **Maya** |
|---|---|
| —— 1. Drinking | —— 1. "Land of make-believe" |
| —— 2. Compassion | —— 2. Cremation |
| —— 3. Devotion | —— 3. Magic |
| —— 4. Rebirth | —— 4. Material forms |
| —— 5. Eating | —— 5. Reality |
| —— 6. Kindness | —— 6. Spiritual |
| —— 7. Snow | —— 7. Illusions |

(continued)

Example 7    (concluded)

| Moksha | | Dharma | |
|---|---|---|---|
| ___ | 1. Reincarnation | ___ | 1. Obedience |
| ___ | 2. "Leave off the mask" | ___ | 2. Station in life |
| ___ | 3. Reunion | ___ | 3. Reunion |
| ___ | 4. No new karma | ___ | 4. Loyalty |
| ___ | 5. Bad karma | ___ | 5. Deeds |
| ___ | 6. Brahman | ___ | 6. Duty |
| ___ | 7. Atman | ___ | 7. Results |

# Structured Overviews

Another technique for previewing vocabulary is the *structured overview*, which has been defined as a "visual and verbal representation of the key vocabulary of a learning task in relation to a more inclusive or subsuming vocabulary or concepts that have previously been learned by the student" (Estes, Mills, and Barron, 1969, p. 41).

The structured overview usually takes the form of a diagram or an outline. It is designed to help students recognize the relationship among words and to relate unfamiliar material to previously learned concepts.

After the vocabulary has been selected, the words are placed on a diagram or outline that reflects their relationships. This task can be done with input from students, who should already have some understanding of the words. As the overview is completed, other related words can be added to it.

The specific directions for constructing and using a structured overview follow. These steps have been adapted from Earle and Barron (1973).

1. Analyze the vocabulary of the learning task and list all words that you feel are representative of the major concepts you want the students to understand.

2. Arrange the list of words until you have a diagram that shows the interrelationships among the concepts particular to the learning task.

3. Add to the diagram any vocabulary concepts you believe are already understood by the students in order to depict relationships between the learning task and the discipline as a whole.

4. Evaluate the overview. Have you depicted major relationships clearly? Can the overview be simplified and still effectively communicate the relationships you consider to be most important?

# Figure 2.6 Structured Overview for Mathematics

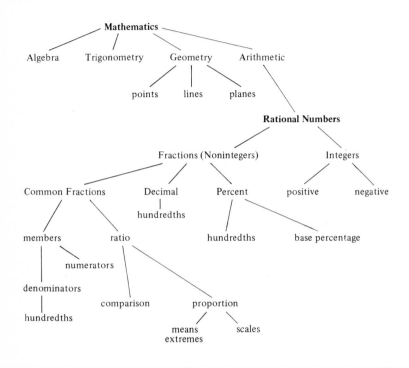

From Richard Earle, "Use of Structured Overviews in the Mathematics Class," in *Research in Reading in the Content Areas*, ed. Harold L. Herber and Peter Sanders (Reading and Language Arts Center, Syracuse University, 1969). Reprinted by permission.

5. When you introduce the learning task, display the diagram to the students and explain briefly why you arranged the words as you did. Encourage the students to supply as much information as possible.

6. During the course of the learning task, relate the new information to the structured overview as it seems appropriate.

Figure 2.6 shows a structured overview developed by Earle (1969) for a mathematics course, and Fig. 2.7 shows one developed for a humanities unit. The narrative that accompanies the latter overview could be included with a student handout of the overview, or it could be used as the teacher's "script" in discussing the overview with students.

# Figure 2.7  Structured Overview for Humanities

*To the student:* The diagram is designed to assist you in learning basic Hindu concepts and in seeing how the concepts relate to each other.

At the top of the diagram is *birth* or *rebirth.* Once born or reborn, the individual experiences *karma,* or a variety of thoughts, words, and actions. These deeds may be either good or bad. The nature of *karma* depends on one's *dharma,* or duty in life. One's *dharma* is determined by one's family position, caste, and age. At some point *samsara* occurs, and the individual experiences rebirth or reincarnation. If one has built up good *karma,* one can expect a higher station in future lives. If one has built up bad *karma,* one can expect a lower station and sorrow in future lives. Throughout the entire birth-rebirth cycle, individuals live in a world of *maya;* that is, they think their world is real, but it is only an illusion. After some time and after good *karma* has been built up, individuals seek a release from the cycle of rebirth and a reunion with God or *moska.* Now *Brahman,* God or ultimate reality, has united with *atman,* the soul or inner self.

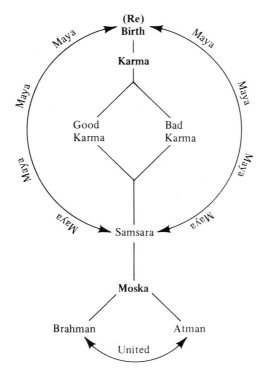

If students were to complete their own structured overviews, as Barron (1979) suggests, a variety of overviews would be produced in one class, but they would contain the same basic vocabulary. This task can be accomplished by placing the words on a ditto master. The words are blocked in with dotted lines. After the master is run off, the students cut out the words and explore ways of arranging their own overviews.

How effective are structured overviews? Hill (1979) believes too little research has been completed on them "to hazard conclusions about (their) effectiveness relative to pupil ability and materials" (Hill, 1979, p. 142). Smith's review of the limited research on structured overviews led her to conclude that the "results of the studies have failed to show that the strategy does indeed facilitate learning on content material" (Smith, 1978, p. 6). On the other hand, Tierney and Cunningham (1980), who also reviewed the research, say there is general support for their use under particular conditions with particular students. Barron (1979), one of the originators of the approach, admits that he was unable to produce consistent, positive results by using structured overviews. However, he feels the major reason for this outcome is that too often teachers, rather than students, manipulated the vocabulary in designing the overviews. His research, unfortunately lacking in detail, indicates that when teachers assist students with the construction of overviews, they attain higher test scores than those students who were exposed to overviews developed exclusively by the teacher or who were exposed to none at all.

## Advanced Organizers

Structured overviews are sometimes considered to be a special type of *advanced organizer*. According to Ausubel (1963), the purpose of an advanced organizer, a short passage containing general concepts, is to relate the content of the reading assignment to what students already know about it. Stated differently, the passage is intended to activate the schema students have for the assigned topic.

This brief passage, written at a higher level of abstraction than the reading assignment, gives the student an advanced, general overview of the more detailed information they will read. The advanced organizer helps students to use their established knowledge in learning the new material. A passage (advanced organizer) like the one that appears in Example 8 could be used to introduce students to the topic of *personality* in a psychology course.

### Example 8   Advanced Organizer

At one time or another you and a friend probably got together and discussed other friends. No doubt you identified those who "have a good personality," those who "have a bad personality," and some who simply "don't seem to have any personality at all.'' Such discussions make you realize that people behave in different ways. Each person in each category (good, bad, no personality) has his own unique personality. Do you know anybody who is exactly like you? Probably not. We all prefer different foods, types of entertainment, and school subjects.

Once you know people, you begin to see that while they have unique personalities, they are also consistent in the way they act. When you go to a party with friends, you probably can predict how each one will act. You come to expect these friends to behave in ways that are consistent with your past observations of them.

People are fascinating. Because they are, you will probably enjoy reading this chapter on personality.

This passage has the characteristics of the advanced organizer as described by Ausubel. It is a brief, written passage prepared by the teacher. Its concepts are general. It is related to the experiences of the students and it relates to the more detailed, specific information that is contained in the reading assignment. It should help students use what they already know in order to master the content of the assignment.

## Advanced Organizers Versus Overviews

Ausubel makes a distinction between his advanced organizers and chapter overviews and summaries:

> In all cases I define advanced organizers as introductory material at a higher level of abstraction, generality, and inclusiveness than the learning passage itself, and an overview as a summary presentation of the principal ideas in a passage that is *not necessarily* written at a higher level of abstraction, generality, and inconclusiveness, but achieves its effects largely by the simple omission of specific detail.
>
> Further, advanced organizers also differ from overviews in being relatable to presumed ideational content in the learner's current cognitive structure. (Ausubel, 1978, p. 252)

Perhaps the distinction between advanced organizers and chapter overviews becomes clearer by reviewing some procedures Ausubel (1960) used in one of his studies on advanced organizers. Prior to reading a passage on steel, Ausubel's experimental subjects read an introductory advanced organizer, while the control subjects read an introductory overview. The advanced organizer was "presented at a much higher level of abstraction, generality and inclusiveness than the [overview] passage. It was designed to serve as an organizing or anchoring focus for the steel material and to relate it to [the student's] existing cognitive structure. Principle emphasis was placed, therefore, on the major similarities and differences between metals and alloys, their respective advantages and limitations, and the reasons for making and using alloys" (Ausubel, 1960, p. 268).

On the other hand, the overview passage read by the control group "consisted of such historically relevant background material as the historical evaluation of the methods used in processing iron and steel. . . . In contrast to the introductory passage given to the experimental group, it contained no conceptual material that could serve as an ideational framework for organizing the particular substantive body of more detailed ideas, facts, and relationships in the learning passage" (Ausubel, 1960, pp. 268–269).

If a science teacher had planned to give a reading assignment on X rays, she could write an advanced organizer that provided examples of energy that can be seen but cannot be sensed by the skin. Examples, such as heat, could be given of energy that can be sensed by the skin but not seen. The idea of an invisible X ray could be developed by linking it with the idea that energy can be directly experienced only when one is equipped with an appropriate sense organ. If the same teacher wanted to write an overview or summary on X rays, she could give a brief history of X rays and summarize the contents of the reading assignment. However, in most cases this background would not be necessary, because most textbook chapters contain either an overview or a summary or both.

The purpose, then, of the advanced organizer is to prepare students for new material by providing them with short passages containing very general concepts that help students grasp the more specific information they will encounter in the reading assignment. Purportedly this passage helps students to link up the new knowledge with what they already know, and it may help them to bring order into the new material.

The research on the effectiveness of advanced organizers is conflicting, confusing, and controversial. After analyzing 32 studies for the purpose of answering the question, "Do advanced organizers facilitate learning?" Barnes and Clawson (1975) concluded that they did not. Tierney and Cunningham (1980) note that despite the hundreds of studies completed on advanced organizers, there still is no real "closure" regarding their instructional value. Hartley and Davies reached a similar conclusion when they said that taken as a whole, the results have generally been favorable, but "more recent studies have increasingly tended to be more inconclusive" (Hartley and Davies, 1976, p. 254).

Sledge (1978) reviewed the more recent research on advanced organizers that was conducted on the secondary level and concluded that the majority of studies indicated that advanced organizers have limited value in helping secondary students with reading comprehension. She did point out that when researchers reported positive findings, it was the less able students who ben-

efited from the approach. Mayer's study (1978) also showed the positive benefits of advanced organizers with low-ability students. Yet Hartley and Davies
(1976) opined that advanced organizers probably work best with students of
above-average ability!

While Mayer (1978) feels advanced organizers are particularly useful when
used with material that is awkward and inconsistent, Hartley and Davies (1976)
think they should be used with material that possesses a dominant structure.

Given the conflicting research on and the difficulty in preparing advanced
organizers, it is easy to understand why few middle and high school teachers
use them unless they are already a part of an instructional packet, such as in
the *Novel Ideas* program.

## Prereading Activities

In the *Novel Ideas* program edited by Savage and Gallo (1980), students are
provided with *prereading activities*. Like advanced organizers, these activities
contain general, familiar concepts that are designed to help students grasp the
important ideas they will encounter in the reading material. However, they are
not limited to brief written passages. They contain activities with which students
become actively involved, which probably enhances the likelihood that they
will link up the new knowledge with what they already know (the schema they
already have for the topic).

Figures 2.8 and 2.9 show prereading activities from the *Novel Ideas* program. Figure 2.8 illustrates the use of a familiar situation of a state lottery in
order to raise issues related to the potential problems that wealth can bring, a
major theme of the assigned short story "The Pearl". Figure 2.9 contains a
checklist and questions designed to stimulate discussion about friendship and
loyalty, important themes in the novel *The Outsiders*.

## Adaptation of the Guided Reading Procedure

Another practical alternative to the advanced organizer, and one that serves
the same purpose, is Spiegel's (1980) adaptation of the *guided reading procedure*. (See Chapter 3 for a complete description of the guided reading procedure.) When the major topic of the reading assignment has been identified,
students volunteer everything they know about it to the teacher. All information
is accepted and recorded on the board. Then students identify recorded information that conflicts and information that seems to be missing. No attempt
is made at this point to resolve the conflicting information or to add the missing
information. Rather an outline is created, with the conflicting information placed
side by side and the missing information listed by headings in the outline. Each
type of problem is keyed with a question mark. The teacher may also want to

# Figure 2.8 Prereading Activity for English

**THE STATE LOTTERY**

 **Congratulations! You have finally hit PAY DIRT! Whoever thought you would win $1,000,000.00 in the State Lottery? The whole town, the entire state is sharing in your excitement. Your lucky win is in all of the newspapers—the news is spreading like an epidemic! Explain how your "win" will affect your life.**

1. What do you plan to do with your newly acquired wealth?

2. What types of problems might you have because of your new wealth?

3. How do you think your friends will now treat you?

4. How do you think people in general will treat you?

5. Describe any "good" this wealth might bring you.

6. Describe any "evil" this wealth might bring you.

7. How do you think this wealth will change you
   socially:

   emotionally:

   mentally/intellectually:

8. Do you wish you had won more money in the State Lottery? Why?

▶ **Write a paragraph describing what you would do with all the money that you have won. (Use a separate sheet of paper if necessary.)**

From Audrey A. Friedman, *Novel Ideas: The Pearl* (Littleton, Mass.: Sundance-Publishers & Distributors of Educational Materials, 1980). Reprinted by permission.

suggest subtopics in order to ensure full coverage of the topic. A sample prereading outline based on the topic *spiders* appears in Fig. 2.10.

Spiegel believes this type of prereading readiness activity helps students develop purposes for reading. For example, they may read to prove that their own information was accurate, to supply the missing information, or to untangle conflicting information. When the unit has been completed, students create a complete, accurate outline.

The procedure can also serve as an informal diagnosis. On the basis of student responses, the teacher may discover that students already know so

# Figure 2.9  Prereading Activity for English

> **When you meet people your own age, what interests you about them? In the list below, check the five qualities that interest you most.**

_____ the way they dress
_____ how they treat people outside their group
_____ their grades in school
_____ what they do for fun
_____ how they are treated by their families
_____ their athletic abilities
_____ what they're interested in

_____ where they hang out
_____ how they treat other members of their group
_____ their physical appearance
_____ their sense of humor
_____ the kinds of homes they live in
_____ the way they talk
_____ how much money they have to spend

> **What other qualities do you look for in a friend? List two or more of them below.**

> **Describe the qualities that are important to the members of a group to which you belong (club, team, friends, etc.).**

> **What would you have to change about yourself if you wanted to join another group?**

From Gwendolyn Kerr, _Novel Ideas: The Outsiders_ (Littleton, Mass.: Sundance-Publishers & Distributors of Educational Materials, 1980). Reprinted by permission.

much about the topic that pursuing it any further would be a waste of time. Conversely, the teacher may discover that students know so little about that topic that pursuing it any further would be too frustrating and more background information would have to be provided.

In summary, the modified guided reading procedure provides teachers with a practical way to activate students' schema for a topic and to develop purposes for reading. It also can be used to informally diagnose student pre-knowledge of the planned assignment.

# Figure 2.10  Prereading Outline

**Spiders**

I.  How They Look
    ?A.  Have six legs/have eight legs
     B.  Have two body parts
    ?C.  Antennae
II.  How They Live
    ?A.  What they eat
     B.  Spin webs
         1.  Made of silk
         2.  Lots of different kinds of webs
         3.  Sticky
             ?a.  What makes them sticky
             ?b.  Why doesn't the spider get stuck

From Dixie Lee Spiegel, "Adaptations of Manzo's Guided Reading Procedure," *Reading Horizons*, vol 20, no. 3(1980):189. Reprinted by permission.

## Previewing Chapters

Previewing chapter summaries and overviews in expository texts may serve the same purpose as the advanced organizer, even though they are written on the same level of abstraction and generality as the rest of the chapter. (Reading summaries and reading overviews, however, are only two steps involved in completing chapter previews.) Previewing allows students to get a quick overview of a chapter before reading it carefully. It is very much like skimming an article or chapter (see Chapter 6). Students can identify some key ideas, determine the author's organizational pattern(s), and get an overall notion of what to expect from a careful reading of the chapter. In short, previewing helps students to read for a purpose, because they begin to think about the author's points as they question the chapter titles, headings, and subheadings; and they begin to understand the relationship between and among headings, subheadings, and the major topic of the chapter. This process also calls relevant schema to the minds of the students. The steps involved in previewing a chapter follow.

1.  Read and analyze the title of the chapter.
2.  Skim the introductory paragraphs, all boldfaced headings, and the first sentences of each paragraph.
3.  Examine visual aids such as charts, graphs, maps, and other illustrations.

4. Read the last few paragraphs in the chapter or sections labeled Summary, Review, or Conclusion.

5. If listed, read the questions at the end of the chapter.

6. Consider how the chapter fits into the context of the entire book. As Howards puts it: "This particular chapter can be thought of as another segment of a total puzzle. Without it, the puzzle would be incomplete and unclear" (Howards, 1980, p. 296).

Steps 1 and 2 are completed quite quickly and with little guidance by the teacher. However, teachers may have to provide some instruction with step 3. Maps, for example, present an enormous amount of information in a very precise manner. Teachers may have to take some time to help students clarify the meaning and use of legends, cardinal and intermediate direction, scales, and grids.

If graphs, such as table, line, bar, and circle, are included in the chapter, teachers should explain how they demonstrate relationships and clarify numerical data. Students should be encouraged to note the title of graphs, identify the source of information contained in the graphs (e.g., U.S. Department of Commerce), look for any keys to symbols used in the graph, evaluate the reliability of the source, and study the labels on the rows and columns.[2]

Roller's (1979) review on graph-reading literature reinforces the need for teachers to point out the presence of graphs, since many readers are reluctant to interrupt their flow of reading the linear text in favor of reading graphic illustrations. Naturally if graphs are analyzed during a preview, there is no interruption, and having already gained some information from a graph during the preview, students may be more willing to analyze them more thoroughly during their more careful reading of the complete chapter. Perhaps if more specific instruction is given on graph reading at the secondary level, students will not, as Vernon (1950) believes, become college students before they become independent readers of graphs and capable of integrating them with the text.

Roller's research, in part, supports Vernon's opinion concerning the integration of graphs with supporting text. In her study Roller found that seventh grade students attained higher scores on graph reading and interpretation when graphs were studied *without* a supporting text. Her students also demonstrated a dependence on the teacher to direct attention to graphs. Given these research results, Roller recommends that teachers should seize the opportunity to improve and reinforce the graph skills of students whenever graphs are encountered in a textbook. Instruction focusing on the graphs will seldom be repetitive

2. For a very comprehensive outline of techniques for explaining graphs and other types of illustrations, see E. G. Summers, "Utilizing Visual Aids in Reading Materials for Effective Learning," in *Developing Study Skills in Secondary Schools*, ed. Harold L. Herber (Newark, Del.: International Reading Association, 1965), pp. 97–155.

or redundant, because each graph, wherever it appears, is unique in terms of the author's and illustrator's purpose.

One reading educator who strongly supports the direct teaching of graph reading (and writing) is Edward Fry (1981). Fry encourages teachers to dedicate themselves to the development of graphical literacy. He feels that, like other basic skills, graph reading will be taught if teachers value teaching it. Those who do, he continues, should follow these procedures:

- Allow some time for graphical literacy in the curriculum.
- Ask reading comprehension types of questions about graphs.
- Select texts that have a good use of graphs.
- Talk to students about the importance of graphs.
- Grade graphs in student papers.
- Work on extending the types of graphs a student uses.
- Have a graphing contest and prizes.
- Invite art and drafting teachers to reading and English classes to talk about graph use and development.
- Use graphs themselves on the chalkboard or the overhead projector in explaining ideas. (Fry, 1981, p. 389)

Fry also has developed a comprehensive taxonomy of graphs (see Figs. 2.11 and 2.12). It is designed to expand students' and teachers' thinking about the kinds of information a graph can communicate and is to be used as the basis of curriculum development.

In addition to graphs, students also should be encouraged to analyze any pictures contained in the chapter and to determine the purpose of the picture, the specifics portrayed in the picture, and any generalizations or inferences that can be made about the picture. Most research indicates that students' comprehension is enhanced when they examine pictures in textbooks (Jenkins and Pany, 1981).

Cartoons are sometimes included in chapters. When they are, teachers can point out their symbolic elements and encourage students to view them critically.

If teachers do not want to spend the time during the preview to analyze graphic materials, they can wait until later when they discuss the chapter with the class. In any case one cannot assume that students know how to interpret graphics. However, if teachers have included graphics as part of their diagnostic group inventory (see Chapter 7), they will have a much better idea of the extent to which they will have to provide assistance in this area.

Step 4 and step 5 of previewing chapters are completed quickly. When students preview chapters, they give themselves the "frame of reference" (step 6) they need for their more detailed, careful analysis of the complete chapter.

# Figure 2.11  A Taxonomy of Graphs

1. *Lineal graphs*—Sequential data
    a. *Simple lineal*—For example, a time line or simple nonbranching flow chart can be used in history, literature (a story line), or directions.
    b. *Multiple lineal*—Parallel lines. For example, a set of three time lines that show terms of office of presidents, with a parallel line showing inventions, and a third parallel line that shows the reigns of English kings or queens.
    c. *Complex lineal*—Complex lines that have branching, feedback loops, and diverse data. For example, a computer programmer's flow chart; a process chart; or a hierarchy chart for a business or governmental organization, a genealogy chart, or a sports tournament elimination chart.
2. *Quantitative graphs*—Numerical data
    a. *Frequency polygon*—gives continuous data, can best show trends. For example, a normal distribution curve, growth curves, stock market fluctuations.
    b. *Bar graph*—Gives discrete data points, can best show the difference between two amounts. For example, it can contrast the size of enrollment for three different years.
    c. *Pie graph*—Best shows percent by various areas.
    d. *Complex numerical graphs*—Engineering graphs, multiple data graphs, higher mathematics graphs. For example, graphs drawn in logarithmic units, multiple line, or multiple variables.
3. *Spatial graphs*—Area and location
    a. *Two-dimensional*—Represent something flat. For example, road maps, floor plans, football plays.
    b. *Three-dimensional*—Represent height or depth plus length and width. For example, a map with contour lines showing mountains or valleys, mechanical drawings, or building elevations that accurately show dimensions.

    Basically, spatial graphs show the location of a point or the location and size of a line (one dimension), area (two dimensions), or volume (three dimensions). By use of special indicators or multiple graphs, different time periods can be shown.
4. *Pictorial graphs*—Visual concepts.
    a. *Realistic*—More or less what the eye would see without significant distortion or elimination of detail. Can have an angle or point of view,

# Figure 2.11 (continued)

selection of subject matter, selection of composition, background, and content. For example, photographs or realistic drawings, single or multiple color.

b. *Semipictorial*—A recognizable image but with noticeable distortions in form, color, content, or omissions of detail. For example, most Picasso paintings, schematic drawings showing cutaway or exploded engine, cartoons, or outline drawings.

c. *Abstract pictorial*—Highly abstracted drawing which, however remote, has some basis in visual reality. For example, a single line across a space might represent the horizon; a vertical line, a person; a series of squares, a row of automobiles. Abstract drawings or graphs nearly always require some context, verbal explanation, or prior experience with the type of abstraction.

5. *Hypothetical graphs*—Interrelationship of ideas
These graphs have little or no basis in visual reality.

a. *Conceptual graph*—An attempt to communicate abstract ideas by using lines, circles, and other forms, with or without words or symbols. For example, a philosopher who labels the sides of a triangle "truth, beauty, justice"; a theoretical model of the reading process with boxes labeled "short-term memory and long-term memory."

b. *Verbal graph*—The use of graphical arrangements of words or symbols to add meaning to the words. For example, a sentence diagram, semantic mapping.

6. *Intentional omissions from the Taxonomy of Graphs*

a. *High verbal omission*—On the borderline between having some graph qualities and being purely verbal would be a typical outline with main idea and supporting details, or posters and advertisements composed with different sizes and styles of type that show emphasis or are aesthetically pleasing.

b. *High numerical omission*—Arrangements composed mostly of numbers, such as statistical tables, are omitted.

c. *Symbols* are omitted because, for all practical purposes, they are the equivalent of a word. Typical examples are rebuses or glyphs (like the outline of a man on a restroom door, a cross on a church building, and road sign arrows).

d. *Decorative design*—Designs whose main purpose is decoration, not conveying concepts, are omitted.

# Figure 2.11 (concluded)

*Combinations*—Nearly any kind of graph can be combined. An example of a combination would be a mechanical drawing, which is a type of spatial graph (3b), but which could approach the reality of a picture (Section 4, Pictorial). Another example would be a bar graph, which is quantitative (2b), but which can use drawings or photographs of images; for example, car production is seen as many little cars piled on top of each other.

From Edward Fry, "Graphical Literacy," *Journal of Reading* 24(1981):386–387. Reprinted with permission of Edward Fry and the International Reading Association.

# Figure 2.12  Illustration of the Taxonomy of Graphs

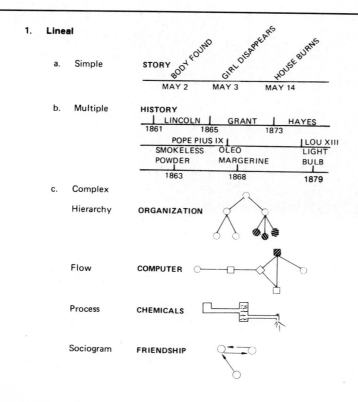

# Figure 2.12  (continued)

2.  **Quantitative**

    a.   Frequency Polygon

    b.   Bar Graph

    c.   Pie Graph

    d.   Complex

3.  **Spatial**

    a.   2 Dimensions

    b.   3 Dimensions

4.  **Pictorial**

    a.   Realistic

    b.   Semipictorial

    c.   Abstract

# Figure 2.12 (concluded)

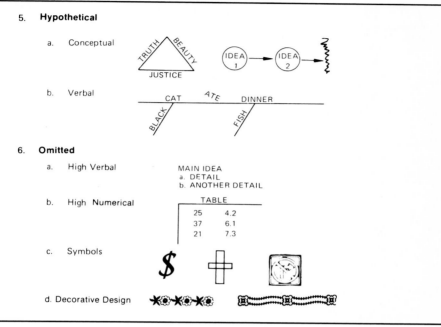

5. **Hypothetical**

   a.   Conceptual

   b.   Verbal

6. **Omitted**

   a.   High Verbal

   b.   High Numerical

   c.   Symbols

   d. Decorative Design

From Edward Fry, "Graphical Literacy," *Journal of Reading* 24(1981):384–385. Reprinted with permission of Edward Fry and the International Reading Association.

# The Group-Directed Reading-Thinking Activity Plan

By completing chapter previews, students can begin developing self-directed purposes for reading, as advocated by Stauffer (1969) in his *group-directed reading-thinking activity (DRTA) plan*. The plan has five major components:

1. Identifying purposes for reading.
2. Guiding the adjustment of rate to purposes and material.
3. Observing the reading.
4. Developing comprehension.
5. Fundamental skill-training activities.

According to Stauffer, "The reading-thinking process begins in the mind of each reader as he experiences a state of doubt or curiosity about what he knows or does not know, and what he thinks will or will not happen" (Stauffer, 1969, p. 25). It has been noted that what readers know about a topic is referred to as their schema for it.

Schema theory is an important consideration in step 1 of Stauffer's plan, because the readers' existing knowledge about a topic to be read will directly influence their purpose for reading about that topic. As Stauffer puts it: "The ideas a pupil declares are *his* ideas; they reflect *his* experience and knowledge, *his* association and projection, *his* ego. He is out to prove himself right or wrong. The self-actualizing tendency of self-declared purposes is enormous" (Stauffer, 1969, p. 25).

Stauffer's second step in the DRTA plan is guiding the adjustment of reading rate to purposes and materials. Once readers have declared their purposes and raised their questions, they adjust their rate of reading accordingly. While previewing a chapter to declare their purposes, most students skim through the material. However, at the stage when students are reading to answer their questions or to verify their predictions, they are engaged in a slower, study type of reading.

For step 3 in the DRTA plan teachers should observe students as they read silently to see if they are adjusting their reading rate to the material and if their declared purposes for reading are appropriate to the content revealed in the chapter. If the answer to the latter question is no, "a few well-chosen questions on the part of the teacher will soon have [them] reading again" (Stauffer, 1969, p. 42).

In step 4 students are asked to defend or refute their declared purposes for reading; they do so by *producing* evidence from the chapter read. Stauffer suggests that teachers can help students produce evidence by raising questions, such as, "Did you find the answers to your questions?" and "Were your predictions correct?" or by directing students to read the parts that prove it.

After a chapter has been read, special attention is given to skills relevant to the chapter (step 5), such as critical analysis, organizational patterns, and various study skills. These skills are discussed in the next four chapters.

Completing a chapter preview can help students declare purposes for reading. By analyzing headings, subheadings, visual materials, overviews, summaries, and so forth, students get an idea of the contents of the chapter, integrate that with their own schema for the contents, and then declare their purposes for reading. When students preview a chapter, they know what to expect, which helps them to locate and identify important pieces of information in the text.

## Student-Generated Questions

After previewing a chapter and making predictions about the content of the entire chapter, students may be motivated to raise further questions to answer during a more complete reading of the chapter. Homer (1979) offered some suggestions on how teachers can help students make these predictions. After students preview the chapter, the teacher asks, "What do you think the author(s) will present in this chapter?" and "Why do you think so?" Their speculations are discussed.

After discussion and before the chapter is read, the teacher asks, "What are some questions you would like to ask about this assignment?" and "Are there some ideas you want to check out?" These ideas and questions are recorded on the board. The responses are grouped according to the concepts presented in the reading assignment. Students who raise similar questions are grouped together.

Once in their small groups, students try to answer these questions and others developed by the group. This small-group inquiry session then develops into a large-group sharing session. Finally, the teacher encourages students to read in order to "find out if your answers were correct."

Recent research indicates that students gain more from their reading when they construct their own questions as opposed to responding to questions given to them (Anderson and Armbruster, 1980; Andre and Anderson, 1978–1979; Homer, 1977). Singer also advocates "teaching students to satisfy their own curiosities by formulating and reading to answer their own questions and thus achieve their own goals in learning from text" (Singer, 1980, p. 9).

# Previewing Books

If teachers guide their students through chapter previews, students soon will develop the habit of doing it automatically and independently. Another related readiness activity, one that actually should precede the teaching of chapter previews, is book previews. This activity, too, should become an automatic, independent student activity once teachers have reviewed it a few times with students.

The steps involved in a book preview follow.

**1. Read the title page.** The title page provides students with the general topic of the book and any particular emphasis it will have. This book, for example, has as its general topic *content area reading* and its specific emphasis is on practical approaches. The title page also indicates who the author and publishers are. For instance, you probably have concluded (I hope) from reading the title page of this book that the author is qualified by virtue of his educational background and experience; and most readers would recognize Addison-Wesley as a reputable publisher. The date on the title page helps the reader to predict, at least to some extent, how contemporary the author's ideas are.

**2. Read the preface and introduction.** The preface of a book provides the reader with the author's ideas about the book—why it was written, the intended audience, the basic point of view, the plan of the book, how it can be used, how it differs from other books of its type, and so on. As Howards says: "The author often gives himself away in his preface or introduction. He tells his bias or his view of the subject about which he is writing. This is good. The author should have some special reason for writing any book, and the reader should know this reason and use it as a guide when he reads the material" (Howards, 1980, p. 291).

The preface of this book, for example, describes typical approaches to teaching reading at the secondary level and how this book will present suggestions for changing or modifying them. The audience is identified: "preservice and in-service reading and content area teachers." The basic content of the book is noted: "specific, practical, and effective techniques for incorporating the teaching of reading with the various academic disciplines." Then a brief definition of reading is given to support the author's approach. After the organization of chapters is discussed, a summary of the book's contents is given.

**3.  Read the table of contents.** Students should view the table of contents as a summary outline of the book. They can also determine the relative importance of the various topics and subtopics by noting the number of pages allotted to each chapter and section. The contents can also help the readers confirm some assumptions about the book's slant that were established from reading the preface. The organization of the chapters also becomes obvious. By reviewing this book's table of contents, for example, readers would note that many chapters deal with "problems" associated with the chapter's topic and that ways of solving that problem are addressed in the sections on "Introducing and Teaching. . . ." In addition, they probably would confirm the author's contention that the book's major emphasis is on practical approaches.

**4.  Skim the index.** Most students realize that the index is an alphabetical listing of topics, events, and persons that are discussed somewhere in the book. They should be alerted to the fact that if an author has devoted several pages to a topic, then it is probably an important topic. Furthermore, if students know that they are going to have an objective type of test, they can use the index to review for the test. For example, suppose the teacher announces that the test will cover pages 100 to 225. Students then can review the index to see what specific topics have been indexed on those pages. They should know or be able to recite what is important about those topics. If they cannot recall the important ideas, they can make a quick review of the topic by referring to the pages listed in the index.

Previewing a book is a simple, but important, process. As was mentioned earlier, teachers should guide students through the steps until they begin to do it on their own.

There is little research on the benefits of completing chapter and book previews, but there is some limited research on one of the major components of a chapter preview, the chapter *overview*. Hartley and Davies (1976) reported that most of the studies showed favorable results when they studied chapter overviews, but the authors feel that more research should be completed on the topic. Tierney and Cunningham (1980) also reviewed the research in this area and found that at times both chapter overviews ("prefatory statements") and the analysis of pictures contained in the chapter facilitated learning.

# Instructional Objectives

*Instructional objectives* are statements of instructional intent that teachers use to focus their teaching lessons. They also help teachers design criterion-referenced or diagnostic tests in their content areas. (See Chapter 7.) However, and perhaps more importantly, when teachers share instructional objectives with students prior to announcing reading assignments, instructional objectives tend to facilitate learning (Kaplan and Rothkopf, 1974; Lindsey, 1980; Rothkopf and Kaplan, 1972).

In studies demonstrating that objectives tend to facilitate learning, Rothkopf and Kaplan used what they called *specific objectives* and *general objectives*. These are somewhat different from the *behavioral* and *descriptive objectives* discussed in Chapter 7. Only Rothkopf and Kaplan's specific and general objectives will be discussed here.

Both specific and general objectives consist of a single sentence or phrase that describes a learning goal. A specific objective is relevant to only one sentence in a reading assignment, while a general objective is relevant to two to five sentences in the reading assignment. An example of a specific objective is, "Learn about the physical appearance of Gothic type." An example of a general objective is, "Learn about the physical appearance of the three kinds of typefaces discussed" (Rothkopf and Kaplan, 1972, p. 296).

In their studies with hundreds of high school students in New Jersey and undergraduate students from Rutgers University, Rothkopf and Kaplan found that when objectives (or goal descriptions) were made available to students, there was a marked increase in the recall of objective-relevant information. However, more intentional learning resulted from specific objectives than from broad objectives. As Rothkopf (1980) later explained, readers can more easily use verbatim identities between specific objectives and text to regulate learning processes than they can use the categorical terms of the general objectives. Another important result of these studies is that when either or both specific and general objectives are given to students, their recall of incidental learning (learning not specified in the objectives) is greater than it is for students who are simply told to learn as much as possible but who receive no objectives. However, according to Rothkopf, this outcome happens only when the text contains incidental segments that include lexical and semantic [vocabulary/meaning] features that overlap the lexical and semantic features identified by the learning goals. . . . This is because the goal-description directions induce inspection of incidental text features under those circumstances. When there is no overlap between the semantic features of the background text and the learning goals, incidental learning is suppressed because the goal-descriptive directions reduce inspection of the incidental text elements. (Rothkopf, 1980, p. 27)

Rothkopf also notes that other studies (Duell, 1974; Rothkopf and Billington, 1975) indicate that sharing objectives with students is of particular value where there is a discrepancy between what the teacher and the student perceive as important in the text. In other words, students adjust and regulate their reading and learning activities in relation to their own perceived importance of text elements. When the teacher states an objective that students may or may not perceive as important, students tend to discriminate between objective-relevant and other text elements. That is, they pay more attention to the text portions that are related to the stated objectives. Rothkopf explains that when students encounter objective-related information in their text, the "target sentence" is read at half the speed of other sentences. The fixation time (the amount of time the eye stops) is lengthened by about 15 seconds and the number of fixations (the number of times the eye stops) nearly doubles.

Hartley and Davies (1976) also reviewed the research on instructional objectives as a preinstructional strategy and claim they "seem" to have a positive effect upon learning. It was difficult for the researchers to be more definitive about the studies because so many different definitions of objectives were used in the studies they reviewed.

Sharing instructional objectives with students before they read appears to be a promising technique. Objectives are relatively easy to write, and most teachers have to write them for their supervisors anyway. Why not share them with students?

## Summary

Readiness for reading middle and secondary content subjects is defined as those capacities or characteristics necessary for the successful acquisition of information and ideas contained in a reading assignment. To prepare students for the acquisition of this new information, teachers should try to help them bridge the gap between what they already know (the schema they have for the major topics in the assignment) and what they should learn from the new information that is contained in the reading assignment.

# A Trip to Mexico, Part II

Judy, a student in Dr. Smith's college class, had just asked the professor why they were discussing the ways they would prepare for a trip to Mexico.

"I thought you'd never ask," answered Dr. Smith. "But before I answer your question, Judy, let me ask you one. If you were in fact going to Mexico, would you look into all these things we have been talking about before you went?"

"Sure."

"Why?"

"Because I'd enjoy the trip more. I'd get more out of it by knowing what to expect when I got there."

"And that's the point. You'd be more 'ready' for the trip. Well, the same is true for reading assignments. If you want your students to get more out of them, you've got to help your students get ready for them—just as you'd get ready for a trip. Now there are several ways we can help students to develop readiness for reading assignments. For example,. . . ."

Teachers can draw on a variety of approaches for increasing their students' readiness for reading assignments. The most traditional approach is to preview the important, new, difficult, or unusual vocabulary that will appear in the reading assignments. Teachers can highlight the vocabulary by emphasizing context clues, structural analysis, wordslips, and gamelike vocabulary exercises.

Teachers and students can take the important vocabulary and develop visual representations of them, such as diagrams and outlines. These visual aids are called structured overviews and are sometimes considered to be a special type of advanced organizer.

When teachers prepare advanced organizers as a readiness activity, they write brief passages at a higher level of abstraction than that in the assigned reading. This passage is designed to help students use their established knowledge in learning the new material.

Readiness activities that do not require much preparation time for teachers are chapter previews and book previews. When students complete a chapter preview, they analyze its title, introductory paragraphs, boldfaced headings, visual aids, summarizing paragraphs and questions. When students complete a book preview, they analyze its title page, preface, table of contents, and index.

Another relatively simple technique for developing readiness for reading assignments is to prepare specific and broad objectives that direct students to the important information contained in the assignments. This procedure is a particularly good technique to use with students who have difficulty differentiating important from unimportant textual information.

A point made at the beginning of this chapter bears repeating: *all* these readiness techniques should *not* be used prior to directing students to read a chapter. Teachers should choose those procedures that match their teaching styles, the nature of the reading assignment, and the needs and learning styles of their students. They should also consider the research that has been completed on these various techniques and the amount of time and effort required to prepare them. In addition, Tierney and Cunningham's (1980) comment that it would be naive to assume that any prereading readiness strategy is sensitive enough to warrant its implementation across all reading situations is well taken.

# Bibliography

Ames, Wilbur S. "The Development of a Classification Scheme of Contextual Aids." *Reading Research Quarterly* 2(1966):57–83.

Anderson, Richard C. "The Notion of Schemata and the Educational Enterprise." In *Schooling and the Acquisition of Knowledge*, edited by Richard C. Anderson, Rand J. Spiro, and William E. Montague. Hillsdale, N.J.: Lawrence Earlbaum Associates, 1977.

Anderson, Richard C., and Peter Freebody. *Vocabulary Knowledge*. Urbana: Center for the Study of Reading, University of Illinois, 1979.

Anderson, Richard C., Ralph E. Reynolds, Diane L. Schallert, and Ernest T. Goetz. *Frameworks for Comprehending Discourse*, Technical Report no. 12. Urbana: Center for the Study of Reading, University of Illinois, 1976.

Anderson, Thomas H., and Bonnie B. Armbruster. "Reader and Text-Studying Strategies." Paper presented at the Conference on Reading Expository Text, November 1980, at the University of Wisconsin-Madison.

Andre, Marli E. D. A., and Thomas H. Anderson. "The Development and Evaluation of a Self-questioning Study Technique." *Reading Research Quarterly* 14(1978–1979):605–623.

Ausubel, David P. "The Use of Advanced Organizers in the Learning and Retention of Meaningful Verbal Material." *Journal of Educational Psychology* 51(1960):267–272.

———. *The Psychology of Meaningful Verbal Learning*. New York: Grune & Stratton, 1963.

———. "In Defense of Advance Organizers: A Reply to the Critics." *Review of Educational Research* 48(1978):251–257.

Barnes, Buckley R., and Elmer U. Clawson. "Do Advanced Organizers Facilitate Learning? Recommendations for Further Research Based on an Analysis of 32 Studies." *Review of Educational Research* 45(1975):637–659.

Barr, Rebecca. "Expository Reading in Classrooms." Paper presented at the Conference on Reading Expository Text, November 1980, at the University of Wisconsin-Madison.

Barron, Richard F. "Research for the Classroom Teacher: Recent Developments on the Structured Overview as an Advanced Organizer." In *Research in Reading in the Content Areas, the Fourth Report*, edited by Harold L. Herber and James D. Riley. Syracuse University Reading and Language Arts Center, 1979.

Dale, Edgar, Joseph O'Rourke, and Henry A. Bamman. *Techniques of Teaching Vocabulary*. Menlo Park, Calif.: Benjamin/Cummings, 1971.

Davis, Frederick B. "Research in Comprehension in Reading." *Reading Research Quarterly* 3(1968):499–545.

Duell, Orpha K. "Effects of Type of Objective, Level of Test Questions, and the Judged Importance of Tested Materials upon Posttest Performance." *Journal of Educational Psychology* 66(1974):225–234.

Earle, Richard E. "Use of Structured Overviews in Mathematics Classes." In *Research in Reading in the Content Areas, First-Year Report*, edited by Harold L. Herber and Peter Sanders. Syracuse University Reading and Language Arts Center, 1969.

Earle, Richard A., and Richard F. Barron. "An Approach for Teaching Vocabulary in Content Subjects." In *Research in Reading in the Content Areas, Second-Year Report*, edited by Harold L. Herber and Richard F. Barron. Syracuse University Reading and Language Arts Center, 1973.

Estes, Thomas H., Daniel C. Mills, and Richard F. Barron. "Three Methods of Introducing Students to a Reading-Learning Task in Two Content Subjects." In *Research in Reading in the Content Areas, First-Year Report*, edited by Harold L. Herber and Peter L. Sanders. Syracuse University Reading and Language Arts Center, 1969.

Fry, Edward. "Graphical Literacy." *Journal of Reading* 24(1981):383–390.

Guarino, Eugene A. "An Investigation of the Effectiveness of Instruction Designed to Improve the Reader's Skill in Using Context Clues to Derive Word Meaning." Ph.D. dissertation, Syracuse University, 1960.

Hartley, James, and Ivor K. Davies. "Preinstructional Strategies: The Role of Pretests, Behavioral Objectives, Overviews and Advanced Organizers." *Review of Educational Research* 46(1976):239–265.

Herber, Harold L. *Teaching Reading in Content Areas*. 2nd ed. Englewood Cliffs, N.J.: Prentice-Hall, 1978.

Hill, Water R. *Secondary School Reading: Process, Program, Procedure*. Boston: Allyn & Bacon, 1979.

Homer, Cynthia L. "A Comparison of the Influence on Reading Behavior of Two Purpose-Setting Procedures for Administering an Informal Reading Inventory." Ph.D. dissertation, Northern Illinois University, 1977.

————. "A Directed Reading-Thinking Activity for Content Areas." In *Reading Through Content*, edited by R. T. Vacca and J. A. Meagher. Storrs: Reading-Study Center, University of Connecticut, 1979.

Howards, Melvin. *Reading Diagnosis and Instruction, an Integrated Approach*. Reston, Va.: Reston, 1980.

Jenkins, Joseph R., and Darlene Pany. "Instructional Variables in Reading Comprehension." In *Comprehension and Teaching: Research Reviews*, edited by John T. Guthrie. Newark, Del.: International Reading Association, 1981.

Kaplan, Elaine M., and Anita Tuchman. "Vocabulary Strategies Belong in the Hands of Learners." *Journal of Reading* 24(1980):32–34.

Kaplan, R., and Ernst Z. Rothkopf. "Instructional Objectives as Directions to Learners: Effect of Passage Length and Amount of Objective-Relevant Content." *Journal of Educational Psychology* 66(1974):448–456.

Langer, Judith A. "From Theory to Practice: A Prereading Plan." *Journal of Reading* 25(1981):152–156.

Lapp, Diane, and James Flood. *Teaching Reading to Every Child.* New York: Macmillan, 1978.

Lawton, Joseph T., and Susan K. Wanska. "Advanced Organizers as a Teaching Strategy: A Reply to Barnes and Clawson." *Review of Educational Research* 47(1977):233–244.

Lindsey, Jimmy D. "Effect of Direction, Text Organization, and Age Level on Reading Comprehension." *Reading Improvement* 17(1980):219–223.

Mayer, Richard E. "Advance Organizers that Compensate for the Organization of Text." *Journal of Educational Psychology* 70 (1978):880–886.

Otto, Wayne, Robert Rude, and Dixie Lee Spiegel. *How to Teach Reading.* Reading, Mass.: Addison-Wesley, 1979.

Reynolds, Ralph E., Marshá A. Taylor, Margaret S. Steffensen, Larry L. Shirey, and Richard C. Anderson. *Cultural Schemata and Reading Comprehension,* Technical Report no. 201. Urbana: Center for the Study of Reading, University of Illinois, 1981.

Roller, Beverly V. "Graph Reading Skills of Seventh Grade Students." In *Research on Reading in Secondary Schools,* Monograph no. 3, edited by Joseph L. Vaughan, Jr., and Paula J. Gaus. Tucson: University of Arizona, 1979.

Rothkopf, Ernst Z. "Adjunct Aids, and the Control of Mathemagenic Activities During Purposive Reading." Paper presented at the Conference on Reading Expository Text, November 1980, at the University of Wisconsin-Madison.

Rothkopf, Ernst Z., and M. J. Billington. "A Two-Factor Model of the Effect of Goal-Descriptive Directions on Learning from Text." *Journal of Educational Psychology* 67(1975):692–704.

Rothkopf, Ernst Z., and R. Kaplan. "An Exploration of the Effect and Density and Specificity of Instructional Objectives on Learning from Text." *Journal of Educational Psychology* 63(1972):295–302.

Rumelhart, David E., and Andrew Ortony. "The Representation of Knowledge in Memory." In *Schooling and the Acquisition of Knowledge,* edited by Richard C. Anderson, Rand J. Spiro, and William E. Montague. Hillsdale, N.J.: Lawrence Earlbaum Associates, 1977.

Savage, John, and Don Gallo, eds. *Novel Ideas.* Littleton, Mass.: Sundance, 1980.

Schallert, Diane L. "Synthesis of Research Related to Schema Theory." Paper presented at the Conference on Reading Expository Text, November 1980, at the University of Wisconsin-Madison.

Singer, Harry. "Towards an Instructional Theory for Learning from Text: A Discussion of Ernst Rothkopf's Adjunct Aids, and the Control of Mathemagenic Activities

During Reading." Paper presented at the Conference on Reading Expository Text, November 1980, at the University of Wisconsin-Madison.

Sledge, Andrea Celine. "The Advanced Organizer: A Review of Research at the Secondary Level." In *Research on Reading in Secondary Schools,* Monograph no. 2, edited by Joseph L. Vaughan, Jr., and Paula Gaus. Tucson: University of Arizona, 1978.

Smith, Anne L. "The Structured Overview: A Prereading Strategy." In *Research on Reading in Secondary Schools,* Monograph no. 2, edited by Joseph L. Vaughan, Jr., and Paula Gaus. Tucson: University of Arizona, 1978.

Smith, Brenda D. *Bridging the Gap: College Reading.* Glenville, Ill.: Scott, Foresman, 1981.

Spearitt, Donald. "Identification of Subskills of Reading Comprehension by Maximum Likelihood Factor Analysis." *Reading Research Quarterly* 8(1972):92–111.

Spiegel, Dixie Lee. "Adaptations of Manzo's Guided Reading Procedure." *Reading Horizons* 20(1980):88–92.

Spiro, Rand J. "Remembering Information from Text: The 'State of Schema' Approach." In *Schooling and the Acquisition of Knowledge,* edited by Richard C. Anderson, Rand J. Spiro, and William E. Montague. Hillsdale, N.J.: Lawrence Earlbaum Associates, 1977.

Stauffer, Russell G. *Teaching Reading as a Thinking Process.* New York: Harper & Row, 1969.

Stevens, Kathleen C. "Can We Improve Reading by Teaching Background Information?" *Journal of Reading* 25(1982):326–329.

Thorndike, R. L. *Reading Comprehension Education in Fifteen Countries: International Studies in Evaluation III.* New York: Halsted Press, 1973.

Tierney, Robert J., and James W. Cunningham. *Research on Teaching Reading Comprehension.* Urbana: Center for the Study of Reading, University of Illinois, 1980.

Vernon, M. D. "The Visual Presentation of Factual Data." *British Journal of Educational Psychology* 36(1950):174–185.

# Chapter 3

# Distinguishing

# Main Ideas

# and Absorbing Data

# A Visitor from Art, Part I

"Why is the art teacher coming to our reading class?" asked Bill.

"I don't know," replied Susan. "But at least it will be a change of pace."

"I guess so. See you tomorrow."

The following day Bill, Susan, and the other 18 students in Miss Drago's reading class began the day with their first-period class in developmental reading. After taking attendance, Miss Drago said, "As I told you yesterday, I've invited our art teacher, Mr. Samuels, to our class to show you some slides. I told you that there would be a connection between his slides and the skills we've been covering in reading. But we'll talk about that tomorrow. Right now, give your undivided attention to Mr. Samuels.

"Thank you, Miss Drago. It's very nice to be here. I see lots of familiar faces. I brought some slides with me today. As we look at them, I would like you to concentrate on how the wholeness of each painting determines the nature of the parts. It is not enough for us simply to study the fragments or parts of the painting without paying attention to the more general context. All artists have this appreciation of part-whole relationships. . . . Maureen, are you listening?"

"Yes, Mr. Samuels."

"Very well. Now, with regard to size in these paintings, you will note that the closer we come to an object, the larger the visual image on the retina becomes. You all know what the retina is?"

"He must think we're dummies," Susan whispered to Bill.

"You must try to keep a stable conceptualizations of objects despite the changes in the size of our visual images. When you do this, you are able to hold onto the concept, in spite of changes in the object's appearance. You're focusing on the general, whole context of your perceptions. Beth, you have a question?"

"Yes, I think I understand what you mean, but do we think about this when it's happening?"

"Good point. This activity happens largely on an unconscious level.

# Introduction to Organizational Patterns

The concept of approaching the teaching of comprehension through an understanding of organizational patterns is based, in part, on ideas drawn from the theory of Gestalt psychology. Gestalt psychology is concerned with perception: its patterns, its organization, and its holistic character. According to

Most of us come to accept change in the environment as a natural condition. But by holding onto a concept, we get a sense of continuity, and it helps us to see orderly relationships. Now I'm going to show you some slides of paintings that will illustrate part-whole relationships. Please flick off the lights. . . . I've got to try to focus this thing. . . . OK, how's that?"

"Good," replied most of the students.

"Let's begin by looking at a portion of a slide. Here you see just the woman's hands from William Glackens's *Chez Monquin*. Notice how her left hand is clutching her right arm. Now look at the entire painting. The couple, obviously at a restaurant, are not at ease with each other. This is the main point. Some of the details include the clutched arm, the sad expressions of the man and woman, and rather than looking at each other, they are looking with disinterest at something else, perhaps entertainment of some sort.

"Here is a close detailed picture of the mother and child from Rubens's *Virgin and Child*. But this close picture of the two faces is only part of the whole picture. Now here's the whole picture. The faces, paradoxically, seem, at once, to look both the same and different. Notice how the general feeling—the main point, if you will—is one of warmth and love. Notice the mother's arms so softly holding the child; and how the child's arm so lovingly and delicately is placed on the mother's neck.

"We will now look at a very detailed painting by Velazquez. Notice the dog. The artist himself is on the left working on a painting of the king and queen of Spain. His picture is reflected in the mirror on the back wall. There is a young princess in the middle of the painting. She is surrounded by people of her court. Now look carefully at all of this. If you were to give this painting a title, what would you call it? Raymond, what do you think?"

"I think I'd call it *Adoration*."

As Raymond answered Mr. Samuels's question, Gary whispered to Mark, "So what's this got to do with our reading class?"

At the end of the chapter you will find out how one student discovered how to apply the art lesson to the reading class.

Clayton, the term *Gestalt* may be translated as "a pattern, configuration or self-regulated organized entity. It implies the priority of units larger than simple sensations and, psychologically, it implies that behavior is more than the simple addition of discrete units. The cliché that the whole is more than the sum of its parts derives from the organizational principle implicit in a Gestalt" (Clayton, 1965, p. 56). The concern of Gestalt psychologists is with relationships and interactions. Humans are organized to see things in relationships.

Students, then, should be taught that when writers express or shape their ideas, they tend to organize them in certain ways, depending on the nature of their message. They don't simply dash off a mass of isolated details or a jungle of ideas; rather they break ideas down and organize them so that readers can perceive how the ideas interact and how they are related. If writers have not done this, they have failed to comply with their "contractual" obligations. (See Chapter 1.) Still, if readers have a knowledge of the different types of organizational patterns, they sometimes can restructure disorganized writing into something intelligible.

Readers have the responsibility to interact with writers in such a way as to concentrate on the important aspects of their message and to recognize that much of the writers' message is supportive of these main concepts. This idea of focusing on the essential thoughts is similar to the psychological phenomenon of *figure ground*. The figure in a perceptual field is clearly outlined, well shaped, and prominent, whereas the stimuli of the ground constitutes the fringe or background.

Artists will use similar colors and shapes in their various paintings, but the placement of them in the paintings gives each work its own unique distinction, configuration, and idea. Steven Sondheim used similar notes when he wrote "Send in The Clowns" and "Being Alive," but the timing and sequence of the notes gave each composition its distinct sound and unique message. Likewise, writers use similar words, phrases, and grammatical structures, but they are organized in a variety of ways in order to express a variety of ideas. And most writers try to focus on main ideas (the figure) that are supported by details (the ground).

# Patterns and Levels of Comprehension

When writers choose to utilize the various organizational patterns, they structure their message so that readers must comprehend their message at either the literal or inferential level of understanding or at both levels. At the literal level readers determine what authors say. This activity is what Edgar Dale (1967) calls *reading the lines*. At the inferential level readers determine what authors mean by what they say. Dale calls this task *reading between the lines*.

The organizational patterns discussed in this and the next two chapters are main idea/details, data, sequence, cause/effect, problem/solution, and persuasive. These patterns are closely related to Barrett's (1972) taxonomy of reading comprehension. His literal and inference categories are reproduced below. The evaluation category is reproduced in Chapter 5. (The taxonomy also includes an appreciation category.)

Barrett wants users of his taxonomy to know that the taxonomy is mainly a teaching tool; that the tasks should not be thought of as discriminate comprehension subabilities, since difficult tasks from one category, such as literal, may be more demanding than easy tasks from another category, such as inferential; and finally that there often is an overlap among the categories (Smith and Barrett, 1979).

Taxonomy of Reading Comprehension

1.0. *Literal Recognition or Recall.* Literal comprehension requires the recognition or recall of ideas, information, and happenings that are explicitly stated in the materials read. *Recognition tasks,* which frequently take the form of purposes for reading, require the student to locate or identify explicit statements in the reading selection itself or in exercises that use the explicit content of the reading selection. *Recall tasks* demand the student to produce from memory explicit statements from a selection; such tasks are often in the form of questions teachers pose to students after a reading is completed. Two additional comments seem warranted with regard to literal comprehension tasks. First, although literal comprehension tasks can be overused, their importance cannot be denied, since ability to deal with such tasks is fundamental to ability to deal with other types of comprehension tasks. Second, all literal comprehension tasks are not necessarily of equal difficulty. For example, the recognition or recall of a single fact or incident may be somewhat easier than the recognition or recall of a number of facts or incidents, while a more difficult task than either of these two may be the recognition or recall of a number of events or incidents and the sequence of their occurrence. Also related to this concern is the hypothesis that a recall task is usually more difficult than a recognition task, when the two tasks deal with the same content and are of the same nature. Some examples of literal comprehension tasks are:

1.1. *Recognition or Recall of Details.* Students are required to locate or identify or to call up from the memory such facts as the names of characters, the time a story took place, the setting of a story, or an incident described in a story, when such facts are explicitly stated in the selection.

1.2. *Recognition or Recall of Main Ideas.* Students are asked to locate or identify or to produce from memory an explicit statement in or from a selection which is the main idea of a paragraph or a larger portion of the selection.

1.3. *Recognition or Recall of Sequence.* Students are required to locate or identify or to call up from memory the order of incidents or actions explicitly stated in the selection.

1.4. *Recognition or Recall of Comparisons.* Students are requested to locate or identify or to produce from memory likenesses and differences among characters, times in history, or places that are explicitly compared by an author.

1.5. *Recognition or Recall of Cause and Effect Relationships.* Students in this instance may be required to locate or identify or to produce from memory reasons for certain incidents, events, or characters' actions explicitly stated in the selection.

1.6. *Recognition or Recall of Character Traits.* Students are requested to identify or locate or to call up from memory statements about a character which help to point up the type of person he or she was when such statements were made by the author of the selection.

2.0. *Inference.* Inferential comprehension is demonstrated when the student uses a synthesis of the literal content of a selection, personal knowledge, intuition, and imagination as a basis for conjectures or hypotheses. Conjectures or hypotheses derived in this manner may be along convergent or divergent lines, depending on the nature of the task and the reading materials involved. For example, inferential tasks related to narrative selections may permit more divergent or creative conjectures because of the open-ended possibilities provided by such writing. On the other hand, expository selections, because of their content, may call for convergent hypotheses more often than not. In either instance, students may or may not be called upon to indicate the rationale underlying their hypotheses or conjectures, although such a requirement would seem to be more appropriate for convergent rather than divergent hypotheses. Generally, then, inferential comprehension is elicited by purposes for reading, and by teachers' questions which demand thinking and imagination which are stimulated by, but go beyond, the printed page. Examples of inferential tasks related to reading are:

2.1. *Inferring Supporting Details.* In this instance, students are asked to conjecture about additional facts the author might have included in the selection which would have made it more informative, interesting, or appealing.

2.2. *Inferring the Main Idea.* Students are required to provide the main idea, general significance, theme, or moral which is not explicitly stated in the selection.

2.3. *Inferring Sequence.* Students, in this case, may be requested to conjecture as to what action or incident might have taken place between two explicitly stated actions or incidents; they may be asked to hypothesize about what would happen next; or they may be asked to hypothesize about the beginning of a story if the author had not started where he or she did.

2.4. *Inferring Comparisons.* Students are required to infer likenesses and differences in characters, times, or places. Such inferential comparisons revolve around ideas such as: "here and there," "then and now," "he and he," "he and she," and "she and she."

2.5. *Inferring Cause and Effect Relationships.* Students are required to hypothesize about the motives of characters and their interactions with others and with time and place. They may also be required to conjecture as to what caused the author to include certain ideas, words, characterizations, and actions in this writing.

2.6. *Inferring Character Traits.* In this case, students may be asked to hypothesize about the nature of characters on the basis of explicit clues presented in the selection.

2.7. *Predicting Outcomes.* Students are requested to read an initial portion of selection, and on the basis of this reading to conjecture about the outcome of the selection.

2.8. *Inferring about Figurative Language.* Students, in this instance, are asked to infer literal meanings from the author's figurative use of language.[1]

The "tasks" from the literal and inference sections of Barrett's taxonomy that will be addressed in this chapter and in Chapter 4 are recognition or recall of details, inferring supporting details, recognition or recall of main idea, inferring the main idea, recognition or recall of sequence, inferring sequence, recognition or recall of cause and effect relationships, inferring cause and effect relationships, recognition or recall of comparisons, and inferring comparisons. Predicting outcomes, recognition or recall of character traits, inferring character traits, and inferring about figurative language are particularly important tasks for the study of literature, but they will not be discussed directly in this or the following chapter.

# Introducing the Concept of Organizational Patterns

Teachers should explain to students that writing moves from the simple organization of a sentence (subject and predicate), to the more complex organization of a paragraph (main idea/supporting details), to the even more complex organization of using main ideas and supporting details to express the relationship of ideas contained in cause/effect, problem/solution, sequence,

---

1. Adapted from Barrett, Thomas C., "A Taxonomy of Reading Comprehension," *Reading 360 Monograph* (1972). Lexington, Massachusetts, Ginn and Company (Xerox Corporation). Reprinted by permission.

data, and argumentative patterns of writing. When teaching the simple pattern of main idea/details or any of the more complex organizational patterns, teachers can use the following introductory lessons.

Allen Sack (1975) introduces the concept of organizational patterns by illustrating the "law of reduction of units." A series of numbers is put on the board or the overhead. Students are asked to memorize the numbers and associate them with something. For example, when the number 177655512126024365 is placed before students, some will group the numbers as shown in the accompanying table. Instead of having 18 individual numbers to memorize, they have only 5 units that must be remembered because each has a meaningful association. Clearly it is easier to remember 5 units than it is to remember 18 numbers.

| Unit | Association |
| --- | --- |
| 1776 | American Revolution |
| 5551212 | Long-distance information |
| 60 | Minutes in an hour |
| 24 | Hours in a day |
| 365 | Days in a year |

Another technique for introducing organizational patterns was originally presented in Scott, Foresman's *Tactics* series. Several designs are presented to students. One or two are clearly organized and the others are very disorganized. (See Fig. 3.1.) Before presenting the designs to the students, the teacher might say: "Let's try a simple experiment. I am going to let you study some designs. After studying each one for about ten seconds, you must try to reproduce it as accurately as possible without looking back at it."

After the students have studied each design and tried to reproduce each one, they usually conclude that they were able to reproduce certain ones, like designs 2 and 4 in Fig. 3.1, because they have some distinct order to them. Others, like designs 1 and 3, are disorganized and are thus difficult to reproduce.

These two exercises in recognizing orderly designs and units of numbers are then applied to recognizing order in writing, as exemplified in the organizational patterns. When readers can perceive a writer's plan and pattern, they understand and retain more of what they read (Bartlett, 1978; Meyer, Brandt, and Bluth, 1980; Taylor, 1980).

## Main Ideas and Details

The first pattern or "task" that we will discuss is main ideas/details because it is subsumed by all the other organizational patterns. [There is some evidence,

# Figure 3.1  Designs for Introducing Organizational Patterns

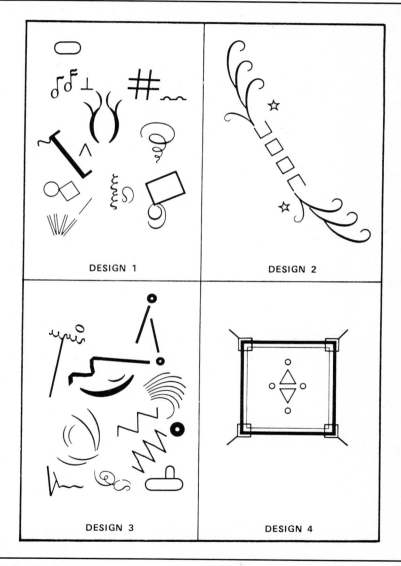

DESIGN 1

DESIGN 2

DESIGN 3

DESIGN 4

From Richard P. Santeusanio, *Developing Reading Skills for Business and Industry*, p. 48. Reprinted with permission. Copyright © 1981 CBI Publishing Co., Inc., 51 Sleeper St., Boston, Mass. 02210.

however, that it may be preferable to introduce the concept of main ideas *after* the major organizational patterns have been introduced to students (Meyer, forthcoming).] The main idea/details pattern is basic to the development of ideas as they are presented in all the other patterns. For example, students who are unable to determine main ideas will have difficulty comprehending cause/ effect relationships, recognizing an author's major assertion in persuasive writing, and identifying an author's solution to a problem.

Students must also be able to read for main ideas and supporting details in order to recall information for review and for examinations. In addition, the skill helps them outline chapters or complete research reports. Finally, the skill is needed by students who wish to use self-directed study techniques such as SQ3R (see Chapter 6). Clearly determining main ideas is a very important skill for students to master.

## Problems in Understanding Main Ideas

You probably have heard it said that some people "can't see the forest for the trees." This adage can be applied to many readers. When they read, they are able to identify and remember details (the trees) but they do not "see" the main point (the forest).

There are a number of reasons why middle and secondary students have difficulty with the skill of determining the main idea. One possible reason is that either the writer or the reader or both have not lived up to their "contractual agreement." Other reasons are related to classroom teaching practices and the nature of some elementary instructional materials that have been used to teach students how to determine main ideas. We will discuss the writer/reader contract first.

## Contractual Agreement

When writers express their ideas poorly, some students will have difficulty determining the main points. Writers may fail to clarify their main ideas with appropriate supportive details. Perhaps they made abrupt changes in their subject matter. Their transitions may be inadequate. This lack of clarity in writing represents one aspect of the authors' contractual agreement that may not have been honored.

Another contractual responsibility of authors is to know the audience for whom their books are intended. Stated differently, they should consider whether or not their readers will have the relevant schemata needed to comprehend their text. If a social studies text, for example, is intended for seventh grade students but the author(s) of the text have little idea of the background knowledge required of seventh-graders who will read their text, then they have not met their contractual obligations. Students who do not have the background related to the topics discussed in a text assigned to them will be unable to determine the main ideas contained in that text.

When students have been assigned well-written textbooks and their experiential background fits that text, they have a "contractual" obligation to determine the main ideas of the text by taking the time to synthesize information, recognize common elements, and fit the parts (details) into a whole (main idea). In other words, they have to apply their reading skills, in this case ability to determine main ideas, to the textbook assignments.

Students also have a responsibility to engage their schemata when, in fact, their experiences are adequate enough to deal with the textbook. Schemata should be engaged prior to, during, and after reading. Learning should occur because the readers' relevant experiences are focused and structured during reading and are integrated with the information contained in the text (Tierney and Pearson, 1981).

Students, then, may have difficulty with determining the main ideas of textbooks because either they or the textbook authors, or both, have violated aspects of the reader/writer contract. Students may also have difficulty with this skill because of the type of questions teachers have asked them in the classroom and the type of instructional materials instructors have used to teach them how to determine main ideas.

## Teachers' Questions

When quizzing students concerning the content of a reading assignment, some teachers tend to ask questions that simply require students to repeat details. Perhaps some of the following questions sound familiar to you. "Give me the date. . . ." "Name the character that. . . ." "List the places. . . ." "Identify the six characteristics of. . . ." Guszak (1968) documented how frequently questions about facts or details are asked by elementary school teachers. He determined that nearly 70% of their questions were ones requiring recognition and recall of factual materials. (If similar studies were to be conducted at the secondary and college levels, the results probably would be similar.) Some teachers do, of course, ask questions about main ideas. However, very often these teachers lose patience when students have to think about their answers. Rather than take the time to elicit main ideas from students, they find themselves supplying the main ideas themselves and letting students supply the details.

## Instructional Materials

The nature of instructional materials used to teach both elementary and secondary reading also contributes to the problem. According to Peterson (1975), research on the contents of basal readers indicates that only three of the nine best-selling basal programs present a systematic approach and sequence to teaching main ideas. (Even teacher-training textbooks reviewed made little or no reference to teaching main ideas.)

Although several supplementary reading skills workbooks claim to teach main idea, a perusal of them indicates that often this is not the case. In the first place, the workbooks usually do not provide students with strategies for selecting main ideas. Typically directions say, "Read the selection and answer the questions that follow." The assumption is made that if students answer enough of these questions about main ideas, they will master the skill and apply it when reading textbooks. This practice is not a teaching procedure; it is more like a testing procedure. It does little to help students learn the skill of determining the main idea. They still do not know *how* to find a main idea.

In the second place, even the questions that purport to be main-idea questions are, in fact, detail questions. Here, for example, are some multiple-choice questions taken from workbook exercises that claim to be teaching the concept of main idea.

## Example 1    Multiple Choice, Selecting a Topic

This story is about:

- (a) A school bus
- (b) A new hogan
- (c) Tom's new school[2]

## Example 2    Multiple Choice, Selecting a Title

The best title for this selection is:

- (a) How You Can Stop Snoring
- (b) The Snoring Problem
- (c) Sleeping Americans
- (d) Inventions[3]

These questions do *not* require students to identify main ideas; the questions simply require students to identify a topic. A main idea expands on a topic; it is a general, declarative statement about the topic. In Example 1 the correct answer is c, "Tom's new school." But the *main idea* of the selection is "Tom's new school is just like your school." In Example 2 the correct answer

2. "Run Deer, the Indian Boy," *New Diagnostic Reading Workbook Series* (Columbus, Ohio: Merrill, 1969), p. 61.

3. "World Wide," *Scope/Reading Skills 1* (New York: Scholastic Book Services, 1967), p. 65.

is b, "The Snoring Problem." Again only a topic is identified. The *main idea* is "No single device can cure all snorers." While it's true that "The Snoring Problem" is a good title, the exercise does not help students achieve the workbook program objective: "Finding the main idea of each article."

There are, of course, some workbooks that ask students to choose from complete, declarative statements, one of which is an accurate statement of the main idea, as shown in the following example.

### Example 3    Multiple Choice, Selecting a Declarative Sentence

The main idea of this passage is that:

(a) Anger is a universal phenomenon among humans.

(b) Psychiatric tests proved that a person who gets angry is well-balanced.

(c) Normal persons are apt to get angry much more easily than abnormal individuals.

(d) Normal persons react more intensely to anger-provoking situations than do abnormal individuals.

(e) None of the individuals tested was able to see that the anger-provoking actions of the experimenters were "rigged."[4]

Each choice in Example 3 is a declarative sentence. The selection's topic, *anger*, is included in each choice. The correct answer (d) is a general statement reflecting the main idea of the passage. This example is a vast improvement over the first two examples.

There is nothing wrong with only asking students to identify the topic of a paragraph or a long reading selection. That, in fact, is the first step in learning how to find main ideas, and it may be the major focus of main-idea instruction in the primary grades. However, students must learn to expand their ability to identify topics to making general, declarative main-idea statements. The true test of whether or not students can apply this skill to the content areas is to ask them to generate their own main ideas based on textbook paragraphs and selections they have read. In other words, they must throw away the crutch of multiple-choice questions, which are so characteristic of workbooks. After all, students will find no multiple-choice questions after every paragraph or two in, for example, their science and social studies books.

Regardless of the reasons for the difficulty some middle school and secondary students have with selecting main ideas, both reading teachers and content teachers will have to provide their students with some assistance.

4. Allan Sack and Jack Yourman, *100 Passages to Develop Reading Comprehension Questions* (New York: College Skills Center, 1965), p. 5.

# Introducing and Teaching Main Ideas

## Simple Activities

Poor readers may need exposure to very simple activities at the beginning of instruction. Categorizing words may help. For example:

Peaches, apples, and plums are all _____ ,

Baseball, hockey, and soccer are all _____ .

You also could help students distinguish between general and specific words, such as Harvard versus university, Nike versus sneakers, Afro versus hairstyle, and blue versus color.

Ask students to identify the topic and main idea of pictures. When using this technique, Moore and Readence (1980) suggest that teachers first model for the students the process of arriving at the main idea of a picture. Teachers can express main ideas by noting how the details in the picture combine to lead to the picture's main point. Taylor (1978) suggests asking students to select at least ten photos they feel they can title. They then write down the number of the picture followed by their title for it.

## Clarification of Terms

When beginning to teach main ideas, teachers should clarify the terms *topic, main idea,* and *details.* The *topic* is the subject matter of the passage, the one or two things the passage is about. It is usually a noun or phrase. When readers ask themselves, "What is this all about?" they are seeking the topic.

The *main idea* is a declarative statement about the topic. This statement reflects the most important idea about the topic. It may be directly stated in a sentence from the passage or it may be implied. When readers ask themselves, "What is the most important idea about the topic?" they are seeking the main idea.

*Details* are bits of information that support, clarify, or explain the main idea. Their function is to tell when, where, how, or why. They also may serve as examples of the main idea. When readers ask, "When did this happen?" or "How did this happen?" or "Where did this happen?" or "Why did this happen?" they are asking questions that require detailed responses. These questions should help them find information that supports their main-idea statements.

## Multiple-Choice Exercises

Putnam (1974) believes teachers can teach main ideas to students by selecting passages from textbooks and developing statements about them, one of which students will select as the best expression of the main idea. One of the statements should have nothing to do with the selection; one should relate minor details; and one should express the main idea. After students practice with this format, teachers change it so that one statement contains minor details, one contains a poorly expressed statement of the main idea, and one contains a well-expressed statement of the main idea. When students have success with this format, they are ready to generate their own main ideas from selections.

Putnam's ideas can be utilized by teams of three students (Dillner and Olson, 1977). One student acts as moderator while the other two participate. The participants can engage in some of the activities suggested above. The moderator, with his or her answer key, tells them which answer is correct. If both students are correct, each is awarded a point. If they disagree, they discuss and defend their choices. The participant with the most points becomes the moderator for the next set of exercises.

Another variation of this game is to have the participants read various textbook passages and then summarize the ideas in the format of a telegram. The participant with the best telegram is awarded a point.

## Signal Words

You can point out that supporting details are sometimes introduced by certain key words (such as *first, second, third, next, then, finally*) and key phrases (such as *one reason, another reason*). Main ideas, on the other hand, are often signaled by phrases such as *thus, in summary, most importantly, in conclusion* (Aukerman, 1972).

## Topic Sentences

Many teachers like to teach students main idea by asking them to locate it in a sentence or sentences in paragraphs. [Despite the apparent widespread use of this technique, Williams and Stevens (1972) found that only 57% of the 531 students they tested could properly identify the topic sentence of paragraphs.] Textbooks on reading instruction often suggest this procedure and offer techniques such as symbolizing and diagraming main ideas. Figure 3.2 illustrates Burmeister's (1978) symbol suggestion, Singer and Donlan's (1980) diagram suggestion, and Aukerman's (1972) diagram suggestion.

The following examples come from content area textbooks; they illustrate main ideas located in various sections of paragraphs. Notice how the details support the main-idea sentences.

### Example 4    Main Idea at the Beginning
of the Paragraph

<u>In examining bits of matter around us, we notice that much of it, in</u> <u>fact most of it, is a mixture of many substances.</u> This is true of most of our foods, our own bodies, concrete, wood, and much of what

# Figure 3.2  Symbols and Diagrams for Main Ideas

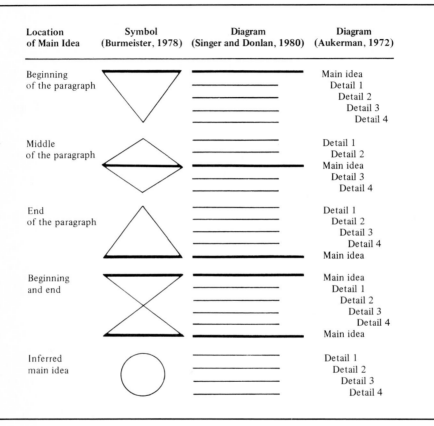

| Location of Main Idea | Symbol (Burmeister, 1978) | Diagram (Singer and Donlan, 1980) | Diagram (Aukerman, 1972) |
|---|---|---|---|
| Beginning of the paragraph | | | Main idea<br>Detail 1<br>Detail 2<br>Detail 3<br>Detail 4 |
| Middle of the paragraph | | | Detail 1<br>Detail 2<br>Main idea<br>Detail 3<br>Detail 4 |
| End of the paragraph | | | Detail 1<br>Detail 2<br>Detail 3<br>Detail 4<br>Main idea |
| Beginning and end | | | Main idea<br>Detail 1<br>Detail 2<br>Detail 3<br>Detail 4<br>Main idea |
| Inferred main idea | | | Detail 1<br>Detail 2<br>Detail 3<br>Detail 4 |

we find in nature. In many of these pieces of matter we can easily see border regions where one substance stops and another begins. The mineral called granite is a good example. Granite is made up of four other minerals—feldspar, quartz, hornblende, and mica. These four ingredients have different colors, textures, and hardness, and so are easily distinguished. Granite is a coarse mixture.[5]

5. Tom R. Thomson, *Ideas from Chemistry* (Menlo Park, Calif.: Addison-Wesley, 1973), p. 7.

## Example 5    Main Idea in the Middle of the Paragraph

On May 17, 1954, the Supreme Court in *Brown v. Board of Education of Topeka, Kansas* ruled that, "in the field of public education the doctrine of 'separate but equal' has no place. Separate educational facilities are inherently unequal. Therefore, we hold that the plaintiffs [Brown and several similar cases] have been depirved of the equal protection of the laws guaranteed by the Fourteenth Amendment." <u>The Brown decision, which was rendered for all the plaintiffs, ruled the state school segregation laws unconstitutional.</u> The Court's decision on public education culminated more than a half century of legal efforts to crack the walls of segregation. It heralded the civil rights revolution of the 1950's and 1960's. The goals and techniques of the movement were many and varied, but this chapter focuses on the United States Supreme Court and public school desegregation.[6]

## Example 6    Main Idea at the End of the Paragraph

If you think you want to stick with writing for a while, there are two things you must continue to do. Write a lot. Read a lot. The best way to connect with the skill and craft and magic of good writing is to read good writers. They cannot give you the experiences to write about. They cannot give you the creative spark, or the talent, or whatever it is that makes a piece of writing memorable. But they can show you how they did it. And a lot can be absorbed by osmosis. Read the master story tellers—Hemingway, Steinbeck, Faulkner, Chekhov, De Maupassant, Somerset Maugham, Eudora Welty, Flannery O'Connor, D. H. Lawrence, Katherine Mansfield. Read stories by writers who are publishing fiction now, in popular magazines like *Esquire, The Atlantic Monthly, Harper's, The New Yorker.* Read the O. Henry Prize collections that come out each year, and Martha Foley's annual collection *The Best American Short Stories.* See if your local bookshop carries any literary magazines, quarterlies, or underground periodicals that include fiction and poetry. <u>The wider</u>

---

6.  Thomas T. Lyons, *The Supreme Court and Individual Rights in Contemporary Society* (Menlo Park, Calif.: Addison-Wesley, 1975), p. 41.

your reading tastes the clearer sense you will have for the possibilities of imaginative writing and what you want to do with it.[7]

## Example 7    Main Ideas at the Beginning and End of the Paragraph

Next in importance to the economic function of colonial women, discussed in Chapter One, was their contribution to the building of communities. As one historian has said, "The participation of women in every sphere of life and labor was absolutely imperative to the success of the American colonies." The Spaniards settled their colonies with soldiers, missionaries, and adventurers, as did the French. In both cases these largely male settlements were outposts for exploitation of the colonies rather than communities. It was the bringing of white women to the British colonies that altered the character of the British settlements. Whether housed in a primitive dugout shelter, a sod lean-to, or a log cabin, women attempted to recreate the life of the Old Country in the wilderness. Anthropologists refer to women as being "culture carriers," whose function it is to transmit the inheritance of culture to the growing child and the environment. Thus, pioneer women were essential not only to the survival of their families but to the building of communities in the New World.[8]

## Example 8    Inferred Main Idea

Then it was over. Creole and Sonny let out their breath, both soaking wet, and grinning. There was a lot of applause and some of it was real. In the dark, the girl came by and I asked her to take drinks to the bandstand. There was a long pause, while they talked up there in the indigo light and after awhile I saw the girl put a Scotch and milk on top of the piano for Sonny. He didn't seem to notice it, but just before they started playing again, he sipped from it and looked toward me, and nodded. Then he put it back on top of the piano. For me, then, as they began to play again, it glowed and shook above my brother's head like the very cup of trembling.[9]

7. James D. Houston, *Writing from the Inside* (Menlo Park, Calif.: Addison-Wesley, 1973), p. 82.
8. Gerda Lerner, *The Women in American History* (Menlo Park, Calif.: Addison-Wesley, 1971), pp. 22–23.
9. James Baldwin, *Going to Meet the Man* (New York: Dial Press, 1965), p. 140.

There are also paragraphs that contain no main idea at all; they simply support a main idea contained in another paragraph, usually the one immediately preceding it. This situation is exemplified in the next passage. The second paragraph consists entirely of details that support the main idea of the first paragraph.

### Example 9    A Paragraph Without a Main Idea

You also have an organization weakness if one or more of the positions that your people hold require unique combinations of abilities. Some salesmen, for example, have excellent ability to open new accounts but poor ability to provide routine service to existing accounts. To resolve this problem, some firms have two kinds of sales positions: one with responsibility primarily for new business and the other with responsibility primarily for servicing existing business. In production, some managers have excellent ability to start up new facilities but poor ability to manage a going operation. To resolve this problem, some firms establish two kinds of production management positions: one with responsibility for start-up activities (and other special projects) and the other with responsibility for managing a going operation.

If you are with a nonprofit organization, you may face a similar weakness in your organization structure. For example, clergymen are often expected to function both as ministers and as administrators even though they may have little interest or training in administration. In universities, professors are sometimes expected to be both excellent teachers and excellent researchers.[10]

In some rare cases an author will highlight the main idea for students by shading it. An example of this technique, used in a mathematics textbook, is show in Fig. 3.3.

## Generating Main Ideas

While locating main-idea sentences is a popular approach, students must be alerted to the fact that the technique does not always work, because authors often do not state clear topic or main-idea sentences in their paragraphs (Braddock, 1974). In addition, looking for one topic sentence can become a me-

10. Raymond O. Leon, *Manage More by Doing Less* (New York: McGraw-Hill, 1964), pp. 235–236.

# Figure 3.3  Shading Main Ideas

| B | A supermarket receipt illustrates an important property of positive numbers. |

| | |
|---|---|
| 0.92 | Prod |
| 1.43 | Prod |
| 2.89 | Meat |
| 1.47 | Groc |
| 6.71 | Total |

Study Mini-Review 26 (Addition of Positive Numbers; Addition of Negative Numbers).

> **Every sum of positive numbers is also a positive number.**

Adding negative numbers is similar. For example, in a football game you could consider yards lost as negative.

| Down | Yards Lost |
|------|-----------|
| 1 | −5 |
| 2 | −1 |
| 3 | −15 |
| | −21    Total yards lost |

> **Every sum of negative numbers is also a negative number.**

To add negative numbers, add their absolute values. Then write the answer with a negative sign.

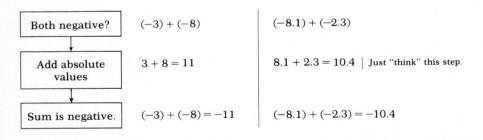

| Both negative? | $(-3) + (-8)$ | $(-8.1) + (-2.3)$ |
| Add absolute values | $3 + 8 = 11$ | $8.1 + 2.3 = 10.4$   Just "think" this step. |
| Sum is negative. | $(-3) + (-8) = -11$ | $(-8.1) + (-2.3) = -10.4$ |

chanical process that discourages readers from mentally interacting with writers. It is Axelrod's (1975) opinion that the topic sentence approach is too gimmicky; the pupil is learning a trick and not a skill.

An alternative to the topic sentence approach is described below. It is based on the premise that ultimately students must be able to determine main ideas on their own. Teachers can help students achieve this goal by teaching them the following steps.

1.  *Find the topic.* Writers usually choose to write about people, things, or concepts. Who or what they write about is the topic. Students can usually determine the topic of a passage by finding a word or phrase that is repeated several times.

2.  *Find the main idea.* To expand on their topic, writers make a certain point or generalization. This point is their main idea. Students can usually determine the main idea of a passage by answering the question "What, in general, does the author tell me about the topic?"

3.  *Complete the checkout.* Writers support or prove their main ideas by using facts, details, examples, illustrations, dates, and sometimes analogies. If students find none of the above to further explain an author's main idea, then they probably have failed to state the main idea correctly. They can complete their checkout by asking, "Does the author tell me more about the main idea? Am I told when, where, how, or why? Does the writer give me any examples?" The checkout step is especially important, because it helps students understand *why* their main-idea statement is right or wrong.

The following examples show how this approach can be used with paragraphs from a business book and a science book.

## Example 10    Generating Main Ideas: Business

Most managers fail to seek ideas from subordinates. Many of those who do, fail to listen effectively when the ideas requested are offered. Discouraging as this conclusion may seem, there is ample evidence of its validity. If you have doubt, ask ten people below middle management in any organization; the results will be devastating. The reasons for this self-defeating behavior range from psychological to pragmatic implications. Some managers are simply self-centered and uninterested in the view of others—particularly their subordinates. Others honestly feel that on many matters the views of their subordinates would be neither relevant nor particularly helpful. Still others fear the impression of weakness that they suspect would result from asking the opinion of a subordinate. Some who solicit opinions with sincere intent find it difficult if not impossible to pay serious attention to the suggestions that are forthcoming.[11]

1. *Find the topic.* What word or phrase is repeated? The word and its pronoun that is repeated is *managers.*

2. *Find the main idea.* The answer to the question "What, in general, does the author say about managers?" is "Most managers fail to seek ideas from their subordinates."

3. *Complete the checkout.* Does the author tell readers where, when, why, or how, or give examples? In this paragraph the author tells the readers *why.* According to the passage, some managers fail to seek ideas from their subordinates because they are self-centered; others feel the views of subordinates are irrelevant; some believe seeking out ideas from subordinates is a sign of weakness. These, then, are details that tell readers more or give them specifics about the main idea. The main idea has been checked out, and now readers know that the other information (details) in the paragraph does give them more specifics about the main idea. They have, therefore, generated the correct main idea.

## Example 11    Generating Main Ideas:
### Science

To his surprise, it was in a slightly different position among the stars the next night. He looked at it *every* clear night and saw that it was moving eastward. Then in early February it reversed its direction, as a planet does. The next November, when the calculations of this wanderer's orbit were completed, it was found to lie at just about 2.8 AU from the sun. It was named Ceres (for the Roman goddess of Sicily), and joyfully hailed as the missing planet. Measurements of its size showed that Ceres is disappointingly small (only about 500 miles across). Even though its orbit lay between those of Mars and Jupiter, both easily visible to the naked eye, Ceres could only be seen with a good telescope.[12]

1. *Find the topic.* What word or phrase is repeated? The word is *Ceres,* which is directly mentioned three times and referred to as *it* eight times.

2. *Find the main idea.* The answer to the question "What, in general, does the author say about Ceres?" is "The planet Ceres was discovered."

11. Charles D. Flory and R. Alec MacKenzie, *The Credibility Gap in Management* (New York: Van Nostrand Reinhold, 1971), p. 90.

12. Lou Williams Page, *Ideas from Astronomy* (Menlo Park, Calif.: Addison-Wesley, 1973), p. 138.

3. *Complete the checkout.* Does the author tell readers where, when, why, or how, or give examples? She tells us *where.* It was discovered "at just about 2.8 AU from the sun. . . . its orbit lay between those of Mars and Jupiter." She tells *when.* It was discovered in November 1801 (1801 was mentioned in the previous paragraph). She tells *how.* "He [Piazzi] looked at it *every* clear night and saw that it was moving eastward." He used a "good telescope." She also tells us *how big* it was: "only about 500 miles across." The main idea has been checked out, and now readers know that the other information (details) in the paragraph gave them more specifics about the main idea. Their main idea is correct.

This process may seem like a lengthy one, but students will find that after they have practiced the technique with the teacher's guidance a few times, the main ideas will come to them very quickly. They will also begin to see that whole paragraphs sometimes do nothing more than give details to support a main idea in another paragraph. In some cases, depending on their purpose for reading the selection, students can merely skim these paragraphs.

## "What Did the Author Say?"

Secondary teachers can help students apply the skill of determining main ideas to textbooks by adapting a technique developed by community college instructor Virginia Moore Shrauger (1975). The technique, entitled "What did the author say?" is designed to help students read actively, to organize, recall, and understand main ideas, and to write, summarize, and outline main ideas. A modification of Shrauger's steps follows.

1. *First session.*
   (a) Students are asked to read a selection from their textbooks containing approximately a thousand words. They should be prepared to recall what they have read.
   (b) About ten minutes are given for the reading.
   (c) After reading, students answer, in writing, the question "What did the author say?"
   (d) No special instructions on reading skills are given.
   (e) Selected student answers are mimeographed and distributed to the class (students' names are omitted).

2. *Second session.*
   (a) The criterion answer is shared with the students.
   (b) Students score the answers by using the scale shown in Fig. 3.4.

# Figure 3.4  Scoring Scale

Scoring Scale for use with "What did the author say?" A score of 1 point is the minimum which can be earned by a student, and no student is to earn less than 1 point. A score of 10 points is the maximum. Scores appearing to fall between number values on the scale are scored at the lower value. Scores are determined by comparing the ideas expressed in the student answer with those included in the criterion answer.

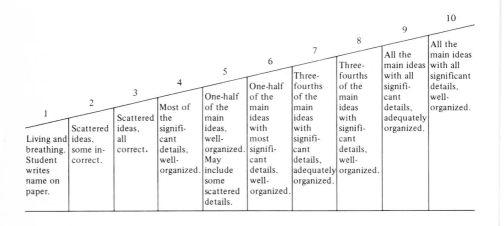

From " 'What Did the Author Say?' A Technique to Organize, Understand and Remember Ideas." Virginia Moore Shrauger. In Roy Sugimoto (ed.), *Proceedings of the Eighth Annual Conference of the Western College Reading Association*, 1975, p. 170. Reprinted by permission.

3. *Third session.* Instruction is given as needed in selecting main ideas and details, paraphrasing, recognizing organizational patterns, and organizing writing. The same article is used, and, if necessary, additional articles are assigned.

4. *Fourth and subsequent sessions.* The steps are repeated at the discretion of the instructor.

According to Shrauger, students enjoy the activity and improve as they gain more experience with it. In fewer than 12 practice sessions the student scores move to the higher end of the scoring scale. Of course, teachers using this activity should be sensitive to the ability level of students. The technique may not work well, for example, in classes containing learning disabled students, who could be embarrassed by the publication of their poorly written work.

# Generic Approaches to Teaching Organizational Patterns

The preceding section included some specific suggestions on how to teach main idea/details, the most basic organizational pattern. This section includes a description of some generic approaches that can be used to teach the main idea/ detail pattern and other organizational patterns to be discussed in the next two chapters. The generic approaches include the direct teaching model, adjunct questions, and reading/study guides. Each approach is discussed and then exemplified in models.

## Direct Teaching Model

The *direct teaching model* for teaching main ideas and other organizational patterns is based loosely on the *Oregon direct instruction model* (Becker and Englemann, 1977). This model emphasizes small-group, face-to-face instruction by teachers who use carefully sequenced lessons in reading. It is based on a behavioristic approach, which maintains that all behaviors are learned and skills must be directly taught if children are to attain specific behavioral objectives. The approach is highly structured; the student's behavior is directly dependent on the teacher's behavior. Reinforcement or rewards are used to encourage desired behaviors.

An important component of direct instruction is the translation of teaching strategies into a *format* that specifies exactly how the teacher is to present the strategy. The format includes what to say, what words to emphasize, what to ask, how to signal (a cue given by the teacher that tells students when to make group responses), and how to correct students appropriately, which is done through praise, probing questions, and rechecking (Carnine and Silbert, 1979).

The success of the direct teaching model for teaching reading has been well established when used with low-income, primary grade students (Guthrie, 1977) and as a prereading program (King, 1978). Although some educators might argue that this approach is appropriate only for use with instructionally naive students, Englemann and Carnine (1976) demonstrated its success with more sophisticated students.

The direct teaching model has been practiced on a very limited basis at the secondary level. However, after citing the success of their model in the primary grades, Becker and Englemann encouraged the extension of their model to higher grades because "schools do not teach the language and conceptual skills that are the building blocks of intelligent behavior. . . . It would seem logical that the model would be a source of expert input about the design of curricula for the higher grades (particularly for teaching the cognitive skills which underlines reading comprehension and largely defines intelligent behavior" (Becker and Englemann, 1977, p. 9).

# Model 3.1  Direct Teaching

**Pattern: Main Idea/Details**
**Content: Social Studies**

*[Here the teacher defines main idea.]*

**Teacher:  I am going to try to help you pick out main ideas in your social studies book. Remember, a main idea consists of the topic of a passage and a general statement about the topic. What is a main idea?**

*Students:  A general statement about a topic.*

*[The process is explained.]*

**Teacher:  We can usually identify a topic by identifying a word or phrase that is repeated. For example, in the first paragraph on this page, what word or phrase is repeated?**

*Students:  African people.*

*[Now students are led through the thinking process.]*

**Teacher:  Good, African people. Now what, in general, does the author tell us about African people?**

*Students:  Many African people produce the things they need in order to live.*

*[Teacher reminds students about the meaning of the checkout.]*

**Teacher:  OK. Now we can see if our main idea is correct by completing the checkout. A checkout can be completed by seeing if the author tells us where, when, why, or how, or gives us examples. How do we complete a checkout?**

*Students:  By seeing if the author tells us where, when, why, or how, or gives us examples.*

---

This direct teaching approach may be an appropriate alternative for those secondary students who are failing to learn from textbooks. According to Carnine and Silbert (1979), the approach is particularly effective with handicapped, bilingual, and economically disadvantaged students. All students could very well benefit from this approach when a particular organizational pattern, as discussed in this and the next two chapters, is being introduced to a class.

A model for teaching main ideas through the use of direct teaching is illustrated in Model 3.1. The dialogue given in the model is an example of a

**Teacher: Good, these are the details that support the author's main ideas. How does the author support his main idea in this passage? Does he tell us where, when, why, or how, or give us examples?**

*[Now students apply the checkout technique.]*

Students: *Examples are given. It says that even today many African people produce their own food, make their own clothes, and build their own homes.*

**Teacher: So our checkout proves we've selected the correct main idea. The author provided us with a term that means "producing goods on your own." What is it?**

Students: *Subsistence economy.*

*[The teacher reviews the process.]*

**Teacher: Fine. Now to review our process. The first step in finding a main idea is what?**

Students: *Find the topic.*

**Teacher: And the topic of this passage was what?**

Students: *African people.*

**Teacher: And what do we do next?**

Students: *Give a general statement about the topic.*

**Teacher: What general statement did we make about African people?**

Students: *Many of them produce on their own the things they need for living.*

**Teacher: Good, and then we were able to check out this main idea because the author gave us details to support the general statement. Now let's move on to another passage.**

*[Teacher provides more than one example.]*

script that teachers can prepare and follow in their teaching. It is designed to help students apply the skill of determining the main idea to a social studies selection. When corrections are necessary, teachers would ask probing questions and recheck student responses.

Note that special insertions have been placed in Model 3.1—and in all other models included in this and the next two chapters. The purpose of these insertions is to alert you to important and unique aspects of the models. These insertions would not, of course, appear in the materials handed to the students.

## Adjunct Questions

The value of using *adjunct questions* (questions read before, during, or after a reading assignment) to enhance student comprehension of text has been fairly well established. Readers recall more when questions are asked about the content of a text than when questions are not used. Questions tend to make readers pay closer attention to the content. Questions increase student inspection time and the expenditure of cognitive effort. Reynolds and Anderson, in explaining the positive results of their study on adjunct questions, state it this way: "Questions cause readers to selectively attend to question-relevant information; and a process supported by the extra attention to question-relevant information causes more of this information to be learned" (Reynolds and Anderson, 1980, pp. 17–18).

After reviewing studies on adjunct questions, Durkin (1981) concluded that using questions appears to be a worthwhile technique for promoting comprehension. Tierney and Cunningham (1980), who reviewed a large number of studies on the use of questions to improve comprehension, also concluded that they have a beneficial effect on learning conditions. They are particularly effective when the material to be read is difficult to read; when the goal of the questions is to learn only the information that is necessary to answer the questions; and when the information tested by the questions is among the most important in the text.

This last point was reinforced by Durkin (1981); she believes that teachers who use questions should select only those that deal with important content. Teachers, she said, should become better questioners if they wish their students to become better comprehenders. Rothkopf (1980) also warns us that questions should be used sparingly. Too many, he says, will slow down the reading process and may interfere with the students' ability to integrate scattered information contained in the text.

The adjunct question models included in this chapter on main ideas/details and those in the following two chapters illustrate how teachers can direct students' attention to the important content in the text as reflected by the nature of the organizational pattern used by the author. Brunner and Campbell offer three principles that should be understood regarding the relationship between teacher questions and reading comprehension.

1. Good questioning techniques result when teachers have consciously thought through their instructional strategies. . . .
2. Since reading is an active process, the more the student understands how specific questions relate to specific comprehension levels (and skills), the more he will be able to guide his reading. . . .
3. Teacher's questions should be based on some understanding of the nature of reading comprehension. (Brunner and Campbell, 1978, p. 111)

A model for teaching main ideas through the use of adjunct questions is given in Model 3.2. Note that in this model not only are students given appropriate questions to respond to, but also page references are included to help them identify the portions of the text that contain the information needed to answer the questions.

## Reading/Study Guides

A *reading/study guide* is designed to enhance students' understanding of their textbooks while simultaneously improving their ability to deal with the different organizational patterns. Herber (1978) contends that this dual development of content understanding and reading ability is accomplished because reading/ study guides give direction to the use of appropriate learning strategies, which leads to an understanding of the specific content information. Further, he believes the key to the success of guides is that they simulate the internal organization of textbook chapters.

Herber defines *simulation* as "an artificial representation of real experience; a contrived series of activities which, when taken together, approximate the experience of the process that ultimately is to be applied independently. As it pertains to the process of comprehension in reading, simulation would be to contrive a set of activities which approximate what one does when one comprehends independently" (Herber, 1975, pp. 515–516).

Guidelines for constructing a reading/study guide follow. They have been adapted from Estes and Vaughan (1978).

1. Carefully analyze the purpose of your lesson and the nature of the reading assignment. Determine its predominate organizational pattern. While various paragraphs may be organized in different ways, usually a single pattern will characterize the entire assignment.

2. Determine the important ideas that are reflected in the assignment. They may be directly stated or implied. Jot these ideas down.

3. Construct a pattern guide that simulates what a reader will have to do in order to comprehend the reading assignment. If, for example, the assignment follows a problem/solution pattern, the guide should clearly indicate that the reader must search out the major ideas associated with the *problem,* the *effects* of the problem, the *cause* of the problem, and the *solution* to the problem.

4. Allow students to use the guide as they read the assignment. They should then discuss their answers in small groups, defend their answers, and resolve their differences.

Estes and Vaughan expressed an important caveat regarding reading/ study guides. They should not be blindly adopted by teachers; rather they

# Model 3.2  Adjunct Questions
**Pattern: Main Idea/Details**
**Content: Social Studies**

*To the student:* All of you have been taught how to select main ideas. Try to apply the skill on your own. The questions below will help you. Consider these questions before and as you read each section.

### Section I: Introduction

Topic: The Executive Branch (p. 209)

1. What two things does the first paragraph say about the executive branch of the U.S. government?

   *[This question points out that an illustration reinforces the main idea.]*

2. How does the artist's picture of the pipes (p. 208) help you to understand the two statements you found in Question 1?

3. What does the reading say you will learn in this chapter?

4. On the basis of these answers, what is the main idea of this section?

### Section II: Two Parts of the Executive Branch

Topic: Department of Defense and Social Security Administration (pp. 209–211)

*[This question helps students check out the main idea.]*

1. What is the main idea that the paragraphs about the Defense Department

---

should be adapted to a set of circumstances. The authors also note several of the guides' advantages. For instance, guides emphasize the interrelationships between content and skills; they tend to facilitate learning; they foster activity and focus on conceptualization; they emphasize process as well as product; they promote problem solving; and they develop reading skills and independence.

What does the research reveal about the effectiveness of reading/study guides? Grant (1979) and Tierney and Cunningham (1980) have reviewed the research on reading/study guides. Grant (1979) feels that although research studies dealing with the use of study guides is far from extensive, some conare trying to tell you? List five details that help to prove the main idea you have identified.

2. What is the main idea contained in the paragraphs about the Social Security Administration? List three details that help to prove the main idea you have identified.

   *[This question encourages inferential thinking.]*

3. Why did the author use these two readings about the Department of Defense and the Social Security Administration? (What was he trying to tell you?)

## Section III: Managing the Bureaucracy

Topic: The Federal Bureaucracy (pp. 211–212)

1. What is the definition of a bureaucracy?
2. What are Clinton Rossiter and President Franklin Roosevelt telling you about the federal bureaucracy?
3. Why is a pyramid used to illustrate the shape of a bureaucracy?

   *[Questions 4, 5, and 6 encourage students to use graphic aids.]*

4. List the levels, from top to bottom, in a federal bureaucracy (see chart page 213).
5. Answer the questions on page 212 about the chart on page 213.
6. According to the last two paragraphs of this section, why is the chart on page 213 somewhat misleading?
7. On the basis of the answers to the above questions, what is the main idea of this section?

clusions still can be drawn from them. "First, the use of study guides does appear to be an aid to comprehension when used in conjunction with group discussions. Second, and perhaps most important, in order for the students to make efficient use of the guides, they should be written on a level commensurate with the students' abilities. Third, guides may function as a pre-reading, pur-pose-setting method and as a post-reading method" (Grant, 1979, p. 58).

Tierney and Cunningham's (1980) interpretation of the research completed on reading and study guides is that it is "encouraging." They feel that more research is needed to discover how different types of guides should be developed so that they will be more consistently effective with students.

# Model 3.3  Reading Study Guide

**Pattern: Main Idea/Details**
**Content: Generic, Applicable to All Content Areas**

*[These questions lead students through
the process.]*

1. *Topic:* What word or phrase is repeated in the paragraph(s)?
2. *Main idea.* What does the author tell you about the topic?
3. *Checkout.* How does the author explain his main idea—where, when, how, why, or give examples?

---

The reading/study guides in Models 3.3, 3.4, 3.5, and 3.6 illustrate how the process of determining main ideas can be simulated for students. The work sheet in Model 3.3 can be used to help students generate their own main ideas from their textbooks. It should be used after the step-by-step process (see pp. 85–87) for selecting main ideas has been explained. Teachers can assign specific paragraphs from expository textbooks and ask students to complete the work sheet after analyzing the paragraphs.

In Model 3.4 the reading/study guide helps students identify the main ideas contained in complexly written material about Islamic family life. Note that the multiple-choice format and the page references simplify the task for students.

Models 3.5 and 3.6 help students identify main ideas and draw conclusions in literature. Model 3.5 helps students draw conclusions about the characteristics of God that are inferred in biblical passages. After students draw their conclusions, they must supply quotes from the passages to justify their choices. Model 3.6 illustrates how one teacher helped his students draw conclusions about the author's purpose for writing a story.

## The Data Pattern

When authors inform readers by presenting a large collection of main ideas that are related but are at the same time relatively independent, they are utilizing the *data pattern* (Santeusanio, 1981). This pattern is also referred to as the informational pattern (Sack and Yourman, 1981) and the simple listing pattern (Niles, 1965).

Writers ordinarily focus on a single major topic that is subdivided into its component parts. Sometimes these topics or subtopics are compared and contrasted. The task of the reader is to recognize the author's major topics and

# Model 3.4 Reading/Study Guide
**Pattern: Main Idea**
**Content: Sociology**

This reading on Islamic family life can be best understood by focusing on the main ideas of each section. A main idea contains a topic (what the paragraph or section is about) and a statement about the topic (a declarative sentence). This guide is designed to assist you. Try to concentrate on main ideas as you complete the reading. Preview it first; then as you read the selection, complete the guide. Some of the multiple-choice answers are accurate details. Don't confuse those statements with statements of the main idea. You will have an opportunity to discuss your answers in a small-group discussion.

### Introduction (pp. 99–100)

Read this section to identify the definition of the family and the overall main idea of the introduction.

1. Definition of marriage (write it).

   *[Each choice is a declarative sentence.]*
2. The main idea of this section is that:
   (a) There are moral advantages of marriage.
   (b) All Muslims must marry.
   (c) Muslims are family-oriented and they see marriage as a religious duty.

### The Meaning of Marriage (pp. 100–101)

   *[Students must carefully inspect the passage to select the correct choice.]*
3. What is the main idea of the first paragraph of this section?
   (a) Marriage is a commitment to each other and God.
   (b) Marriage is mainly a commitment partners make to each other.
   (c) Marriage is mainly a commitment to God.
4. What is the main idea of the second paragraph of this section?
   (a) Celibacy is recommended for both men and women.
   (b) Marriage is mainly an economic transaction.
   (c) Although marriage provisions apply to men and women equally, there is no community property.

# Model 3.5  Reading/Study Guide
## Pattern: Main Idea/Details
## Content: Bible as Literature

The selections from the Scriptures depict God in a variety of ways. As you read them, try to decide what major characteristic of God the passage illustrates. For each passage, first select the characteristic. Then select some quotes from the passage that support your choice or prove that your choice is correct.

### Genesis 1:1–5, 24–28

*[Students must carefully inspect the passage to justify their choice.]*

1.  In this passage the characteristic attributed to God is:

    (a) Passion.

    (b) Creator.

    (c) Guardian.

    (d) Shepherd.

*[Students generate their own answers.]*

2.  Here are some quotes to support my choice.

### Genesis 6:5–8

3.  In this passage the characteristic attributed to God is:

    (a) Passion.

    (b) Creator.

    (c) Guardian.

    (d) Shepherd.

4.  Here are some quotes to support my choice.

---

subtopics, identify the main ideas related to these topics, and then synthesize the main ideas. The reader moves from identifying main ideas of individual paragraphs to identifying main ideas of complete sections of an article or chapter.

Chapters or articles written in the data pattern can be likened to a university with its various schools. When students first enter college, they find the college (major topic) has different schools (subtopics). These schools may include the

# Model 3.6 Reading/Study Guide
**Pattern: Main Idea/Details**
**Content: World Literature**

Many stories that are read by or to Indian children have been written for a specific purpose. Some of those purposes are listed below. Review the list of purposes. Then read each story. Decide what the author's main purpose was in writing the story. Place the number of the purpose next to the title of the story. There may be more than one purpose for each story. Be prepared to discuss and *justify your answers* in a group discussion.

> *[Follow-up discussion will contribute to student understanding of the text and of the process of selecting main points.]*

### Purpose of Story

1. To stir the emotions of children.
2. To teach children about holy places of pilgrimage.
3. To teach children about great scholars.
4. To teach children about great heroines or heroes.
5. To teach children about traditional Indian attitudes toward life.

_____ "The Mud Pie and the Dry Leaf" (p. 82)
_____ "The Fable of Kanya Kumari" (p. 83)
_____ "Panni" (p. 83)
_____ "The Turtle Who Fell off a Stick" (p. 84)

schools of education, liberal arts, business, law, and so on. The schools may even be further divided into departments (sub-subtopics). The school of education probably has departments of administration, counseling, curriculum, reading, special education, and so forth.

Authors who organize their ideas by using the data pattern begin with a major topic. A social studies author, for example, may choose to write on "immigration." This major topic can then be broken down into its component parts or subtopics, such as "reasons for immigration," "colonial immigration," "pre–Civil War immigration," "recent immigration," "number of immigrants," "where they settled," and "assimilation of immigrants."

# Figure 3.5  A Portion of a Table of Contents

By examining the table of contents of a text, as we suggested in Chapter 2, students can often get a quick glimpse of how an author is going to break down his major topics. For example, a portion of a table of contents from an economics book is reproduced in Fig. 3.5. Notice how the major topic "wheat" in Chapter 3 is clearly subdivided into those who grow it, buy it, mill it, bake it, and buy it.

# Introducing and Teaching the Data Pattern

Before introducing the data pattern, teachers may have to review the skill of reading for main ideas. After that is done, teachers can alert students to the fact that chapters and articles written in the data pattern consist mainly of a collection of straightforward main ideas that are relatively easy to follow as long as students recognize when writers move on to new topics. Naturally if students fail to recognize when authors move to new topics, they fail to comprehend the material. The teacher's primary responsibility, then, is to help students recognize changes in the author's thinking—that is, when the author has moved on to a new topic or subtopic. The relationship of subtopics to main ideas and details can be illustrated to students by presenting them with a diagram such as the one that appears in Fig. 3.6.

## Survey the Material

If the chapter or article that students have been asked to read contains well-organized major headings and subheadings, then surveying the material will help students focus on the author's major topics. The steps involved in surveying a chapter are discussed in Chapter 2 on pages 48–50.

## Reading/Study Guides

If the reading assignment is quite complex and contains few or no boldface headings, the teacher can prepare a reading/study guide that highlights the major topics for the students. In other words, the teacher shows the students when the author's thinking has changed (i.e., when he has moved on to a new subtopic).

A business teacher, for example, decided to assign to her students an article entitled "The Masterminds of Management" (*Dun's Review*, July 1976). This article discusses five men who made contributions to the field of management. The article contains no boldface headings, so a simple reading/study guide was prepared to help the students identify the major subtopics (each of the men) and the important main ideas and details related to each subtopic (their contributions to management). Example 12 illustrates the guide.

# Figure 3.6 Relationship of Main Ideas to Data Pattern

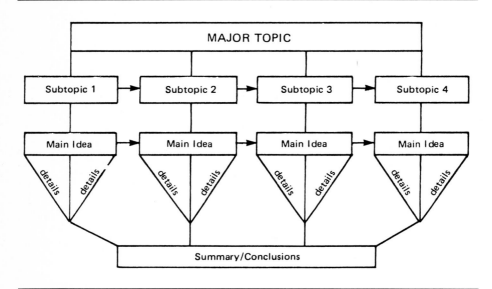

From Richard P. Santeusanio, *Developing Reading Skills for Business and Industry*, p. 151. Reprinted with permission. Copyright © 1981 CBI Publishing Co., Inc., 51 Sleeper St., Boston, Mass. 02210.

## Example 12    Reading/Study Guide for "The Masterminds of Management"

*Subtopic:* Mastermind

*Contribution:* In your own words, write the major contributions of each man.

J. Edgar Thompson

Andrew Carnegie

Frederick Taylor

Pierre duPont

Alfred Sloan, Jr.

# The Guided Reading Procedure

When students are required to recall a great deal of data—a large collection of main ideas and details—Manzo (1975) recommends that they interact with their teachers by using the guided reading procedure (GRP). According to Manzo, by using this procedure, students will recognize implicit questions, increase concentration during reading, practice self-correction, and organize new information.

In this procedure, which is recommended for use no more than once a week, students read a brief passage and then try to recall what was read without any aid. Intermediate students read approximately 500 words for 5 minutes; junior high students read approximately 700 words for 7 minutes; senior high students read approximately 2000 words for 10 mintues; and college students read approximately 2500 words for 12 minutes.

The steps in the procedure follow.

1. Set a purpose for reading (see Chapter 2). The teacher may choose to offer a general purpose: "Read in order to remember all that you can." Students close their books when the reading time has elapsed.

2. Students are asked to recall what they have read. The student responses are recorded on the board in an abbreviated form. All answers, regardless of their accuracy, are accepted. Answers should be numbered for ease of reference.

3. When the students run out of main ideas and details, they analyze their responses in order to determine inconsistencies and incomplete information. At this point they look back at the assignment to make their corrections or additions.

4. Students now organize the revised information into some structural form such as an outline, diagram, or map (see Chapter 6).

5. If students do not seem to have gained full understanding of the data, the teacher asks questions requiring synthesis and integration of the new information with previously learned data.

6. A traditional test, objective or essay, is administered to evaluate short-term memory. A similar test is administered at a later date to evaluate medium- or long-term memory.

Manzo (1975) reported "routinely positive accounts from field studies" of the GRP, and Bean and Pardi (1979) and Ankney and McClurg (1981) also reported significant student success when they used the procedure. The latter researchers also made the following points about the GRP.

- It is time-consuming but thorough.
- It is an interesting way of dealing with highly factual prose, especially in science and social studies textbooks.
- Students are eager to verify information and look for more data.
- It does not encourage learning at higher levels of comprehension, as Manzo has suggested.
- An aide or student should record student responses on the board. (Teachers may want to have two people recording so that twice as many answers can be recorded in the same amount of time.)

## Three-Level Guides

Material written in the data pattern lends itself well to analysis at three levels of comprehension—literal, inference of interpretive, and applied. This analysis can be accomplished by using the *three-level guides* described by Herber (1978). Three-level guides may also be prepared for material written in the other organizational patterns.

Three-level guides are a variation of reading/study guides that were discussed earlier in this chapter. They consist of declarative statements based on a reading selection written in the data pattern. The statements reflect what can be literally understood from the selection, what can be inferred from the selection, and what the reader may be able to apply from the selection. The applied level of comprehension is "the process of taking what has been known and applying it to what has just been learned, then evolving ideas which encompass both but extend beyond them" (Herber, 1978, p. 47). Readers can apply what they learn to their own lives, to something else they have read, or to solving a real problem.

## Constructing Three-Level Guides for the Data Pattern

Before preparing a three-level guide, teachers first analyze the information they feel students should learn from the reading selection. They identify important data that have been stated literally and data that require students to make inferences. Then in light of both the important literal and inferred ideas they have identified, teachers consider issues that will generate the application of those ideas.

Declarative statements are used when preparing the guides because, according to Herber (1978), they give students the feeling of what it is like to comprehend at each of the three levels. However, when teachers are encouraging thinking at the applied level, sometimes regular open-ended, free-response questions can stimulate more creative thinking than declarative statements can.

Teachers can prepare appropriate items for each level of comprehension by first asking themselves questions (Herber, 1978). For the literal level ask, "What important data are directly stated?" For the interpretive level ask, "What important data are implied or hinted at?" For the applied level ask, "What broad principles and applications can be generated from the information in this selection?" The answers to these questions will provide the teacher with items for each level of the guide.[13]

Once students have read the selection and completed their guides they can discuss their responses in small groups. During these discussions students share their reasons for accepting or rejecting the statements in the guide.

Example 13 illustrates a three-level guide.

## Example 13    Three-Level Guide for Social Studies

Part I: Literal Level

*Directions:* Place a check on the line before each statement that represents what was directly stated in Chapter 11. Do not put a check before those statements that do not represent what was stated in the chapter.

_____ 1. Andrew Jackson was very popular with the people.

_____ 2. Cotton was the leading crop of the South after 1800.

_____ 3. South Carolina opposed the tariff and threatened to secede from the Union.

_____ 4. John Q. Adams had a very successful term as our sixth president.

_____ 5. The election of 1824 represented the unity of our country.

_____ 6. Senators Webster and Calhoun disagreed on the issue of states' rights.

_____ 7. The rise of the common people brought about the growth of democracy.

_____ 8. The Whig party was founded to oppose the Democratic party's growing power.

_____ 9. The panic of 1837 was an economic depression.

_____ 10. William Henry Harrison won the election of 1840.

13. Readers who wish to have a more detailed description of three-level guides are referred to Chapter 3 of Harold Herber's *Teaching Reading in the Content Areas,* 2nd ed. (Englewood Cliffs, N.J.: Prentice-Hall, 1978).

Part II: Interpretive Level

*Directions:* Read the following statements. On the basis of what you read, place a check before the statements you feel the author would agree with. Be prepared to defend your answers.

_____ 1. The election of Andrew Jackson was a victory for wealthy southern planters.

_____ 2. The nominating convention gave more people the chance to choose candidates for president.

_____ 3. Jackson and Jefferson had the same ideas of democracy.

_____ 4. Jackson considered himself a servant of the people.

_____ 5. People in 1830 felt that the Indian Removal Act would solve Indian conflicts east of the Mississippi River.

_____ 6. Congressional leaders did not take South Carolina's threat to secession seriously.

_____ 7. The workers in the eastern states distrusted Jackson.

_____ 8. The cartoon of Andrew Jackson on page 235 shows the attitude of a majority of people in the United States since 1836.

_____ 9. During an economic panic such as in 1819 and 1837, all people experienced hard times.

_____ 10. Jackson's spoils system brought about an increase in democracy to the United States.

Part III: Applied Level

*Directions:* Check the statements you agree with. Be prepared to defend your answers.

_____ 1. The process of social mobility discussed in this chapter still works in American society today.

_____ 2. Jackson's techniques for handling problems should be adopted by our current president.

_____ 3. The political presidential campaign of 1840 was very similar to the campaign of 1980.

_____ 4. Political patronage is inevitable.

*Discussion questions.*

1. If you were a Cherokee Indian in 1834, would you have been outraged by the Indian Removal Act?

2. Are there groups in modern society who face problems similar to those faced by the Cherokee tribe? If so, in what ways are the problems similar?

# Graphic Organizers

Alvermann (1982) has developed and tested a way of helping students determine main ideas contained in material written in the data or simple-listing pattern. She suggests that prior to asking students to read such material, teachers can provide students with a partially completed *graphic organizer*. (Alvermann uses the term *graphic organizer* synonymously with the term *structured overview*, which is discussed in Chapter 1, pages 39–42.)

The key words or concepts contained in the graphic organizer are structured so that they reflect either a comparison/contrast or cause/effect ideational relationship among the terms. The teacher deliberately omits some of the key terms and replaces them with boxes. This technique encourages students to read for the purpose of filling in the missing information on the graphic organizer.

Next the teacher provides students with a simple introductory lesson that reviews the concept of comparison/contrast or cause/effect relationships. For example, teachers might ask students to compare and contrast two of their favorite television programs, or they may ask students to analyze what causes some teenagers to rebel and how this rebellion affects themselves and others.

Now the teacher displays the partially completed graphic organizer or an overhead, the blackboard, or a mimeographed handout. The students are reminded to keep the comparison/contrast or cause/effect organizer in mind as they read their assignment. They are also encouraged to remember the key terms from the organizer, because these terms will help them remember contrasting or cause/effect terms and relationships from the textbook. Students should be mentally filling in the empty slots contained in the graphic organizer.

At this point students read the material organized in the data pattern. After they have completed their reading, students discuss how the organizer helped them to understand the reading, or the teacher can have the students demonstrate in writing their ability to recall the material.

Based on her research involving only a small number of students, Alvermann feels this technique can help students recall the main ideas contained in writing that is organized in the data pattern. She believes this technique works this way because the imposed structure created by the teacher highlights ideational relationships of high-level information and this structure may serve as a cuing device that helps students to access main ideas and related details.

# Absorbing Data in Mathematical Problems

According to Earle (1976), when students are confronted with data in mathematical word problems, they must synthesize all three levels of comprehension in order to carry out the problems. For example, listed below are seven steps for solving word problems. Students must respond at the literal level for steps

1, 2, and 3, at the interpretive level (analyzing relationships among explicitly stated details) for steps 4 and 5, and at the application level for steps 6 and 7.

- *Step 1.*   Read through the problem quickly. Try to obtain a general grasp of the problem situation and *visualize* the problem as a whole. Don't be concerned with the actual names, numerals, or values.
- *Step 2.*   Examine the problem again. Try to understand exactly *what you are asked to find.* This may be stated as a question or command. Although it often comes at the end of the problem, it may appear anywhere in the problem.
- *Step 3.*   Read the problem again to note what *information is given.* At this point you are looking for exact numbers and values.
- *Step 4.*   Analyze the problem carefully to note the *relationship* of information given to what you are asked to find (Steps 2 and 3). Note information which seems to be missing. Also [note] surplus information.
- *Step 5. Translate* the relationships to *mathematical terms.* Indicate both the values and operations. This almost always involves planning a *sequence* of steps which correspond to the operations. The end result will be one or more mathematical sentences or *equations.*
- *Step 6.*   Perform the necessary *computation.*
- *Step 7.*   Examine the solution carefully. *Label* it to correspond to what the problem asks you to find. Finally, check the value against your grasp of the problem situation to judge whether it seems *sensible.*[14]

## Mathematics and Three-Level Guides

Both Earle (1976) and Riley and Pachtman (1978) feel that some students may not be able to synthesize and transfer general directions to problem solving and that reading guides can provide students with more guidance. Riley and Pachtman (1978) purport that three-level mathematics guides tell students *how* to do problems as opposed to just telling them *what* to do. The guides, they say, provide more guidance for students because rather than generate alternatives themselves, students simply have to recognize correct alternatives.

They also believe that three-level mathematics guides encourage students to see relationships among the various aspects of the problem, including the facts, the ideas, and alternative ways of solving the problem. A three-level mathematics guide, created by Riley and Pachtman, is reproduced in Fig. 3.7.

14.  Richard A. Earle, *Teaching Reading and Mathematics* (Newark, Del.: International Reading Association, 1976), pp. 49–50. Reprinted with permission of Richard A. Earle and the International Reading Association.

# Figure 3.7  Three-Level Guide for Mathematics

## Word Problem Reading Guide

Problem: A printing press which Ralph works can print 15,000 sheets of paper per hour. How many sheets can the press print per minute?

Part I. Facts of the problem.
  Directions: Read the word problem above. Then, under column A, check those statements that contain the important facts of the problem. Refer back to the problem to verify your responses. Under column B, check those statements you think will help you solve the problem.

| A<br>Facts | B<br>Will help | |
|---|---|---|
| ——————— | ——————— | 1. The printing press can print 15,000 sheets per *minute*. |
| ——————— | ——————— | 2. The printing press can print 15,000 sheets per *hour*. |
| ——————— | ——————— | 3. The problem asks how many sheets can be printed in one minute. |
| ——————— | ——————— | 4. Ralph works at a printing company. |

Part II. Mathematical ideas and interpretation.
  Directions: Check the statements that contain math ideas related to this problem. Refer back to Part I (Column B) to verify your responses. (You may wish to change some of your responses in Part I.)

————————  1. There are 60 seconds in one *minute*.
————————  2. The word "per" often suggests division.
————————  3. Division is the opposite of multiplication.
————————  4. "Per" may suggest a proportion.
————————  5. There are 60 minutes in one *hour*.
————————  6. Since a minute is less than an hour, the answer will be less than 15,000.

Part III. Numerical depictions.
  Directions: Below are possible ways of computing a solution. Check those that apply to this problem. Refer back to Parts I (Column B) and II to verify your responses. (You may wish to change some of your responses in Part I or II.)

————————  1. $60 \times ? = 15,000$
————————  2. $\dfrac{15,000}{60} = ?$
————————  3. $15,000 \div 60 = ?$
————————  4. $15,000 \times 60 = ?$
————————  5. $\dfrac{15,000}{?} = 60$

Based on your responses to Parts I, II and III, compute the answer to the problem.

From James D. Riley and Andrew B. Pachtman, "Reading Mathematical Word Problems: Telling Them What to Do Is Not Telling Them How to Do It," *Journal of Reading* 21(1978):532. Reprinted with permission of James Riley, Andrew Pachtman, and the International Reading Association.

---

## Figure 3.8  PQ4R Outline Sheet

---

1. Preview:
   a.   First reading of problem
   b.   List unknown words and phrases for possible discussion:
      1) consecutive _____
      2) even _____
      3) integers _____
      4) _____

2. Question:
   a.   Second reading
   b.   Write direct question of problem:
      Find 3 consecutive even integers _____

3. Read:
   a.   Third reading
   b.   List all word facts of problems in some logical order:
      1) 4 times the first _____
      2) decreased by the second _____
      3) is 12 more than _____
      4) twice the third _____
      5) _____

---

Despite the apparent virtues of a guide like this one, Riley (1979) was unable to demonstrate the clear superiority of guides over the more traditional direct reading method that consists of a simple work sheet containing three questions: (1) What are the facts of the problem? (2) What are the numerical expressions related to the problem? (3) What are the mathematical concepts that can be applied to the problem?

## Mathematics and PQ4R

Maffei (1973) offers a clear-cut method for absorbing, analyzing, and applying data found in mathematics problems. He does this by applying Thomas and Robinson's (1977) PQ4R method, a variation of the SQ3R study approach.

4. Reflect:

    a.  Fourth reading

    b.  What is x, the unknown quantity, representing?

        Let $x$ = 1st consecutive even integer: $x$, $x + 2$, $x + 4$

    c.  Translate word facts into algebraic facts with the use of x:

        1) $4(x)$ _____

        2) $-(x + 2)$ _____

        3) $= 12 +$ _____

        4) $2(x + 4)$ _____

        5) _____

5. Rewrite:

    a.  Rewrite algebraic facts in terms of a "balanced" equation and then solve
        for x:

$$4x - (x + 2) = 12 + 2(x + 4)$$
$$=$$
$$=$$
$$x = 22$$

6. Review:

    a.  Substitute value of x in equation to check for true sentence:

        Check: $4(22) - (22 + 2) = 12 + 2(22 + 4)$

    b.  Does the problem make sense in terms of the question? 22, 24, and 26
        are 3 consecutive even integers such that. . . .

From Anthony C. Maffei, "Reading Analysis in Mathematics," *Journal of Reading* 16(1973):547. Reprinted with permission of Anthony C. Maffei and the International Reading Association.

The six components of PQ4R are preview, question, read, reflect, recite, and review. For mathematics problems Maffei changes *recite* to *rewrite*.

    When using this approach, teachers should provide students with a PQ4R outline sheet (see Fig. 3.8) and then follow the steps below.

    1. *Preview.* After reading the problem for general ideas, students write down next to their P step unfamiliar words and phrases. From context clues or with the help of another student, the teacher, or a dictionary, the words are defined.

2. *Question.* As students reread the problem, they zero in on the specific questions to be answered.

3. *Read.* During this third reading of the problem students identify and write down specific phrases and sentences related to the problem, such as "less than" and "as much as."

4. *Reflect.* At this point the teacher asks students to reflect on the type of word problem they are handling. Relationships are analyzed (motion, mixtures, areas, unknown quantity, etc.).

5. *Rewrite.* After students read the problem for the final time, they rewrite the numerical information as a balanced equation.

6. *Review.* Students substitute the known value of $x$ into the equation. They also see if their work makes sense in terms of the question in step 2.

# Comparing and Contrasting Data

## Introduction

Rather than simply present data in a straightforward fashion, some writers may compare and contrast it. This presentation can confuse some students, because they can lose track of the author's thoughts, especially if the author compares (shows similarities) and contrasts (shows differences) more than two people, events, concepts, or ideas.

Confusion may also result when authors compare or contrast data and integrate it with other ideational relationships such as cause/effect. Example 14 is a case in point.

### Example 14    Conflicting Ideational Relationships

In the passage below the author first makes a *comparison* (both the chromosphere and the corona were "first observed only during total eclipses"). Then a *contrast* is made at the same time that a *cause/effect* relationship is discussed (the "corona extends out farther than the chromosphere" gives the contrast and the cause; the corona "can be seen when the chromosphere and the photosphere are both covered by the moon" gives the effect). In the next sentence a *cause/effect* relationship is used to explain a *comparison* ("Like the chromosphere, it [the corona] is usually invisible" gives the comparison and the effect; "the photosphere is so bright" gives the cause.)

Like the chromosphere, the corona was first observed only during total eclipses. Because the corona extends out farther than the chro-

mosphere it can be seen when the chromosphere and the photosphere are both covered by the moon. Like the chromosphere, it
is usually invisible because the photosphere is so bright.[15]

While this example illustrates how authors can inadvertently confuse their
readers, Fig. 3.9 shows how an author clarifies comparative and contrasting
data by use of visual aids. The charts nicely highlight the similarities and differences among three different types of city governments.

## Signal Words

Teachers can help students recognize when data is being compared or contrasted or both by familiarizing them with *signal words* associated with this
pattern. These words include *however, but, although, yet, unless, while, similarly, like, same, different, but also, not only, conversely, as well as, on the
other hand, by contrast.*

Example 15 reprints some passages from a biology text. The signal words
the author used to make the comparison have been circled.

### Example 15    Signal Words: Biology

The origin and structure of cilia and flagella seem to be fundamentally
the (same.) In each case they grow out of basal bodies. These have
the (same) structure as centrioles and are formed by them.

The cilium of flagellum itself has not only the outer ring of nine
microtubules (each now with just *one* accessory tubule attached to
it) (but also) two central fibrils that are (identical) to microtubules in
their construction (Fig. 5.22). In (both) cilia and flagella, the entire
assembly is sheathed in a membrane which is simply an extension
of the cell membrane.

The (similarities) between the structure of cilia, flagella, basal
bodies, and centrioles and the structure of microtubules suggest that
we are dealing with another one of the fundamental architectural
components of cells.[16]

Some passages from a sociology text are given in Example 16. The signal
words the author used to make the contrasts have been circled.

15. Lou Williams Page, *Ideas from Astronomy* (Menlo Park, Calif.: Addison-Wesley, 1973),
    p. 165.
16. John W. Kimball, *Biology*, 4th ed. (Reading, Mass.: Addison-Wesley, 1978), pp. 78–79.

# Figure 3.9 Comparison/Contrast of Three Types of City Government

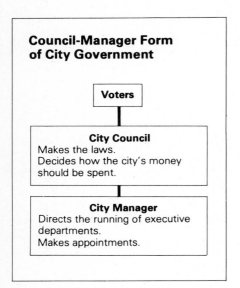

**Council-Manager Form of City Government**

Voters

**City Council**
Makes the laws.
Decides how the city's money should be spent.

**City Manager**
Directs the running of executive departments.
Makes appointments.

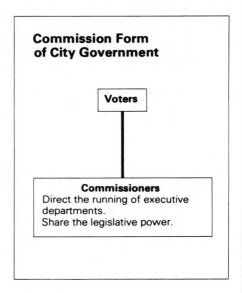

**Commission Form of City Government**

Voters

**Commissioners**
Direct the running of executive departments.
Share the legislative power.

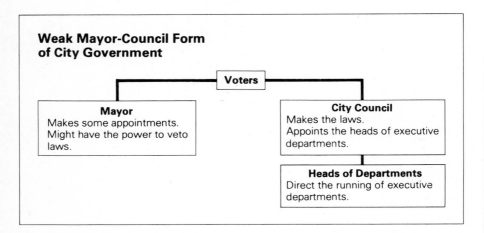

**Weak Mayor-Council Form of City Government**

Voters

**Mayor**
Makes some appointments.
Might have the power to veto laws.

**City Council**
Makes the laws.
Appoints the heads of executive departments.

**Heads of Departments**
Direct the running of executive departments.

## Example 16   Signal Words: Sociology

An **in-group** is *any group or social category to which a person feels he or she belongs*—family, members of the (same) sex, people of the (same) age, those who share the (same) religious or ethnic background, fellow construction workers or graduate students or mothers, fellow countrymen. (Conversely,) an **out-group** is *any group or social category to which a person feels he or she does not belong*—other families, the opposite sex, those higher (or lower) in the company, people from other nations. Out-groups include (both) those people an individual rejects or ignores and those who reject or ignore that individual. [17]

Back in 1909, Charles Horton Cooley coined the term **primary group** to describe *a small, intimate group of people who relate to one another in direct, personal ways*—for example, a family, a child's play group, peer groups, work groups, friends, neighbors (in the traditional sense), and lovers. Cooley wanted to (distinguish) these groups from *secondary groups* in which relationships are formal and impersonal—committees, business acquaintances, professional associations, and neighbors who are cordial but distant. The chief (difference) between the two kinds of groups lies in the quality of relationships between members and the degree of individual involvement. [18]

Sometimes writers will compare or contrast ideas *without* the use of signal words. Notice how mass and weight are contrasted without signal words in Example 17, which reprints a paragraph from a physics text. In cases like this it is possible that some students would not infer that two topics are being contrasted.

## Example 17   No Signal Words

In the last section, the relation between weight and mass was discussed briefly. As we saw, mass is a fundamental property of an object and does not depend on where the object is; weight is the

17. Ronald C. Federico, *Sociology*, 2nd ed. (Reading, Mass.: Addison-Wesley, 1979), p. 257.
18. *Ibid.*, p. 260.

pull of gravity on an object and depends on the distance between the object and the body that is exerting the pull. Weight is measured in units of force, since it is a measure of a gravitational force; mass is measured in units of force divided by units of acceleration.[19]

The next example also shows concepts being contrasted (connotations versus denotations) without the use of signal words.

### Example 18    No Signal Words

You have seen that a message often conveys more than the literal meaning of its words. This is true partly because of the **connotations** attached to particular words. Words commonly have both **denotations** and connotations. The denotation of a word is the referent for the word—the object or idea to which the word refers. The words *clothing, dresses, gowns,* and *attire* all can have the same referent; all might be used to refer to the same objects. The connotation of a word is the added suggestiveness, in addition to denotation, that a word may carry.[20]

## Signal Words: Modified Cloze Procedure

The significance of signal words in the comparison and contrast pattern can be highlighted by using the *modified cloze procedure.*[21] (The cloze testing procedure is discussed in Chapter 7.) These exercises are designed so that students will focus on context clues, grammatical structure, and syntax in order to predict the signal words the author used in writing the passage. Students first are given the opportunity to read a selection that contains some signal words. Then they are given the same selection, but this time blanks appear where the signal words were. Students are to fill in the blanks with the correct signal word or select the correct one from a choice of four. A discussion should follow that demonstrates why answers are right or wrong (Jongsma, 1980). The passages in Example 19 illustrate how this technique can be used with content area textbooks.

19. Robert J. Hulsizer and David Lazarus, *The World of Physics* (Menlo Park, Calif.: Addison-Wesley, 1977), p. 130.

20. Bernard R. Tanner and Robert E. Shutes, *Looking at Language* (Menlo Park, Calif.: Addison-Wesley, 1973), p. 55.

21. For other suggestions on using the modified cloze procedure to teach reading skills, see Jacqueline L. Marino, "Cloze Passages: Guidelines for Selection," *Journal of Reading* 24(1981):479–483; Florence G. Schoenfield, "Instructional Uses of the Cloze Procedure," *Reading Teacher* 34(1980):147–151; Keith Thomas, "Modified Cloze: The Intralocking Guide," *Reading World* 19(1979):19–26.

## Example 19   Modified Cloze Procedure

So far in this chapter we have only discussed our economy. It is important to understand that not all economic systems are the same as the one in our country. Throughout history, people have developed [_____1_____] economic systems. Today, in the industrial countries there are two major types of economic systems—*market economies* (like ours) and *command* economies.

1. (a) foolish
   (b) similar
   (c) weak
   (d) strong
   (e) different

A command economy is quite [_____2_____] from our economy. In our economy no single authority makes the economic decisions. Producers own factories and tools, and they are free to invest their money to produce what they think will sell. Consumers can choose what they want to purchase from the variety of products offered for sale.[22]

2. (a) different
   (b) smaller
   (c) larger
   (d) similar
   (e) faster

## Paragraph Frames

Nichols (1980) suggests that teachers can sensitize students to the comparison/contrast pattern and other organizational patterns by using paragraph frames. A *paragraph frame* "resembles the cloze procedure in that spaces are provided for student insertions and that the surrounding words are designed to provide clues to what should fill the spaces" (Nichols, 1980, p. 229). However, the basic intent of the frame is to help students paraphrase material organized in the comparison and contrast or other organizational pattern.

Figure 3.10 illustrates an incomplete, comparison/contrast frame; Fig. 3.11 shows a completed comparison/contrast frame. Paragraph frames appear to

---

22. Elmer U. Clawson, *Our Economy: How It Works* (Menlo Park, Calif.: Addison-Wesley, 1980), pp. 38–40.

## Figure 3.10 Incomplete Comparison/Contrast Frame

_____ are different from _____ in several ways. First of all _____
while _____.
   Secondly, _____
while _____.
   In addition, _____
while _____.
   Finally _____
while _____.
   So it should be evident that _____
_____

## Figure 3.11 Completed Comparison/Contrast Frame

**Content Area: Biology**
**Grade Level: Freshman**

**Topic: Cold- and Warm-Blooded Animals**

**Assignment: Essay (Summary: Comparison-Contrast Pattern)**

_Mammals_ are different from _reptiles_ in several ways. First of all _mammals are warm-blooded which means that they maintain a relatively constant body temperature independent of surrounding temperature_ while _reptiles are cold-blooded which means that their body temperature depends on their surroundings._

In addition, _mammals are more adaptable and are found all over the earth_ while _reptiles are generally limited. Reptiles are usually not found in the coldest regions and hibernate in cool winter areas._

Finally, _mammals generally have their young develop within the female's body. The young are born live_ while _reptiles lay eggs._

So it should be evident that _although reptiles millions of years ago were the ancestors of mammals that they are very different today._

From James N. Nichols, "Using Paragraph Frames to Help Remedial High School Students with Written Assignments," _Journal of Reading_ 24(1980):230. Reprinted with permission of James N. Nichols and the International Reading Association.

have the potential to improve both the reading and the writing skills of stude
Nichols found them to be particularly effective when used with remedial hi
school students.

## Manipulative Exercises

White and her colleagues (1980) suggest using teacher-made cards to teach
comparison/contrast and other comprehension skills. The cards, containing
significant events from a reading selection, are manipulated by students in
groups of three or four. As students sort the cards, the teacher encourages
them to interact and to resolve differences regarding the correct placement of
cards. Students must justify their placement with information from the reading
selection. The developers of this approach feel that this type of manipulative
exercise stimulates thinking, because students move from being passive to being
active participants in the learning process.

Figure 3.12 shows an example of a manipulative exercise for the com-
parison/contrast pattern as developed by White and her colleagues. It was
based on Faulkner's story "A Rose for Emily." The teacher first provides appropriate background information on the culture of the old South and the
author. Then after key vocabulary words are pretaught, students read the short
story.

## Reading/Study Guides

Guides that highlight contrasting ideas may be helpful to students. Example 20
shows how a social studies teacher used a reading/study guide to help students
focus on the points of distinction of four caste systems.

### Example 20　Reading/Study Guide for Comparison and Contrast

*Directions:* The four basic castes are *Brahmin, Kshatriya, Vaishya, Shudra.*
Complete the chart below by filling in the "point of distinction" for each caste.
Two have been done for you.

| Point of Distinction | Brahmin | Kshatriya | Vaishya | Shudra |
|---|---|---|---|---|
| Once-born or twice-born? | | Twice-born | | |
| Color | White | | | |
| Twice-born ceremony | | | | |

# Figure 3.12  A Manipulative Exercise

## A Rose for Emily

## Compare/Contrast Card Activity

Various artists have dealt with themes of unrequitted love, madness, and life in small towns. Helen Reddy's song "Delta Dawn" provides some interesting parallels to "A Rose for Emily."

Play the song (on tape from the Media Center).

Briefly discuss initial reactions students have to the comparison between Delta Dawn and Emily Grierson.

Divide class into groups of 2–5 and pass out cards.

*Directions:* You have sixteen cards with phrases from the song and story.

1. Divide the cards into 2 groups of 8 cards, one group being phrases from the story, the other group, phrases from the song.

2. Match cards between these groups to show either similarities or differences between the two women.

3. You will end with 4 pairs of cards showing similarities, and 4 pairs of cards showing differences.

When students have completed the task to their satisfaction, the teacher may quickly check arrangements and ask for rationale for several placements in order to confirm that students do have reasons to support their conclusions. Pass out the Student Check List ditto so that students can check their own arrangements.

The one pairing of cards that may give students trouble is ". . . walks downtown with a suitcase in her hand . . ." with "She plans to kill him." Clarify that Delta Dawn behaves in a passive way, while Emily Grierson is active.

See below for student check list (answer key).

**Student Check List: "Delta Dawn"/"A Rose for Emily"**
**Comparison/Contrast**

Your cards should be arranged as follows (slight variation is acceptable only if you have satisfactory reasons for the variation).

Comparison between two selections:

| "All the townsfolks say she's crazy." | "We did not say she was crazy then. |
|---|---|

"a faded rose from days gone by"

". . . valance curtains of faded rose color . . . rose-shaded lights. . . ."

"Man of low degree. . . ."

". . . a Northerner, a day laborer."

"Daddy still calls her baby."

Her father ruled her life.

Contrasts between two selections:

" . . . mysterious dark-haired man. . . ."

". . . his hat cocked and a cigar in his teeth, reins and whip in a yellow glove."

". . . promised to take her for his bride."

"He said he was not a marrying man."

". . . prettiest woman you ever laid eyes on. . . ."

"She looked bloated, like a body long submerged in motionless water. . . ."

". . . walks downtown with a suitcase in her hand. . . ."

She plans to kill him.

(continued)

---

## Figure 3.12 (concluded)

---

*Paragraph assignment:* If you choose to write your paragraph on this topic, you might use this as a topic sentence:

There are a number of similarities and differences between Delta Dawn and Emily Grierson.

---

Reprinted by permission of Carol Ann Cramer and Robert K. Green, Ypsilanti High School. From materials developed through Title IV–C Project Read.

## Generic Approaches to Applying the Data Pattern to Content Areas

Earlier in this chapter some generic approaches to teaching the main idea/details pattern were explained and illustrated with models. Two of these approaches, adjunct questions and reading/study guides, are illustrated in Models 3.7 through 3.11 to show how these approaches can be used by teachers when assigning materials written in the data pattern.

Model 3.7 shows how adjunct questions are used to guide student learning of science material written in the data pattern. Notice that page references are provided and that the questions encourage both literal (questions 1 and 2, for example) and interpretive (questions 4 and 7, for example) responses. Students are also given the opportunity in the "On Your Own" section to apply the information in the reading assignment to their own lives and to react critically to the material.

Model 3.8 illustrates how a reading/study guide clarifies a literary selection that contains information on several events that have taken place during the life of an individual. The information is presented through the words of a dying, incoherent woman. The guide could also be classified as a sequence guide (see Chapter 4).

Model 3.9 and Model 3.10 illustrate the use of reading/study guides designed to facilitate the learning of contrasting data found in social studies selections. In Model 3.9 students are assisted in contrasting five different reformation movements. In Model 3.10 students are provided with help in contrasting two Buddhist groups. Notice how the teacher has assisted students by filling in some of the information on the guide.

Finally, Model 3.11 shows a reading/study guide that leads students through an understanding of comparative and contrasting ideas found in a business text. Notice how the format of this guide differs from the format of the previous two guides.

# Model 3.7  Adjunct Questions
**Pattern: Data**
**Content: Science**

### Science Through Discovery (pp. 235–247)

As you read, keep in mind and refer to the questions below. In several instances the page number has been given to assist you in locating or interpreting the answer. If the page number has not been given, it means you should try to produce your own ideas.

1.  What is air pollution?
2.  What is an aerosol? Where does it come from? (p. 236)
3.  How does natural pollution differ from industrial pollution? (p. 237)

*[Students interpret data.]*

4.  Read paragraph 3 on page 239. Which type of particle—the dust or smoke—would be more of a problem as an air pollutant? Explain.

*[Students directed to visual aid.]*

5.  Using the chart on page 240, explain what particles are most likely to cause a problem of air pollution.
6.  What is the most important chemical change that produces air pollutants? (p. 242)
7.  Why is the burning of fuels by industry, homes, and motor vehicles such a great factor in causing air pollution? (p. 242)
8.  How do changes in the speed and direction of the wind have an effect on what happens to pollutants? (p. 245)
9.  What are some other factors that influence the dispersal of pollutants? Explain your answer. (pp. 245–246)

## On Your Own!

*[Students apply data.]*

10.  What are some of the sources of air pollution in your community?
11.  What do you feel are the major problems caused by pollution? Explain your answer.
12.  In what ways does air pollution affect a family's cost of living?
13.  What do you think could be done to control air pollution?

*[Critical thinking emphasized.]*

14.  Who, in your opinion, has the responsibility for preventing air pollution? Explain your answer.

# Model 3.8  Reading/Study Guide

**Pattern: Data**
**Content: English**

*Directions:* In the story "The Jilting of Granny Witherall," the author, Katherine Ann Porter, attempts to get inside the mind of a woman who is dying. How does she feel? What does she think about? The author's Granny does almost all the talking. She manages, in her ramblings, to give us a capsule version of her entire life. She doesn't set it up in any logical order though, so it is up to the reader to sift through what she says and determine the various aspects of Granny's life.

Your task is to place the number of each quote from the story under the appropriate heading.

*[Major aspects (subtopics) of Granny's life highlighted.]*

| The Jilting | Granny as Young Mother | Granny as Mother with Grown Children | Granny as a Dying Woman |
|---|---|---|---|
| | | | |

*[Helps students put order into Granny's ramblings.]*

1. "I'm not going, Cornelia. I'm taken by surprise. I can't go."
2. "Will you stop that nonsense? I'm a married woman."
3. "Such a fresh breeze blowing, and such a green day with no threats in it."
4. "This is the very last of your mother, children."
5. "I want you to pick all the fruit this year, and see that nothing is wasted."
6. "Go wash your face, child, you look funny."
7. "I pay my own bills and I don't throw my money away on nonsense."
8. "Don't let your wounded vanity get the upper hand of you."

9. "So good and dutiful that I'd like to spank her."
10. "Look here, daughter, how do ants get in this bed?"
11. "There, wait a minute, here we are!"
12. "You never saw him, so how do you know how he looked?"
13. "Who's birthday is it? Are you going to have a party?"
14. ".  .  . sitting up nights with sick horses and sick Negroes and sick children and hardly ever losing one. John, I hardly ever lost one of them!"

This model was prepared by Mary Dier Donovan.

## Model 3.9  Reading/Study Guide
**Pattern: Data/Contrasting Ideas**
**Content Area: Social Studies**

### The Reformation

Five reformation movements are discussed in this reading: Lutheranism, Calvinism, Anglicanism, Anabaptism, and Roman Catholic Reform. The author discusses each with particular emphasis on the worship service, governmental structure, biblical emphasis, sacraments, creeds, clerical life-style, and salvation. Statements related to each of these characteristics are listed below. Identify the reformation movement to which the statement applies by using the following abbreviations: L for Lutheranism; C for Calvinism; Ag for Anglicanism; Ab for Anabaptism; and R for Roman Catholic. The first statement has been completed for you. A statement can apply to more than one movement.

*[Helps students contrast more than two ideas.]*

1. *Worship service:*
   (a) __C__ Ceremonies are simplified.
   (b) _____ Highly liturgical.
   (c) _____ English language is used.
   (d) _____ Singing of hymns encouraged.
   (e) _____ Services are translated into the language of the people.
2. *Governmental structure:*
   (a) _____ Pope's authority removed.

(continued)

# Model 3.9 (concluded)

    (b) _____ Government by bishops.

    (c) _____ Pope is the leader.

3. *Biblical emphasis:*

    (a) _____ Only the Latin Vulgate version of the Bible was authoritative.

    (b) _____ Doctrine of the Holy Bible is accepted.

    (c) _____ If not commanded by the Bible, it is removed from the church.

4. *Sacraments:*

    (a) _____ Lord's Supper and Holy Baptism are basically symbolic.

    (b) _____ Baptism rejected.

    (c) _____ Baptism and Holy Communion are most important.

    (d) _____ All seven sacraments are important.

    (e) _____ Through bread and wine, one receives the body and blood of Christ.

5. *Creeds:*

    (a) _____ Historical creeds accepted.

    (b) _____ Wide range of philosophies accepted.

6. *Clerical life-style:*

    (a) _____ Strict discipline required of priests.

    (b) _____ Clergy married.

    (c) _____ Missionary work emphasized.

7. *Salvation:*

    (a) _____ Only those predestined by God can be saved.

    (b) _____ Salvation is gained through faith in Christ.

8. *Other characteristics:*

    (a) _____ Church is totally independent from the state.

    (b) _____ List of heretical books published.

    (c) _____ Church must be pure; people must be pacifists.

    (d) _____ Study of the Bible is an individual responsibility.

    (e) _____ Jesuits try to regain "wanderers."

    (f) _____ All would be "equal" for the thousand years of Christ's ruling.

# Model 3.10  Reading/Study Guide
**Pattern: Data/Contrasting Ideas**
**Content Area: Social Studies**

### Big Raft and Little

After the reasons for the Buddhism split are explained (pp. 39–40), the author discusses the differences between the two major Buddhist groups, *Theravada* and *Mahayana*. As you read, or after you read this selection, complete the chart below. Some portions of the chart have been completed for you. The chart will help you recognize the differences between the two groups with respect to various issues related to Buddhism.

**[Students generate contrasting data.]**

| Issue | Theravada | Mahayana |
|---|---|---|
| Concept of the person | Each person is an individual | |
| Attainment of Nirvana | | Can attain with assistance from others |
| Key virtue | | |
| Religion for whom? | | Primarily for laymen |
| Ideal type | | |
| Metaphysics (speculation) | Avoided | |
| Ideal model of Buddha | | |
| Form of prayer | Meditation | |
| Use of texts | | |

---

# Model 3.11 Reading/Study Guide
## Pattern: Data/Comparing and Contrasting Ideas
## Content: Business

---

*Directions:* As you read the assigned chapter, note how corporations differ from partnerships. Use this guide to help you. As you read, or after you read, this chapter, place a C before the statements below that apply to corporations and a P before those that apply to partnerships. Place a B before those that apply to both.

*[Alerts students to find both comparisons and contrasts.]*

_____ 1. Two or more persons voluntarily combine skill, labor, and capital for the purpose of conducting, as co-owners, a business for profit.

_____ 2. This organization may be formed without meeting any special requirements, such as permission from local authorities.

_____ 3. This organization is looked upon as an individual existing separate and apart from its owners.

_____ 4. This type of business organization must obtain governmental permission to conduct business.

_____ 5. This organization is the oldest and most familiar type of business.

_____ 6. This business organization is not affected by the death of a stockholder and may sue or be sued in its own name.

---

# Summary

By understanding how authors organize their writing, students can begin to sort out information. They can see how ideas are related and how they support each other. These ideas can be stated literally or inferentially.

Teachers should introduce students to the concept of organizational patterns and then emphasize to students that the pattern of main idea/details is basic to an understanding of all the other patterns. (This idea is continuously reinforced in the next two chapters on organizational patterns.) Although students often have difficulty with the basic main idea/details pattern, there are ways the concept can be clarified.

Teachers can start by having students complete simple categorizing exercises and discuss the main points of pictures. The terms *topic, main idea,* and

# A Visitor from Art, Part II

A student in Miss Drago's class is about to explain the application of the art lesson to the reading class.

"I hope you all enjoyed the slides yesterday. Now, how was what you learned from Mr. Samuels similar to what we've been doing in *our* regular reading class? . . . Joan, what do you think?"

"Well, you've been showing us how, when we read, we should recognize the main point of paragraphs and whole chapters; and we should see how the details help to explain the main point. It's sort of the same way when looking at art. . . ."

"How so?" asked Miss Drago.

"Mr. Samuels showed us how the details in a painting help the artist to get across his general idea. We saw close-up details of parts of paintings; and then we were able to see how close-up details worked in with the whole picture."

"Excellent. Now let's turn to. . . ."

*details* can be clarified. A discussion of multiple-choice questions based on regular textbooks can help lead students through the thinking process of arriving at main ideas. This task also helps them to differentiate main ideas from details. Teachers can also point out to students that certain signal words can help them identify main ideas. They may also benefit from practice in finding the topic sentence in paragraphs.

Ultimately, however, students *must* generate their own statements of the main idea. A three-step approach can help them to do so. They first find the topic, then recite a general declarative statement (main idea) about the topic, and finally complete a checkout by finding the details that support the main-idea statement. These three steps can be introduced as part of a technique called "What did the Author Say?"

Generic approaches to teaching the main idea/details and data patterns include the direct teaching approach, adjunct questions, and reading/study guides. There is some research to support the use of all three approaches. Teachers should not focus exclusively on any one approach, though. Rather teachers should vary the approaches according to the needs and abilities of students and the nature of the content.

When students are confronted with reading material written in the data pattern, they must realize when the author is shifting to a new subtopic. For each of the author's subtopics the reader must generate the important main ideas and details.

Teachers can help their students comprehend material written in the data pattern by encouraging them to survey chapters that highlight subtopics in boldface type. When material is not highlighted in this way, teachers can prepare reading/study guides for their students.

When material contains a particularly high dosage of data, the guided reading procedure can be used. This technique helps students concentrate on the material and organize the data. If teachers wish to help their students respond to data at different levels of comprehension, then three-level guides will help them reach this goal. Three-level guides, or adaptations of the PQ4R system, may help students absorb the highly detailed data contained in mathematics problems. Research, however, has not conclusively substantiated the effectiveness of such procedures.

Sometimes authors choose to compare or contrast data, or both. Teachers can help students with this type of data pattern by alerting them to signal words and having them complete paragraph frames, modified cloze exercises, and manipulative exercises.

# Bibliography

Alvermann, Donna E. "Restructuring Text Facilitates Written Recall of Main Ideas." *Journal of Reading* 25(1982):754–758.

Ankney, Paul, and Pat McClurg. "Testing Manzo's Guided Reading Procedure." *Reading Teacher* 34(1981):681–685.

Aukerman, Robert C. *Reading in the Secondary School Classroom.* New York: McGraw-Hill, 1972.

Aulls, Mark W. *Developmental and Remedial Reading in the Middle Grades.* Boston: Allyn & Bacon, 1978.

Axelrod, Jerome. "Getting the Main Idea Is Still the Main Idea." *Journal of Reading* 18(1975):383–387.

Barrett, Thomas C. "Taxonomy of Reading Comprehension." In *Reading 360 Monograph.* Lexington, Mass.: Ginn, 1972.

Bartlett, Brendon J. "Top-Level Structure as an Organizational Strategy for Recall of Classroom Text." Ph.D. dissertation, Arizona State University, 1978.

Bean, Thomas W., and Rick Pardi. "A Field Test of a Guided Reading Strategy." *Journal of Reading* 23(1979):144–147.

Becker, Wesley C., and Siegfried Englemann. *The Oregon Direct Instruction Model.* Eugene: University of Oregon Follow-Through Project, 1977.

Bernard, Harold W. *Psychology of Learning and Teaching.* 3rd ed. New York: McGraw-Hill, 1972.

Braddock, Richard. "The Frequency and Placement of Topic Sentences in Expository Prose." *Research in the Teaching of English* 8 (1974):287–302.

Brunner, Joseph F., and John J. Campbell. *Participating in Secondary Reading: A Practical Approach.* Englewood Cliffs, N.J.: Prentice-Hall, 1978.

Burmeister, Lou E. *Reading Strategies for Middle and Secondary School Teachers.* 2nd ed. Reading, Mass.: Addison-Wesley, 1978.

Carnine, Douglas, and Jerry Silbert. *Direct Instruction Reading.* Columbus, Ohio: Merrill, 1979.

Clayton, Thomas E. *Teaching and Learning, A Psychological Perspective.* Englewood Cliffs, N.J.: Prentice-Hall, 1965.

Dale, Edgar. "The Critical Reader." In *Critical Reading,* edited by Martha L. King, Bernice E. Ellinger, and Willavene Wolf. Philadelphia: Lippincott, 1967.

Dillner, Martha H., and Joanne P. Olson. *Personalizing Reading Instruction in Middle, Junior and Senior High Schools.* New York: Macmillan, 1977.

Durkin, Delores. "What Is the Value of the New Interest in Reading Comprehension?" *Language Arts* 58(1981):23–43.

Earle, Richard A. *Teaching Reading and Mathematics.* Newark, Del.: International Reading Association, 1976.

Englemann, Siegfried, and Donald Carnine. "A Structural Program's Effect on the Attitudes and Achievement of Average and Above-Average Second Graders." In *Formative Research Studies,* Technical Report 76-1, edited by W. C. Becker and S. Englemann, Appendix B. Eugene: University of Oregon Follow-Through Project, 1976.

Estes, Thomas H., and Joseph L. Vaughan, Jr. *Reading and Learning in the Content Classroom.* Boston: Allyn & Bacon, 1978.

Grant, Jodi. "Study Guides as Aids to Learning: A Review of Research." In *Research on Reading in Secondary Schools,* Monograph no. 3, edited by Joseph L. Vaughan, Jr., and Paula J. Gaus. Tucson: University of Arizona, 1979.

Guszak, Frank J. "Teacher Questioning and Reading." *Reading Teacher* 21 (1968):227–234.

Guthrie, John T. "Follow Through: A Compensatory Education Experiment." *Reading Teacher* 30(1977):240–244.

Herber, Harold L. "Questioning Is Not the Answer." *Journal of Reading* 18 (1975):512–517.

————. *Teaching Reading in the Content Areas.* 2nd ed. Englewood Cliffs, N.J.: Prentice-Hall, 1978.

Jongsma, Eugene. *Cloze Instruction Research: A Second Look.* Newark, Del.: International Reading Association, 1980.

King, Ethel M. "Prereading Programs: Direct Versus Incidental Teaching." *Reading Teacher* 31(1978):504–510.

Maffei, Anthony C. "Reading Analysis in Mathematics." *Journal of Reading* 16(1973):546–549.

Manzo, Anthony V. "Guided Reading Procedure." *Journal of Reading* 18(1975):287–291.

McNiff, Shaun A. *Looking at Art.* Newport, R.I.: Harvast Labs, undated.

Meyer, Bonnie J. F. "Organizational Aspects of Text: Effects on Reading Comprehension and Applications for the Classroom." In *Reading Comprehension,* edited by James Flood. Newark, Del.: International Reading Association, forthcoming.

Meyer, Bonnie J. F., David M. Brandt, and George J. Bluth. "Use of Top-Level Structure in Text: Key for Reading Comprehension of Ninth-Grade Student." *Reading Research Quarterly* 16(1980):72–103.

Moore, David W., and John E. Readence. "Processing Main Ideas Through Parallel Lesson Transfer." *Journal of Reading* 23(1980):589–593.

Nichols, James N. "Using Paragraph Frames to Help Remedial High School Students with Written Assignments." *Journal of Reading* 24(1980):228–231.

Niles, Olive Stafford. "Organization Perceived." In *Developing Study Skills in Secondary Schools,* edited by Harold Herber. Newark, Del.: International Reading Association, 1965.

Peterson, Verna R. "A Comparison Between Two Instructional Approaches to Teaching Topic and Main Idea." Master's thesis, University of Minnesota, 1975.

Putnam, Lillian R. "Don't Tell Them To Do It . . . Show Them How." *Journal of Reading* 18(1974):41–43.

Reynolds, Ralph E., and Richard C. Anderson. *Influence of Questions on the Allocation of Attention During Reading.* Urbana: Center for the Study of Reading, University of Illinois, 1980.

Riley, James D. "The Effects of Reading Guides and a Directed Reading Method on Word Problem Comprehension, Problem Solving Ability, and Attitude Toward Mathematics." In *Research in Reading in the Content Areas, The Fourth Report,* edited by Harold L. Herber and James D. Riley. Syracuse University Reading and Language Arts Center, 1979.

Riley, James D., and Andrew B. Pachtman. "Reading Mathematical Word Problems: Telling Them What to Do Is Not Telling Them How to Do It." *Journal of Reading* 21(1978):531–534.

Rothkopf, Ernst Z. "Adjunct Aids, and the Control of Mathemagenic Activities During Purposive Reading." Paper presented at the Conference on Reading Expository Text, November 1980, at the University of Wisconsin-Madison.

Sack, Allan. *Manual for Teacher-Trainers* New York: College Skills Center, 1975.

Sack, Allan, and Jack Yourman. *The Sack-Yourman Developmental Speed Reading Course.* New expanded ed., New York: College Skills Center, 1981.

Santeusanio, Richard P. *Developing Reading Skills for Business and Industry.* Boston: CBI, 1981.

Shrauger, Virginia Moore. " 'What Did the Author Say?' A Technique for Learning to Organize, Understand and Remember Ideas." In *Proceedings of the Eighth Annual Conference of the Western College Reading Association,* edited by Roy Sugimoto. Whittier, Calif., 1975.

Singer, Harry, and Dan Donlan. *Reading and Learning from Text.* Boston: Little, Brown, 1980.

Smith, Richard J., and Thomas C. Barrett. *Teaching Reading in the Middle Grades.* 2nd ed. Reading, Mass.: Addison-Wesley, 1979.

Taylor, Barbara M. "Children's Memory for Expository Text After Reading." *Reading Research Quarterly* 15(1980):399–411.

Taylor, Marilyn J. "Using Photos to Teach Comprehension Skills." *Journal of Reading* 21(1978):514–517.

Thomas, Ellen Lamar, and H. Alan Robinson. *Improving Reading in Every Class.* 2nd ed. Boston: Allyn & Bacon, 1977.

Tierney, Robert J., and James W. Cunningham. *Research on Teaching Reading Comprehension.* Urbana: Center for the Study of Reading, University of Illinois, 1980.

Tierney, Robert J., and P. David Pearson. *Learning to Learn from Text: A Framework for Improving Classroom Practice.* Urbana: Center for the Study of Reading, University of Illinois, 1981.

White, Judith, Eva Swenarton, Beverly Riordan, Carol Morgan, and Trudy Adams. "A Comprehensive Secondary Reading Model." Paper presented at the International Reading Association Convention, May 1980, St. Louis.

Williams, Maurice, and Virginia M. R. Stevens. "Understanding Paragraph Structure." *Journal of Reading* 15(1972):513–516.

# Chapter 4

# Recognizing

# Sequence

# and Cause/Effect

## An NBC News Report, Part I

"I think you know by now," said Mr. Champa, high school social studies teacher, "that I'm not a big TV fan. But I'm actually going to make watching TV a homework assignment."

"Oh, come on, Mr. Champa, you're not serious. What do you want us to watch, reruns of 'Charlie's Angels'?" asked Steven Cassidy.

Some students chuckled while others encouraged Steven with comments like "Right on" and "*All* right."

"No, Steven," continued Mr. Champa. "I don't want you to watch 'Charlie's Angels.' "

"Aw," responded the class in unison.

"I want you to watch a special NBC news report. I'll tell you why in a few minutes. We have been studying presidential elections—how and why candidates are elected. What did we say regarding how candidates once could finance their campaigns? . . . Marilyn."

"It was mainly through donations. Many donations were unbelievably large. Didn't some insurance man give Nixon millions of dollars?"

"Yes," replied Mr. Champa, "an insurance executive, W. Clement Stone, donated almost five million dollars in Nixon's 1968 and 1972 campaigns. Was that why, Billy, new campaign finance laws were passed?"

"Yeah, I guess so."

"Do you all agree with Billy? How about you, Ralph?"

"That may have had something to do with it. But what really ticked them off was that they found Nixon's campaign received almost twenty million dollars in illegally, undisclosed contributions."

"That's right. This is basically what caused Congress to pass a set of strong new campaign finance laws. Who remembers some of the details of the laws? For example, what is the limit on personal contributions? Yes, Sandy."

"It's two . . . , no, a thousand dollars."

## Introduction

Because the organizational patterns of sequence and cause/effect appear so often in secondary textbooks, there is a great need for teachers to assist their students in these reading comprehension skills areas. In an informal study conducted by Niles (1965), sequence, or time order, and cause/effect were among the four most frequent organizational patterns found in social studies, science, and language textbooks.

Steven raised his hand, and before Mr. Champa acknowledged him, he asked, "Does that mean that each angel can only give each candidate a thousand dollars?"

"Yes," replied Mr. Champa, trying not to crack a smile. He continued, "What about committee contributions?"

"Ten thousand."

"No, who can help him? Jean."

"It's five."

"Right. What must candidates do when they receive contributions that exceed two hundred dollars? . . . Doesn't anyone remember? Yes, Joan."

"Don't they have to keep some kind of record or something?"

"Yes, very strict records, indeed. And you will recall that candidates who are eligible and accept federal matching funds are bound by federal regulations to a ceiling on what they can spend on the primaries this year—fourteen million, seven hundred thousand dollars, to be exact. Now let's review a little bit. The main *cause* for the passage of the new finance laws was the controversy over Nixon's illegal contributions. Now, however, the new laws are having some profound *effects* on the primaries this year. And that's why I want you to watch the NBC news report. It's called 'Is There A Better Way?' I think it's on at 10, on channel 4. As you watch it, I want you to jot down the effects these new laws have had on the candidates and their campaigns. We'll discuss the program tomorrow. The program will also cover the importance of the New Hampshire primary. What's unique about that primary, Sam?"

"It's a number one, man!"

"Cut out the 'man' business, OK? Also, watch and listen to find out the significance of the first primary as opposed to the middle and late primaries. And . . . well, there goes the bell. . . ."

At the end of the chapter you will find out what the students learned regarding the effects the new finance laws had on the primaries.

When using material dealing with a series of events, the teacher must decide whether the events have a *sequence* relationship (succession of events not related by causality) or a *cause/effect* relationship (succession of events linked by causal relationships). The point to consider is whether the events necessarily follow one another like a line of dominoes toppling each other over (cause/effect) or whether they just happen to occur in a particular order.

In a few cases in which there are vague or unimportant causal relationships between the events, it is often better to treat the situation as a sequence. For example, it is more important to emphasize the *order* in which ingredients are mixed together in a recipe than it is to explain *why* the yolks have to be folded in later than the egg whites. In many cases it is more important to make up mnemonic devices or to encourage students to create their own devices, establishing a sequence in their memories that way, than to insist on an insignificant or hard-to-grasp causal connection between the items.

Most students do not have difficulty with ordering simple events. But when printed materials become more complex, as they do in many secondary textbooks, students sometimes lose their sense of sequence. Therefore when secondary content materials are written in a sequence pattern, whether the sequence is stated explicitly or implicitly, teachers must provide students with some guidelines on how to proceed.

# Problems in Learning Sequence

When the townwide criterion-referenced reading comprehension test results of an elementary school system were recently analyzed (Santeusanio, 1980), it was found that at all grade levels students scored lowest on the skill of sequencing ideas. Pearson and Johnson, recalling their classroom teaching experiences, noted that "no skill seemed as difficult for our intermediate-grade students as placing a list of events from a story in the sequence in which they occurred. Nearly as difficult was the task of answering *when, what happened before* . . . , and *what happened after* . . . questions" (Pearson and Johnson, 1978, p. 116). These types of questions continue to plague a significant number of secondary students.

## Reversibility of Events

Pearson and Johnson (1978) attribute much of the difficulty students have in this area to the concept of *reversibility of events*. Reversible events are those that can occur in any order. For example, the events in the following sentence are reversible.

Joe and Jane brushed their teeth after they played tennis.

The order of these events is not predictable. Therefore retelling the sequence of the events could cause difficulty for some students, because unless they just remember what happened first, there is no way they can reconstruct the sequence through logic. The order of events is arbitrary.

## Stated Versus Actual Order

Another factor mentioned by Pearson and Johnson that affects comprehension of sequential events is whether the actual order of occurrence matches the order presented in the text. For example, in the following sentences the order presented in the text does *not* match the actual order of occurrence.

David and John played soccer. Earlier they had their piano lessons.

Because playing soccer is presented first in the text, some students mistakenly assume that the soccer playing preceded the piano lessons.

Here is an example from an economics textbook in which the stated order varies from the actual order of events.

## Example 1   Stated and Actual Orders Vary

Before logs are transported to paper or lumber mills, they must be sorted by intended use and graded for quality. Truckloads of logs, 25 tons at a time, are brought into the sorting yard. They are weighed, graded, marked, sorted into stacks, and reloaded onto other trucks in a matter of minutes.[1]

The reader of this passage could mistakenly conclude that logs are first transported to paper or lumber mills and then sorted. In fact, the first activity mentioned in the paragraph actually happens last. The author then wrote two more paragraphs before he returned to the idea of transporting logs. Notice that in this paragraph (Example 2) the author writes the events in the order that they actually occurred.

## Example 2   Stated and Actual Orders Agree

Once sorted and graded, the logs must again be transported, this time to a mill. Some of the mills may be in other countries. Others may be in the same area as the logging. Logs are transported by truck, railcar, and ship, or they are floated on a river, lake, or stream.[2]

The next example, taken from a literature textbook, again shows a passage in which the actual order of events does not match the order presented in the text.

## Example 3   Stated and Actual Orders Vary

When Bosman finally was able to move clear of his howling, hugging teammates, he walked toward the dugout. Just before he stepped

---

1. Elmer U. Clawson, *Our Economy: How It Works* (Menlo Park, Calif.: Addison-Wesley, 1980), p. 150.
2. Elmer U. Clawson, *Our Economy: How It Works* (Menlo Park, Calif.: Addison-Wesley, 1980), p. 150.

in, he raised both arms, like a victorious fighter—which he was—
to the fans.[3]

## Implicit Sequence

Peters (1977) believes that identifying the correct sequence of events causes
difficulty for some readers when the sequence is presented implicitly rather than
explicitly. This situation requires students to complete the difficult task of im-
posing the organizational structure of the material themselves. Unfortunately,
many students do not have the ability to do so.

The following passages from textbooks supply us with examples of implicitly stated sequential events. In Example 4 the cycle of plant growth is
implied; in Example 5 the sequence of events leading to the production of
electric currents is implied. This latter paragraph is particularly difficult to read
because it contains so much information. (Have the authors met their contractual obligations?)

### Example 4    Implied Sequence: Ecology

Along the northern border of North America, Europe, and Asia is
a region of very low temperatures and slight precipitation: Much of
the soil remains frozen throughout the year, though the upper few
centimeters melt for a few months during the summer. Temperatures
are high enough to permit the growth of plants only during about
60 days of each year. Although few species are able to withstand
this harsh environment, and the community is a simplified one, life
is by no means rare in this *arctic tundra* biome.[4]

### Example 5    Implied Sequence: Physics

What exactly is it that flows inside the wires? How does connecting
wires to a battery make a current flow? Wires are made of metals,
and as we saw in Section 8.6, metals are called conductors because
some of the electrons inside them are free to move around within
the metal. The electrons can move in all directions equally easily,
so left to themselves, they move in all directions inside the conductor.
If we want to make a current flow, we have to furnish an electrostatic
force to push them all in the same direction. It is the battery or the
machine behind the wall plug which furnishes such a force. It creates

3. Hal Lebovitz, "Don't Jinx the No-Hitter," in *Shapes*, ed. Mary Lenarz, Molly Wigand, and
   Jan Alexander (Minneapolis: National Computer Systems, 1978), p. 18.
4. Lawrence W. McCombs and Nicholas Rosa, *What's Ecology?* (Menlo Park, Calif.: Addison-
   Wesley, 1973), p. 145.

an electric field between the ends of the wire, and the electrons move in the direction opposite to that of the field. (Remember, the direction of the field is the direction of the force on *positive* charges, so the negative electrons feel a force in the opposite direction.) Electrons are held inside a metal by strong electric forces. They can't leak out unless the metal is heated to a high temperature. In fact, work must be done to remove electrons from a metal.[5]

## Multiplicity of Sequential Events

Difficulty in identifying sequence may also arise when a great many events are discussed sequentially. In this case students may have trouble keeping the events in order. In a discussion of mitosis, for example, the author of a biology text guides the student through the four phases that occur during mitosis: prophase, metaphase, anaphase, and telephase. However, each phase has its own sequence of events (sequence within a sequence). In Example 6, which gives the sequence of events during the prophase period, notice how the author has used signal words, such as *onset, begin, while, previously,* and *at this time,* in an effort to minimize the problem of multiple sequences.

### Example 6    Multiple Sequences

**Prophase.**  The onset of mitosis is marked by several changes. The nucleoli begin to disappear while the chromosomes themselves begin to appear. The previously extended strands of the chromosomes coil up into a helix, that is, like a cylindrical spring (Fig. 14.9). In so doing, they become shorter and thicker and thus more easily visible. At this time, the nuclear membrane begins to disappear.[6]

## Need for Focused Instruction

Perhaps secondary students would have less difficulty with the skill of sequence if they had had more *focused instruction* on it in the elementary grades. Otto and Kamm (1977) suggest a carefully developed program that begins in kindergarten with oral activities and ends in the late intermediate grades or early secondary grades. In their program, concepts such as *first, last, before,* and *after* are emphasized; calendar markers are taught; explicit cue words such as *next* and *later* are pointed out; and instruction in implicit cues is provided.

5.  Robert I. Hulsizer and David Lazarus. *The World of Physics* (Menlo Park, Calif.: Addison-Wesley, 1972), pp. 246–247.

6.  John W. Kimball. *Biology.* 4th ed. (Reading, Mass.: Addison-Wesley, 1978), p. 253.

Even if all students were to receive this type of instruction on the skill of sequencing, they would still need assistance in applying the skill to the content areas. In social studies, for example, students are often exposed to the concepts of the economic growth and the political development of nations. Teachers can facilitate the teaching of these concepts with reference to the skill of sequence. According to DeCaroli (1972), if time and chronology (sequence) are specifically taught by the teacher, the students' understanding will be far greater than it would be if these concepts were left to incidental learning.

# Introducing and Teaching Sequence

## Types of Sequence

The two types of sequence patterns discussed by Burmeister (1978) are chronological and spatial. When writers use the *chronological pattern*, they may state events in a clear-cut fashion from beginning to end; they may present them in reverse; or, as is done in literature, they may use the flashback technique.

The *spatial pattern* is used when writers wish to emphasize a sequence of area to area or region to region. For example, the author of a history text might discuss the route followed by frontiersmen, or a scientist might discuss the parts of the body through which food travels as it is digested.

## Simple Activities

One of the best ways to introduce the skill of sequencing is to cut up comic strip frames, mix them up, and ask students to place them in the correct sequence. Students should not arbitrarily sequence the frames; they should be encouraged to recognize the logic of the sequence. This task usually serves as a good motivational activity, and it works particularly well with poor readers at the secondary level.

Peters (1977) uses mysteries to introduce the skill of sequence. Short and easy-to-read mysteries are read by the students. Then the events are presented to the students in inverted order. Students solve the mystery by arranging the clues in their proper sequence. After the mystery is solved, students are usually able to list the events in their proper sequence.

## General Suggestions

When assigning materials written in the sequence pattern, teachers can encourage their students to notice the order in which the events happen. They can also suggest that text material written in the sequence pattern should be read slowly and cautiously, especially if that material is science. (Consider the possible ramifications of completing a scientific experiment out of sequence!) Rereading steps in a sequence should be encouraged, because sometimes what readers think is a step may not really be one, and when order is necessary, they must determine the correct order of the steps.

Group discussions can be used to provide practice in sequencing. The teacher can ask for a retelling of events from a reading assignment. If events are either omitted or changed, the misunderstandings can be noted and corrected through discussion and rereading. Harris and Sipay (1975) believe that this technique is the most natural and effective way to provide practice in sequencing.

# Relating Sequence to Main Ideas

Teachers can point out to students how the main idea/details pattern relates to the sequence pattern. In other words, important main ideas and details are often the important steps involved in the sequence pattern. The next example, based on a social studies text,[7] illustrates this point.

### Example 7    Relating Sequence to Main Ideas

Major Topic: Development of Paper

| Sequence Step | Main Idea/Details |
| --- | --- |
| 1. Oldest written records | The oldest written records were made by ancient Sumerians. They used clay tablets. Egyptians later used papyrus. |
| 2. A.D. 105 | Ts'ai made significant strides in using wood as raw material for making paper. He was dissatisfied with silk and bamboo. |
| 3. Twelfth Century | Ts'ai's idea finally reached Europe, where rags were being used to make paper. |
| 4. 1800s | Kellar invented a machine for making wood pulp. A chemical process was added, resulting in the production of paper. |
| 5. Late 1800s | One papermaking machine is in use in the United States. |
| 6. Present day | There are 875 paper mills in the United States. Half the world's paper is produced there. |

7. Elmer U. Clawson, *Our Economy: How It Works* (Menlo Park, Calif.: Addison-Wesley, 1980), pp. 139–142.

# Figure 4.1 The Relationship of Main Ideas to the Sequence Pattern

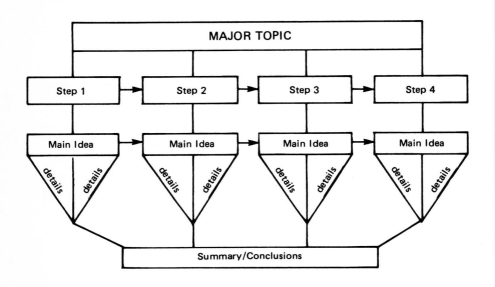

From Richard P. Santeusanio, *Developing Reading Skills for Business and Industry*, p. 196. Reprinted with permission. Copyright © 1981 CBI Publishing Co., Inc., 51 Sleeper St., Boston, Mass. 02210.

Presenting a diagram such as the one depicted in Fig. 4.1 can help students visualize the relationship between sequence and main idea/details.

## Signal Words: Modified Cloze Procedure

The importance of signal words can be pointed out to students. These words include *first, second, third, later, beginning, end, finally, next, soon, while, when, until, as soon as, during, meanwhile*. The significance of these signal words can be highlighted by using the modified version of the cloze procedure, as discussed in Chapter 3. The next examples illustrate the technique. For convenience the correct answers appear in parentheses in the blank spaces. Some teachers may prefer to give students choices from which to choose the correct answer rather than ask students to fill in the blank on their own.

### Example 8    Modified Cloze Procedure:
### Social Studies

The petition for naturalization is sent to a federal court near where the person lives.    (Then)    there is a wait of about one month.    (During)    this time, the Immigration and Naturalization Service checks up on the person. Then there is a    (final)    hearing.    (When)    the person becomes a citizen, he or she must swear to be loyal to the United States, and to give up loyalty to his or her old country.[8]

### Example 9    Modified Cloze Procedure:
### Social Studies

The    (end)    of the war saw women firmly entrenched in several new fields of work, particularly office work, government service, and retail trade. Northern women in great numbers flocked to the South as teachers for the freedmen.    (Later)    southern women took their place in that region's newly-formed public schools. By the turn of the    (century)    the majority of the nation's public school teachers were women. Associated with this development was the entry of women into higher education, the establishment of coeducational schools, women's colleges, and teacher training institutions, and the acceptance of some pioneering women in professional schools.[9]

## Paragraph Frames

As we discussed in Chapter 3, students can become familiar with certain organizational patterns by working with paragraph frames. The purpose of the paragraph frame is to help students paraphrase text material organized in the sequence and other patterns. Nichols (1980) illustrates use of paragraph frames with the sequence pattern. Figure 4.2 shows an incomplete frame; Fig. 4.3 shows a completed sequence frame.

## Manipulative Exercises

In Chapter 3 we discussed White and her colleagues (1980) manipulative exercises for teaching comprehension skills. Examples of lessons designed to

8. Richard E. Gross, *American Citizenship, The Way We Govern* (Menlo Park, Calif.: Addison-Wesley, 1979), p. 274.
9. Gerda Lerner, *The Women in American History* (Menlo Park, Calif.: Addison-Wesley, 1971), p. 93.

---

## Figure 4.2 Incomplete Sequence (Time Order) Frame

---

At the end of _____ what happened was that _____ .
    Previous to this _____
_____ .

    Before this _____
_____ .

    The entire chain of events had begun for a number of reasons including
_____
_____ .

    Some prominent incidents which helped to trigger the conflict were ____
_____ .

---

From James N. Nichols, "Using Paragraph Frames to Help Remedial High School Students with Written Assignments," *Journal of Reading* 24(1980):229. Reprinted with permission of James N. Nichols and the International Reading Association.

teach the data (comparison and contrast) pattern were provided. Figure 4.4 shows an exercise designed to assist students with sequencing events.

A variation of this approach is to place illustrations related to a reading assignment on the cards. These cards also can be manipulated by groups of students, leading to greater comprehension of the material. Science and social studies materials lend themselves particularly well to this activity. Two examples of the technique follow.

In Fig. 4.5 illustrations of the phases of stellar evolution are shown. These illustrations could be placed on cards. Students would be required to sequence the cards correctly.

In Fig. 4.6 the various stages involved in making paper from wood are shown. This illustration could be reproduced, cut into parts, and placed on cards. Students would be required to sequence the cards correctly.

## Internal Textbook Aids

It should be pointed out that some textbooks contain built-in aids to assist students with the sequencing of ideas. The use of flow charts, for example, is a popular technique. Figure 4.7 shows a flow chart that illustrates the steps

# Figure 4.3 Completed Sequence (Time Order) Frame

**Content Area: American History**
**Grade Level: Sophomore/Junior**

**Topic: World War I**
**Assignment: Essay (Summary: Time Order Pattern)**

At the end of *World War I* what happened was that *the various peace treaties, such as the Treaty of Versailles, radically changed the face of Europe and began many social, political and economic changes.*

Previous to this *German resources had been exhausted and German morale had collapsed.* This had resulted in *Germany surrendering and the war ending without a single truly decisive battle having been fought.*

Before this *the "Great War" had raged from 1914–1918 chiefly in Europe among most of the great Western powers.*

The entire chain of events had begun for a number of reasons including *imperialistic, territorial, and economic rivalries which had been growing since the late nineteenth century.*

Some prominent incidents which helped trigger the conflict were *the assassination of the Archduke Francis Ferdinand of Austria-Hungary in 1914 and the sinking of the Lusitania in 1915.*

From James N. Nichols, "Using Paragraph Frames to Help Remedial High School Students with Written Assignments," *Journal of Reading* 24(1980):230. Reprinted with permission of James N. Nichols and the International Reading Association.

involved for a bill to become a law; Fig. 4.8 is a flow chart that gives the steps involved in completing a mathematics word problem.

An example of a reading type of exercise used in a social studies textbook is shown in Fig. 4.9. The exercise helps the student with sequencing the stages of a bill.

Figure 4.10 is an illustration from a textbook that provides the student with a clear idea of the sequence of events involved in carrying out an application of Charles's law. (The volume of a gas being heated is increased by 1/273 of its volume at zero degrees Celsius for each degree on the Celsius scale.)

And finally, some authors help to clarify the sequence of ideas by using calendar markers in their writing. In Example 10 notice the references to "winter," "May," "June," and "October."

# Figure 4.4  A Manipulative Exercise
## "A Rose for Emily"
## Sequencing Card Activity

This activity is designed to clarify for students the correct time-sequence of the events in the story, "A Rose for Emily." Since this story is told by a townsperson who seems to be remembering random details about Miss Emily, it is difficult for students to comprehend which events happen in close or distant time relationship with other events.

Directions: The story is not told in chronological order (events are not revealed in the time order in which they happened). You are given a set of 17 cards. Arrange them in the time sequence in which the events occurred. You may use your books to refer to details which give time references.

Teacher's role: Circulate and observe as students work on the task. As they indicate completion, check their arrangement. There will undoubtedly be errors. Assign individuals in the group to look in the book for specific phrases. Key phrases to find are:

Miss Emily buys arsenic.

Miss Emily's cousins arrive.

The Board of Aldermen call on Miss Emily to collect her taxes.

There is a terrible smell at Miss Emily's house.

Miss Emily gives china-painting lessons.

Miss Emily's hair turns grey.

Let the class continue working, leaving 15–20 minutes at the end of the hour to clarify the correct order of events. Go through each event asking students for page and paragraph references that indicate time.

Students should come away from this activity with an understanding of the following:

1. Homer Baron arrived shortly after Miss Emily's father died.
2. His body is upstairs for about 40 years.
3. She continues to visit that room (and evidently lay in the bed) for a quite period of time (at least 6+ months because of her grey hair).

See below for proper arrangement of cards.

### Chronological Order of the Cards from "A Rose for Emily"

1. Miss Emily's father dies.
2. Colonel Sartoris says Miss Emily does not need to pay her taxes.

3. Homer Baron comes to town.

4. Miss Emily and Homer Baron take Sunday rides together.

5. Miss Emily's cousins arrive.

6. Miss Emily buys toilet articles and a man's suit.

7. Miss Emily buys arsenic.

8. Homer Baron returns to Jefferson after a short absence.

9. Homer Baron dies.

10. There is a terrible smell at Miss Emily's house.

11. Miss Emily's hair turns grey.

12. Miss Emily gives china-painting lessons.

   *[Items 13 and 14 are interchangeable.]*

13. The Board of Aldermen call on Miss Emily to collect her taxes.

14. Miss Emily refuses to allow a mailbox and house numbers to be attached to her house.

15. Miss Emily dies at age 74.

16. Townspeople break into the upstairs room.

   *[Put item 17 anywhere between 11–15.]*

17. A grey hair falls on the pillow next to Homer's body.

## "A Rose for Emily": Chronological order of the Cards (with Page References)

1. Miss Emily's father dies.
   She is about 48–50 years old when the Board of Aldermen call; the smell occurs 30 years before this (p. 38, part II); Homer Baron arrives after her father dies.

2. Colonel Sartoris says Miss Emily does not need to pay her taxes.
   Not an exact time placement for this—Colonel Sartoris is a contemporary of her father's. Most likely he remitted her taxes shortly after the town realizes she has no money.

3. Homer Baron comes to town.
   Homer Baron arrives the summer after her father's death (p. 40, last line).

4. Miss Emily and Homer Baron take Sunday rides together.
   "Presently we began to see . . ." (p. 41, top).

5. Miss Emily's cousins arrive.
   Ladies were upset about the "disgrace and bad example" of Miss Emily

(continued)

---

# Figure 4.4 (continued)

---

and Homer Baron riding around town. They call the cousins (p. 42 bottom–p. 43 top).

6.  Miss Emily buys toilet articles and a man's suit.
    Female cousins were still there: "They are married. . . . We were glad because. . . ." (p. 43, end of 1st paragraph).

7.  Miss Emily buys arsenic.
    "While her two female cousins were visiting her" (p. 41, last line). It makes sense that Miss Emily bought the gifts first; Homer Baron told her he did not plan to marry her; she bought the arsenic.

8.  Homer Baron returns to Jefferson after a short absence.
    Cousins depart; Homer Baron returns three days later (p. 43, paragraph 2 middle).

9.  Homer Baron dies.
    "That was the last we saw of him" (p. 43, last paragraph).

10. There is a terrible smell at Miss Emily's house.
    Homer Baron causes the smell.

11. Miss Emily's hair turns grey.
    "When next we saw her . . ." (p. 44 top—see previous paragraph for confirmation that this occurred after Homer Baron dies).

12. Miss Emily gives china-painting lessons.
    "From that time on . . ." (p. 44, paragraph 2).

13. The Board of Aldermen call on Miss Emily to collect her taxes.
    "The door through which no visitor had passed . . ." (p. 37, paragraph 3).

14. Miss Emily refuses to allow a mailbox and house numbers to be attached to her house.
    "The front door closed (after china-painting lessons) . . . and remained closed." "When the town got free postal delivery . . ." (p. 44, end of paragraph 2).

15. Miss Emily dies at age 74.
    "And so she dies . . ." (p. 44, bottom). "Up to the day of her death at seventy-four . . ." (p. 44, paragraph 1).

16. Townspeople break into the upstairs room.
    (p. 45, 3rd paragraph)

17. A grey hair falls on the pillow next to Homer's body.
    Put this somewhere between 11 and 15.

Extra challenge: For those students who are willing and able, the following exercise calls for some extremely careful reading and thinking.

Identify Miss Emily's age and the year (where possible) for these 6 events (there are some key clues to make this task possible).

Age references (at best as can be determined from available information):

| | Miss Emily's Age | Year | |
|---|---|---|---|
| Father dies | 26–28 | | |
| Sartoris remits taxes | 26–28 | 1894 | |
| Homer Baron dies/smells | 28 | | |
| China-painting lessons | 40 | 1906 | (approx.) |
| Board of Aldermen call | 48–50 | 1914–1916 | (approx.) |
| Miss Emily dies | 74 | 1940 | (approx.) |

Reprinted by permission of M. Trudy Adams and Nancy E. Goff, Ypsilanti Public Schools. From materials developed through Title IV–C Project Read.

# Figure 4.5  Illustrations for a Sequencing Activity

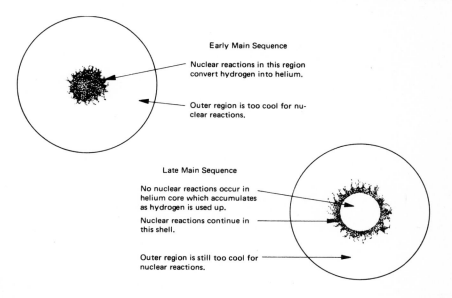

Early Main Sequence

Nuclear reactions in this region convert hydrogen into helium.

Outer region is too cool for nuclear reactions.

Late Main Sequence

No nuclear reactions occur in helium core which accumulates as hydrogen is used up.

Nuclear reactions continue in this shell.

Outer region is still too cool for nuclear reactions.

(continued)

# Figure 4.5 (concluded)

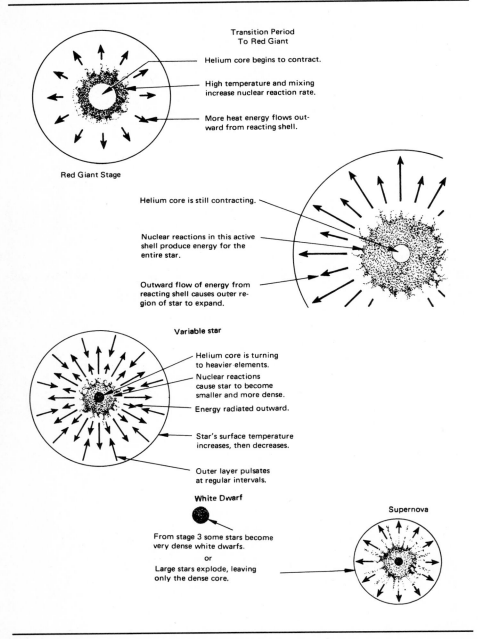

Transition Period
To Red Giant

Helium core begins to contract.

High temperature and mixing
increase nuclear reaction rate.

More heat energy flows outward from reacting shell.

Red Giant Stage

Helium core is still contracting.

Nuclear reactions in this active
shell produce energy for the
entire star.

Outward flow of energy from
reacting shell causes outer region of star to expand.

Variable star

Helium core is turning
to heavier elements.

Nuclear reactions
cause star to become
smaller and more dense.

Energy radiated outward.

Star's surface temperature
increases, then decreases.

Outer layer pulsates
at regular intervals.

White Dwarf

From stage 3 some stars become
very dense white dwarfs.

or

Large stars explode, leaving
only the dense core.

Supernova

From *Ideas from Astronomy* by Lou Williams Page, pp. 186, 188, 190. Copyright © 1973 by Addison-Wesley Publishing Company, Inc. Reprinted by permission.

# Figure 4.6 Illustrations for a Sequencing Activity

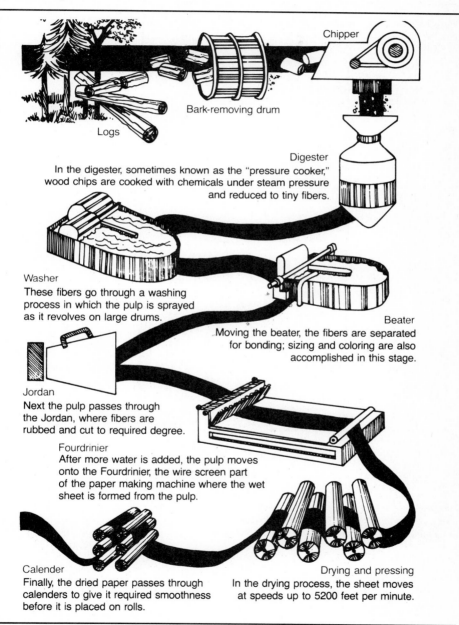

Chipper

Bark-removing drum

Logs

Digester
In the digester, sometimes known as the "pressure cooker,"
wood chips are cooked with chemicals under steam pressure
and reduced to tiny fibers.

Washer
These fibers go through a washing
process in which the pulp is sprayed
as it revolves on large drums.

Beater
Moving the beater, the fibers are separated
for bonding; sizing and coloring are also
accomplished in this stage.

Jordan
Next the pulp passes through
the Jordan, where fibers are
rubbed and cut to required degree.

Fourdrinier
After more water is added, the pulp moves
onto the Fourdrinier, the wire screen part
of the paper making machine where the wet
sheet is formed from the pulp.

Calender
Finally, the dried paper passes through
calenders to give it required smoothness
before it is placed on rolls.

Drying and pressing
In the drying process, the sheet moves
at speeds up to 5200 feet per minute.

# Figure 4.7  Flow Chart Sequence

**How a Bill Becomes a Law**

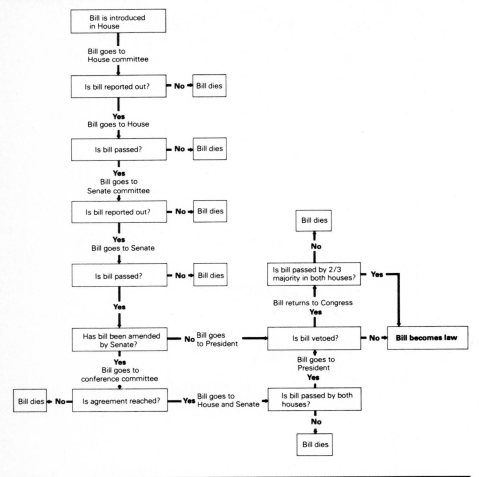

From *American Citizenship. The Way We Govern* by Richard E. Gross, p. 94. Copyright © 1979 by Addison-Wesley Publishing Company, Inc. Reprinted by permission.

# Figure 4.8  Flow Chart Sequence

## SUMMARY

Some word problems can be solved by writing and solving systems of equations.

Sid and Sam are professional basketball players. The sum of their heights is 415 centimeters. Sid is 19 centimeters taller than Sam. How tall is each?

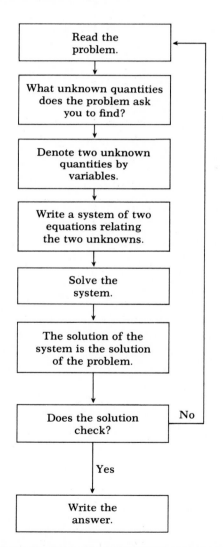

Find:  Sid's height
       (in centimeters)
       Sam's height
       (in centimeters)

Let  $x$ = Sid's height,
     $y$ = Sam's height.

$$\begin{cases} x + y = 415 \\ x - y = \ \ 19 \end{cases}$$ ←*Sum of heights is 415 cm.*

*Sid is 19 cm taller than Sam.*

$\begin{aligned} x + y &= 415 \\ x - y &= \ \ 19 \\ \hline 2x &= 434 \\ x &= 217 \end{aligned}$      $\begin{aligned} 217 + y &= 415 \\ y &= 198 \end{aligned}$

217 cm = Sid's height
198 cm = Sam's height

*Sum of their heights is 415.*

$217 + 198 = 415$ ✔

$217 - 198 = \ \ 19$ ✔

*Sid's height is 19 cm more than Sam's.*

Sid is 217 centimeters tall. Sam is 198 centimeters tall.

# Figure 4.9 Reading Exercise for Sequencing

**In What Stage Is the Bill?**

There are three general stages a bill goes through in order to become a law.

Stage A:  The bill is written and prepared for the House or Senate to consider.

Stage B:  The bill is introduced and discussed, and possibly amended in committees.

Stage C:  The bill is discussed, possibly amended, and voted upon in both houses of Congress.

Read each activity below, and tell what stage the bill is in.

1. Congresswoman Howard studied the material on schools that John Porter brought from the Library of Congress.
2. Congresswoman Howard placed her bill in the hopper.
3. In the House there was a general debate on the Howard bill.
4. A conference committee changed the wording of the Senate amendment.
5. The clerk of the House gave the Howard bill the number H.R. 9,999.
6. The House committee held public hearings on the Howard bill.
7. The House committee studied the Howard bill after hearings were over.
8. Some committee members suggested amendments to the Howard bill.
9. A Senate committee studied the Howard bill.
10. In order to stop the Howard bill, some senators held a filibuster.

From *American Citizenship, The Way We Govern* by Richard E. Gross, p. 104. Copyright © 1979 by Addison-Wesley Publishing Company, Inc. Reprinted by permission.

## Example 10    Sequencing by Calendar Markers

Ground squirrels hibernate in their burrows through the long winter. In May they emerge and mate. The young are born in mid-June. By the beginning of October, the young have reached adult size, and all of the ground squirrels return to their burrows for the winter

# Figure 4.10 Sequence of Events in Charles's Law

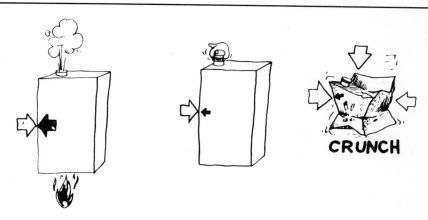

If you boil an inch or so of water in a gallon can, the water vapor will drive most of the air from the can. If the can is quickly capped (to prevent air from returning), a partial vacuum is created as the water vapor condenses back to water. At this point the air pressure outside the can is so much greater than the pressure of the vapor and the little air left inside the can that the can is crushed, as if by a giant hand.

From *Ideas from Chemistry* by Tom R. Thomson, p. 69. Copyright © 1973 by Addison-Wesley Publishing Company, Inc. Reprinted by permission.

hibernation. Many other animals of the tundra remain active through the winter.[10]

Teachers should point out these internal textbook aids to their students. They should also continuously encourage their students to attend to these aids. Otherwise students will not take advantage of them.

# Generic Approaches to Applying the Sequence Pattern to Content Areas

Chapter 3 contains a discussion of some generic approaches to teaching the main idea/details and data patterns in different content areas. These approaches—direct teaching, adjunct questions, and reading/study guides—are

10. Lawrence W. McCombs and Nicholas Rosa, *What's Ecology?* (Menlo Park, Calif.: Addison-Wesley, 1973), p. 145.

# Model 4.1 Direct Teaching

**Pattern: Sequence**
**Content: Science**

---

**Teacher:** Today we are going to learn more about sequence. Sequence in reading means to remember events in their correct order. What does sequence mean?

> *[Sequence defined.]*

*Students:* To remember events in their correct order.

> *[Teacher may ask individuals or the group to repeat the definition.]*

**Teacher:** We learned that sometimes certain signal words help us with remembering the sequence of events. The words *first, second,* and *third* are some. What are some signal words?

*Students:* First, second, and third.

> *[Signal words stressed.]*

**Teacher:** Others are *next, then,* and *later.* Repeat.

*Students:* Next, then, and later.

**Teacher:** Good. We are going to read an article entitled "Counting Fish in the River." Your task is to find the signal words in the article. What is your task?

*Students:* To find signal words in the article.

> *[Skill applied to text, not workbook.]*

---

applied to content materials written in the sequence pattern in Models 4.1 through 4.8. You may wish to review Chapter 3 for the rationale for using these teaching approaches. As you review these models, notice that they contain special inserts that highlight their uniqueness and particular virtues. These inserts would not appear on the actual materials handed to students.

Model 4.1 demonstrates the use of the direct teaching approach to help students comprehend scientific information written in the sequence pattern. The model exemplifies a script that teachers can prepare and follow in their teaching. Teachers would, of course, stray from the script when corrections were necessary.

**Teacher: Excellent. Now read the article and circle all the signal words you can find.**

> *[After the students read the selection, the dialogue continues.]*

**Teacher: What are the signal words in the first paragraph?**

*Students: There are none.*

**Teacher: What are the signal words in the second paragraph?**

*Students: First, second, next, and then.*

**Teacher: Correct. What are the signal words in the third and fourth paragraphs?**

*Students: Later, then, now, finally.*

> *[Signal words help students learn concept.]*

**Teacher: These signal words helped you to put in order the steps for counting rules. What is the counting rule called?**

*Students: Recapture counting.*

> *[If students fail to recall, refer them to paragraph 1.]*

**Teacher: What would happen if we didn't follow the steps in sequence?**

*Students: The count would not be right.*

> *[Teacher can continue with further questions to ensure comprehension.]*

---

Adjunct questions are used to assist students with the sequence pattern in Models 4.2 and 4.3. Chronological or temporal sequence in science material is stressed in Model 4.2. Notice that, unlike some of the other adjunct question models in this text, page references are not provided. Thus the teacher is providing students with less direct assistance.

Spatial sequence is highlighted in Model 4.3. Students gain practice in following directions in a real life situation. This model also gives students practice in reading a map.

Model 4.4 is an example of how the familiar time line format assists students with ordering historical events.

# Model 4.2  Adjunct Questions
## Pattern: Sequence
## Content: Science

*To the Student:* Before reading "Bacteria," preview the questions that appear below. The questions are designed to help you identify the proper sequence of events in the selection "Bacteria."

*[Questions stress sequence and help students become aware of the importance of sequence in this paragraph.]*

1. Describe the three steps that must be followed in order to make cheese from milk.
2. Name the type of cheese made when these steps are not followed.
3. How does the cheese maker control what type of cheese is made?
4. In which step in the sequence does this happen?
5. List the proper sequence of steps that must be taken to produce vitamins from bacteria.
6. What happens *after* vitamins are removed?

Several activities are incorporated in Models 4.5 and 4.6. In Model 4.5 students number the sequence of events. Then a fill-in activity that requires students to use signal words is provided. Finally, adjunct questions are incorporated into the guide's third section. Model 4.6 also begins with numbering events in sequential order. Then in Part II students inspect pairs of events and decide which occurred first. The third part requires students to decide which events occurred *before* a certain date.

Model 4.7 illustrates how a typical English lesson, teaching the parts of the plot, relates to the sequence pattern. Students examine quotes from a play and decide where these quotes fit with respect to the different parts of the plot ranging from *exposition* to *resolution.*

In Model 4.8 business students are helped to follow the steps involved in preparing a six-column work sheet. Notice that because of the nature of the subject matter, students are required to respond only at the literal level of comprehension.

# Model 4.3  Adjunct Questions
Pattern: Sequence
Content: Real Life

## SEQUENCE MAPS

Sequence is the order in which one thing follows another. All of us use sequence in everyday living situations. For example, we use sequence whenever we give or follow directions to get from one place to another.

Suppose you have just arrived at the Camp Nelson office. It is 3:00 P.M. The camp guide has given you the map below and the following information:

* Check in at the Health Cabin first.
* You are assigned to Cabin 8.
* The swimming pool and sports field close at 5:00 P.M.

If you want to swim before the pool closes, you will first go from the Health Cabin to your cabin to change your clothes. Then you will head for the swimming pool. By using the camp map, you will be able to find the quickest way to get from one place to another. This will give you more time for swimming and fun.

**Read and study the camp map shown below. Then complete the exercises on the following page.**

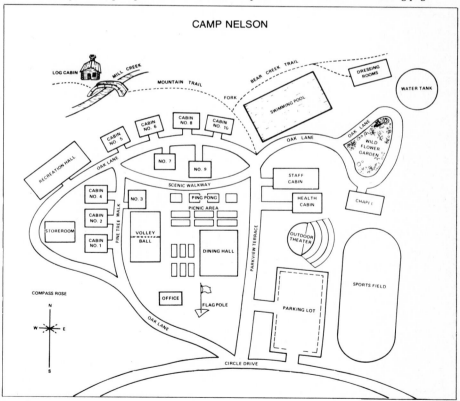

CAMP NELSON

# Model 4.3 (concluded)

## SEQUENCE MAPS

**DIRECTIONS:** Use the information on the opposite page to complete this lesson. Write the letter of each correct answer on the PAIR Answer Sheet. The first two items have been done for you.

1. If you walk north on Pine Tree Walk from Cabin 2, the first building you pass will be _____

   **a.** Cabin 4        **b.** Cabin 3        **c.** Volleyball Court        **d.** Cabin 1

   **ANSWER:** **b.** Cabin 3 is the first building north of Cabin 2.

2. Still going north on the same walk, the next building will be _____

   **a.** Storeroom        **b.** Cabin 5        **c.** Cabin 4        **d.** Recreation Hall

   **ANSWER:** **c.** Cabin 4 is the next building you will pass as you walk north.

- - - - - - - - - - - - - - - - - - - - - - - - - - - - - - - - - - - -

3. As the campers walked east on Oak Lane and then south on Parkview Terrace, they passed several buildings. The cabin they passed just before reaching the Staff Cabin was _____

   **a.** Cabin 2        **b.** Cabin 7        **c.** Cabin 8        **d.** Cabin 10

4. As the campers walked northwest on Mountain Trail, the last thing they passed before coming to the fork at Bear Creek Trail was the _____

   **a.** flagpole        **b.** dressing room        **c.** bridge        **d.** swimming pool

5. A group of campers had permission to hike as far as Mill Creek. They promised to turn back at the bridge. If they kept their promise, they did not pass the log cabin because it is _____ the bridge.

   **a.** until        **b.** before        **c.** beyond        **d.** below

6. After the hike, the group was hungry. They walked south on Parkview Terrace to the picnic area to wait for the dining room to open. The building they passed after the Staff Cabin is the _____

   **a.** Cabin 7        **b.** Health Cabin        **c.** Office        **d.** Chapel

7. The Ping-Pong tables are _____ of Scenic Walkway.

   **a.** west        **b.** south        **c.** north        **d.** east

8. The dining hall is located _____ the picnic area and the flagpole.

   **a.** beyond        **b.** before        **c.** following        **d.** between

From *EDL Pair Competency Program* (New York: EDL/McGraw-Hill, 1979), pp. 54–55. Reprinted by permission of the Office of Instruction, Los Angeles Unified School District.

# Model 4.4 Reading/Study Guide
## Pattern: Sequence
## Content: Social Studies

*Directions:* This guide is designed to help you identify the significant historical events of Judaism. First read the selection carefully. Then complete the chart below. The time line shows six historical periods of Judaism. Fill in the appropriate events from the following list under each period in the time line. If necessary, refer to the reading. Event no. 1 has been done for you.

**[Placing events on time line helps students order events correctly.]**

### Significant Events

1. Emphasis on education in the Jewish ghettos produced scholars like Joseph Caro.
2. Persecution of Jews exemplified by Pope Innocent III's decree that no kindness be extended to Jews.
3. The Golden Age of Jewry exemplified by the words of Maimonides Rashi and Gabriol.
4. Talmud created.
5. Belief in one God emerges.
6. Moses liberates Jews from Egypt (Passover).
7. Maccabees' victory over the Syrians gives Jews freedom to practice their own religion.

### Historical Periods

| Biblical Period (ca. 2500–300 B.C.E.) | Hellenistic Period (ca. 300 B.C.E.–135 C.E.) | Talmudic Period (ca. 135–600) | Judeo-Islamic Age (7th–13th Centuries) | European Age (13th–18th Centuries) | Modern Age (18th Century to the Present) |
|---|---|---|---|---|---|
| | | | | | 1. Emphasis on education in the Jewish ghettos produced scholars like Joseph Caro. |

# Model 4.5  Reading/Study Guide
## Pattern: Sequence
## Content: Social Studies

**The Sabbath: The Cycle of the Week (pp. 75–84)**

In this section the author describes the events associated with the Sabbath. The correct *sequence* of events is important. Below is a list of the major Sabbath events. Read these statements and then read pages 75 to 84. You should number the events in correct order by placing a 1 next to the event that happens first, a 2 next to the event that happens second, and so forth.

\_\_\_\_\_ The Sabbath candles are lit.

\_\_\_\_\_ Kiddush is recited.

\_\_\_\_\_ Appropriate preparations are made.

\_\_\_\_\_ Haudalah is recited.

\_\_\_\_\_ Participate in morning services.

\_\_\_\_\_ Participate in evening services.

**The Sabbath Eve and the Evening Service (pp. 76–78)**

Review this section to identify the correct sequence of events. Then complete the exercises below. Fill in the blank with either the word *before* or *after*.

*[Importance of signal words reinforced.]*

1. The Sabbath candles are lit approximately twenty minutes _____ sundown.
2. Candles may no longer be lit _____ sundown passes.
3. Benediction is recited _____ the candles are lit.
4. Members of the household greet each other with the words "Shabbat Shalom" _____ the candles are lit.
5. _____ dinner, members of the household attend evening services.

**Concluding the Sabbath (pp. 83–84)**

*[Students generate their own answers.]*

Answer the following questions.

1. When is Haudalah recited?
2. When is the candle held? When are the fragrant spices smelled?
3. When are the hands examined?

# Model 4.6 Reading/Study Guide
**Pattern: Sequence**
**Content: Social Studies**

In Chapter 1, "The Beginning of Our Nation," the sequence of events is stressed. This guide is designed to help you place historical events in the correct chronological order.

> *[Variety of exercises makes the guide more interesting to complete.]*

## Part I
Below is a list of historical events listed in incorrect order. Number them from 1 to 6 according to the correct chronological order.

_____ Boston Tea Party.

_____ St. Augustine founded by Spanish.

_____ Concord and Lexington.

_____ Maryland gave religious freedom to Christians.

_____ Jamestown.

_____ Mayflower.

## Part II
In each of the following pairs, put a check beside the one that happened *first*.

1. _____ (a) Pilgrims landed at Plymouth.
   _____ (b) Henry Hudson sailed into what is now called the Hudson River.
2. _____ (a) Ponce de Leon discovered Florida.
   _____ (b) Hernando Cortes took over the Aztecs.
3. _____ (a) New Hampshire becomes a separate colony.
   _____ (b) Massachusetts started public education.
4. _____ (a) French and Indian War.
   _____ (b) Sugar Act repealed.
5. _____ (a) The Boston Massacre.
   _____ (b) Declaration of Independence.

## Part III
The following are all colonies. Put a check beside those that were settled *before* 1650.

_____ Massachusetts

_____ Delaware

_____ North Carolina

_____ Maryland

_____ Pennsylvania

_____ New Jersey

# Model 4.7  Reading/Study Guide
## Pattern: Sequence
## Content: English

### "The Ceremony" by Nigel McKeand
(From the TV series "The Waltons"; anthologized in *This Land Is Our Land: The American Dream*, pp. 38–53.)

*Directions:* Read the information below on the parts of the plot. Then write the plot parts from "The Ceremony" on the dotted lines on the diagram. Use the lines of dialogue to make your decisions. Each sentence of the dialogue fits under a part of the plot in the diagram, but the sentences are not in correct order. Write the sentence numbers on the diagram's solid short lines. Be sure to put them under the correct part of the plot. The sentences will not necessarily be in chronological order.

### *[Plot parts clearly explained.]*

### Sequential Parts of the Plot
The *exposition* usually comes at the beginning of the play, although bits of exposition will occur throughout the play. A good script writer often gives us a bit of exposition just before we need to know it to appreciate an important moment in the play. The exposition usually deals with what has happened in the past; it explains all that is necessary to understand what follows (setting, mood, main character, point of view, background).

The *complication* is the next part of the teleplay or script. It presents the problem or conflict implied in the beginning situation. In George M. Cohan's terminology, you "get your man up a tree."

The *turning point* or crisis is the third part of the story, the part that takes a decisive turn. In George M. Cohan's scheme, this is the point at which "you throw rocks at the man in the tree." The turning point in tragedy was identified long ago by the Greek philosopher Aristotle. "Reversal of Situation is a change by which the action veers round to its opposite, subject always to our rule of probability or necessity . . . Recognition . . . is a change from ignorance to knowledge, producing love or hate between persons destined by the poet for good or bad fortune. The best form of recognition is coincident with a reversal of the situation. This recognition, combined with Reversal, will produce either pity or fear in a tragedy."

The *climax*, the point of highest emotional intensity, is the point of highest suspense. Sometimes this moment coincides with the turning point. In other stories it replaces the resolution, as in stories that have an exciting ending, particularly twist endings.

The final section is the *resolution* or *denouement*, the part where the author unravels the complication and thus provides the answer to the main questions. This part is where George M. Cohan "gets the man down from the tree." This resolution in fairy tales (and other stories) is the and-they-lived-happily-ever-after part.

## Lines from the Ceremony

1. *David:* (holding out the gift, a prayer shawl) I bought this for you a long time ago.

2. *Jim-Bob:* His daddy won't let him have his birthday.

3. *News Announcer:* . . . in Adolf Hitler's Germany, the persecution of the Jews goes on. Jews are forbidden to marry non-Jews. No Jew may teach or hold public office. Meanwhile, books by foreign authors are disappearing from Germany. One night recently, in Berlin, more than 20,000 books were burned.

4. *Grandpa:* If you deny your heritage, you'd be false to yourself. It would fester inside you like a disease.

5. *Paul:* Today I am thankful for many things—my father and mother for bringing me through these troubled times to manhood . . . and my friends here for giving us back our faith in people.

6. *Paul:* You see . . . I am a Jew.

7. *Ike:* They just arrived in the United States. Doc Harrison's lending them his summer cottage here.

8. *Paul:* John-Boy helped me find the rabbi. I talked to him about my Bar Mitzvah. He says it is the birthright of every Jew to have a Bar Mitzvah. He says I can have it even if my father is not present.

9. *Grandpa:* You know, Professor, all my life I've lived in the shadow of this mountain. My father—and his father before him—were born here. Generations of Waltons rest up there in the family graveyard. This is my heritage. Compared to yours it's small, but it's mine. If my ancestors had ever denied who they were, my grandchildren wouldn't be the people they are today. I think those same feelings are in your heart . . . just as they've been in the hearts of your people for five thousand years.

10. *Eva:* We loved Germany. It was our native land. Suddenly, everything changed. My husband, for no reason, was forced out of his job. In school, Paul was taunted. On the streets, our neighbors turned away and would not speak to us.

    Then one night every window of our house was smashed. Our door was smeared with paint and filthy words.

(continued)

# Model 4.7 (concluded)

11. *Paul:* You mean I can't have my Bar Mitzvah?
    *David:* Not even that. We cannot take any more risks.

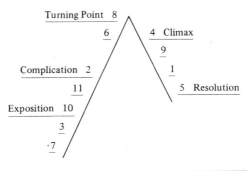

# Model 4.8 Reading/Study Guide
**Pattern: Sequence**
**Content: Business**

*Directions:* This reading guide is provided to help you see how the writer organized his thoughts. In this case the sequential pattern begins with an Introduction in which the writer presents a background to the six-column work sheet and the sequence of steps that are needed to prepare a six-column work sheet. In each step of the sequence (steps 1–9) you are required to read each question and place your answer(s) in the space provided. The purpose of this guide is to help you understand and retain the information in this chapter. Review the guide *before* reading the chapter. Then complete the guide.

**Background**
Answer T for true or F for false in the following statements.

_____ 1. The owner of every business wants to know from time to time how well the business is doing.

_____ 2. A paper with several amount columns, used for analysis purposes, is known as a work sheet.

_____ 3. The length of time for which an analysis of business operations is made is called a fiscal period.

_____ 4. All the ledger account balances are sorted and summarized in the balance sheet section.

_____ 5. The completed work sheet is used in preparing the financial reports at the end of the fiscal period.

*[Students generate answers themselves.]*

## Sequence of Order

*Step 1.* What are the three lines of the heading?

(a) _____

(b) _____

(c) _____

*Step 2.* What are the column headings, reading from left to right, on a standard six-column work sheet?

(a) _____

(b) _____

(c) _____

(d) _____

(e) _____

*Step 3.* What is step 3?

_____

*Step 4.* What is extended from the balance sheet items into the balance sheet section?

(a) _____

(b) _____

*Step 5.* What is extended from the income and expense items into the income statement section?

(a) _____

(b) _____

# Problems in Learning Cause/Effect

Cause/effect is vastly more complicated than sequence, but it is a very common pattern and is extremely important for students to master. Some reading educators even believe that the skill is the *most* important aspect of comprehension instruction (Pearson and Johnson, 1978).

Before teachers can present material in the proper perspective, they must consider all the possible pitfalls and misunderstandings to which the student is liable. Only then are they able to determine how many of the complexities of the situation the students would benefit from considering.

## Implied Cause/Effect

Sometimes we can be misled into believing that understanding causal relationships is a simple process because they are often signaled by clue words such as *hence, since,* and *therefore.* However, many cause/effect relationships are not signaled; they are implied. For example, there are no signal words in the following sentences: "Harry's arm pained him for several days. He decided to consult a doctor." Students must make the inference that Harry consulted the doctor (effect) because of the pain he was feeling in his arm (cause).

Research completed by Irwin (1980) supports the notion that causal statements that are both implied and reversible are particularly difficult for students. Irwin, who studied both fifth grade and college-level students, recommends that writers of textbooks at all levels avoid implicit causal statements, particularly reversible ones. Causal relationships should be explicitly stated, even if to do so authors must write longer sentences. Irwin warns us, however, that fifth grade students also have difficulty comprehending explicit causal relationships.

See if you can find the four implied cause/effect relationships in Example 11.

### Example 11    Cause/Effect Relationships

During the winter, phytoplankton populations dwindle. Days are short; there is not much sunlight for photosynthesis. Surface water temperatures are low. However, nutrients are being released to the water by decomposer bacteria. With the first temperature rise of spring, there is usually a sudden bloom of phytoplankton. Days are longer, and there is more sunlight for photosynthesis. This blooming may continue into the early summer if nutrients are plentiful. Where upwelling brings nutrient-rich deep water to the surface, the blooms are especially dense and long lasting.[11]

11. Lawrence W. McCombs and Nicholas Rosa. *What's Ecology?* (Menlo Park, Calif.: Addison-Wesley, 1973), p. 119.

The four implied cause/effect relationships are these:

1. Lack of sunlight (cause) results in dwindling phytoplankton.
2. The rise in temperature and increased sunlight causes phytoplankton to bloom.
3. Blooming will continue (effects) if nutrients are plentiful (cause).
4. When upwelling brings nutrient-rich deep water to the surface (cause), the result is dense, long-lasting blooms (effect).

## Reversible Causal Relations

Some students might be confused by writers who place the effect before the cause, although this technique is a common way of expressing the relationship in writing. See if you can find the reversible causal relations in Examples 12 and 13.

### Example 12   Effect Placed Before Cause

The fact that English is spoken widely throughout more than a quarter of the earth's surface results from the history, development, and expansion of the British Empire. Such names as Sir Francis Drake, Captain Cook, Admiral Bligh, and Doctor David Livingstone figure in this colorful history. The map on page 5 showing the Commonwealth of Nations in 1969 gives some idea of how far Britain's sphere of influence spread after the sixteenth century.[12]

### Example 13   Effect Placed Before Cause

Bitter presidential-Senate conflicts followed over the nominations of two Southern conservative federal judges to the high Court—Clement F. Haynsworth, Jr., of the Fourth Circuit Court of Appeals in Richmond and G. Harrold Carswell of the Fifth Circuit Court of Appeals in New Orleans. In November, 1969, the Senate rejected Haynsworth 55–45 because of charges of conflict of interest—that he had presided in cases in which he had a financial interest. The following April the Senate turned down Carswell 51–45 when it was discovered that he had run for the Georgia legislature on a white supremacy platform in 1948, had recently helped organize a whites-only golf club in Tallahassee, Florida, and possessed a mediocre record as a judge. In the twentieth century only one other Supreme Court nomination, that by President Herbert Hoover of North Car-

12.  Bernard R. Tanner and Robert E. Shutes. *Looking at Language* (Menlo Park, Calif.: Addison-Wesley, 1973), p. 4.

olina's racist and anti-labor Judge John J. Parker in 1930, was rejected by the Senate.[13]

In the first sentence of Example 12 the author supplies us with an effect first: "English is spoken widely throughout more than a quarter of the earth's surface." The second part of the sentence tells us that this result was caused by the history, development, and expansion of the British empire.

The first three sentences of Example 13 also contain reversible causal relations. In the first sentence the effect, bitter presidential-Senate conflicts, is stated first; then the cause, nominations of two Southern conservative federal judges to the high court, is stated. In the next sentence the effect, Senate rejection of Haynsworth, is stated first. The cause, charges of conflict of interest, is stated second. A similar reversal occurs in the third sentence. The effect, Carswell is turned down, comes first; and the causes, Carswell's white supremacy poilitical platform, association with a whites-only golf club, and mediocre record, are stated second.

The first and third sentences in Example 13 are especially difficult because the causal relations are both reversible *and* implied. (Did you notice that my last sentence was also a reversible causal relationship?)

## Causal Versus Enabling Factors

Teachers should make students aware of the *post hoc ergo propter hoc* (after this, therefore because of this) fallacy, even if they do not want to burden the pupils with the Latin terminology. Students should be warned not to assume that sequence implies cause. Just because one event preceded another, they cannot be sure, without strong evidence, that the earlier event caused the later one. Superstitions are the classic example of this fallacy. I am mistaken if I believe that my breaking a mirror on Friday the thirteenth caused my house to burn down on Saturday the fourteenth. Teachers might construct reading guides that require students to distinguish *causes* of a given event from events that merely antedate it.

Pearson and Johnson (1978) address this issue in another way when they discuss how causal factors can be mistaken for *enabling factors*. To illustrate, read the passage below and answer the question that follows it.

> Frank Jones read the Sunday newspaper. He noticed an ad for an adult reading improvement course that was sponsored by a local university. He was eager to improve his reading efficiency. Frank enrolled in the course. When the course ended ten weeks later, his reading efficiency had improved by 50%.

13. Thomas T. Lyons. *The Supreme Court and Individual Rights in Contemporary Society* (Menlo Park, Calif.: Addison-Wesley, 1975), pp. 267–268.

Question: Why was Frank able to improve his reading efficiency?

Select the correct answer.

1. Because he successfully completed an adult reading improvement course.
2. Because he read an ad in the paper.
3. Because he was eager to improve.

Answers 2 and 3 are incorrect. They are contributing factors that enabled Frank to improve his reading, but they did not cause him to improve his reading. Pearson and Johnson would probably suggest that they were *necessary* but not *sufficient* conditions that enabled Frank to improve his reading efficiency. What *caused* Frank to improve his reading was the fact that he successfully completed a reading improvement course.

Burmeister also alludes to the distinction between causal and enabling factors in her example concerning drugs: "People can become drug addicts only if drugs are available to them. Yet the mere availability of drugs does not mean that people will become addicts. The availability of drugs is a necessary, but not a sufficient condition to establish or even assume a cause/effect relationship. However, availability of drugs must *precede* addiction" (Burmeister, 1978, p. 238).

Burmeister points out another example of mistaken causal relationships— the case where students assume a cause/effect relationship exists when only a *correlation* exists. She provides the example of the well-known correlation between possessing a large vocabulary and success, which leads some people to assume that the large vocabulary caused the success. She continues: "The fact may be that the two factors interface—the more successful people are, the more experiences they have, and the larger their vocabularies are likely to be. Moreover, both success and a large vocabulary may be caused by high intelligence, insatiable curiosity, and drive. These may be the real causes of *both* the success *and* the large vocabulary" (Burmeister, 1978, p. 273).

# Introducing and Teaching Cause/Effect

## Simple Activities

The concept of cause/effect relationships will have to be introduced carefully to some students. A good way to introduce the concept dramatically is to poke a pin in an inflated balloon. Braver teachers may choose to enter class by slipping on a banana peel. In either case, the point is well made.

Another introductory activity that helps students understand the concept was suggested by Spache (1976). She recommends letting students interview senior citizens to learn facts about the history of their community. The students discuss or display in pictures the changes that have taken place in the community and then explain the causes of the changes.

When introducing cause/effect, teachers should be sure students understand that "effect" is what happens (a balloon breaks; teacher falls down) and "cause" is the reason something happens (a pin is poked into a balloon; a banana peel was left on the floor).

## Chain Reactions

Teachers can also point out how cause/effect events can form a *chain reaction*. Most students can relate to an example from their home life: girl comes in late for supper; parent reprimands girl; girl takes out her anger over reprimand by picking on younger brother; younger brother sticks tongue out at older sister; and on and on it goes. Students will be able to supply their own colorful examples of cause/effect chain reactions. Also, students can fill in flow charts or diagrams that require an awareness that the effect on one situation became the cause of another effect. These exercises will help to reinforce their knowledge of the chain reaction concept.

Example 14 illustrates the chain reaction concept.

### Example 14   Chain Reactions

Between 1909 and 1913 militant strikes of garment workers in Baltimore, Chicago, Philadelphia, and New York focused national attention on the horrors of sweatshop labor. The NWTUL gave active support to the strikers—raising funds, providing legal counsel, running relief kitchens, and educating and organizing the public in support of the strike. It mobilized the goodwill, economic resources, and influence of society and club women on behalf of union women and was invaluable in providing organizational continuity in the fight for protective labor legislation. The 1911 Triangle Shirt Waist factory fire in which 147 workers, most of them young girls, died because of inadequate fire escapes, overcrowding, and locked exits, awoke a shocked nation to the need for legislative protection of workers. Improved fire protection laws in New York and several other states were the direct result of the NWTUL's unremitting efforts after the disaster.[14]

14.  Gerda Lerner. *The Women in American History* (Menlo Park, Calif.: Addison-Wesley, 1971), p. 135.

Did you notice these chain reactions?

Cause:  Factory fire, poor fire escapes, overcrowding, locked exits.
Effect:  Young girls died.
Cause:  Young girls died.
Effect:  Nation shocked.
Cause:  Nation shocked.
Effect:  NWTUL makes unremitting efforts to improve situation.
Cause:  NWTUL makes unremitting efforts to improve situation.
Effect:  New York gets improved fire protection laws.

Students should also realize that several events may converge to produce a single result; similarly, a single cause may have many repercussions. The assassination of Archduke Ferdinand was the immediate cause of World War I, but a student who went away believing it was the sole and ultimate cause of the war would be greatly misguided. Questions that emphasize a plurality of causes help to reinforce an awareness of multiple causes (for example, "Which one of the four statements below *does not* describe a cause for the South's attempts to secede from the Union?").

# Relating Cause/Effect to Main Ideas

As with the sequence pattern, teachers can show how the cause/effect pattern relates to the main idea/details pattern. For example, both a cause and an effect can be considered main ideas, as they are in Example 15. The main idea of the first paragraph (British sailors and merchants could not communicate with people from various parts of the Pacific and the Far East) is a cause. The main idea of the second paragraph (pidgin English developed) is the effect.

### Example 15    Cause/Effect and Main Idea/Details

The English dialects of Australia, New Zealand, South Africa, Canada, and the United States developed principally among settlers who came from the British Isles. But from the seventeenth century British sailors and merchants were trading goods extensively throughout the Far East, the islands of the Pacific, and the west coast of Africa. Their problem was how to communicate with people whose languages were entirely different from the European languages, people who sometimes found it nearly impossible to reproduce certain sounds.

Out of this interaction arose what is known as pidgin English. The word *pidgin* is itself a Cantonese corruption of the English *business;* pidgin English started out therefore as a language of business, using for the most part English words with Chinese arrangement and syntax. Since that time it has spread throughout the Pacific.[15]

Presenting a diagram such as the one in Fig. 4.11 can help students visualize the relationship between cause/effect and main idea/details patterns.

## Paraphrasing Exercises

Pearson and Johnson (1978) suggest using a *paraphrasing exercise* to teach causal relations. Teachers can extract cause/effect relations from content area textbooks and ask students to paraphrase them. If that task is too difficult for students, teachers can provide paraphrased statements and ask students to identify the one that accurately matches the causal statement in the text. Here is an example from science.

### Example 16    Paraphrasing

Statement from text: "When rising moist air is cooled below its dew point, clouds are formed."

Question: Which statement means the same as the statement from the text?

1. When rising moist air rises above its dew point, clouds are formed.
2. Clouds are formed because the rising moist air is cooled below its dew point.
3. Clouds will form regardless of the air's dew point.

## Signal Words

Before students are asked to determine cause/effect relationships from textbooks, they may need practice in identifying cause/effect relationships in simple sentences that have signal words such as *because, if, consequently, led to, as a result, since, so,* and *therefore.* Using passages such as those in Examples 17–19, the teacher can ask students to place one line under the cause, place two lines under the effect, and circle the signal words.

---

15. Bernard R. Tanner and Robert E. Shutes, *Looking at Language* (Menlo Park, Calif.: Addison-Wesley, 1973), pp. 23–24.

# Figure 4.11 The Relationship of Main Idea/Details Pattern to Cause/Effect Pattern

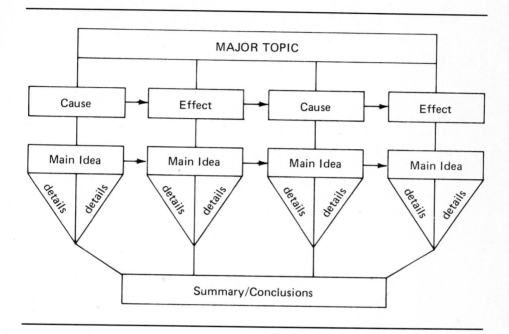

## Example 17    Finding Cause, Effect, and Signal Words: Simple Sentences

Wanda became angry (because) someone had borrowed her bicycle without asking her permission. (Because) Wanda was really very upset, she slammed her hand hard against a nearby brick wall. (As a result of) banging her hand against the wall, Wanda cut and scraped her hand.

When students are ready, they can complete similar exercises from textbooks. Some examples from different content areas follow.

### Example 18    Finding Cause, Effect, and Signal Words: Social Studies

In the earliest history of humans, there were no farmers. People got their own food by hunting animals and gathering grains, fruits, and other plants. (Since) they had no idea that plants and animals could be raised in one area, they were forced to follow the food supply. As animals migrated, or natural plants ripened in different places, the hunters and gatherers were required to move. (If) they didn't, they starved. The life of these early people was one of constant moving and seaching for food supplies.[16]

### Example 19    Finding Cause, Effect, and Signal Words: Science

Raising the temperature invariably increases the tendency for matter to expand or change from one state to another that occupies more volume (space). This is (because) particles move faster at higher temperatures. (As a result) the particles tend to break away from one another or at least "stretch" the bonds or forces holding them together.

On the other hand, we can raise the temperature of a system only by putting energy into it. Likewise, to cool a system, we have to take energy out of it, allowing the energy to spread.[17]

## Modified Cloze Procedure

The modified cloze procedure discussed earlier can help sensitize students to cause/effect signal words. Notice the signal words that can be deleted in Example 20.

### Example 20    Modified Cloze Procedure

Air and water pollution and the ugly accumulation of trash can be blamed mostly on how things are calculated in deciding what should

16. Elmer U. Clawson, *Our Economy: How It Works* (Menlo Park, Calif.: Addison-Wesley, 1980), pp. 97–98.
17. Tom R. Thomson, *Ideas from Chemistry* (Menlo Park, Calif.: Addison-Wesley, 1973), p. 17.

be produced for sale in the market, how much should be produced, and what production methods should be used. That is also the <u>reason</u>, I believe, for the damage done by the widespread use of inorganic fertilizers and by the accumulation of insecticides in animals. All these harmful practices <u>result</u> mainly from a combination of two things: a high level of activity in producing goods and services and consuming them (economic activity), and applying scientific knowledge and techniques in ways harmful to the environment.

An economist, someone who studies the way we manage our resources, would say that such harmful practices have occurred <u>because</u> we ignore externalities. An externality is defined as something "outside," or "extra," that a person does not consider when he figures his profit or loss. It can be either good or bad, and usually costs or benefits someone else.[18]

# Problem/Solution Pattern

The cause/effect pattern is often a component of the *problem/solution pattern*. When writers choose to use this pattern, they wish to discuss problems related to their discipline. For example, a chapter in a business text dealt with the *problem* of poor morale among employees. This led to a discussion of the *effects* of the problem, which were low worker output and a subsequent loss in the company's profit. The author then focused on the *causes* of the problem: workers were too closely supervised and their goals were in opposition to those of management. The *solution* was for management to discover ways of involving workers in planning, organizing, and controlling their own work.

The problem/solution pattern is easy to identify because the problem is often stated in the title of the article or chapter. Once students realize that the content deals with some type of a problem, they know that their purpose for reading is to seek out the causes, effects, and solutions to the problem. The solutions to the problem most often are found at the end of the article or chapter, while the causes and effects are most often found in the middle.

It is also possible that one aspect of the problem/solution pattern will be treated in an entire chapter. For example, in the textbook *Exploring Earth and Space* (Magnoli, Ellis, and Douglass, 1978), Chapter 19 is entitled "Solving Problems with Fresh Water." This chapter follows a chapter called "Problems with Fresh Water," which details the problems connected with fresh water, the causes of the problems, and the effects of the problem.

18. Ansley J. Coalet, adapted by George M. Clark, "Our Economy: An Essential Cause of Pollution," in Biological Sciences Curriculum Study. *The Environment: Some Viewpoints* (Menlo Park, Calif.: Addison-Wesley, 1975), p. 34.

# Figure 4.12 The Relationship of Main Ideas to the Problem/Solution Pattern

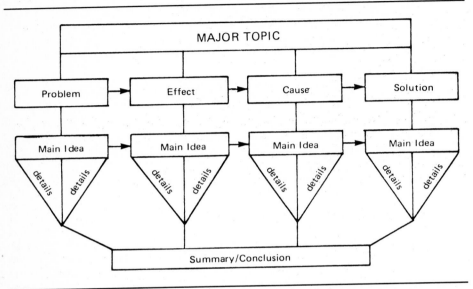

From Richard P. Santeusanio. *Developing Reading Skills for Business and Industry.* p. 51. Reprinted with permission. Copyright © 1981 CBI Publishing Co., Inc., 51 Sleeper St., Boston, Mass. 02210.

## Relating Problem/Solution to Main Ideas

The relationship between the main idea/details pattern and the problem/solution pattern can be illustrated with a visual aid such as the one that appears in Fig. 4.12.

## Manipulative Materials

Teachers may wish to develop some manipulative materials such as those discussed earlier in this chapter. Figure 4.13 presents another example from the work of White and her colleagues (1980). In this lesson the problem is discrimination against Mexican-American migrant workers as discussed in an American history textbook. The teacher provides background information on Mexican-American migrant workers. Then students are encouraged to read the

# Figure 4.13 Manipulative Exercise for Problem/Solution Pattern; Card Information and Answer Key

Problem: Discrimination against Mexican-American migrant workers in the 1960s.

**Causes**

| |
|---|
| "Anglos" took away property and rights from Mexican-Americans. |

| |
|---|
| Mexican Revolution in 1916 created an image of Mexicans as bandits or rebels. |

| |
|---|
| Radio, TV, and other media's false presentation of Mexican life-style. |

| |
|---|
| Migrant workers let themselves be exploited by American farmers. |

**Effects**

| |
|---|
| Low-paying jobs. |

| |
|---|
| Poor educational opportunity. |

| |
|---|
| Mexican-Americans must live in poor areas. |

| |
|---|
| Mexicans are viewed as second-class citizens. |

**Solutions**

| |
|---|
| Chicanos try to increase sense of identity and unity of Mexican-Americans. |

| |
|---|
| Chavez sets up United Farm Workers organizing committee. |

| |
|---|
| Workers strike. |

**Outcome**

| |
|---|
| 1970 owners recognize Union of United Farm Workers Committee. |

Reprinted by permission of Carol Ann Cramer and Robert K. Green, Ypsilanti High School. From materials developed through Title IV–C, Project Read.

chapter and look for causes of the discrimination, effects of it, solutions, and final outcome.

When they finish the reading, groups of students manipulate the information and heading cards so that proper information is placed under each of the heading cards "causes," "effects," "solutions," and "outcome." One student in each group is designated as leader and checks the groups' work to make sure the group members can support their placement of cards with evidence from the reading material. The proper match of heading cards and information is shown in Fig. 4.13.

## Generic Approaches to Applying the Cause/Effect Pattern to Content Areas

The models in this section illustrate how the three generic approaches—the direct teaching approach, adjunct questions, and reading/study guides—are used to assist students comprehend discourse written in the cause/effect pattern. In Model 4.9 a script is shown that is designed to help students recognize cause/effect relationships in English. Notice how the inserts in this and the other models point out their virtues and uniqueness.

Models 4.10 and 4.11 highlight the use of adjunct questions. In Model 4.10 the questions assist students with understanding cause/effect relationships in English. Many of the questions are designed to assist students with inferred cause/effect relationships. On the other hand, in Model 4.11 questions related to a real life situation emphasize literal cause/effect relationships.

Models 4.12 through 4.16 exemplify the use of reading guides to assist students with comprehending cause/effect relationships. Model 4.12 encourages students to focus primarily on effects since the guide itself states the causes. One of the purposes of the next guide, Model 4.13, is to help students differentiate between statements of cause and statements of effect. Page references are provided in this guide because the text is very complex.

Model 4.14, which contains a variety of exercises, encourages students to focus primarily on causes. Model 4.15 helps students comprehend a science chapter that is written at the beginning in the sequence pattern and then changes to the cause/effect pattern. The guide's exercises help students realize that the change has taken place.

Finally, Model 4.16 illustrates a guide that simulates the thinking involved in ideas expressed in the problem/solution pattern. The guide clearly identifies the various components of the pattern.

# Model 4.9  Direct Teaching
**Pattern: Cause/Effect**
**Content: English**

**Teacher: We have been studying how a knowledge of certain writing patterns can help us with our reading. Cause/effect has been one of them. Remember, an effect is something that happens. What is an effect?**

> *[Distinction made between cause and effect.]*

*Students: Something that happens.*

**Teacher: Good, an effect is something that happens. The cause is the *reason* something happens. Repeat with me. . . .**

*Students and Teacher: The cause is the reason something happens.*

**Teacher: Cause precedes effect; cause comes first. What comes first, cause or effect?**

*Students: Cause.*

> *[Alerts students to reversibility.]*

**Teacher: Let's remember our generalization, cause precedes effect, but the effect may be *written* first.**

*Students: Cause precedes effect, but the effect may be written first.*

> *[Purpose set for reading.]*

**Teacher: Good. We are going to read a brief selection abut the author O. Henry. We will find that many events in his life, things that happened in his life, were caused by unpleasant situations. Read, now, to find some cause/effect relationships.**

> *[After students read the selection, the dialogue continues.]*

**Teacher: What caused O. Henry to move to Texas?**

*Students: His health condition.*

**Teacher: Correct: The *cause* was poor health; the *effect* was moving to Texas, where he became a bank teller. Now why did he go to South America?**

*Students: Because he was accused of embezzlement.*

(continued)

# Model 4.9  (concluded)

*[Questions relate directly to stated purpose for reading.]*

**Teacher: Good. Now what was the *effect*?**

*Students: The effect was moving to South America.*

**Teacher: Right, and what was the *cause*?**

*Students: Being accused of embezzlement.*

**Teacher: Excellent. What led to his conviction?**

*Students: His wife became ill. He returned to Texas and was convicted.*

**Teacher: What, then, is the *effect* here?**

*Students: The conviction.*

**Teacher: Good, and the *cause*?**

*Students: His wife's illness, which made him return to Texas.*

**Teacher: What was a positive *effect* of his imprisonment?**

*Students: He began to write.*

**Teacher: Fine. We can see, then, that many cause/effect relationships are apparent in this selection on O. Henry. Your awareness of these relationships can lead to better comprehension and retention of ideas.**

# Model 4.10  Adjunct Questions
**Pattern: Cause/Effect**
**Content: English**

*To the Student:* As you read "Casey at the Bat," refer to the questions below. They will help you identify the cause/effect relationships in the selection.

*[Questions alert students to cause/effect relationships.]*

1. An event was taking place in Mudville; briefly describe what was happening.
2. In the first verse, what happened to Cooney and Burrows?

3. What was the effect upon the spectators?
4. What caused the crowd to fall into an even greater melancholy?
5. What was the natural expected outcome of the batter's trips to bat?
6. What really did happen to Jimmy and Flynn?
7. As a result of this event, how did the crowd react?
8. When Casey arrived at bat, he tipped his hat to the crowd. What caused him to do so?
9. What effect did this act have on the crowd?
10. Why do you suppose Casey let the first two balls go by?

Each of the following numbered items contains a cause/effect relationship. Read each item carefully. If the underlined part of the sentence is a cause, write the letter C on the line before the item. If the underlined part of the sentence is the effect, write the letter E.

\_\_\_\_\_ 1. The umpire called "Strike one" and the crowd shouted, "Kill him!"

\_\_\_\_\_ 2. Because Casey was confident of his ability, he let the first two balls go by.

\_\_\_\_\_ 3. There is no joy in Mudville—mighty Casey has struck out.

\_\_\_\_\_ 4. Since Casey has two strikes against him, the sneer is gone from his lips.

\_\_\_\_\_ 5. The crowd called the umpire a fraud, because he called strike two.

This model was prepared by Margaret Richter.

# Model 4.11 Adjunct Questions
**Pattern: Cause/Effect**
**Content: Real Life**

Before reading the information about a wasp/hornet killer, preview the following questions. Answer them after you read the passage.

1. What happens when you fire Jet Stream at pests?

*[Questions alert students to typical cautions found on labels.]*

(continued)

# Model 4.11 (concluded)

2. What particular ingredient has this effect on pests?
3. Why should you apply the stream at night?
4. What could cause the Jet Stream can to catch fire?
5. What could happen if the can is exposed to very high temperatures?
6. What do you think would happen if Jet Stream were sprayed on plants?

# Model 4.12  Reading/Study Guide
## Pattern: Cause/Effect
## Content: Social Studies

Listed below are some situations that are related to ideas you found in this chapter. Study the situation and complete the guide by providing what you think may have caused the situation or what you think would be an effect of the situation.

1. (a) *Causes.* The city of Pittsburgh depends on the production of coal and steel. As of yesterday, all mines have dried up.

   (b) *Effects.*

   *[Students generate answers themselves.]*

2. (a) *Causes.* Crayton is a small town. Recently a large corporation discovered rich deposits of raw materials (various metals and petroleums) within and around the town. The town is situated near the Mississippi River, and one can reach it by taking a train. The next largest city is five hundred miles away.

   (b) *Effects.*

3. (a) *Causes.* Electricity is no longer transmitted by wires. Everyone now gets their energy directly from the sun.

   (b) *Effects.*

4. (a) *Causes.* A law has been passed. Zinc and lead are poisons. They must be taken out of all products.

   (b) *Effects.*

# Model 4.13  Reading/Study Guide
**Pattern: Cause/Effect**
**Content: Humanities**

### Gods and Goddesses Among the Hindus, Past and Present

*Directions:* Each of the following items contains a cause/effect relationship. Read each item carefully. If the underlined part of the sentence(s) is a cause, write the letter C on the line before the item. If the underlined part of the sentence(s) is an effect, write the letter E.

*[Questions help students distinguish between cause and effect.]*

_____ 1. The New Hinduism . . . had accepted as legitimate more of the religion of the people than had Brahmanism. In so doing, it had developed its characteristic tolerance of widely different beliefs. (p. 21).

_____ 2. This constant tendency toward imitation (by the lower castes) of the "higher" religion and of the "higher" castes has created a certain degree of unity within the heterogeneous mass of Hinduism. (p. 22)

_____ 3. . . . What might be called Hindu "orthodoxy" has been increasing rather than decreasing as more people have gained access to the Sanskrit texts in the original or in translation. (p. 22)

_____ 4. These spirits . . . are not adored or worshipped, but feared. The various rites, ceremonies and superstitious practices with which they are approached are attempts to control them and avert their wrath. (pp. 22–23)

*Directions:* The questions below deal with cause/effect relationships discussed in the "Village Cults" section. Answer them in complete sentences.

### *[Students generate their own answers.]*

1. What has *caused* village Hinduism to be largely unknown in the West?

2. What, according to some village people, *causes* smallpox? What are the *effects* of this belief?

3. What *causes* Indian villages to continue to believe in magic and witchcraft?

4. Many of the villagers hold strong superstitions. What *effect* has this factor had on their health care practices?

# Model 4.14 Reading/Study Guide
Pattern: Cause/Effect
Content: English

### "A Game of Catch"

*To the Student:* Before reading the story, preview the guide below. It will help you understand the cause/effect relationships that occur in the story. Read the story and then complete the guide. Refer to the story if necessary.

*[Variety of exercises makes the guide interesting to complete.]*

### Part I

Read pages 72 and 73 and then answer the questions below. Check either "yes" or "no."

|  | Does (a) cause (b)? |  |
|---|:---:|:---:|
|  | **Yes** | **No** |
| 1. (a) Monk and Glennie were seventh graders. | | |
| (b) They were good baseball players. | ——— | ——— |
| 2. (a) Glennie saw that Scho had nothing to do. | | |
| (b) Glennie invited Scho to play. | ——— | ——— |
| 3. (a) Scho didn't have a glove. | | |
| (b) Glennie and Monk threw easy grounders to Scho. | ——— | ——— |
| 4. (a) Scho missed a hard grounder. | | |
| (b) Glennie and Monk threw the ball to Scho more carefully. | ——— | ——— |
| 5. (a) Glennie didn't think three-way catch was working out well. | | |
| (b) The boys agreed to take turns playing two-way catch. | ——— | ——— |

### Part II

Read pages 74–76 and then answer the questions below in complete sentences.

1. What *caused* Scho to go up the tree?
2. What *caused* Scho to say "I can make you two do anything I want."
3. What was the *effect* of Scho's teasing the boys?

4. What *caused* Monk to climb the tree?

5. What happened as a result of Scho's falling off the tree?

**Part III**

Reread the paragraph below from the story. Put one line under the words that express the *cause* and two lines under the words that express the *effect*. Circle the *clue word* that signifies a cause/effect relationship.

> "I found a wonderful seat up here," Scho said loudly. "If I don't fall out." Monk and Glennie didn't look up or comment and so he began jouncing gently in his chair of branches and singing "Yo-ho, heave ho" in an exaggerated way.

# Model 4.15 Reading/Study Guide
## Pattern: Cause/Effect and Sequence
## Content: Biology

In this chapter the authors present information on alcohol. The first section emphasizes the sequence of ideas (a discussion of what happens to the body when alcohol enters it). The second section emphasizes cause/effect relationships (the effects of alcohol upon the body and what causes each effect). Use the guide below to assist you as you read this chapter.

*[Guide simulates thinking for two different organizational patterns.]*

**Section I**

The following list describes things that happen to the body when alcohol is consumed. The statements are not in the correct sequence. You are to number the statements from 1 to 8 according to the correct sequential order.

_____ Presence of alcohol in cells.

_____ Alcohol enters blood.

_____ Temperature of blood rises.

_____ Increased circulation to the skin.

_____ Alcohol delivered to tissues.

_____ Heat released from cells.

_____ Alcohol absorbed by cells.

_____ False impression of warmth.

# Model 4.15 (concluded)

**Section II**

Below are listed some effects of alcohol upon the body. Match the cause with the effect by placing the letter of the cause next to the effect.

Effects

_____ 1. Temperature of blood rises.

_____ 2. Alcoholic flush.

_____ 3. Internal organs deprived of adequate blood supply.

_____ 4. Alcoholic breath odor.

_____ 5. Tissues become dehydrated.

_____ 6. Gastritis.

_____ 7. Emotional control loss.

_____ 8. Vision and speech become blurred and slurred.

_____ 9. Muscle coordination fails.

Causes

(a). Alcohol increases stomach secretions.

(b). Cerebellum becomes affected by alcohol.

(c). Excess heat produced from oxidation of alcohol.

(d). Blood rushes to skin.

(e). Oxidation of alcohol produces water.

(f). Cerebrum becomes affected by alcohol.

(g). Alcohol that is not oxidized is released from lungs.

(h). Frontal lobe becomes affected by alcohol.

# Model 4.16 Reading/Study Guide
**Pattern: Problem/Solution**
**Content: Health/Business**

Use this guide to assist you in ascertaining the important ideas from the selection "The Trouble with Drugs."

*[List logically guides students through each component of the pattern.]*

1.  The *problem* discussed in this article is:
    (a)  Drinking on the job.
    (b)  Sleeping on the job.
    (c)  The use of wet and dry drugs on the job.

**[Items 2 and 3 indicate that problem has effects on different people.]**

2.  The *effect* on the employee is:
    (a)  A change in one's mood and a bending of one's mind.
    (b)  The loss of the job.
    (c)  The loss of self-respect.

3.  The *effect* on the employer is a:
    (a)  Great loss of money.
    (b)  Great loss in prestige.
    (c)  Great loss of interest in the company.

4.  Select *two* statements that represent *causes* of the problem.
    (a)  Drugs are accessible in the street and in drug stores.
    (b)  Workers go to bed too late.
    (c)  Drugs are accessible on the job.
    (d)  Employers are indifferent to employees' problems.

5.  Select *five* statements that represent *solutions* to the problem.
    (a)  Develop an Alcoholics Anonymous program.
    (b)  Develop an official policy with respect to the problem.
    (c)  Prescreen to detect potential problem employees.
    (d)  Provide rehabilitation programs.
    (e)  Make pep pills available to employees.
    (f)  Immediately fire the problem employee.
    (g)  Look for early signs of illness.
    (h)  Create a good system for evaluating work performance.
    (i)  Avoid discussing the problem.
    (j)  Stay away from quack counselors.

# An NBC News Report, Part II

Mr. Champa is about to discuss a TV program he asked his students to watch. Their primary purpose for watching was to discover the effects the new finance laws had on the primary elections.

"I hope you all enjoyed the program. It focused mainly on finance laws. Who makes sure that candidates comply with these new laws? Rick?"

"There's something called the Federal Election Commission. It's got over two hundred fifty people working for it."

"Yes. Now I asked you to look for some of the effects that the new laws and the FEC have had on the candidates. Now we'll break up into groups of five. One person should be chosen as recorder. I want each group to try to recall as many effects as possible that were mentioned on the program. I'll give you ten minutes or so; then we'll get back together and review your lists."

After the groups worked together for ten minutes, Mr. Champa said, "I think that's enough time. Let's go around to each group. We'll get at least one effect from each group. The group's recorder should report. OK, Margaret. Give us one that your group came up with."

"Somebody on the program mentioned that the candidates had to spend so much time on campaigning . . . something like a third of their time. And this meant that they couldn't really get their ideas on issues out to the public."

"OK, so what effect did this have? Group 2 . . . Donald."

"Let me check my notes here. Well, one thing we've got is that the candidates had less time to get briefed on issues and to meet with their constituents."

"What else? Group 3?"

"Well, they practically had to go around begging for money."

"What else happened to some candidates because of the laws? Group 4, Eva it's your turn."

"Some of them, John Connally for example, had to drop out of the race early."

## Summary

Sequence and cause/effect are two patterns of organization that frequently appear in middle and secondary school textbooks. Sometimes cause/effect relationships are expressed in chapters or articles that focus on problems and offer solutions to them. Writers who discuss problems inevitably explain their

"What would have happened to Connally under the old system?"

"Oh, I know," said Eva. "They said he could have received lots of money from friends. But that's not legal now. He probably would have stayed in the race much longer."

"Now Group 5. Did you come up with what happened to one of the fellows who placed a newspaper ad in California? Jayne?"

"Let's see . . . Is that the one about the guy the commission investigated?"

"Yes, go on."

"I guess he had to spend thousands of dollars to defend himself. It seems it involved some minor technicality."

"What else did your group come up with?"

"That part where they said it cost almost two million dollars for the candidates to make their reports to the FEC."

"Right. Does anybody remember what Charles Keating, Connally's former chief operating officer, said about the psychological effects of the law and the FEC? . . . What did he say pervaded the whole campaign? Arthur."

"Fear," said Arthur. "Everybody was worrying about being investigated."

Mr. Champa continued for a while with the discussion and then broached the subject of the timing of primaries.

"Now who remembers what was said about the first primary as opposed to the last primaries? . . . George."

"If you were first in New Hampshire, you'll probably be your party's candidate."

"Does winning in New Hampshire cause you to become the nominee?"

"Well, maybe not directly. But it sure helps. The media stomps to New Hampshire. The winners get all sorts of publicity. They said that since 1952 every man elected president had won his party's primary in New Hampshire!"

"Indeed. Let's now take a look at. . . ."

causes and the *effects* of the problems. Several reasons can be cited to explain why students sometimes have difficulty comprehending material written in these patterns, and there are a number of techniques teachers can use to help their students overcome the problem.

Teachers can, for example, begin with rather simple activities and proceed to show the relationship of these patterns to main ideas. They can teach signal words, use a modified cloze procedure, prepare manipulative exercises, and use direct instruction, adjunct questions, and reading/study guides. By using a variety of approaches based on their students' regular classroom textbooks, teachers will be able to help their students comprehend material written in the complex sequence and cause/effect patterns.

# Bibliography

Burmeister, Lou E. *Reading Strategies for Middle and Secondary School Teachers*. 2nd ed. Reading, Mass.: Addison-Wesley, 1978.

DeCaroli, Joseph. "What Research Says to the Classroom Teacher: Time and Chronology." *Social Education* 36(1972):312–313.

Estes, Thomas H., and Joseph L. Vaughan, Jr. *Reading and Learning in the Content Classroom*. Boston: Allyn & Bacon, 1978.

Harris, Albert J., and Edward R. Sipay. *How to Increase Reading Ability*. 6th ed. New York: McKay, 1975.

Irwin, Judith W. "The Effects of Explicitness and Clause Order on the Comprehension of Reversible Causal Relationships." *Reading Research Quarterly* 15(1980):477–488.

Magnoli, Michael A., Doris M. Ellis, and Linda Douglass. *Exploring Earth and Space*. River Forest, Ill.: Laidlaw, 1978.

Nichols, James N. "Using Paragraph Frames to Help Remedial High School Students with Written Assignments." *Journal of Reading* 24(1980):228–231.

Niles, Olive Stafford. "Organization Perceived." In *Developing Study Skills in Secondary Schools*, edited by Harold Herber. Newark, Del.: International Reading Association, 1965.

Otto, Wayne, and Karlyn Kamm. *Wisconsin Design for Reading Skill Development, Teacher's Planning Guide: Comprehension*. Minneapolis: NCS Educational Systems, 1977.

Pearson, P. David, and Dale D. Johnson. *Teaching Reading Comprehension*. New York: Holt, Rinehart and Winston, 1978.

Peters, Charles W. "The Comprehension Process." In *Reading Problems, a Multidisciplinary Perspective*, edited by Wayne Otto, C. W. Peters, and N. Peters. Reading, Mass.: Addison-Wesley, 1977.

Santeusanio, Richard P. "Report on Reading Programs." Paper presented to the Danvers Subcommittee on Curriculum, December 1980, Danvers, Mass.

Spache, Evelyn B. *Reading Activities for Child Involvement*. 2nd ed. Boston: Allyn & Bacon, 1976.

White, Judith, Eva Swenarton, Beverly Riordan, Carol Morgan, and Trudy Adams. "A Comprehensive Secondary Reading Model." Paper presented at the International Reading Association Convention, May 1980, St. Louis.

# Chapter 5

## Evaluating

## Persuasive

## Techniques

# Madison Avenue, Part I

Why does Mr. DePietro have so many strange hats and head gear piled up on the table in front of his classroom? This was the question on the minds of his eighth grade students as they paraded into his classroom.

Mr. DePietro took attendance, then donned his first hat, a chef's hat, and said, "I'm going to try to sell you some products today. I want you to pay careful attention to the techniques I use and tell me which is your favorite. The first product I have for your consideration is Chef DePietro's spaghetti sauce.

"I know all you teenagers really love spaghetti. It's a favorite dish in our house, where we use Chef DePietro's scrumptious spaghetti sauce. And you don't have to be Italian to make it. It's as easy as one-two-three.

"Just open the bottle, pour the delicious contents into a sauce pan, heat, and serve over your favorite spaghetti. You'll love the magnificent aroma that permeates your kitchen as you sit down to enjoy the most satisfying spaghetti dish of your life."

Switching to a cab driver's hat, Mr. DePietro continued, "My cabs are the cleanest, smoothest-riding cabs in town and used by the mayor and

# Introduction

When writers use the organizational patterns of main idea, sequence, cause/effect, problem/solution, and data, their main purpose is to *inform* rather than to persuade their readers. This chapter deals with modes of communication writers and speakers use when they wish to sell their ideas.

When writers wish to persuade their readers, they organize their material in much the same way that advertisers organize their ads. They begin by making an *assertion*. While the advertiser may write, "The Gale Department Stores are special," an author may write, "When business managers adapt their leadership style to various situations, they are more effective in reaching personal and organizational goals."

How are these assertions *supported*? The advertiser may support the assertion that the department store is special by noting the store's personalized and fast services to customers. The writer may support the assertion regarding leadership style by reporting interviews, citing research, quoting authorities, or providing personal, subjective reasons.

What *outcome* does the advertiser expect? He expects the public to shop at Gale Department Stores. The writer, on the other hand, expects his readers his staff all the time. Why, when Robert Redford and Jane Fonda come to town, they always ask for DePietro's cabs."

Next Mr. DePietro placed a hockey helmet on his head, and as he banged a hammer on it, he said, "See, you can even hear how sturdy this helmet is. Not like those ridiculous, worthless helmets by Hoppy. Why, Hoppy doesn't even know how to spell helmet, never mind make them. I wouldn't tell my worst enemy to use a Hoppy helmet! Now you've seen and heard how sturdy the DePietro helmet is. Let's try the same test on this weak, cheap, unsafe Hoppy helmet."

After smashing a Hoppy helmet into many pieces, Mr. DePietro modeled more hats and headgear and continued to amuse his class. The students then volunteered reasons why they liked certain ads and commented on their teacher's selling techniques. Toward the end of class Mr. DePietro summarized the seven basic propaganda techniques and gave his students a writing assignment.

"For homework I want you to write a brief ad and use one or two of the propaganda techniques we discussed today."

At the end of the chapter you will find samples of the homework Mr. DePietro collected from his students.

to accept the theory or opinion and, in some cases, to act on it. For example, if the readers are managers, they may in fact decide to adopt the adaptive leader behavior model espoused in the article.

To sum up, writers who wish to persuade their readers first make an *assertion,* a positive, forceful opinion, theory, conclusion, or declaration. Next they *support* their assertion with subjective reasons, objective research, interviews, or expert testimony. Finally, the writers have an expected *outcome,* which may be either stated directly or implied. Readers may simply agree with the author's ideas or they may take some action. On the other hand, they may critically read the article and note some flaws in the writer's reasoning or research. In such cases they reject or modify the assertion and do not act or think as the writer would like. The writer, therefore, has not been successful in attaining his or her expected outcomes.

The major difference between the persuasive pattern and the other informational patterns we have discussed lies in the writer's motivation or purpose for writing. When writers choose to utilize the persuasive pattern, they wish to move the reader to some action or belief. (This motivation sometimes is also the case with the problem/solution pattern.) Writers utilize other writing patterns when their purpose is mainly to inform the reader.

Whatever pattern writers choose, readers should analyze critically the writers' ideas or information. However, materials written in the persuasive pattern lend themselves more readily to evaluative reading. As soon as a reader comprehends a writer's assertion, opinion, or theory, the reader's purpose should be to understand and carefully evaluate the writer's supportive statements. The reader's evaluation should include judgments about the reasonableness, soundness, logic, validity, and reliability of statements writers use to support their assertions. These steps are the essence of critical reading. However, because readers approach the written word with their own experiential background, tastes, and temperament, each is capable of interpreting the author's "proof" or supportive statements differently.

Teachers should stress to their students that people who promote their ideas are not necessarily bad. In fact, much persuasive writing is intended to protect us, as in the myriad of publications that come from Ralph Nader and his associates. Most authors choose a topic to write about because they strongly believe in the ideas they are trying to promote. After a careful, critical reading of these ideas, readers can choose to accept or reject them. Readers who reject ideas without carefully considering the author's supporting statements have not met their contractual obligations. Similarly, readers who accept ideas before examining them carefully are not fulfilling their contractual obligations either.

Several reading educators have stressed the importance of critically analyzing persuasive and other types of writing. Almost two decades ago the late reading educator Nila Banton Smith felt so strongly about it that in a speech she delivered to the International Reading Association, she referred to critical reading as a "national obligation." More recently Turner noted that developing critical readers is a major purpose of a reading program, and the skills of critical reading are the "bread and butter tools needed by the individual in modern society" (Turner, 1980, p. 173). After a panel of 14 reading experts analyzed the most recent test data on a broad sample of nine-, thirteen-, and seventeen-year-olds that was released by the National Assessment of Educational Progress, the panelists concluded that classroom instruction should focus more on critical reading and thinking skills (Micklos, 1982). It is important that students learn how to use some norm or standard in evaluating written discourse. They must be given opportunities to judge, inspect, compare, analyze, and accept or reject the ideas people have put into writing.

## Tasks in Critical Reading

What are some of the tasks involved in critical or evaluative reading? Perhaps this is a good point to return to Barrett's taxonomy (see Chapter 3). Note below the various tasks Barrett associates with the evaluation component of his taxonomy of reading comprehension. These tasks are essential aspects of critical reading, and an awareness of them can help students become more critical, probing, and active readers.

3.0. *Evaluation.* Evaluation is demonstrated by students when they make judgments about the content of a reading selection by comparing it with external criteria—for example, information provided by the teacher on the subject, by authorities on the subject, or by accredited written sources on the subject; or with internal criteria—for example, the reader's experiences, knowledge, or values related to the subject under consideration. In essence, evaluation requires students to make judgments about the content of their reading, judgments that have to do with its accuracy, acceptability, worth, desirability, completeness, suitability, timeliness, quality, truthfulness, or probability of occurrence. Examples of evaluation tasks related to reading are:

3.1. *Judgments of Reality or Fantasy.* Students are requested to determine whether incidents, events, or characters in a selection could have existed or occurred in real life on the basis of their experience.

3.2. *Judgments of Fact or Opinion.* In this case, students are asked to decide whether the author is presenting information which can be supported with objective data or whether the author is attempting to sway the reader's thinking through the use of subjective content that has overtones of propaganda.

3.3. *Judgments of Adequacy or Validity.* Tasks of this type call for the readers to judge whether the author's treatment of a subject is accurate and complete when compared to other sources on the subject. In this instance, then, the readers are called upon to compare written sources of information with an eye toward their agreements or disagreements, their completeness or incompleteness, and their thoroughness or superficiality in dealing with a subject.

3.4. *Judgments of Appropriateness.* Evaluation tasks of this type require the students to determine whether certain selections or parts of selections are relevant and can contribute to resolving an issue or a problem. For example, students may be requested to judge the part of a selection which most appropriately describes a character. Or they may be called upon to determine which references will make significant contributions to a report they are preparing.

3.5. *Judgments of Worth, Desirability, or Acceptability.* In this instance, students may be requested to pass judgments on the suitability of a character's action in a particular incident or episode. Was the character right or wrong, good or bad, or somewhere in between? Tasks of this nature call for opinions based on the values the readers have acquired through their own personal experiences.[1]

## Internal and External Criteria

When students engage in the evaluation tasks, they make judgments about their reading by using either external criteria or internal criteria (Smith and Barrett, 1979). *External criteria* consist of information gained from outside authorities and from those with good reputations in a given field. When students acquire information from outside sources, they are better able to make judgments on a writer's supporting evidence, reasons, or logic. For example, students in a high school health class were asked to read a selection about an individual's theory on what caused alcoholism. The theory stressed physiological causes of alcoholism as opposed to psychological causes. The students then read authoritative accounts on the causes of alcoholism, and using this information as their criteria, they evaluated the evidence the writer used to support his theory on the causes of alcoholism.

    *Internal criteria* consist of the reader's own knowledge, experiences, and values. Also influencing their judgments are their own biases, beliefs, or preferences. Because of the nature of the criteria used, *internal criteria* are more subjective than *external criteria*. Students may choose to evaluate the theory on alcoholism, for example, by drawing on their own experiences. They may be acquainted with some alcoholics, and on the basis of their experiences with them, they could decide on the validity or reasonableness of the theory of alcoholism presented in the article. Obviously, the utilization of external criteria and internal criteria does not have to be an either/or choice when evaluating written communication. Both kinds of criteria can and should be used.

## Problems in Reading Critically

### Reader Predisposition

The difficulties that both adolescents and adults have with critical reading may be related more to their attitudes and characteristics than to the complexity of the process of critical reading itself. Some readers, unfortunately, have a narrow, preconceived view of the world. They are caught in their own biases that often

---

1. Adapted from Barrett, Thomas C., "A Taxonomy of Reading Comprehension," *Reading 360 Monograph* (1972). Lexington, Massachusetts, Ginn and Company (Xerox Corporation). Reprinted by permission.

prevent them, even at a literal level of understanding, from entertaining the ideas of those with opposite or different views. They are unable to suspend judgment; they are quick to disagree or simply unable to understand.

Eller and Dykstra (1959) have considered the issue of the effects of read-ers' attitudes on critical-reading ability. Two of the studies they cite are pertinent. One study demonstrated that ninth grade students who had a negative attitude toward blacks were significantly less able to read critically about them than those whose attitudes were indifferent. The other study indicated that the majority of people who were predisposed against minority groups were unable to identify the theme of a series of cartoons depicting "Mr. Biggott." On the other hand, most of these who were sympathetic toward minority groups were able to interpret the cartoons correctly.

The effects of reader attitudes on critical-reading ability were discussed more recently by Reynolds (1981) and his colleagues, who reviewed Read and Rosson's unpublished research on this topic. In this study the researchers used a questionnaire to identify people who were either strongly in favor of or opposed to nuclear power. These people were asked to read a passage about a fire at a nuclear power station. When the subjects completed a multiple-choice test immediately after the passage, there was no correlation between reader predisposition and test scores. However, when the test was delayed one or two weeks, people had a tendency to distort the passage in a manner consistent with their beliefs. Those favoring nuclear power were able to reject antinuclear statements that had no basis in the passage, but they had a tendency to accept spurious, pronuclear statements. Subjects who opposed nuclear power produced the opposite pattern.

Artley (1959) also reviewed studies on the predisposition of readers and concluded that the more personal, immediate, or intense one's negative feelings are on a given topic, the less likely it is that one can make an accurate interpretation of material written on that topic.

After reviewing many studies on reader predisposition, Eller and Dykstra concluded that

> a critical reading curriculum cannot ignore the reader-predisposition factor. The teacher may compensate by deluding himself into thinking he faces a class of essentially homogeneous personality; however, the public school class of today is rare that does not contain critical divisions along the lines, not only of intelligence differences, but of racial differences, family socioeconomic status differences, religious differences, a generous variety in degrees of psychological adjustment, and, of course, sex differences. This should be enough to convince one of the heterogeneous nature of the psychological response of a class to the content of any given piece of printed matter. (Eller and Dykstra, 1959, p. 28)

## Other Causes

Other reasons that some students have problems reading critically include a lack of emphasis on it in their teachers' education courses, the fact that some school systems avoid controversial topics in their curricula, the paucity of commercial materials designed to teach critical reading, the lack of research on the topic, and confusion surrounding the concept.

The recent emphasis on accountability in education is another reason. Since standardized tests are often used to measure accountability, teachers tend to teach the skills emphasized on the test. With the possible exception of the subskill area of fact and opinion, most standardized reading tests do not attempt to measure critical reading because the divergent thinking required in critical reading cannot be measured on a multiple-choice test. Hence the skill is not stressed in the curriculum.

In a study related to this issue of emphasis on critical reading in the curriculum, Davis (1969), after studying elementary children's ability to distinguish between fact and opinion, concluded that there is an obvious need to help students improve in this skill. All students need direct instruction, encouragement, and an opportunity to apply the skill.

Not surprisingly, Wolf, Cansneder, and Cansneder (1967) were able to demonstrate that when critical reading is taught regularly to children throughout the school year, they display a significantly greater ability to read critically than those who do not receive regular instruction.

# Introducing and Teaching Critical Reading

## Propaganda Techniques

One of the best ways of introducing the concept of critical reading is to review the various propaganda techniques. When doing so, teachers should keep in mind Postman's definition of propaganda, which, he said:

> refers not to the goodness or badness of causes but exclusively to a use of language designed to evoke a particular kind of response. We might say, for example, that propaganda is language that invites us to respond emotionally, more or less immediately, and in an either-or manner. It is distinct from language which stimulates curiosity, reveals its assumptions, causes us to ask questions, invites us to seek further information and to search for error. From this perspective, we eliminate the need to distinguish between good and bad propaganda (except in the sense that "good" propaganda works and "bad" doesn't). We eliminate the need to focus on causes and

actions and the precarious issue of which ones are in whose enlightened self-interest. (Postman, 1979, pp. 129–130)

The seven major propaganda techniques are outlined below.

1. *Name calling*. Writers or speakers use disagreeable words to arouse anxiety, hate, and disapproval. ("If we cut local taxes, our children will fail in school and police and fire protection will fall to dangerous levels. Do we want disasters to occur in our community?") Very often little or no evidence is given to support the point they are making.

2. *Glittering generalities*. Writers use pleasant, agreeable words to arouse good feelings, approval, and respect. ("The food is succulent, the atmosphere is dreamy, and the service is friendly.") The statements are often sweeping and meaningless. This technique is sometimes called "glad names."

3. *Transfer*. Writers try to get readers to transfer the respect, admiration, or sympathy they have for one thing to the idea they are proposing. For example, an editorial writer might describe a day that a candidate for public office spent with his or her family on a picnic. The writer's goal is to have the readers transfer their admiration for clean family living to the candidate and therefore vote for the candidate. This technique is sometimes called "favorable association"; the idea or plea is associated with socially acceptable activities, principles, individuals, or objects.

4. *Testimonial*. Writers try to get readers to accept an idea by stating that well-known people agree with it. For example, a person may try to get people to accept her new theory and book on weight reduction by quoting famous people who accept the idea. The use of famous people who support certain products is well known to everybody and is sometimes called "endorsement."

5. *Plain folks*. Writers associate their ideas with people "just like you and me" so that we will accept them. That candidate for office is associated with the good old plain folks he joined at the picnic. He's just like us!

6. *Card stacking*. Writers present only one side of the issue or selectively quote others. This technique is very evident in articles we read on nuclear energy, abortion, gun control, the draft, and other highly emotional issues. Statistics are often misused or incorrectly interpreted, but many readers are impressed by them.

7. *Bandwagon*. Writers try to get their readers to accept an idea because everybody else is enthusiastic about it. Writers draw on people's desire to do what the great majority is doing. Proponents of certain educational approaches could influence teachers by citing the "hundreds of school systems using the XYZ method." They are led to believe that they are out of step if they are not using the method.

Smith (1963) suggests that teachers present students with five questions to help them analyze propaganda.

1. Who is the propagandist?
2. Whom is the propagandist serving?
3. What is the aim of the propagandist in writing on this subject?
4. To what human interests, desires, emotions does the propagandist appeal?
5. What techniques does the propagandist use?

When teachers guide students in detecting propaganda techniques, they should keep the following ideas in mind. First, the categories are not mutually exclusive. Several of the techniques may be present in the same selection or portion of a selection. Second, there may be propaganda devices that do not fit neatly into any of the seven categories. Students should be encouraged to create their own labels for these devices. Third, communicators who use these devices are not necessarily evil or dishonest. As Steinfatt (1979) queries: Would Lyndon Johnson have been "guilty" of the bandwagon technique if he had said he received a mandate from the people by virtue of winning a strong majority of the vote in the 1964 presidential election? Would Chavez have been "guilty" of employing the plain folk device if he referred to his background as a migrant worker in his efforts to win farm laborers to his cause? The propaganda devices, then, can be applied to both discourse that readers consider to be false and discourse they consider to be true.

It is relatively simple for students to analyze propaganda techniques in advertisements. However, many textbook authors do not use propaganda techniques when writing their textbooks. Teachers are more apt to find the opportunity to help students apply their knowledge of propaganda techniques when supplementary sources such as newspapers and magazines are used in the classroom.

## Communication Manipulation

An alternative approach to analyzing propaganda is offered by Rank (1976). He encourages students to recognize that writers and speakers manipulate communication to (1) intensify their own "good," (2) intensify others' "bad," (3) downplay others' "good," and (4) downplay their own "bad." Rank believes that everybody naturally engages in intensifying and downplaying communications and that applying the four-part schema to communications does not necessarily mean that one is making moral or ethical judgments about the communication. Applying the schema helps students recognize their own efforts at language manipulation as well as those of others.

Writers can *intensify* their own goodness or the badness of others by using the communication techniques of repetition, association, and composition. Obviously if the reader or listener is going to remember the message of the communicator, it will have to be repeated. This principle is well known to advertisers: "It's the real thing." "Plop, plop, fizz, fizz." "You asked for it, you got it." We hear these messages repeated so often that some of us begin to think that the products *must* be good.

Writers can also intensify by association, as we discussed above in the section on propaganda techniques. Finally, they can intensify by their choice of words such as certain adverbs and adjectives. For example, the candidate for office can be described as *extremely well* qualified or as a *super* person. Words connoting goodness can be used to describe him. He is a *family man* and a *regular churchgoer.*

Writers can *downplay* their own badness and the goodness of others by using the communication techniques of omission, diversion, and confusion. If there is negative information about them or the ideas they are promoting, they can simply omit it; or if there is positive information about one's opponent or an opposing idea, that too can be omitted. Downplaying can also be achieved by diverting the attention of the reader or listener, by introducing irrelevant side issues, or introducing humor into the message. Perhaps the most common technique used in downplaying is to confuse the reader or listener by introducing "*faulty logic, shifting definitions, equivocation, circumlocution, multiple diversions, contradictions, inconsistencies, jargon,* or anything which obscures clarity or understanding" (Rank, 1976 p. 13).

Example 1 gives some specific illustrations of Rank's four-part schema in communication manipulation. In a typical lesson students could review these simple examples. Then they might analyze more complex material, like that in Example 2, which is a portion of a lesson designed to help secondary and middle school students with the application of the seven traditional propaganda techniques and Rank's schemata for analyzing propaganda. Ronald Reagan's and Jimmy Carter's 1980 presidential nomination speeches were used in this lesson. For each quotation extracted from the speeches, students were asked to categorize it according to Rank's classification scheme and, if applicable, to one or two of the seven propaganda techniques.

## Example 1   Communication Manipulation

When we write or speak, very often we manipulate the way we communicate our message.

1. We may *intensify* our own "good."

> We won the hockey game yesterday. I was goalie. The other team didn't score any goals.

2. We may *intensify* others' "bad."

> We lost the hockey game yesterday, by one goal. I was goalie. If that kid on the other team had not screened my vision on the last goal, we would not have lost.

3. We may *downplay* others' "good."

> We lost the hockey game yesterday. We should have won; they were just lucky.

4. We may *downplay* our own "bad."

> We lost the hockey game yesterday, but it wasn't an important game. Our record is six wins and two losses.

## Example 2   A Lesson in Communication Manipulation

**Reagan: I know we have had a quarrel or two in our party, but only as to the method of attaining a goal. There was no argument about the goal.**

*Downplay own bad: Diverts attention away from squabbles within the party.*

**Reagan: I will not stand by and watch this great country destroy itself under mediocre leadership that drifts from one crisis to the next, eroding our national will and purpose.**

*Intensify others' bad: Describes Democratic leadership as "mediocre" and responsible for destruction and erosion of country (name calling).*

**Reagan: But back in 1976, Mr. Carter said, "Trust me." And a lot of people did. Now, many of those people are out of work. Many have seen their savings eaten away by inflation. Many others on fixed incomes, especially the elderly, have watched helplessly as the cruel tax of inflation wasted away their purchasing power.**

*Intensify others' bad:  Describes Carter's inability to control inflation (card stacking).*

**Reagan:  Those who preside over the worst energy shortage in our history tell us to use less, so that we will run out of oil, gasoline and natural gas a little more slowly. Conservation is desirable, of course, for we must not waste energy. But conservation is not the sole answer to our energy needs.**

*Downplay others' good: Downplays Carter's plea for energy conservation by saying it is "not the sole answer to our energy needs." Omits any other conservation proposals made by Carter (card stacking).*

**Reagan:  It is impossible to capture in words the splendor of this vast continent which God has granted as our portion of his creation. There are no words to express the extraordinary strength and character of this breed of people we call Americans. Everywhere we have met thousands of Democrats, Independents and Republicans from all economic conditions and of life, bound together in that community of shared values of family, work, neighborhood, peace and freedom.**

*Intensify own good:  Associates his candidacy with the "strength and character" of American people; he is "good" because he has met so many thousands of people (bandwagon, plain folks, glittering generalities).*

**Carter:  We're Democrats. And we've had our differences, but we share a bright vision of America's future—a vision of a good life for all our people—a vision of a secure nation, a just society, a peaceful world, a strong America—confident and proud and united.**

*Downplay own bad:  Acknowledges that the Democratic party has had its differences, but all Democrats "share a bright vision" (glittering generalities).*

**Carter:  And we have a memory of Franklin Roosevelt forty years ago when he said that there are times in our history when concerns over our personal lives are overshadowed by our concern for "what will happen to the country we have known." This is such a time—and I can tell you that the choice to be made this year can transform our own personal lives and the life of our country as well.**

*Intensify own good: Associates his candidacy with the name of a revered president (transfer, testimonial).*

**Carter:  And I have learned that the presidency is a place of compassion. My own heart is burdened for the troubled Americans. The poor, the jobless and the afflicted—they have become part of me. My thoughts and my prayers for our hostages in Iran are as though they were my own sons and daughters.**

*Intensify own good:  Infers that he is "good" because of his concern for "The poor, the jobless and the afflicted" (plain folks).*

**Carter:  In their fantasy America, inner city people, and farm workers and laborers like women and children, are to be seen but not heard. The problems of working women are simply ignored. The elderly do not need Medicare. The young do not need more help in getting a better education. Workers do not require the guarantee of a healthy and a safe place to work.**

*Intensify others' bad: Uses phrase "fantasy America" in the pejorative sense to emphasize the "bad" world we would have should his opponent be elected (glittering generalities, card stacking).*

**Carter: Along with this gigantic tax cut, the new Republican leaders promise to protect retirement and health programs and to make massive increases in defense spending, and they claim they can balance the budget. If they are serious about these promises—and they say they are—then a close analysis shows that the entire rest of the government would have to be abolished—everything from education to farm programs to the GI Bill to the night watchman at the Lincoln Memorial. And the federal budget would still be in the red.**

*Downplay others' good: Downplays the attractive proposals of the Republicans by saying that if they were to be implemented, "the entire rest of the government would have to be abolished" (card stacking).*

## Fact Versus Opinion Continuum

Teachers can also improve the critical ability of their students by providing them with direct instruction on the difference between statements of fact and statements of opinion. Good readers actively seek both the facts and the opinions of writers. For example, they want the *facts* about the day's happenings, but they also want someone's *opinions* with respect to these facts. Readers wanted the facts regarding the hostages in Iran, and they also wanted opinions regarding their psychological well-being and alternative approaches to freeing them. Americans continue to be fascinated with opinionated articles written on possible conspiracies connected with the assassination of President Kennedy.

When introducing fact/opinion lessons to students, teachers should indicate that it is not always possible to categorize statements neatly into a fact category or an opinion category. As Pearson and Johnson (1978) suggest, a continuum is more appropriate whereby a statement is either *more of a fact* or *more of an opinion*.

Turner (1980) offers criteria that students can use when trying to place statements on the fact/opinion continuum. Some are listed below.

- The statement comes from a believable authority. ("Have you read Farmer Jones's recent article on how to grow tomatoes?" versus "Have you read Farmer Jones's recent article on how to extract a tooth?")

- The statement is substantiated by other evidence or other authorities. ("There is evidence that smoking causes lung cancer," versus "There is evidence that laetrile can help to cure cancer.")

- The statement is reconcilable with what we know from personal experience. ("I read that rewarding children for their good behavior gives you well-behaved children. That's just what happens in our family"; versus "I read that allowing children to make choices at an early age builds responsibility. That doesn't work in our family.")

- The statement seems logical and reasonable. ("Keeping a checking account helps to balance your household budget," versus "If you use all the grocery coupons you find in the paper, you'll save lots of money.")

- The statement is generally accepted to be true or accepted by those we trust. ("The sun is about 93 million miles from earth," versus "UFOs are commonplace.")

- The statement is open to few or no exceptions. ("Eating a balanced diet will help to keep you healthy," versus "Participating in hockey builds good character.")

- The statement has been repeated often with little or no contradiction to this point. ("In the long run you'll save money if you insulate your home," versus "Nuclear energy is the answer to our energy crisis.")

- The statement can be checked. ("The Kansas City Royals defeated the New York Yankees in the first two games of the 1980 eastern division baseball play-offs," versus "George Brett is a fair third baseman.")

## Questions to Guide Critical Reading

Any time teachers give students reading assignments that seem to lend themselves particularly well to critical analysis, they can ask them to keep some of the following questions in mind as they read.

1. Is the author qualified to write on this topic?
2. What are the author's motives in writing on this topic?
3. Does the author use extravagent expressions (*only, never, absolutely, always, unconditionally, every, completely, positively,* and so on) to support his or her point of view?
4. Am I interpreting the author's ideas objectively? Do I fully understand his or her message before criticizing it?
5. Does the author give enough examples or studies to prove the assertion or theory?
6. Does the author present views contrary to the one he or she is espousing?
7. When the author uses quotations, does the author reflect the point of view of the person being quoted or has that person been quoted out of context?
8. If the author uses research studies to prove a point, are they up to date?
9. What is the policy or point of view of the publishing company, newspaper, or magazine for whom the author is writing?
10. Does the author use emotionally charged words instead of real evidence to support his or her theory?
11. Is the evidence used by the author relevant to the theory?

Students respond best to these questions and the general content of the reading selection when they are given the opportunity to engage in small-group discussions. Critical reading requires the kind of divergent thinking that group discussions foster, such as sharing ideas, comparing evaluations, and convincing others.

# Relating the Persuasive Pattern to Main Ideas

Students can be shown how main ideas relate to the persuasive organizational pattern. Displaying a chart like the one in Fig. 5.1 will help students perceive the relationship. Then teachers can guide students through an analysis of a selection, as is done with a business-related article in Example 3.

### Example 3    Persuasion and Main Ideas

In this article the writer voices an opinion or theory that he wants to convey; thus he chose to use the persuasive pattern to convey his message. The important main ideas and details in the article are listed below. Notice how they are associated with the different components of the persuasive pattern.

| Pattern Component | Main Ideas and Details |
|---|---|
| Assertion | The corporation is under attack from the government, stockholders, and economists. |
| Support of assertion | (1) The government is establishing more and more laws and regulations. (2) Congress is anti-business. (3) Galbraith and Goodwin call for greater government control of business. (4) Harrington believes businessmen are a threat to free enterprise. (5) Heilbroner predicts greater economic planning on the part of government. |
| Expected outcomes | If you are a businessperson, you should improve communication with both the public and the government in order to improve your image and to soften the attack. (Santeusanio, 1981, pp. 91–92) |

## Figure 5.1  Relationship of Main Ideas to Persuasive Pattern

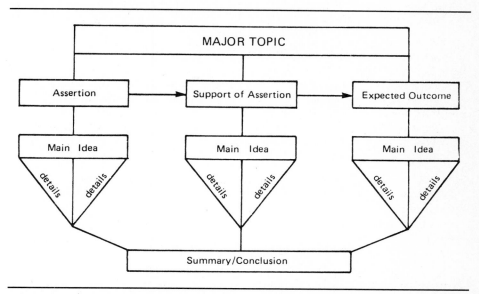

From Richard P. Santeusanio, *Developing Reading Skills for Business and Industry*, p. 89. Reprinted with permission. Copyright © 1981 CBI Publishing Company, Inc., 51 Sleeper St., Boston, Mass. 02210.

# Critical Reading and the Data Pattern

While it has been suggested that critical reading is best taught in conjunction with material written in the persuasive pattern, teachers should not ignore it when assigning material written in the data pattern. The following critical analysis by Neil Postman (1979) of an informational or data passage is quoted extensively here because it illustrates so well the importance of this point.

> The propaganda was intended to give us some background information on George Jackson, who was for a time a charismatic leader in the movement for black liberation. We are informed that Jackson was a choirboy, that his father was a post office employee, and that Jackson subscribed to conventional values when he was young. We are also told that the circumstances of Jackson's first serious crime were these: One night a friend whom Jackson had invited for a ride

in his car ordered him to stop at a gas station. The friend went inside and stole seventy dollars; then he told Jackson to drive away. Although Jackson was convicted for robbery, we are led to believe that he was entirely innocent. The following paragraph telling of Jackson's early life was included in the piece as part of our background information:

When Jackson was 15, still too young to drive legally, he had a slight accident in his father's car, knocking a few bricks out of the outside wall of a small grocery store near his home. His father paid the damages, the store owner refrained from pressing charges, but he was still sent to reform school for driving without a license. Three years later, shortly after his release from reform school, he made a down payment on a motorbike, which turned out to have been stolen. His mother had the receipt and produced it for the police, but Jackson was sent back to reform school, this time for theft.

I believe that this paragraph is one of the great propagandistic passages of all time, and is deserving of being included in the *Joseph Goebbels Casebook of Famous Boondoggles*. Let us do a small explication of it:

When Jackson was 15, still too young to drive legally. . . .

Well, now, what does this imply? That Jackson was a competent driver, but that the laws governing these matters are unreasonable? Why not, "still too young to drive"? Who or what is in need of correction here, Jackson or the Motor Vehicle Bureau?

. . . he had a slight accident in his father's car, knocking a few bricks out of the outside wall of a small grocery store near his home. . . .

The diminutives are almost oppressive: a *slight* accident, a *few* bricks, a *small* grocery store. One almost expects to read that someone's *trivial* leg was *barely* fractured. And what is a slight accident, anyway? Dislodging even a few bricks from an *outside* wall (It wasn't, for God's sake, an *inside* wall!) doesn't sound awfully slight to me. And why are we told it was "near his home"? Are we being led to believe that he had only driven around the block?

Best of all is the phrase "in his father's car." Does this imply that George really had nothing to do with the accident, that it happened *to* him while he was innocently sitting in his father's car? Why not, "He had a slight accident when he stole his father's car"? Or did George's father approve of his taking the car?

His father paid the damages. The store owner refrained from pressing charges, but he was still sent to reform school for driving without a license.

The "still" is a wonderful piece of propaganda here. It leads us to believe that everything had been settled to everyone's satisfaction, but that the police and the courts were simply being vindictive. After all, it was a *small* crime, and George *was* a choirboy. Why the big deal?

Three years later, shortly after his release from reform school, he made a down payment on a motorbike, which turned out to have been stolen.

First of all, I'd like to know how "shortly" after his release. It sounds as if George was in reform school for almost three years. Is this true? And why is the information being kept from me?

Second, the word "down payment" is simply marvelous. It conjures an image of a responsible businessman engaged in a wholly legitimate transaction. But George obviously didn't buy the motorbike at Macy's. He must have bought it from someone on the streets who was giving him a "real bargain." But, the "turned out to be stolen" suggests that choirboy George never suspected, not even for a moment, that anyone could traffic in stolen property. Where did George grow up, in Beverly Hills?

His mother had the receipt and produced it for the police, but Jackson was sent back to reform school, this time for theft.

The implication here is that the evidence George's mother produced should have been enough for any reasonable policeman. But apparently it wasn't. What was the evidence against George? Was he convicted of theft without a trial? What did the police have to say at the trial? We are told nothing, left with the impression that George was possibly framed and certainly the victim of a system that was out to get him.

Let me stress, in case you have gotten the wrong impression, that I do not know much about the late George Jackson, and some of what I do know evokes my admiration. What I am talking about is a method of propagandizing which attempts to conceal itself as information. The response that is asked for here is, "Believe this. You are being given all the information you need to know." But I can sooner believe that a soldier would go to war for Mom's apple pie than that a friend of George invited him for a ride, "ordered" him to stop at a gas station, held up the place, and told him to drive away, while all the time George thought his friend was only going to the bathroom. I would guess that you couldn't get away with that kind of stuff in Indianapolis. . . . In New York, it's easy.[2]

Postman has done a splendid job of illustrating the importance of critically analyzing everything we read. A passage that appears at first glance to be just

---

2. Neil Postman, "Propaganda." Reprinted from *Et cetera*, Vol. 36, No. 2, pp. 131–133, by permission of the International Society for General Semantics.

"information" related to the life on an individual turns out to be a subtle piece of propaganda. This is the most dangerous type of propaganda because we do not realize how our thinking has been colored or swayed.

# Generic Approaches to Applying the Persuasive Pattern to Content Areas

The generic approaches—direct teaching, adjunct questions, and reading/study guides—to teaching the persuasive pattern in a variety of content areas are exemplified in Models 5.1 through 5.9. The rationale for using these approaches is discussed in Chapter 3. As you review the models, note that they contain inserts that highlight their uniqueness and virtues. These inserts would not appear in material presented to students.

Model 5.1, a direct teaching model, helps students differentiate fact from opinion in a social studies lesson. The teacher carefully discusses definitions and examples and then leads students through an application of the lesson to a newspaper article.

Critical analysis of literature is stressed in Model 5.2 and 5.3, which use adjunct questions. Students are encouraged to respond critically to Swift's famous satirical essay *A Modest Proposal* in Model 5.2. They are encouraged to do the same in Model 5.3 as they read Cormier's modern novel *The Chocolate War*. In Model 5.2 students are asked to find examples of propaganda devices that Swift uses in his essay. In Model 5.3 students are given the opportunity to use propaganda devices themselves in brief creative-writing exercises.

Model 5.4 through 5.6 illustrate how reading/study guides can help students analyze written discourse organized in the persuasive pattern. In Model 5.4 students are asked to rate how well the writer supports her thesis or assertion. In Model 5.5 students are given the opportunity to analyze critically conclusions and arguments that are based on statements taken from a news story.

In Model 5.6 students analyze statements that reveal the attitudes of an artist. After they study the statements, students inspect some statements written by the teacher. Students decide whether the artist would have agreed with the statements. If students believe the artist would have agreed, they must cite quotations from the artist that supports their decision. Finally, they are given the opportunity to express their own opinions on the statements.

Students also get an opportunity to express their own opinions in Model 5.7, which stresses critical reading in science. Differentiating fact from opinion is stressed again in Model 5.8, this time in science. Finally, in Model 5.9 students are asked to analyze critically arguments given in support of and against gun control.

# Model 5.1  Direct Teaching

Pattern: Persuasive
Content: Social Studies

*[Terms defined and examples given.]*

**Teacher:  In today's lesson we will focus on differentiating between facts and opinion. A fact is a statement that is true. It is something that can be proven. What is a fact?**

*Students: Information that is true.*

*[Terms defined and examples given.]*

**Teacher:  An opinion is what a person feels or thinks about something. But it has not been proven. Listen to this statement: "In five years the United States will be able to produce enough oil to supply all its citizens. We will not have to depend on any foreign imports." This is an opinion. It's what the author believes. It has not been proven to be true. Can any of you make a statement that could be categorized as an opinion.**

*[Students provide their own examples.]*

*Students: (Various responses.)*

**Teacher:  Good. Now give me an example of a fact.**

*Students: (Various responses.)*

**Teacher:  Fine. On the board are two words that signal to us that information is an opinion. They are *believe* and *seem*. Can you think of any other words?**

*[Key words highlighted.]*

*Students: (Various responses; list should include* feel, think, perhaps, maybe, it appears, probably.)

**Teacher:  Yes, all these words indicate that the writer or speaker is offering an opinion. Who can give me some examples of opinions using some of these words?**

*Students: (Various responses.)*

**Teacher:  Sometimes writers will use certain emotional words when expressing their opinions. Here are two words on the board: *best* and *most*. We might say, for example, "This is the best ice cream I've ever had." Or we might say, "The Cabot Theater shows the most exciting movies." Think of some other emotional words and use them in a sentence. I'll make a list of these words on the board.**

(continued)

# Model 5.1 (concluded)

*Students: (Various responses; list should include words like* favorite, worst, terrible, wonderful, strongest, weakest, poorest, valuable, nicest.*)*

**[Definitions reviewed.]**

**Teacher: Fine. When writers use these words they are indicating to us that they are making a judgment or offering an opinion. Now, what is an opinion?**

*Students: It's what the writer believes.*

**Teacher: Yes, and what's a fact?**

*Students: It's information that is true.*

**[Lesson applied to newspaper article.]**

**Teacher: Writers usually state opinions in what we call persuasive writing. Persuasive writing is used when writers want to convince us that something is true, such as in advertising and political speeches. Let's look at this article entitled "Arms Race or Human Race? A Year of Decision." Read the first two paragraphs. What is the author's opinion?**

*Students: The worldwide arms race is out of control.*

**Teacher: Good! What are some emotionally charged statements the author uses in the first two paragraphs to try to get us to accept his opinion?**

*Students: (Various responses; they should include phrases like* cancerous spread, before it is too late, threatened with disaster, disaster of nuclear war.*)*

**Teacher: Are any facts quoted in the article?**

*Students: (Responses might include statements like "Worldwide weapon expenditures are estimated at about $350 billion"; "The bomb in Hiroshima killed 140,000 people.")*

**Teacher: Do you think these facts help the writer to convince his reader?**

*Students: (Accept variety of responses.)*

**Teacher: Find another opinion in the next-to-last paragraph.**

*Students: "It is time to stop this insanity."*

**Teacher: When authors use persuasive writing, they often want to move the reader to some action. What action would this writer like his readers to take?**

*Students: Work for disarmament.*

# Model 5.2  Adjunct Questions
**Pattern: Persuasive**
**Content: Literature**

*Directions:* Read and be prepared to answer the questions below. They are designed to help you to critically analyze Jonathan Swift's *A Modest Proposal.*

*[Students support opinion.]*

1. Do you think Swift has made a good proposal? Why or why not?

*[Students consciously look at the other side of the argument.]*

2. Assume you disagree with Swift's proposal that beggar children should be sold as meat. Given this assumption, how would you answer Swift's final two challenges:

    (a) How can Ireland provide food and clothing for a "hundred thousand useless mouths"?

    (b) Shouldn't politicians first ask the beggars now living whether or not they would have preferred to have been eaten as a one-year-old child rather than to have lived fifty or sixty years of unrelieved misery?

*[Students asked to analyze data objectively.]*

3. Assess Swift's arguments from a strictly logical point of view. Given the statistics as he presents them, do his conclusions make good logical sense? Can you find any minor internal logical inconsistencies? (Example: Though the basic proposal is to sell children for meat, one of the supposed advantages is to prevent "that horrid practice of women murdering their bastard children.")

4. Do you think these "inconsistencies" were slipups on Swift's part or are they deliberately introduced as ironic humor? (Irony is defined as "a pretense of ignorance or stupidity assumed in order to make another's false conceptions conspicuous" or "the use of words to express something other than and especially the opposite of the literal meaning.")

*[Students determine writer's purpose.]*

5. What was Swift's real purpose in writing this *Modest Proposal?*

*[Students judge effectiveness of the propaganda itself.]*

(continued)

---

# Model 5.2 (concluded)

6. Do you think that Swift's totally unemotional presentation of the miseries of the poor is more or less effective than a more straightforward or more emotional appeal on their behalf might have been? Give reasons for your answers.

*[Students use internal criteria.]*

7. A practiced critical reader can judge any given work in the light of many different sets of standards or criteria. Assess Swift's *Modest Proposal* in terms of practicability. Identify the passages in which Swift makes practical suggestions about remedying the plight of the poor and starving of Ireland. (Remember, this would not include the ostensible suggestion that the children be sold for food.) Once you have identified the cleverly disguised practical suggestions of Swift, give your own reasons for supporting or not supporting Swift's ideas and rate the worthiness of Swift's "practical" suggestions.

8. Can you find evidence in the essay that Swift's own sensible, practical suggestions turn out not to be practical? What reasons does Swift give?

9. Swift uses many rhetorical devices that we are familiar with from the advertising of our day. Find examples of the following devices:

*[Propaganda techniques applied to the selection.]*

   (a) Extravagance of expression.
   (b) Faulty cause-to-effect reasoning.
   (c) Testimonial.
   (d) Card stacking. (Authors only present what is favorable to their purpose. Often to avoid the appearance of card stacking, authors pretend to consider points that seem to contradict their central points, but if you continue reading, you'll find that they usually manage to turn the argument around to their own advantage and still leave you with the impression that they have considered both sides of the question.)

---

This model was prepared by Christopher Harding.

# Model 5.3  Adjunct Questions
## Pattern: Persuasive
## Content: Literature

### THE CHOCOLATE WAR

**"To Sell or Not to Sell?"**

▶ You have decided to support Jerry in his decision not to sell chocolates. You need to muster as much support as possible to help Jerry and his cause. One way is to launch a poster campaign. Each statement below is an idea that should be emphasized in the poster. Next to each idea, create a catchy slogan or saying that will convince other students *not to sell* chocolates.

1. Refusing to sell chocolates is an example of individualism!

2. The cost of the chocolates is too much, and the number of boxes is too many.

3. There are more important things in life than selling chocolates!

4. If Brother Leon wants the chocolates sold, let Brother Leon sell them!

▶ You disagree with Jerry and have joined The Vigils' poster campaign. Create a slogan or saying that reflects the stated idea and will convince the other students to *sell* chocolates.

1. Selling chocolates reflects true Trinity spirit!

2. The Vigils will make it "very difficult" for anyone who refuses to sell chocolates.

3. Brother Leon supports those who support him and his chocolate sale.

4. Everyone needs a cause; make selling chocolates your cause.

---

From Audrey A. Friedman, *Novel Ideas: The Chocolate War* (Littleton, Mass.: Sundance-Publishers & Distributors of Educational Materials, 1980). Reprinted by permission.

# Model 5.4  Reading/Study Guide
**Pattern: Persuasive**
**Content: Mathematics**

In the article you are about to read, the author takes a stand on the place of calculators in the classroom. After you have determined her position, critically examine the *supporting* arguments she uses and consider the *expected outcomes* that could take place if her position is generally accepted. Use the guide below to assist you as you read the article.

> *[Guide simulates persuasive organizational pattern.]*

1. Check the author's major *assertion*.

    (a) _____ Calculators have no place in the classroom.

    (b) _____ Calculators will have no effect on methods of teaching mathematics.

    (c) _____ Calculators in the classroom can enhance student learning.

2. Check the statements below that the author used to *support* her assertion. For those you checked, decide if the argument she used was a strong or weak argument. In the blank preceding those statements, write S if the argument is strong and W if the argument is weak.

    (a) _____ Students still have to master the basic algorithms used to run the calculator and thus have to learn basic procedures.

    (b) _____ Calculators hinder abstract learning.

    (c) _____ When students learn to perform rapid operations on the calculator, they learn patterns and rules quickly.

    (d) _____ Student motivation is increased when calculators are used in the classroom.

    (e) _____ Students quickly tire of calculators.

    (f) _____ Slide rules actually are more valuable because they force students to use more common sense.

    (g) _____ Use of calculators aids the electronics industry to invent new technology for the classroom.

    (h) _____ Calculators are conveniently used in conjunction with individualized learning packages.

    (i) _____ Inexpensive calculators can be purchased by nearly anyone and thus are readily available for use.

    (j) _____ Use of the calculator in difficult classes would improve learning because of the increased motivation factor.

3. Which of the two "scenarios" described below can we expect if the author's theory is generally accepted?

  (a) _____ School systems will save money by keeping electronics out of the classroom.

  (b) _____ The mathematics curricula will change, reflecting the widespread use of calculators in the classroom.

  *[Teachers have the opportunity here to ask students to use both internal and external criteria.]*

4. Do you think calculators should be used in the classroom? Support your answer.

  *[Students offer their own opinions.]*

---

# Model 5.5  Reading/Study Guide
## Pattern: Persuasive
## Content: Business

---

## Part I: Evaluation of Conclusions

*Directions:* Each exercise below consists of a short paragraph taken from a news story we have read. Following each paragraph you will find some statements. Judge whether or not each of the proposed conclusions logically follows the idea(s) contained in the paragraph. If you think it does, write "yes" next to the statement; if you think it does not, write "no." Be prepared to defend your answers during our class discussion.

1. "Witco will go head-to-head against the big three of the detergent field—Procter & Gamble, Lever Bros., and Colgate-Palmolive—without the benefit of the millions of dollars these companies spend annually in consumer advertising."

  *[Students given opportunity to use logic.]*

  _____ (a)  Witco has a unique philosophy toward advertising, which is remarkably different from the advertising procedures used by the leading three detergent companies.

  _____ (b)  Active will give consumers a cleaner wash than the other leading detergents.

  _____ (c)  Active will offer keen competition to the leading detergent companies without spending nearly as much money on consumer advertising as these companies do.

# Model 5.5 (continued)

2. "Instead, Witco will rely on shelf position, bold, aggressive package design, word of mouth, and intensive public relations efforts through consumer spokespeople in the major areas where Active will be sold."

_____ (a)   Witco places large emphasis on consumer relations and gives the consumer more authority and say about its product.

_____ (b)   Witco will depend on the bad-name technique to discourage consumers from buying the competitors' products.

_____ (c)   Witco will try to win approval by the traditional testimonial advertising.

3. "The woman who buys Tide, Fab, or Cheer will switch around for the best cents-off deal; price plays an important role in this inflationary economy."

_____ (a)   People are concerned about inflation and will experiment with products to find out which products are the best values.

_____ (b)   The bandwagon technique, or buying what the great majority is buying, is important in advertising.

_____ (c)   Consumers are doing more intense thinking about the products they buy.

4. "The grocer will make 16 percent to 18 percent on Active as opposed to a mere $6\frac{1}{2}$ percent to $7\frac{1}{2}$ percent on a typical advertised brand."

_____ (a)   If you want to be assured of a top shelf position in a grocer's store, you should try not to advertise.

_____ (b)   A grocer can save between 8.5 percent and 11.5 percent on an unadvertised product as opposed to a typically advertised product.

_____ (c)   An important means of making a profit is through the propaganda technique of transfer.

## Part II: Evaluation of Arguments

_[Terminology reviewed.]_

_Directions:_ An argument is weak if it is not directly related to the question. An argument is strong if it is important and relevant to the question. Below are some questions. Each question is followed by several arguments. The problem is to decide whether it is a strong or a weak argument. Mark S if it is strong and mark W if it is weak. Be prepared to defend your answers.

_[Students given opportunity to evaluate arguments.]_

1. Should all companies try not to advertise?
   - _____ (a)   Yes; advertising costs add to the price of the product.
   - _____ (b)   No; many people enjoy watching ads on TV.
   - _____ (c)   Yes; if fewer companies advertised, maybe more people would concentrate on the content of the product.
2. Do you think that Active will make it on the market?
   - _____ (a)   Yes; it offers a refreshing philosophy that makes good sense and is unique to advertising.
   - _____ (b)   Yes; it has a nice name.
   - _____ (c)   No; I don't believe people will buy a product that is not drilled into their heads through advertising. People depend on advertising and believe in it.

---

## Model 5.6  Reading/Study Guide
**Pattern: Persuasive**
**Content: Art History**

---

*Directions:* Here are some statements from "I Am for an Art . . ." made by the artist Claes Oldenburg. The statements concern his attitudes toward art.

(a). "I am for art that is smoked, like a cigarette, smells, like a pair of shoes."

(b). "I am for art you can sit on. I am for art you can pick your nose with or stub your toes on."

(c). "I am for an artist who vanishes, turning up in a white cap painting signs or hallways."

(d). "I am for art that is political-erotical-mystical, that does something other than sit on its ass in a museum."

(e). "I am for art that helps old ladies across the street."

(f). "I am for Kool-art, 7-UP art, Pepsi-art, Sunshine-art, 39 cents-art, 15 cents-art, . . . Menthol-art, L&M-art, Exlax-art. . . ."

1. Consider the statements in the table. Do you think Claes Oldenburg would have agreed with them? In column A, put an A if you think he would agree or a D if you think he would disagree.

   **[Students justify choice.]**

2. In column B, write the letter of the quotation(s) above by the artist which supports your decision in column A.

# Model 5.6 (concluded)

*[Students make their own evaluation.]*

3. In column C, write whether you personally agree or disagree with the statement and briefly say why.

|  | A | B | C |
|---|---|---|---|
| 1. An artist is a special, elite individual who cannot and should not function in society like the average person. |  |  |  |
| 2. I go to as many museums as I possibly can to get aesthetic inspiration. |  |  |  |
| 3. Art is for the masses. |  |  |  |
| 4. A good piece of art should be protected, at all cost, from being damaged through human contact. |  |  |  |
| 5. I like to portray in my art the ideal aspects of human nature and avoid the commonplace. |  |  |  |
| 6. Everybody should be able to meaningfully relate their lives to art. |  |  |  |
| 7. For a piece of art to be valid, today's artist must be acutely aware of the many aspects of our twentieth-century life-styles and values. |  |  |  |

This model was prepared by Debra Cohen. Format of the guide is an adaptation of one appearing in Harold Herber's *Teaching Reading in the Content Areas* (Englewood Cliffs, N.J.: Prentice-Hall, 1978).

# Model 5.7  Reading/Study Guide
**Pattern: Persuasive**
**Content: Science**

## Section I

*Directions:* You are going to read an article about dung beetles. This guide is designed to help you read the article critically. Below are some statements related to the article. If you think the author would *want you to agree* with the statement, write "yes" next to the letter (a); if you think the author would *want you to disagree* with the statement, write "no" next to the letter (a). Then next to the letter (b) write "yes" if you personally agree with the statement and "no" if you personally disagree with the statement. Be prepared to defend your answers.

Read the article carefully. None of the statements below are direct quotations from the article. They are possible implications of the author's statements in the article.

*[Students focus on author's purpose; students also offer their own opinions.]*

1. The United States can benefit from dung beetles.

   (a) _____     (b) _____

2. Countries without dung beetles but with manure decomposers can benefit by the dung beetle because of its other attributes (i.e., insect regulation).

   (a) _____     (b) _____

3. The measures taken by the Australians in regulation of the contaminated beetles make any possibility of disease almost nonexistent and therefore safe.

   (a) _____     (b) _____

4. Eventually it appears that hoof-and-mouth and other serious diseases will reach Australia through someone's careless action.

   (a) _____     (b) _____

5. The dung beetle is valuable because it decomposes cow dung and can control diseases of both animals and humans by controlling insects.

   (a) _____     (b) _____

## Section II

In a short paragraph, state whether or not you can justify the relocation of animal species.

*[Reading and writing integrated.]*

# Model 5.8  Reading/Study Guide
**Pattern: Persuasive**
**Content: Science**

*Directions:* We have already discussed the differences between fact and opinion. This article on ecology includes several statements of both fact and opinion. Read the statements below before you read the article. Place an F in the blank if you think it is a fact and an O if you think it is an opinion. Place these letters on the left-hand side, the prereading column. After you read the article, do the same in the postreading column. See if you changed your mind. Also, check the statements you marked F during the prereading to see if any of these factual types of statements were inaccurate representations of the facts.

*[Guide combines readiness activity with critical reading.]*

| Prereading | | Postreading |
|---|---|---|
| _____ | 1. Ecology is the most important subject to study in life. | _____ |
| _____ | 2. The study of ecology teaches students about man and his interaction with nature. | _____ |
| _____ | 3. Every student should take a course in ecology in high school. | _____ |
| _____ | 4. Ecology is not valuable for a student because he or she cannot stop pollution. | _____ |
| _____ | 5. The sun is our best source of energy. | _____ |
| _____ | 6. Radiant energy comes from the sun. | _____ |
| _____ | 7. Organisms get their matter from the earth. | _____ |
| _____ | 8. Calcium compounds have the worst effect on man. | _____ |
| _____ | 9. Calcium and carbon each have to go through cycles at the same time. | _____ |
| _____ | 10. Water is beneficial to our bodies. | _____ |

This model was prepared by Betsy McGregor.

# Model 5.9  Reading/Study Guide
Pattern: Persuasion
Content: Sociology

*Directions:* Read the two articles from the *Boston Globe* on gun control; one is for gun control, while the other is against it. Then read the arguments below that are used to support each position. Try to keep your own position on this issue in the background as you evaluate each argument. If you believe the statement is a strong argument, place an S before the statement; if you believe it is a weak argument, place a W before the statement. Be prepared to defend your answers during our class discussion.

*[Students compare two points of view on the same topic.]*

1. Arguments used to support the position that there *should not be* gun control.

   _____ (a)   All major police organizations and chief of police in Massachusetts are opposed to the banning and confiscation of handguns.

   _____ (b)   The criminals will not be disarmed, and hence the law-abiding citizens will be in great danger.

   _____ (c)   Under the Second, Fourth, Fifth, Ninth, and Fourteenth Amendment to the Constitution, we have a right of private property (gun) and the protection of the owner's right to bear arms.

   _____ (d)   If handguns are banned, people will kill each other with different means.

2. Arguments used to support the position that there *should be* gun control.

   _____ (a)   A reverence for life and its preservation is the cornerstone of the concept to ban handguns in Massachusetts.

   _____ (b)   Handguns are the major cause of death in crimes of passion and arguments among friends and family members.

   _____ (c)   With the ban on handguns 55 to 120 lives are estimated to be saved and 445 to 765 injuries can be prevented yearly.

   _____ (d)   A onetime cost for banning handguns is balanced by a yearly $13 million cost benefit from savings in wages lost, taxes, criminal justice costs, hospital and welfare costs.

   _____ (e)   The U.S. Constitution on the issue of banning weapons has been upheld four times by the Supreme Court.

3. What is *your* position on gun control? Be prepared to defend it!

*[Students do their own persuasive writing.]*

# Madison Avenue, Part II

Mr. DePietro had assigned his students to write an ad by using some of the propaganda techniques he had taught them. Below are some samples of the ads his students wrote. (These ads were actually written by eighth grade students in Danvers, Massachusetts.)

Here we are at the Johnson's home seeing which kind of pickle they prefer. "Well Mrs. Johnson, do you prefer pickle A or pickle B?"

"I think pickle A has a refreshing flavor. It's so crunchy, and delicious. Pickle B has a dull taste, nothing like pickle A."

"Well Mrs. Johnson, you picked the Puckers Pickle. We guarantee our pickles to be the crunchiest, most flavorful pickle you have ever had. And since our pickle sells the most with people just like you and me, it must be the best. So, go on out and buy a jar of Puckers Pickles."

Laurie

"Dick I see your skin has cleared."

"Yes, now that I use Zit-Away I haven't had pimples for weeks, and since then I have become president of the Student Council, I made the football team, and I was given a full scholarship to Harvard University. Why don't you try it Jane?"

"Thanks, Dick I think I will."

USE ZIT-AWAY TODAY!

Miriam

Why risk the chance of becoming a ninety-pound weakling. Eat the power-packed, crunchy, munchy, chewy, gooey, muscle-building cereal Tutti-Frutti Frute Brute. It's superman's favorite breakfast cereal. Look what its done for Clark Kent. Imagine what it can do for you!

Jill

GET-AWAY-FROM-IT-ALL MOBILE—A Product of Clair Motors

Kids! Are you frustrated because you can't drive? Well now you can! Because Clair Motors has made this new product, a get-away-from-it-all mobile. Everyone's using it! And they all have found that the sofa, the push-button town to towner, the soda fountain, the popcorn maker, the extra bunk, and the doghouse for Fido come in handy. All you do is press the button that goes to the place you want to go and it will take you there! No steering wheel! So be with everyone else and get into the latest style, buy a Get-Away-From-It-All Mobile at your nearest Clair Motors car dealer.

NOTICE! It has a very important feature: The door is too small for grown-ups to fit into.

Clair

## Malus Vitamins

Do you feel dragged out emotionally and physically on those Monday mornings when your alarm abruptly awakens you from a peaceful slumber? Well, Dundy and Dundy has the solution to keep you alive every Monday morning. The product is called Malus Vitamins—guaranteed to make your co-workers admire you when you come in Monday morning cheerful and lively.

Everybody uses Malus Vitamins; even Ronald Reagan does. People always wonder how he looked so young and tireless during his campaign. Well, now you know the secret—he uses Malus Vitamins every morning, Wouldn't you like to work eight hours and still have enough energy to work another ten hours? Here is your chance to do so. Dundy and Dundy guarantees success the first morning you use Malus Vitamins. Look what it did for Reagan!

Amy

## Zip Soap

If you want lather and protection, buy Zip Soap. It will make you feel fresh and energetic. Bruce Jenner used Zip Soap and look what happened to him. He won the marathon in the 1976 Olympics.

Scott

# Summary

When authors use the persuasive pattern for communicating their ideas, their purpose in writing is to convince their readers of something. They have an assertion, opinion, theory, idea, or product they wish to "sell" to their readers. All communication, but particularly this type, should be critically analyzed. However, regardless of what the purpose of any writing may be, readers have the responsibility of first understanding what the authors' ideas are. They then can and should critically analyze the ideas. Readers should also realize that those who promote their ideas are not necessarily "bad." In fact, writers have a responsibility to present their ideas in the best possible light.

Adolescents and adults sometimes have difficulty reading critically because of their own biases, attitudes, and predispositions. The lack of emphasis on critical reading in both teacher education programs and in the middle and secondary curricula are other contributing factors to the problem. Teachers can, however, foster critical thinking in the classroom by exposing their students to the propaganda techniques, the use of communication manipulation, the fact/opinion continuum, and evaluative types of questions. Direct teaching, adjunct questions, and reading/study guides can also help to promote their critical-reading and -thinking skills.

# Bibliography

Artley, A. Sterl. "Critical Reading in the Content Areas." In *Critical Reading, An Introduction*, E. Elona Sochor, chairman. Urbana, Ill.: National Council of Teachers of English, 1959.

Barrett, Thomas C. "Taxonomy of Reading Comprehension." In *Reading 360 Monograph*. Lexington, Mass.: Ginn, 1972.

Davis, John E. "The Ability of Intermediate Grade Pupils to Distinguish Between Fact and Opinion." *Reading Teacher* 22(1969):419–422.

Eller, William, and Robert Dykstra. "Persuasion and Personality: Readers Predispositions as a Factor." In *Critical Reading, An Introduction*, E. Elona Sochor, chairman. Urbana, Ill.: National Council of Teachers of English, 1959.

Micklos, John J., Jr. "A Look at Reading Achievement in the United States." *Journal of Reading* 25(1982):760–762.

Pearson, David P., and Dale D. Johnson. *Teaching Reading Comprehension*. New York: Holt, Rinehart and Winston, 1978.

Postman, Neil. "Propaganda." *ETC* 36(1979):128–133.

Rank, Hugh. "Teaching About Public Persuasion: Rationale and Schema." In *Teaching About Doublespeak*, edited by Daniel Dieterich. Urbana, Ill.: National Council of Teachers of English, 1976.

Reynolds, Ralph E., Marshá A. Taylor, Margaret S. Steffensen, Larry L. Shirey, and Richard C. Anderson. *Cultural Schemata and Reading Comprehension*, Technical Report no. 201. Urbana: Center for the Study of Reading, University of Illinois, 1981.

Santeusanio, Richard P. *Developing Reading Skills for Business and Industry.* Boston: CBI, 1981.

Smith, Nila Banton. *Reading Instruction for Today's Children.* Englewood Cliffs, N.J.: Prentice-Hall, 1963.

Smith, Richard J., and Thomas C. Barrett. *Teaching Reading in the Middle School.* 2nd ed. Reading, Mass.: Addison-Wesley, 1979.

Steinfatt, Thomas M. "Evaluating Approaches to Propaganda Analysis." *ETC* 36(1979):157–180.

Turner, Thomas N. "Critical and Creative Reading." In *Teaching Reading,* edited by J. Estill Alexander. Boston: Little, Brown, 1980.

Wolf, Willavene, Bernice Cansneder, and Bruce M. Cansneder. *Critical Reading Ability of Elementary School Children.* Columbus: Ohio State University Research Foundation, 1967.

# Chapter 6

# Developing

# Self-Directed

# Study Techniques

## The Metamorphosis of Mrs. Hood, Part I

Peg, a reading specialist, was enjoying her free period, and as she sat in the high school teacher's lounge, she was reviewing some notes.

"What are you up to?" asked Bill, a science teacher.

"Oh, I'm just going over a presentation I have to make tonight in my grad course at State," replied Peg.

"What are you doing it on?"

"I was asked to talk about our program in reading in the content areas. May I try it out on you?"

"Fine with me."

"I think I'll begin with a brief statement of how the program is organized. I'm going to tell them how I rotate from teacher to teacher and work with them and their classes."

"Do you do the same thing in every class or do you first talk it over with each teacher, as you did when you visited my class?"

"Oh, we always have the conference first to see what the teacher wants to focus on. It's usually comprehension or study skills. Lately study skills seem to be a big concern. As a matter of fact, I'm going to give as a sort of case study the program I worked out with Judy Hood."

"You mean the stuff you did with her slow class?"

"Yes. You know what a good teacher Judy is; but she admits she has never had all that much patience with slower classes. She sort of expected the same performance from all her classes."

"Sometimes that's not such a bad idea."

"True, but I'm afraid this one class just wasn't delivering. I think half the class flunked first term. That's when Judy asked me for some help. She really wanted the kids to pass her tests, which she thought were easy."

"Were they?" interrupted Bill.

"They weren't all that rough," replied Peg. "But her students were overwhelmed by all the material they had to study. They just got frustrated when it came time to study for a test."

"I know the feeling. . . ."

"I do too. I'm not sure Judy does; you know how sharp she is."

## Introduction

While reading guides, directed lessons, and adjunct questions are all very valuable teaching tools, students should reach a point where they can begin to develop study skills so that they can independently learn information from textbooks and other sources. As Walter Pauk says: "Real learning takes place

"So what did you and Judy decide to do?"

"Well, I told her that the key would be for her students to have knowledge of the criterion task."

"Huh?"

"You know what I mean. If the kids know precisely what they will be tested on, they'll perform better. Then they tend to read and study with a purpose; they seek answers to questions that are likely to appear on a test."

"Who decides on what the questions will be?"

"The teacher can raise the questions, or the students can; and sometimes they do it together. That's how Judy and I finally decided to do it in her class. At first she wanted to present the questions, but then she saw a greater payoff when she and the class went through the process together."

"How so?"

"First, I took over the class and taught them how to preview a chapter. Then I taught them how to turn subheadings into questions. But we did it together. At this point Judy took over the class. Instead of raising just one question for the subheading, the class and Judy considered a few. Then they read the section to find the answers to the questions. After that they decided on the best question. Then they wrote the question on the left side of their notebook paper and the answer on the right side. So they ended up with a study guide for each chapter. Judy then used some of these questions on her exams and it made quite a difference."

"Sounds neat," said Bill.

"It worked out really well. I wish I could bring some of the students into class with me tonight to talk about it. But I think they would be too embarrassed. But I do have a little essay that one of the students wrote. She said I could make copies of it for the class if I didn't identify her as the writer."

"Are you going to do it?"

"Sure, why not?"

At the end of the chapter you will find the essay that Peg reproduced for the graduate school class.

only through self-teaching. The instructor may pour forth the choicest words of wisdom, and the student may hear them, and even write them in his notebook, but unless he takes these words, and rethinks them in his own words, visualizes them, crystallizes and assimilates them, internalizes them, the words from lectures or books will make no positive difference in his life, academic or otherwise" (Pauk, 1980, p. 303).

Students cannot continue indefinitely to lean on teachers for assistance. Moreover, most teachers have neither the time nor the inclination to develop study aides for every reading assignment they give. On the other hand, if teachers wish their students to become independent learners, they will have to invest some time in teaching study skills. This chapter is designed to assist teachers in their efforts to teach the important study skills.

# SQ3R

By far the best-known study method is the *SQ3R technique,* which was first introduced to college students in 1941 by Francis Robinson. It is still a popular topic in college reading programs and now is presented to thousands of students in the intermediate, middle, and secondary grades. SQ3R is designed to give students a system for studying that will increase their level of learning.

Below is an adaptation of Robinson's (1970) SQ3R method.

- S: *Survey.* Students first preview the chapter as discussed on pages 48–50. They should quickly review the chapter title, diagrams, charts, maps, illustrations, introductory paragraphs, boldfaced headings, the summary, and study questions. The purpose of this quick review is to give students an advance notice of what will appear in the chapter.

- Q: *Questions.* Headings are turned into questions; this technique should arouse the student's curiosity. For instance, a heading like "Transporting Oil" might be turned into the question "How is oil transported?"

- R1: *Read.* Keeping their questions in mind, the students read the section. They find the answers to their questions as well as other major ideas. Students usually write the answers to their questions. They can develop their own study guide by writing their questions on the left side of their notebook paper and the answers on the right side, as shown in Fig. 6.1.

- R2: *Recite.* After they have completed their study guides, students can cover the right-hand side of their papers and test their recall by orally reciting the answers to their questions. They can check their oral response with their written answers.

- R3: *Review.* The recite step can be reviewed some time later and certainly before an exam. As they review their questions and answers, students should see the relationships among their various questions and answers.

## SQ3R for Essays

The SQ3R approach was basically designed to be used with expository textbook material. Taylor (1973) has adapted the approach for use with essays and other materials that lack headings, pictures, and other features utilized in the survey step. The approach, with slight modifications, follows.

# Figure 6.1  SQ3R Study Guide

| Questions | Answers |
|---|---|
| What are the major forest types and how do they differ? | The two types are coniferous (evergreens spruce, and Douglas firs) and deciduous (beech, oak, and maple)  Differences |

| Coniferous | deciduous |
|---|---|
| • thick overhead | • leaves fall |
| • crowded needles intercept light and rainfall | • much light and rain-fall |
| • few shrubs and plants | • many plants |
| • forest warm | • forest windy |
| • large animals | • small animals, insects, birds |

1. *Question the title.* The titles often provide clues, especially when they are of a provocative nature, such as "Nibbling Away at the West" and "Dilemma of the Black Policeman." The title gives clues to the author's purpose for writing the article and his or her point of view. Students raise a question or questions they think will be answered in the selection.

2. *Skim the article.* Using the techniques discussed in the section "Reading Rate and Flexibility" (pp. 263–265), students skim the article. This step includes a rapid reading of the first few paragraphs, the first sentence of

some paragraphs, subheadings if any are present, and concluding paragraphs.

3. *Determine tentative answer(s) to the question(s).* As a result of the skimming, readers usually can state tentative answers to the question(s) raised in step 1. They also may have formulated some new questions.

4. *Read the entire article.* At this point the readers either confirm or alter their answers to the questions raised.

5. *Reread the selection (optional).* Some readers may wish to read the selection again for another reason. Perhaps they want to take notes on the article or critically respond to specific sections of the article.

## SQ3R for Mathematics

Some content areas have special organizational patterns that call for students to modify their usual approach to reading. Mathematics word problems present one such special pattern. An adaptation of SQ3R for mathematics problems has been offered by Burg and colleagues (1978). Their steps are as follows:

Survey:
Skim to get general idea of the problem.

Question:
What is the question or questions?
What facts are needed for solution?
What order of steps are necessary for solution?

Read to:
Clarify the question.
Identify the needed facts.
Determine steps for solution.

Review:
On what does the answer depend?

Reconstruct:
State the problem in your own words without using numbers.
State procedures for solution.
Estimate the answer. (Burg et al., 1978, p. 95)

## OK5R

Many authors have developed variations of SQ3R. One, developed by Walter Pauk (1974), is outlined below. As you read the steps in Pauk's *OK5R approach,* compare it to Robinson's SQ3R.

- O: *Overview.* The overview is essentially the same as Robinson's survey step.

- K: *Key ideas.* Students should be prepared to find main ideas, supporting material, and transitions. Main ideas should be separated from the supporting material.

- R1: *Read.* Students should read small sections of the text for main ideas. Key topics are written in their notebooks. They then repeat the procedure with the next small section in their text.

- R2: *Record.* Students can summarize main ideas and details in their notebooks.

- R3: *Recite.* Using the key topics as a stimulus, students now cover their notes and check their recall of the material.

- R4: *Review.* Students now review their notes for the entire chapter to get the whole picture and to counteract forgetting.

- R5: *Reflect.* At this point, ideas from the chapter are compared, contrasted, organized, reorganized, and considered in light of the students' existing knowledge.

## SQ3R Versus OK5R

You probably recognized many similarities and some differences between the SQ3R and OK5R approaches. Both suggest that students preview chapters in the survey and overview steps. Both suggest in their read step that the chapter be read entirely. Both suggest that students take notes on the reading: Robinson in his recite step and Pauk in his record step. Both suggest in their review step that students review their notes.

The major difference occurs with Robinson's question step and Pauk's key ideas step. Unlike Robinson, Pauk does not suggest turning headings into questions to be answered. Pauk encourages students to read for main ideas and then to summarize them in their own words. In his reflect step Pauk also encourages readers to respond to chapters at Barrett's higher levels of comprehension: inference, evaluation, and appreciation. Robinson, on the other hand, appears to encourage readers to respond mainly at the literal level.

## Research on SQ3R

In the last decade at least three reviews of research on the SQ3R technique have been completed (Johns and McNamara, 1980; Johnson, 1973; Spencer, 1978). Johnson's (1973) review of research led her to conclude that the research evidence does not support the widespread use of SQ3R as a total method for improving reading achievement, but the value of the component parts is generally substantiated. After Spencer (1978) reviewed the research, he stated that he concurred with Albert Harris's assertion that SQ3R "seems to be well grounded in the experimental psychology of learning, but has not been subjected to much experimentation" (Harris, 1971, p. 440).

In a more recent review Johns and McNamara (1980) noted that while SQ3R is a popular study method, its popularity stems not from carefully controlled research studies but from endorsements from reading educators like Burmeister (1978), Courtney (1965), and Spache (1963).

Allan Sack (1975) may have explained why there is a clear lack of research support for SQ3R when he noted its weaknesses.

1. It does not produce a clear-cut grasp of the *organization* of a chapter in its surveying instructions.
2. By emphasizing each sub-head and each sub-section of the chapter the SQ3R does not help the student to tie the organization of the chapter together.
3. The SQ3R requires the student to turn a heading into a question and then read for the answer. What happens when there are no headings?
4. The SQ3R method is somewhat slow because each sub-section is considered individually and action is taken on the basis of each sub-section.
5. The SQ3R is somewhat artificial in the sense that it asks the student to take a sub-heading, turn it into a question and read for the answer. Students are loath to do this sort of thing when not under the stern eye of their teacher. (Sack, 1975, p. 29)

Anderson and Armbruster (1980) have similar reservations about the SQ3R study method. They note that transforming headings into questions may be of limited value because the questions often do not represent what the teacher will use as test items and, as Sack noted, the topic headings often do not represent the main points about the chapter section. Also, by focusing on separate subheadings, students will not be well prepared for questions that ask for the integration of information from two or more sections of the chapter. Finally, they question students' ability to transform headings into good questions.

Despite the research reviews and the opinions of some reading educators, Martha Maxwell (1980) staunchly defends the SQ3R method.

The SQ3R method has often been criticized by skills experts because it has not been systematically researched as a total method, although there is research to support each of the separate steps. But the critics miss the point. For the fearful student, faced with a long, difficult text to read, the SQ3R method provides a technique for getting started. Moreover, it makes explicit the steps that a skilled learner automatically follows. So even if students grumble that it takes too long or that underlining passages in their textbooks is quicker and easier, they will find that, when all else fails, using SQ3R will help them gain a better understanding from their reading. I have found that many students modify the method but that when they are desperate—that is, when faced with an examination that will determine whether they pass or fail a course or when in a situation in which they must make a high grade—using the original SQ3R without modification pays off. (Maxwell, 1980, p. 306)

## SQ3R: To Teach or Not to Teach?

Given the lack of research evidence to support the effectiveness of SQ3R, should classroom content teachers even bother introducing the approach in their classrooms? They probably should if they intend to use the student-developed questions as test items on an examination. This is an especially effective approach for slower students. When these students know their own questions will appear on a test, their motivation and attention increase. One teacher who was introduced to SQ3R and used it this way said it changed her class atmosphere (and grades!) tremendously. Teachers may have to assist students in developing "good" questions, but this assistance can only help students with their comprehension of the text. Teachers also should point out to students those headings that reflect the essence of the textbook sections.

Should reading teachers teach SQ3R to students? They should, but first they should share the technique with the subject matter teachers and find out which ones think the technique will help students enrolled in their classes. The reading teachers could then share this information with their students by saying, "This method will be especially helpful to you in Mrs. Blake's class, Mrs. Tye's class, and Mr. Lillo's class; but it probably won't help you in Mr. Tiernan's class and Miss Russick's class." In the final analysis, the students themselves will decide whether or not the technique is helpful or parts of the technique are helpful.

One aspect of both the SQ3R and OK5R approaches that seems to be particularly helpful to students is self-questioning. Anderson (1978) cites at least four studies that demonstrate that when students *formulate* questions during study by either writing them down or verbalizing the questions to a friend, they score significantly higher on tests than students using other techniques.

SQ3R or OK5R (or both) can be presented as a study technique, but teachers should expose students to other study skills such as note taking, underlining, and outlining.

# Note Taking

*Note taking* from books, like SQ3R, can be an effective study strategy if the nature of the students' notes is compatible with the demands of teachers as reflected in their tests (Anderson and Armbruster, 1980). For example, if students take notes on main ideas, and the teacher tests for main ideas, then the technique works well. However, if the teacher tests for details rather than main ideas, the technique obviously does not work well.

Teachers, then, should encourage students to take notes in a manner that will be most likely to assist them in passing a test. Statements such as "Be sure your notes reflect cause/effect relationships," "Your notes should include specific sequence with dates," and so forth will give students the proper direction. Teachers would be wise to encourage students to paraphrase their notes, especially if they plan to administer essay types of exams.

# The Cornell Method

One technique for taking textbook notes that can be useful for recording details, main ideas, and organizational relationships is Pauk's (1974) *Cornell method*. (This approach can also be used for taking lecture notes.)

First students rule their papers with a 2½-inch margin on the left, leaving about a 6-inch area on the right for recording notes. Before students take notes, they should preview the whole chapter. Then after reading a full paragraph or a headed section, they begin to *record* their notes. As they record their notes, they should try to be selective, remembering to record what their teachers have deemed important (relationships, details, main ideas). Students should use their own words when recording ideas. According to Pauk, students should write full sentences, because that is the way they will have to write on their exams. (He is assuming the exam will be the essay type.)

After students have recorded their notes for the entire chapter, they should *reduce* their notes to concise topics in the 2½-inch cue column. They can then use this column to *recite*. The main column (6-inch column) is covered.Using the topics in the 2½-inch column as cues, the students try to recall the contents or their notes as fully as possible. At this point the students can *reflect* on their notes by adding their own thoughts on the topic. Finally, students can review their notes every so often before the exam. The format of the Cornell note-taking system appears in Fig. 6.2.

Teachers may want to introduce this approach as a group activity. Using their textbook as a source, they can focus on a few pages from it and, with participation from the class, decide on what to record and what terms to use in the reduce or cue column. This informatin can be placed on an overhead projector. After the students have been led through this procedure a few times, students will probably have more success using the procedure independently.

# Figure 6.2  Cornell Note-Taking Format

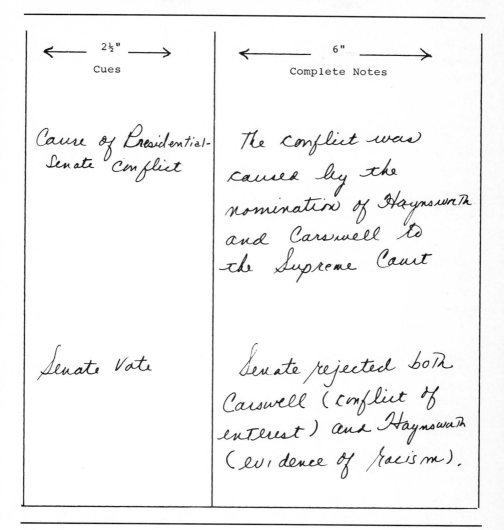

| ← 2½" → | ← 6" → |
| Cues | Complete Notes |
| Cause of Presidential-Senate Conflict | The conflict was caused by the nomination of Haynsworth and Carswell to the Supreme Court |
| Senate Vote | Senate rejected both Carswell (conflict of interest) and Haynsworth (evidence of racism). |

## Research on Note Taking

Very little research has been completed on the effectiveness of note taking; however, one purpose of a study completed by Kulhavy, Dyer, and Silver (1975) was to compare the student test performance of those who studied by using a note-taking technique with the test performance of those who underlined their texts and those who just read the text. After analyzing the test scores of 144 junior and senior high school students, the researchers concluded that the students who took notes learned more than those who underlined, but those who took notes needed more study time. The researchers also found that students who underlined learned more than those who merely read, which lead the researchers to conclude that "apparently, the very act of overtly attending to the material while reading is enough to increase later test performance" (Kulhavy, Dyer, and Silver, 1975, p. 365).

## Lecture Notes and Listening

Some middle and high school teachers require their students to take notes on their lectures as well as from textbooks. Students can be taught to use the same note-taking formats for lecture notes that they use for textbook notes. However, if students are to take satisfactory lecture notes, they must be able to listen well. Devine (1981) offers a number of suggestions that help students improve their ability to listen.

According to Devine, one of the keys to improving students' listening skills is to *prepare* them for a listening experience such as a lecture. Before presenting their lectures, teachers can summarize the major points of the lecture, clarify difficult vocabulary and concepts, provide some questions that students can keep in mind during the lecture, set up a purpose for listening to the lecture, and encourage students to relate the lecture topic to their own experiences. Teachers can help students to anticipate what will be included in the lecture by giving them a brief outline of it.

Students will be more active, interested listeners if their teachers improve the quality of their presentations. Teachers can, for example, augment their lectures with relevant visual aids such as pictures, graphs, tables, diagrams, and charts. These can be displayed on overheads or copied and handed out to students.

Teachers can also make their lectures more interesting by humanizing them. An effort can be made to relate the content of the lecture to the lives of the students by making comments like "You probably had something like this happen to you." The lecture becomes more immediate to students when their teachers interject personal references like *I* and *you*. Nothing heightens the attention of listeners better than a touch of humor.

Students should also feel free to react during and after the lecture. They may want to ask a question, have a word defined, have an idea clarified, or offer an opinion.

If teachers implement some of these suggestions, their lectures will improve, students will listen better, and, it is hoped, the quality of the students' lecture notes will be enhanced. Readers can find more suggestions about teaching listening skills and a review of research on the topic by referring to Devine's (1981) text.

# Underlining and Outlining

According to Anderson and Armbruster's (1980) review of the research, *underlining* is at least as effective as other study techniques. Its effectiveness may be due to the fact that when students underline, they tend to process the text more thoroughly than they would otherwise. In general, students learn more when they underline the texts themselves as opposed to reading texts that have been underlined or highlighted for them.

Most secondary teachers cannot consider this technique very seriously because their students do not own their textbooks. However, *outlining,* a more formal way of recording notes, may help circumvent this problem. When teaching outlining, teachers should reinforce the importance of previewing chapters. Previewing will give students an overview of the entire chapter, including its organizational pattern. It helps give students a sense of direction and a purpose for reading.

Once the preview is completed, students can read paragraphs or entire sections, trying to focus on main ideas. These main ideas should be paraphrased by students and identified with Roman numerals. If there are details deemed important, they can be identified with capital letters. If further important related information is required, it should be recorded and identified with numbers. The form might look like this.

I. Major topic and main idea
   A. Important detail
   B. Important detail
      1. Related detail
      2. Related detail

Some students develop their own forms; this is fine as long as the students understand the relationship indicated by their outline markings.

Outlining can help students summarize information authors present in the various organizational patterns. Possible forms are illustrated in the following examples.

## Example 1   Sequence Pattern

I. Main idea, *event 1*
   A. Important detail
   B. Important detail
II. Main idea, *event 2*
   A. Important detail
      1. Related detail
      2. Related detail
   B. Important detail

## Example 2   Cause/Effect Pattern

I. Main idea, *cause*
   A. Important detail
      1. Related detail
      2. Related detail
   B. Important detail
II. Main idea, *effect 1*
   A. Important detail
   B. Important detail
III. Main idea, *effect 2*

## Example 3   Problem/Solution Pattern

I. Main idea, *problem*
   A. Important detail
      1. Related detail
      2. Related detail
   B. Important detail
II. Main idea, *effects*
   A. Important detail
   B. Important detail
   C. Important detail
III. Main Idea, *causes*
   A. Important detail
   B. Important detail
IV. Main idea, *solutions*
   A. Important detail
   B. Important detail

## Example 4   Persuasive Pattern

I. Main idea, *assertion*
   A. Important detail
   B. Important detail

II. Main idea, *support*

    A. Important detail

        1. Related detail

        2. Related detail

    B. Important detail

III. Main idea, *expected outcome*

    A. Important detail

    B. Important detail

### Example 5   Data Pattern

I. Main idea, *subtopic 1*

    A. Important detail

    B. Important detail

        1. Related detail

        2. Related detail

II. Main idea, *subtopic 2*

    A. Important detail

    B. Important detail

III. Main idea, *subtopic 3*

    A. Important detail

    B. Important detail

## Research on Outlining

After reviewing the research on outlining, Anderson and Armbruster (1980), not surprisingly, concluded that students can use outlining as an effective device when they receive fairly extensive training in how to process information logically. However, they warn us that when students are told to outline but are given no training in how to do so, they may use the format of an outline but only process the text superficially. They also point out that outlining is time-consuming.

Other studies have shown the importance of teaching outlining. One old but convincing study on outlining (Barton, 1932) was completed with almost one hundred high school students. About half of them received direct instruction on outlining; the others received no such training. The students who had outlining training in their social studies classes scored significantly higher on tests in those subjects than the matched group who received no outlining training.

One way teachers can assist students with outlining is to hand them a partially completed outline based on a text selection. For example, the partially completed outline in Example 6 helps students organize, outline, and attend to a mass of information contained in a rather sophisticated reading selection. The partial outline is based on "The Goals of Hindu Life" by Huston Smith.[1] Students were instructed to first preview the chapter, then read it to get the whole picture, and finally read it a second time. As they read the selection the second time, they were to complete the outline form.

### Example 6    Partially Completed Outline

I. Path of desire (pleasure and success).
   A. Man seeks pleasure (goal 1).
      1. Strengths.
         a.
         b.
         c.
      2. Limitations (p. 32).
         a.
         b.
         c.
   B. Man seeks success (goal 2).
      1. Strengths (p. 33).
         a.
         b.
         c.
      2. Weaknesses (see numbered items on pp. 33–34).
         a.
         b.
         c.
   C. Hindu attitude toward path of desire (p. 35).

## Mapping

An alternative approach to note taking and outlining is *mapping* or *diagraming* information from textbooks, lectures, and class discussions. Instead of using numbers and letters to organize their notes, students make a diagram or a map.

1. *The Hindu Tradition* (Niles, Ill.: Argus Communication, 1978).

This approach is particularly useful for those students who are uncomfortable with the highly structured nature of formal outlines. Hanf (1971) offers these suggestions for mapping.

1. Identify the major idea of the lecture, discussion, chapter, or section. This is the starting point. This major idea or topic may be written anywhere on the paper as long as additional information can be built around it.
2. Draw a conspicuous circle around the major topic or idea.
3. Determine secondary related categories. Chapter subheadings may help to determine these categories.
4. Connect the secondary categories to the major topic or idea.
5. Determine supportive details.
6. Connect the details to the ideas or categories they support.
7. Connect all notes to some other note in a way that makes sense. Students can devise their own organizational system.

An example like the one that appears in Fig. 6.3 will help students with the concept of mapping.

Anderson and Armbruster (1980) cite their own research on the positive effects of mapping for middle school students. They feel it works well because it forces students to attend to and process the relationships among *all* idea units in order to translate writing into a coherent diagram. But they also feel the benefits of this intense processing should be weighed against the cost: students must spend considerable time constructing a visual presentation.

According to Anderson (1978), mapping techniques should be flexible, simple, and capable of representing a variety of organizational patterns. He tells us that students must

> learn a set of relational conventions (symbols), which at the simplest level indicate how two ideas are related, but at the text level can show the complex relationship among many ideas. This scheme has seven fundamental relationships between two ideas, A and B: when B is an instance of A, B is a property or characteristic of A, A is similar to B, A is greater or less than B, A occurs before B, A causes B, and A is the negation of B. In addition, two special relationships show when idea A is an important idea, or a definition. The logical connectives *and* and *or* are also used. (Anderson, 1978, p. 26)

Anderson offers a map illustration (see Fig. 6.4) that represents ideas organized in a variety of organizational patterns. In the box headed "material possessions," the text is describing or giving examples of main ideas. Students would use this mapping style when recording ideas from the data pattern. On the other hand, when the map shows a series of boxes connected by arrows,

## Figure 6.3  The Concept of Mapping

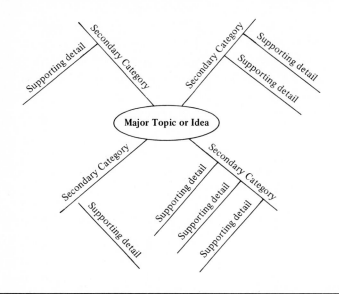

such as those on the right side of Fig. 6.4, students would be mapping ideas from the sequence, cause/effect, and problem/solution patterns.

Anderson believes mapping entire chapters is too time-consuming. He advocates mapping those portions of the chapter that are related to items from a study guide (student-generated items that reflect important ideas based on lecture notes, course guides, and objectives). For example, if teachers provided students with instructional objectives, as we discussed in Chapter 2, students could identify the appropriate data from the text and then construct a short map. Or, as Anderson puts it, one map could be constructed "for each item that might be on a chapter test. Roughly this translates into one map for each entry on the study guide" (Anderson, 1978, p. 27).

Figure 6.5 illustrates the mapping of cause/effect ideas from a social studies text (see the passage on pp. 173–174). Figure 6.6 illustrates the mapping of sequential steps from a science text (see the passage on pp. 158–159). Note that arrows are used to illustrate both cause/effect and sequential relationships. The word *step* is enclosed in each major idea box in the sequence map. This technique differentiates that map from the cause/effect map.

# Figure 6.4  Map of Text

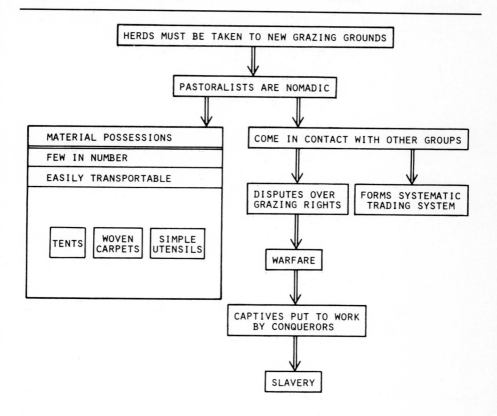

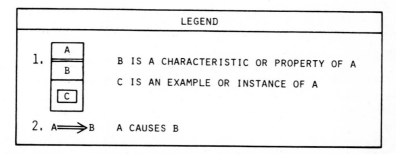

From Thomas H. Anderson, "Study Skills and Learning Strategies," in *Cognitive and Affective Learning Strategies,* ed. H. F. O'Neil and C. D. Spielberger (New York: Academic Press, 1979), p. 94. Reprinted by permission.

# Figure 6.5  Map of Cause/Effect Passage

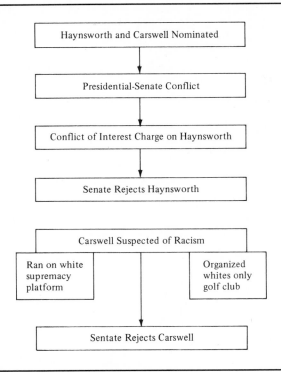

## Comprehension Monitoring

To have success with the study skills discussed in this chapter, students must be capable of monitoring their comprehension. *Comprehension monitoring* involves evaluating and regulating one's ongoing comprehension process (Baker, 1979b). *Evaluating* involves keeping track of the success with which one's comprehension is proceeding. *Regulating* involves ensuring that the process continues smoothly by taking some kind of action, like rereading, when comprehension fails. According to Baker: "Readers who monitor their comprehension of text are likely to know when they understand, when they don't understand, and when they partially understand. In addition, they know to test

# Figure 6.6 Map of Sequence Passage

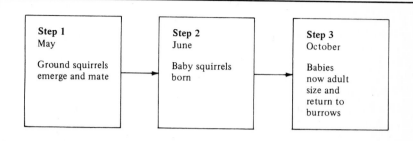

whether their understanding is adequate for the purpose at hand, and when and how to deal with comprehension difficulties" (Baker, 1979b, p. 2).

Students should be able to monitor their comprehension relative to the various taxonomic comprehension levels and tasks that were discussed in previous chapters. Readers, for example, must keep track of their success in recognizing and inferring main ideas, cause/effect relationships, and comparative data.

Baker (1979a) conducted a study on comprehension monitoring with college students. She gave them passages to read from a history text that contained inconsistent information, where ideas in one sentence conflicted with those of another; unclear references, where the context did not specify which of several previously introduced nouns was the referent of a nonspecific phrase; and inappropriate logical connectives, where a connective like *however* that should logically have appeared was replaced with a connective like *therefore*.

Baker concluded from her study that

> college students can and do monitor their comprehension, though not always consistently. If they experience difficulty in understanding, they have a variety of procedures available to assist them in coming up with a plausible interpretation of the text. Moreover, these procedures are sometimes applied so automatically that readers are unaware that their interpretation of the text may not be what the author intended to convey. Finally there are large individual differences in the way readers monitor their comprehension. (Baker, 1979a, p. 32)

An important aspect of this study was that those students who did not notice the confusions during their first reading of the passages were able to do so when specifically instructed to find them during a second reading. Therefore they probably are capable of comprehension monitoring but do not choose to do it when completing reading assignments independently. Why is this so?

Baker offers several explanations. Students may be exposed to poorly written, hard-to-understand material that discourages them from monitoring. They may have unquestioning belief in the printed word, which results in passive reading. Sometimes their comprehension is monitored for them by their teachers, who tend to keep track of what students comprehend, particularly during oral reading. Since the teachers are monitoring comprehension for them, students do not bother doing it themselves. An additional and important factor may be that the students simply are not interested in the reading assignment and are reading it not to learn but to just get the assignment out of the way.

## Test-Taking Skills

Content teachers and reading specialists can make their students' study time more profitable by helping them in the art of test taking. Very often students claim they studied "for hours" but get only C's or, even worse, fail exams. Sometimes their problem stems from the fact that they do not know how to approach the task of answering different types of test questions.

## Test-Taking Tips

Teachers should let their students know what their tests will be like. Are they going to emphasize details, major ideas, relationships, or a combination? What study techniques will be helpful—outlining, mapping, SQ3R, the Cornell method? What test format will be used? Will it be multiple-choice, essay, short answers, or a combination?

The following outline contains some suggestions for taking tests that could be shared with students. Portions of the outline have been adapted from Millman and Pauk's (1969) book *How to Take Tests*.

I. General guidelines.
   A. Be sure you know how long you have to complete the test.
   B. Read all the directions and questions fully before writing any answers. Do not hesitate to ask the teacher questions if you do not understand the directions.
   C. Once you are ready to answer questions, move quickly.
   D. Do not dwell on questions that puzzle you. Leave space on your answer sheet and go back to them later. Guess if you don't know, especially on true/false and multiple-choice questions. Try to answer all questions.

E. If you have enough time, check your answers at the end of the exam period.

II. Essay questions.

A. First organize your answer, perhaps in outline form.

B. If you have memorized important facts or formulas, write them immediately on the back of the examination.

C. Read the question carefully. Be sure to prepare and approach your essay in the way designated by the key term in the question. There are different types of key terms.

1. *Identification* (short-answer). These questions require you to get right to the point. Your concise answer may be a date, name, place, or condition. For example, the test question might be "List four conditions that led to the Watergate scandal." Some terms of identification are these:

| | |
|---|---|
| cite | indicate |
| define | list |
| enumerate | mention |
| give | name |
| identify | state |

2. *Description.* These questions also require you to get to the point, but you can usually amplify your answer to some extent. For example, the test question might be "Describe the responsibilities of a collection agency." Some terms of description are as follows:

a. "Describe" or "Discuss." These questions give you some freedom in organizing and answering the question.

b. "Diagram," "Illustrate," or "Sketch." These questions require concise answers with some examples. They may also mean that you should actually make a drawing. When in doubt, ask your teacher what he or she means.

c. "Develop," "Outline," or "Trace." These questions require you to supply the information in sequential order. You should stick to the order of events and not get sidetracked with related but unimportant issues.

3. *Relation.* These questions usually require more time to organize because they are more complex and analytical than the other types of questions. For example, the test question might be "Analyze the characteristics of the Doric and Ionic columns and show how they reflect the Greek culture of that period." Some terms of relation are as follows:

a. "Contrast," "Differentiate," or "Distinguish." These questions require you to focus on differences.

b. "Compare." This term usually means that you should point out both similarities *and* differences; to be certain, check with your teacher.

c. "Analyze." These questions require you to point out the essential features of something.

d. "Relate." This term means that you should give an account of happenings, events, and circumstances, or, more commonly, it means that you should show how the happening, event, or characteristic is related to another.

4. *Demonstration.* These questions require you to support a theme, principle, idea, or assertion. You must be able to support your answer by citing evidence, arguments, and research. For example, the test question might be "Demonstrate how Hemingway's own life-style is reflected in his writing." Some terms of demonstration are these:

| | |
|---|---|
| demonstrate | prove |
| explain why | show |
| justify | support |

5. *Evaluation.* These questions require you to express an opinion or make a judgment. Your opinion or judgment must be supported. Always try to acknowledge the opposing point of view and remember that if the term *criticize* is used, it is expected that you will express both good and bad points. For example, the question might be "Criticize John Kennedy's foreign policies during 1961 and 1962." Some terms of evaluation are these:

| | |
|---|---|
| assess | evaluate |
| comment | interpret |
| criticize | propose |

D. Once your answer is organized, answer the question directly in the first few paragraphs. The remaining paragraphs can be used to support, amplify, and modify your main points. Use the last few paragraphs to summarize your answer. Write clearly and legibly.

III. Objective questions.

A. Multiple-Choice.

1. Try first to answer the question *without* looking at the alternatives.

2. Then read *all* the alternatives, selecting the one you feel is correct.

3. If you do not know the answer, guess. You will probably be able to narrow your choice down to two answers that appear very similar. Choose one of them.

B.  True/False.

1.  Always look for qualifiers or determiners in true/false questions. If an exact qualifier is used, the test maker is saying that the statement is always true or *never* true. A single exception makes the statement false. Some exact qualifiers are these:

| | | | |
|---|---|---|---|
| all | must | no | only |
| alone | necessarily | none | without excep- |
| always | never | not | tion |

2.  *Indefinite* qualifiers make the test question difficult to answer because there is no clear-cut way to determine its truthfulness or falseness. Some indefinite qualifiers are these:

| | | | |
|---|---|---|---|
| frequently | most | quite often | some |
| infrequently | much | rarely | sometimes |
| less | often | seldom | usually |

# Desensitization Programs

For some students poor test scores may be attributable, in part, to feelings of anxiety they experience when taking a test; no matter how well they know the material or how familiar they are with test-taking strategies, they still freeze up during an exam.

Sarason defines anxiety as "a response to a perceived danger and inability to handle a challenge or unfinished business in a satisfactory manner" (Sarason, 1980, p. 6). He further lists the characteristics of anxiety.

1.  The situation is seen as difficult, challenging, and threatening.
2.  The individual sees himself as ineffective, or inadequate, in handling the task at hand.
3.  The individual focuses on undesirable consequences of personal inadequacy.
4.  Self-deprecatory preoccupations are strong and interfere or compete with task-relevant cognitive activity.
5.  The individual expects and anticipates failure and loss of regard by others. (Sarason, 1980, p. 6)

One way to help test-anxious students is to offer them desensitization programs. *Desensitization programs* are based on the belief that test anxiety is a conditioned, emotional reaction resulting from a single (or multiple) aversive learning experience in examination-related situations (Allen, 1971). Students in these programs receive an explanation of the program and participate in relaxation training. They complete test anxiety questionnaires from which a

# Figure 6.7  Test Anxiety Scale

*Directions:* Answer the following questions as truthfully as possible. Blacken out the T if the statement is *generally true* for you; F if the statement is *generally false.*

**Key**

T    1. While taking an important exam, I perspire a great deal.     T   F

T    2. I get to feel very panicky when I have to take a surprise exam.     T   F

T    3. During tests, I find myself thinking of the consequences of failing.     T   F

T    4. After important tests, I am frequently so tense that my stomach gets upset.     T   F

T    5. While taking an important exam, I find myself thinking of how much brighter the other students are than I am.     T   F

T    6. I freeze up on things like intelligence tests and finals.     T   F

T    7. If I were to take an intelligence test I would worry a great deal before taking it.     T   F

T    8. During course examinations, I find myself thinking of things unrelated to the course material.     T   F

T    9. During course examinations, I frequently get so nervous that I forget facts that I really know.     T   F

F    10. If I knew I was going to take an intelligence test, I would feel confident and relaxed beforehand.     T   F

T    11. I usually get depressed after taking a test.     T   F

T    12. I have an uneasy, upset feeling before taking a final.     T   F

F    13. When taking a test, I find my emotional feelings do not interfere with my performance.     T   F

T    14. Getting a good grade on one test doesn't seem to increase my confidence on the second test.     T   F

T    15. After taking a test, I always feel I have done better than I actually did.     T   F

T    16. I sometimes feel my heart beating very fast during important examinations.     T   F group hierarchy of test anxiety is formed. The hierarchy is constructed by ranking several common examination situations from least to most anxiety producing. Some of the situations include midsemester exams, final exams, feelings the night before exams, and feelings during the exam. The hierarchy provides a list of priorities from which desensitization sessions are planned.

According to Osterhouse (1972), the counselor begins with the least anxiety-provoking scenes. The scenes are presented in sequence while students are in a deep state of relaxation. The counselor reads a standard five-to-six-sentence description of each hierarchy item. The items are repeated as many as four times or until none of the subjects indicate any further anxiety as they visualize themselves in the situation. The counselor continues relaxation instructions between each presentation of a hierarchy item.

Both Allen (1971) and Osterhouse (1972) reported successful desensitization programs with college students, with Allen reporting that the program was more successful when combined with training in study skills. Others (Curtis, 1974; Enright, 1976) have also reported successful desensitization programs.

Rosenthal (1980) maintains that desensitization programs can work well by using *positive imagery*. For example, test-taking scenes are depicted as pleasant by having students imagine being successful on the tests. He cites research demonstrating that positive imagery works as well as relaxation training and it may even require less time.

Rosenthal also describes a *vicarious desensitization program* involving test-anxious junior high students who observed peers who were involved in either individual or group desensitization programs. Such vicarious experiences proved to be as effective as direct experiences, and students involved in both experiences surpassed those involved in neither on "fear ratings" and "work-sample exams."

Since there is ample research on the positive effects of test anxiety desensitization programs, it would behoove middle and high school administrators to consider implementing and evaluating them, provided their schools are staffed with qualified guidance counselors. Teachers may be better able to identify potential candidates for such programs by administering Sarason's (1972) Test Anxiety Scale (see Fig. 6.7). Wark and Bennett (1981) recommend a score of 11 or higher for identifying potential candidates among college students. However, research has not been completed for determining a cutoff score for middle and secondary students.

# Reading Rate and Flexibility

This author has tested hundreds of adolescents and adults on the reading flexibility section of Raygor's (1970) *McGraw-Hill Basic Skills Reading Test* and on an informal test of reading flexibility (Santeusanio, 1981). It is quite evident from these tests that many people are *inflexible readers*. They do not adjust their reading speed to their purpose for reading, their knowledge of the subject matter, and the difficulty of the material. (In fairness, it should be mentioned that the two tests cited above base their flexibility score entirely on the last factor, difficulty of the material.) This result is probably due to the fact that reading speed and flexibility of reading rate are rarely included in the typical high school curriculum.

Every reader should be able to read at four different reading rates: skimming, scanning, rapid, and study type. *Skimming* is reading at the fastest possible rate. It is usually done when one is trying simply to get the gist of the material or to raise questions to be answered during a more careful reading of the material. Readers deliberately leave out chunks of material when they skim.

*Scanning* is reading at the fastest possible rate when one is seeking specific information such as a telephone number or capital of a state. One can skim and scan at thousands of words per minute.

*Rapid reading* is reading as fast as possible in order to comprehend main ideas and some details. Readers usually skip little or no material, and they do not expect to be subjected to a future test on the material. Rapid reading is often the rate one uses for pleasure reading. Collins and his colleagues (1977) associate rapid reading with "reading for meaning." The maximum rapid-reading rate is approximately 800 words per minute when reading all the words in the selection. Depending on their purpose for reading, knowledge of the subject matter, and difficulty of the material, good rapid readers read between 300 to 600 words per minute.

*Study-type reading* is reading at a slow rate when one must follow directions, retain information, and read in anticipation of a future test. Collins and his colleagues call it "reading for doing" or "reading for remembering." Study-type reading is usually completed at rates below 300 words per minute. The rate is *extremely* slow when students feel they need to reread. Looking back should be encouraged for those students who recognize that a breakdown in comprehension has taken place. Alessi, Anderson, and Goetz refer to this technique as a "fix up" strategy employed by those readers who "re-read the sentence or paragraph perhaps engaging in careful analysis strategies such as thinking about the meaning, paraphrasing, drawing diagrams or using mental imagery" (Alessi, Anderson, and Goetz, 1979, p. 7). In fact, their research with college freshmen indicated that certain comprehension failure can be remedied by "lookbacks." However, still to be determined is whether or not readers can be taught to initiate correctly and to direct lookbacks themselves and, if this *can* be done, whether or not it will result in increased student achievement. From a commonsense point of view, one would suspect that it would pay for the miscomprehending student to sacrifice speed for comprehension by looking back.

# Sensitizing Students to Rate Flexibility

One way to sensitize students to reading rate flexibility is to present students with hypothetical situations and ask them to determine the types of reading rate called for in each situation. Here is an example.

### Example 7    Rate Flexibility Exercise

*Directions:* For each situation listed below, decide the most desirable reading rate. Write S if the material should be skimmed or scanned; write Q if the material should be read quickly but completely; and write C if it should be read carefully and slowly. Two answers may be appropriate for some situations. Be prepared to defend your answers.

_____ 1. You are going to read several difficult articles in order to form your own opinion on the merits of nuclear power.

_____ 2. You want to determine if an author is consistent and logical in his or her thinking.

_____ 3. You want to widen your range of interests.

_____ 4. You want to appreciate the poet's emotions in different poems.

_____ 5. You want to have a good laugh.

_____ 6. You want to outline an author's thoughts.

_____ 7. You want to read some sources for a speech you have to give.

_____ 8. You want to find out how to pronounce a word.

_____ 9. You want to read a book to find out how to lose weight.

_____ 10. You want to find out where you can buy an outdoor grill.

_____ 11. You want to understand the steps involved in the growth of a pumpkin seed.

_____ 12. You want to check on some facts.

_____ 13. You want to put your ten-speed bicycle together.

_____ 14. You want to determine when the sale at Sears ends.

# Skimming

If students can comprehend well but are chronically slow readers of everything they read, you can teach them how to skim and read more rapidly. But students must also realize that most of the reading they do in school requires the slower, study-type reading rate.

The following guidelines for skimming chapters and articles can be presented to students.

1.  Read the title.
2.  If a beginning *summary* or *overview* appears, read it completely.
3.  Quickly read the first few opening paragraphs to get a good introduction to the article and a sense of the writer's style and organization.
4.  Read all boldfaced subtitles. They give you summarized ideas and more hints about the writer's organizational pattern.
5.  Float over the material quickly to pick up images of what is involved. While you consciously skip much material, try to pick out phrases that might answer some important questions about the article.

    (a)  *Who* the article is about.
    (b)  *What* the article is about.
    (c)  *When* certain events have taken place.
    (d)  *Where* the events have taken place.
    (e)  *Why* certain events have taken place.
    (f)  *How* the article is organized.

6.  Read quickly all the final paragraphs or the sections labeled *Summary* or *Conclusions*. They add more detail to what you learned from reading the beginning summary or overview.

Edward Fry's (1978) "How You Might Skim an Article" can help students understand the skimming process. It is reproduced in Fig. 6.8.

## Pacing

One way teachers can help students increase their speed of reading relatively easy material is to prepare *pacing* exercises. Pacing exercises are designed to force students to read at a speed considerably faster than that to which they are accustomed. Teachers can accomplish pacing by limiting the amount of time they allow students to read each page or column of a reading selection. Here is how pacing exercises can be prepared.

Teachers should select relatively easy material from newspapers and periodicals that is related to their content areas. Textbooks are *not* recommended. After a teacher has chosen a selection, he or she determines the numbers of words in it. The number of words can be estimated by measuring an inch of column type from the beginning, middle, and end of the reading selection. Count the total number of words in each measured inch of print and determine the average words per inch from the three samples. Next measure the total number of inches of type in the entire selection; and multiply this number by

# Figure 6.8  How You Might Skim an Article

| | | |
|---|---|---|
| Usually the first paragraph will be read at average speed all the way through. It often contains an introduction or overview of what will be talked about.<br><br>Sometimes, however, the second paragraph contains the introduction or overview. In the first paragraph the author might just be "warming up" or saying something clever to attract attention.<br><br>Reading a third paragraph completely might be unnecessary but  ...   ...   ...   ...   ...<br>...   ...   ...   ...   ...   ...<br>...   ...   ...   ...   ...   ...<br>...   ...   ...   ...   ...   ...<br>the main idea is usually contained in the opening sentence<br>...   ...   ...   ...   topic sentence   ...   ...   ...   ...<br>...   ...   ...   ...   ...   ...<br>...   ...   ...   ...   ...   ...<br>...   ...   ...   ...   ...   ...<br>...   ...   ...   ...   ...<br>Besides the first sentence the reader should get some but not all the detail from the rest of the paragraph  ...   ...   ...<br>...   ...   ...   ...   ...   ...<br>...   ...   ...   ...   ...   ...<br>...   ...   ...   ...   ...   ...<br>...   ...   ...   ...   ...   ...<br>...   ...   ...   ...   ...   ...<br>...   ...   ...   ...   ...   ...<br>...   ...   ...   names   ...   ...<br>...   ...   ...   ...   ...   ...<br>...   ...   ... dates   ...   ...<br>...   ...   ...   ...   ...   ...<br>...   ...   ...   ...   ... ...<br>This tells you nothing   ...   ...<br>...   ...   ...   ...   ...   ... | ...   ...   ...   ...   ...   ...<br>...   ...   ...   ...   ...   ...<br>hence sometimes the main idea is in the middle or at the end of the paragraph.<br><br>Some paragraphs merely repeat ideas   ...   ...   ...<br>...   ...   ...   ...   ...   ...<br>...   ...   ...   ..,   ....<br>Occasionally the main idea can't be found in the opening sentence. The whole paragraph must then be read.<br><br>Then leave out a lot of the next paragraph   ...   ...   ...<br>...   ...   ...   ...   ...   ...<br>...   ...   ...   ...   ...   ...<br>...   ...   ...   to make up time.<br>...   ...   ...   ...   ...   ...<br>...   ...   ...   ...   ...   ...<br>Remember to keep up a very fast rate   ...   ...   ...   ...<br>...   ...   ...   ...   ...   ...<br>...   ...   ...   ...   ...   ...<br>...   ...   ...   800 w.p.m.<br>...   ...   ...   ...   ...   ...<br>...   ...   ...   ...   ...   ...<br>Don't be afraid to leave out half or more of each paragraph<br>...   ...   ...   ...   ...   ...<br>...   ...   ...   ...   ...   ...<br>...   ...   ...   ...   ...   ...<br>Don't get interested and start to read everything   ...   ...   ...<br>...   ...   ...   ...   ...   ...<br>...   ...   ...   ...   ...   ...<br>...   ...   ...   ...   ...   ...<br>...   ...   ...   ...   ...   ...<br>skimming is work   ...   ...   ... | ...   ...   ...   ...   ...   ...<br>...   ...   ...   ...   ...   ...<br>...   ...   ...   ...   ...   ...<br>...   ...   ...   ...   ...   ...<br>...   ...   ...   ...<br>Lowered comprehension is expected   ...   ...<br>...   ...   ...   50%   ...   ...<br>...   ...   ...   ...   not too low<br>...   ...   ...   ...   ...   ...<br>Skimming practice makes it easier<br>...   ...   ...   ...   ...   ...<br>...   ...   ...   ...   ...   ...<br>...   ...   gain confidence   ...<br>...   ...   ...   ...   ...   ...<br>...   ...   ...   ...   ...   ...<br>Perhaps you won't get anything at all from a few paragraphs   ...   ...   ...   ...<br>...   ...   ...   ...   ...   ...<br>...   ...   ...   ...   ...   ...<br>...   ...   ...   don't worry<br>...   ...   ...   ...   ...   ...<br>Skimming has many uses   ...<br>...   ...   ...   ...   ...   ...<br>...   ...   ...   reports   ...<br>...   ...   newspapers   ...   ...<br>...   ...   ...   supplementary<br>... text   ...   ...   ....<br>The ending paragraphs might be read more fully as often they contain a summary.<br><br>Remember that the importance of skimming is to get only the author's main ideas at a very fast speed. |

From *Skimming and Scanning* by Edward B. Fry, Ph.D., p. 13. Copyright © 1978. Jamestown Publishers, Providence, R.I. Reprinted by permission.

## The Metamorphosis of Mrs. Hood, Part II

In her graduate class at State College Peg, a high school reading teacher, is finishing her report on reading in the content areas. Her fellow students and professor have been most interested in how her program is organized and implemented.

"So that's how we worked out a program in Mrs. Hood's class. I'm going to hand out a copy of a brief essay one of her students wrote. I didn't edit it at all. I think it nicely summarizes how most of the students feel about Mrs. Hood's new approach."

(This essay was actually written by a high school student.)

I am a junior at Danvers High School and I am in one of Mrs. Hood's history classes. For the past two years of high school, I have done very bad on all my tests because I never knew how to study for them. My way of studying used to be to pick up the papers or books, look them over, and then go out. About two

the average number of words per inch. The result gives the approximate number of words in the reading selection.

Next the teacher selects a predetermined rate, usually between 400 and 800 words, and determines how long it would take to read the selection at that rate. The teacher would then give students only that amount of time to read the article. Comprehension should always be tested after each pacing exercise.

For example, let us say an article has been selected that contains approximately 2000 words, and the teacher would like to pace the students' reading at 500 words per minute. The teacher would give the students only 4 minutes to read the article:

$$\text{reading time} = \frac{\text{words}}{\text{determined rate}} \quad \text{or} \quad 4 = \frac{2000}{500}$$

If the article had four pages containing approximately the same number of words, then the teacher could give students a minute to read each page. The teacher could press them to read more quickly by saying "Next page" after each minute; the students' task then is to get to the end of the page before the teacher says "Next page." Students *must* move on to the next page at that time.

minutes' work. I dreaded the days when I had to take a test and decided to skip them instead of failing them. Especially on exam days! In two years of high school I've taken maybe two exams and skipped the rest but now I'm sort of looking forward to them. Well when I got into my history class and she showed us her way of studying, I decided to try it. I went from getting 60's to 65's to getting 95's to 100's! Well then I figured that if it worked for history it could work for English, Science, etc. as well. Well I'll tell you one thing: if you really want to do good try making two columns. One side for the questions and the other for the answers. Read the questions and fold the answers in back. If you can't guess then look back. I guarantee you'll know the answers faster this way and the funny thing about it is you'll remember them three weeks later. I get better marks so you can too. Also whatever Mrs. Hood gives us to study, that's exactly what's on the test and its not worded so you can't understand it. Well try it once and if you don't like it go back to your old way but I think you'll find it much better. Well.

Good Luck!

## Summary

SQ3R and OK5R are two study approaches that teachers can introduce to students. Despite the lack of research support for these methods, they can be effective approaches when student-generated questions are used as classroom examination test items.

Note taking is an important study skill. One useful note-taking technique is the Cornell method. Mapping or diagraming what is read is an alternative to traditional note-taking techniques. Students can also use underlining or outlining as study techniques.

Study skills cannot be used effectively unless students monitor their comprehension by evaluating and regulating ideas contained in print. In fact, prior to teaching study skills, teachers must be certain that their students have the basic skill of main idea/details mastered, as well as an understanding of how this skill relates to the basic organizational patterns.

Some students have good study techniques but poor test-taking skills. Teachers can share test-taking techniques with these students. Some of these students might also benefit from desensitization programs that have been developed for test-anxious students.

Students must also learn how to become flexible readers. They must know when to skim, when to scan, when to read rapidly, and when to read slowly. The pacing technique can be used to increase the reading rates of students who comprehend well but read everything slowly.

Study systems, note taking, mapping, underlining, outlining, test-taking techniques, and rapid reading are all useful study skills. But like other skills discussed in this text, they should not be taught in isolation or as an end in themselves. Rather they should be taught as the need arises and in conjunction with meaningful subject matter material.

# Bibliography

Alessi, Stephen M., Thomas H. Anderson, and Ernest T. Goetz. *An Investigation of Lookbacks During Studying,* Technical Report no. 140. Urbana: Center for the Study of Reading, University of Illinois, 1979.

Allen, George J. "Effectiveness of Study Counseling and Desensitization in Alleviating Test Anxiety in College Students." *Journal of Abnormal Psychology* 77(1971):282–289.

Anderson, Thomas H. *Study Skills and Learning Strategies,* Technical Report no. 104. Urbana: Center for the Study of Reading, University of Illinois, 1978.

Anderson, Thomas H., and Bonnie B. Armbruster. "Reader and Text—Studying Strategies." Paper presented at the Conference on Reading Expository Text, November 1980, at the University of Wisconsin-Madison.

Baker, Linda. *Comprehension Monitoring: Identifying and Coping With Text Confusions,* Technical Report no. 145. Urbana: Center for the Study of Reading, University of Illinois, 1979a.

———. *Do I Understand or Do I Not Understand: That Is the Question,* Reading Education Report no. 10. Urbana: Center for the Study of Reading, University of Illinois, 1979b.

Barton, W. A., Jr. *Outlining as a Study Procedure.* New York: Columbia University Bureau of Publications, 1932.

Burg, Leslie, Maurice Kaufman, Blanche Korngold, and Albert Kovner. *The Complete Reading Supervisor.* Columbus, Ohio: Merrill, 1978.

Burmeister, Lou E. *Reading Strategies for Middle and Secondary School Teachers.* 2nd ed. Reading, Mass.: Addison-Wesley, 1978.

Collins, Allan M., Ann L. Brown, Jerry L. Morgan, and William F. Brewer. *The Analysis of Reading Tasks and Texts,* Technical Report no. 43. Urbana: Center for the Study of Reading, University of Illinois, 1977.

Courtney, Brother Leonard. "Recent Developments in Reading Instruction in the Content Areas." In *Recent Developments in Reading,* edited by H. Alan Robinson. University of Chicago Press, 1965.

Curtis, Joan M., "Test Anxiety Reduction Programs and Prognostications for College Reading Labs." In *Proceedings of the Seventh Annual Conference of the Western College Reading Association,* edited by Gene Kerstiens. Santa Fe Springs, Calif., 1974.

Devine, Thomas G. *Teaching Study Skills, A Guide for Teachers.* Boston: Allyn & Bacon, 1981.

Enright, Gwyn. "The Study Table and Panic Clinic." In *Proceedings of the Ninth Annual Conference of the Western College Reading Association,* edited by Roy Sugimoto. Santa Fe Springs, Calif., 1976.

Fry, Edward. *Skimming and Scanning.* Providence, R.I.: Jamestown Publishers, 1978.

Hanf, M. Buckley. "Mapping: A Technique for Translating Reading into Thinking." *Journal of Reading* 14(1971):225–230, 270.

Harris, Albert J. *How to Increase Reading Ability.* 5th ed. New York: McKay, 1971.

Johns, Jerry L., and Lawrence P. McNamara. "The SQ3R Study Technique: A Forgotten Research Target." *Journal of Reading* 23(1980):705–708.

Johnson, Sue. "A System for the Diagnosis and Treatment of Test Study Problems." In *Proceedings of the Sixth Annual Conference of the Western College Reading Association,* edited by Gene Kerstiens. Santa Fe Springs, Calif., 1973.

Kulhavy, R. W., J. W. Dyer, and L. Silver. "The Effects of Notetaking and Test Expectancy on the Learning of Text Materials." *Journal of Educational Research* 68(1975):363–365.

Maxwell, Martha. *Improving Student Learning Skills.* San Francisco: Jossey-Bass, 1980.

Millman, Jason, and Walter Pauk. *How to Take Tests.* New York: McGraw-Hill, 1969.

Osterhouse, Robert A. "Desensitization and Study Skills Training as Treatment for Two Types of Test-Anxious Students." *Journal of Counseling Psychology* 19(1972):301–307.

Pauk, Walter. *How to Study in College.* Boston: Houghton Mifflin, 1974.

———. "The Super-Glue of Study Skills." *Reading World* 19(1980):303–304.

Raygor, Alton L. *McGraw-Hill Basic Skills Reading Test.* Monterey, Calif.: McGraw-Hill, 1970.

Robinson, Francis P. *Effective Study.* 4th ed. New York: Harper & Row, 1970.

Rosenthal, Ted L. "Modeling Approaches to Test Anxiety and Related Performance Problems." In *Test Anxiety: Theory, Research, and Applications,* edited by Irwin G. Sarason. Hillsdale, N.J.: Lawrence Earlbaum Associates, 1980.

Sack, Allan. *Manual for Teacher-Trainers.* New York: College Skills Center, 1975.

Santeusanio, Richard P. *Developing Reading Skills for Business and Industry.* Boston: CBI, 1981.

Sarason, Irwin G. "Introduction to the Study of Test Anxiety." In *Test Anxiety: Theory, Research, and Applications,* edited by Irwin G. Sarason. Hillsdale, N.J.: Lawrence Earlbaum Associates, 1980.

———. "Experimental Approaches to Test Anxiety: Attention and the Uses of Information." In *Anxiety: Current Trends,* vol. 2, edited by C. D. Spielberger. New York: Academic Press, 1972.

Spache, George D. *Toward Better Reading.* Champaign, Ill.: Garrard, 1963.

Spencer, Frank. "SQ3R: Several Queries Regarding Relevant Research." In *Research on Reading in Secondary Schools,* Monograph no. 2, edited by Joseph L. Vaughan, Jr., and Paula J. Gaus. Tucson: University of Arizona, 1978.

Summers, Edward G. "Utilizing Visual Aids in Reading Materials for Effective Learning."

In *Developing Study Skills in Secondary Schools,* edited by Harold L. Herber. Newark, Del.: International Reading Association, 1965.

Taylor, Hansley P. "Beneath and Beyond SQ3R: A Reading Approach to Nonfiction." In *Proceedings of the Sixth Annual Conference of the Western College Reading Association,* edited by Gene Kerstiens. Santa Fe Springs, Calif., 1973.

Wark, David M., and J. Michael Bennet. "The Measurement of Test Anxiety in a Reading Class." *Reading World* 20(1981):215–222.

# Chapter 7

# Identifying

# Student Needs

# The Accident, Part I

"They think she will be fine. She may be able to have visitors in a week or so." Drew Keohane, principal of the Galloway Middle School, was talking to Nora Ellsworth, one of his reliable substitute teachers.

"Oh, that's good to hear. I'll be sure to visit her. I hope she's well enough to give me a rundown on her students. You know, it's tough taking over classes in the middle of November, especially Nancy's."

"True," replied Drew. "We both know how much the kids love Nancy. They were really shook up when we told them about her accident. But you'll have them eating out of your hands in no time."

"I'm not worried about that. But I am concerned about getting to know my classes—you know, what they can and cannot do. That's one reason I'm eager to talk with Nancy."

"I'm afraid you won't get much information from her."

"What are you talking about? I thought you said she was going to be OK."

"She's going to be OK physically. But her family tells me she has had a memory loss."

"Oh dear! Does she recognize her family?"

"Yes, but she's hazy on lots of things—how the accident occurred, where she teaches, and many things about her past. So I rather doubt that she'll be able to give you a rundown on her 125 students."

"For sure! Well, I guess I can always go to the old cumulative files."

"True, but you'll only get some achievement test scores and some anecdotal comments from teachers here and there. What you really need to do is to find out how well Nancy's students can handle those science books we use."

"I agree. But how?"

At the end of the chapter you will find out how Nora Ellsworth solved her problem.

# Introduction

When content teachers and reading specialists begin each school year, they meet many of their students for the first time. The vast majority of these teachers want to become familiar with their students as soon as possible. They want to get an idea about the general ability of their classes and the specific strengths, weaknesses, and learning styles of individuals within their classes. They know that each student in *every* class is unique. Some can study independently; some cannot. Some will respond well to the textbook; others will not. Reading, writing, and spelling abilities will vary as well as areas of interest. There are, then, many questions concerning their students that teachers want answered.

Instructors can get the answers to these questions from a variety of evaluation instruments, including standardized achievement tests, individual assessments, group skills tests, cloze tests, and learning style inventories. Achievement tests and learning style inventories are available from many publishing companies. The other types of instruments are developed by the content teacher or the reading specialist. Each instrument is discussed in this chapter.

## Achievement Tests

Teachers are probably most familiar with *achievement tests,* an evaluation instrument designed to help teachers make comparisons among their students and between their students and others in the country. Achievement tests in reading are also used to evaluate district-wide developmental and remedial reading programs, screen students for remedial reading programs, and place students in levels of academic subjects.

The test items included in an achievement test range from easy to moderately difficult to very difficult. This range allows for a test score variance. That is, most students will answer the easy items correctly, some will answer the moderately difficult ones correctly, and a minority will answer the very difficult items correctly.

Before an achievement test is made available to school systems, it is administered to many students across different parts of the country. These students comprise the *norm group* that is needed to convert *raw scores* (the actual number of items answered correctly by students) to grade equivalents, percentiles, and stanines.

## Reporting Scores

When teachers read a student's *grade equivalent* on a standardized test, they have found out that the student has correctly answered the same number of items as the average examinee from the norm group at that grade level. For example, if Christine's grade equivalency on a reading test is 10.2, that score means that the number of items she marked correctly is equal to that of the average norm group examinee enrolled in the second month of the tenth grade.

Unfortunately, grade equivalency scores are often misinterpreted. For example, let us assume Christine was in grade 8 when she took the test. Her test probably contained material written at the sixth, seventh, eighth, and ninth grade levels. Her grade equivalent of 10.2, then, cannot be interpreted as meaning that she can read tenth grade material because she was not even tested on tenth grade material. We simply found out that Christine correctly answered test items from sixth, seventh, eighth, and ninth grade materials as well as the average students in the second month of the tenth grade answered these test items. Because grade equivalency scores are so often misinterpreted, the editors of the most recent editions of *Standards for Educational and Psychological Tests and Manuals* urge test publishers to abandon or discourage the use of grade equivalents (Pyrczak, 1979). The Board of Directors of the International Reading Association (1980) recommend that those who administer standardized reading tests abandon the practice of reporting grade equivalency scores and that test authors and publishers eliminate grade equivalency interpretations from their tests. When making comparisons between and among students, percentile rank and stanine scores are preferable.

When teachers read a student's *percentile rank* on a standardized test, they have found out the percent of examinees in a norm group that scored below and above that student. If Christine's percentile rank on the reading test was 93, it means that her performance on the test was better than that of 92% of the examinees in the norm group and poorer than 6%. A score at the 50th percentile is considered average.

When teachers read a student's *stanine score* on a standardized test, they have found out where he or she places relative to categories ranging from 1 to 9. A score of 4 to 6 is average. Stanine categories below 4 are considered below average, and those above 6 are considered above average. If Christine's stanine score was 9, it means that her performance on the test was in the top 4% of those in the norm group. Pyrczak (1979) notes that stanines are especially useful when broad groupings of examinees are desired. The chart below should give readers a clearer indication of the meaning of stanines.

| Stanine | 1 | 2 | 3 | 4 | 5 | 6 | 7 | 8 | 9 |
|---|---|---|---|---|---|---|---|---|---|
| Percent of Norm Group | Bottom 4% | 7% | 12% | 17% | Middle 20% | 17% | 12% | 7% | Top 4% |

## Validity and Reliability

Test developers normally go to great lengths to make their tests valid and reliable. A test is *valid* if it in fact measures what it purports to measure. For example, does a seventh grade reading test measure reading skills that are representative of reading skills required of seventh grade students? In short, is the test suitable for the purpose for which it will be used?

A test is *reliable* if its test results are consistent. If a group of students take a test today, will their scores be about the same as they would be if they were to take the same test tomorrow or a week later?

There are various ways to determine a test's validity and reliability. The interested reader can learn about these techniques by consulting books on educational testing and statistics. Teachers who use standardized tests should review the data on validity and reliability that are included in the technical manuals that accompany standardized achievement tests.

## Usefulness and Limitations

While secondary reading achievement tests of reading vocabulary and comprehension are satisfactory for making comparisons and predicting future success in reading, they are not good diagnostic instruments. One of the major factors that influences understanding of a text, as we have discussed in this book, is the reader's background and knowledge relative to the text's topic. This factor can interfere when a teacher is trying to make diagnostic decisions from achievement test results. As Royer and Cunningham note: "Failure [on achievement tests] could occur—due to lack of relevant world knowledge—when the student had perfectly good reading comprehension skills. We really do not know if failure on the reading comprehension component of an achievement test is due to an inability to decode words, an inability to comprehend ideas expressed in print, or an inability to comprehend ideas because the reader does not have the prior critical world knowledge needed to interpret the test passages" (Royer and Cunningham, 1978, p. 30). This factor is also a problem with cloze tests and group inventories. It is less of a problem with individual reading inventories because they are administered on an individual's basis, which allows the teacher to learn more about the student's background.

There are several secondary achievement tests in reading. Some are listed with their publisher's address at the end of the Bibliography (pp. 310–311). A more complete list can be found in Oscar Buros's (1978) *Eighth Mental Measurements Yearbook*. These yearbooks also contain critical reviews of the tests.

In summary, the major questions that an achievement test will answer for the teacher are, "How do my students compare with others?" and "What are the reading levels of the students in my class?" But the answers to these questions will not tell the content teachers and reading specialists whether or not their students can read the textbooks that will be used in their classes. To get a better estimate of this factor, teachers can devise a cloze test or a group inventory.

## Cloze Test

The term *cloze* comes from the Gestalt concept of "closure" (see Chapter 3). Humans have a tendency to form complete wholes by filling in a structure's empty spaces—they wish to arrive at closure.

The *cloze procedure* was introduced by Taylor (1953) as a readability measure. Since its introduction in 1953, a great deal of research has been completed and many articles have been written on the cloze procedure. Bormuth's (1967, 1968) work probably has given the greatest impetus to the current widespread use of cloze tests.

A *cloze test* constructed from a textbook should consist of about 250 to 275 words from a textbook passage. The passage is mutilated by deleting every fifth word and replacing that word with a blank space. The students' task is to try to fill in the empty space with the exact word that was deleted. They are trying to arrive at closure.

The rationale behind the cloze test is that readers will be able to predict the deleted words to the extent that their background experiences, interests, and language ability match those of the author's. The better the match, the more likely it is that the readers will be able to interact successfully with the textbook.

The following sections outline the steps one should follow when constructing, administering, and scoring a cloze test.

## Construction

Teachers can construct a cloze test by extracting a passage from a textbook they plan to assign to their students. When constructing the test, they should follow the steps listed below.

1. Plan to type your passage on a ditto master or stencil.
2. Select a reading passage from the textbook you plan to use in your class. The passage should consist of 250 to 275 words. Students should not have read the material.
3. Leave the first sentence intact. Select at random one of the first five words of the second sentence. This word will become your first underlined blank space (which should consist of 15 spaces).
4. After you have chosen your first blank, delete every fifth word thereafter. Continue deleting until you have 50 underlined blanks (each of which is 15 spaces long, regardless of the length of the word).
5. Do not begin a blank on one line and continue it on the next line; some students will then think two words should be filled in. If you cannot fit the 15 spaces on a line, begin a new line and type the blank there.
6. Do not place numbers on the lines (e.g., _ 1 _, _ 2 _, etc.). The numbers can be distracting to students.
7. After you type the sentence that contains the 50th blank, type one more sentence intact.

## Administration

Teachers can easily administer a cloze test in their own classrooms. When doing so, they should consider the following:

- Do not allow students to use their books when completing the cloze exercise.
- Before administering the test, give examples that all students can relate to:

  > Please turn on the _____ . I want to watch the news.
  >
  > The umpire called, "Strike _____ ." Joe struck out again.

- Emphasize that students can get many clues from the context of the reading selection.
- Tell students that the results of the cloze exercise have nothing to do with their course grade and will not be placed in their permanent record file.
- Explain that they are not expected to fill *all* the spaces correctly. They should, however, try not to leave any space blank.
- Indicate that spelling mistakes will be noted but not counted against them.
- If students need the time, allow them to use the entire period to complete the test. Many, of course, will finish early.
- You may want to administer more than one cloze test based on the textbook. Several tests will probably give you more valid results.

## Scoring

When scoring cloze tests, teachers should keep in mind the guidelines that follow.

1. After students complete the test, you can ask them to transfer their answers to an answer sheet to facilitate scoring.
2. Count only exact replacements as correct. (See below for possible exceptions.) This procedure helps you remain objective and allows for a valid interpretation of test results. (In addition, you might go daffy trying to judge the correctness of synonyms.)
3. The total number of exact word replacements should be multiplied by two. Use the guidelines in the accompanying table to interpret scores.

| Score | Interpretation |
|---|---|
| 0–38% | Frustration level: the student probably would be frustrated when trying to read the textbook |
| 40–56% | Instructional level: the book probably is suitable for this student when he or she also gets instruction from the teacher |
| 58% and above | Independent level: the book is probably easy for the student and he or she can read it independently |

Because we tend to associate certain percentage scores with success and failure (e.g., 90% is excellent; 50% is failure), the scores that students attain on cloze tests may be misleading to both the teacher and the student. Bormuth (1968) has suggested some "equivalency" scores. A score of 38% on a cloze test is equivalent to a score of 65% on a multiple-choice test. Therefore students who score 38% or lower on a cloze test would likely be frustrated when trying to read the textbook. A score of 44% on a cloze test is equivalent to a score of 75% on a multiple-choice test. Therefore students who score between 40% and 56% would find that they would benefit from using the book with instruction from the teacher. A score of 58% on a cloze test is equivalent to a score of 90% on a multiple-choice test. Therefore students who score 58% or higher would probably find the book easy to read and understand and could use it without teacher assistance.

Perhaps Bormuth's equivalency scores should be shared with students so that they understand that their scores of 50 and 60, for example, do *not* mean they have failed the test.

The validity of the cloze test has been established as a result of studies such as the one completed by Rankin (1970). He found high correlations between cloze scores and standardized reading test scores.

In addition to ascertaining a student's reading level (frustration, instructional, and independent) with respect to a particular textbook, a teacher, by carefully studying student responses on a cloze test, can gather some other information, such as the following:

- The student's ability to use context clues. The lack of this skill is particularly evident when the inserted word is grammatically correct but the word makes little sense.
- The student's skill in spelling. This skill can be determined by examining the spelling of both correct and incorrect insertions and analyzing the student's spelling of both technical and nontechnical words.
- The student's ability to perceive grammatical structure. This skill can be determined by examining blanks that require noun-verb agreement and those requiring articles, prepositions, adjectives, and adverbs.

Babcock (1975) even feels teachers can sometimes determine a student's attitude toward particular courses by analyzing cloze responses. She demonstrated how, by their choice of certain words, some high school seniors enrolled in a social science course revealed their attitudes toward material possessions, religion, the poor, and law enforcement. For instance, the comments of two students, Babcock said, indicated that they "had arrived at some emotional involvement with the topic." Although this is a very interesting use of the cloze test, such an analysis is very subjective, and teachers using it would have to interpret responses cautiously.

While we have suggested that only exact words be counted as correct when scoring a cloze test, it would probably be wise to follow Thelen's (1976) advice. She advocates reevaluating the tests of those who score at the frustration level. Many of these students are able to replace deletions with acceptable synonyms. If they are able to do so to a significant degree (e.g., if counting synonyms as correct changes their reading level to either the instructional or the independent level), it seems fair to conclude that the book, in fact, would not be frustrating to them. Some teachers have reported that some of their best readers score poorly on cloze tests because synonyms are not counted as correct answers.

Example 1 illustrates the cloze test procedure with a passage taken from an ecology textbook.

## Example 1   Sample Cloze Test for Science

Along the coastal plains of the Atlantic and Gulf coasts to the south, scrub-pine forests are common. However, where these _____ are not disturbed by _____ or by fires, they _____ be replaced over a _____ of years by hardwoods _____ as hickory, oak, and _____ .

Of course, each of _____ kinds of forest could _____ further subdivided. The divisions _____ them are not abrupt. _____ are regions where mixtures _____ two kinds of forest _____ . Yet it is clear _____ it would be possible _____ divide the forest into _____ based upon the major _____ of trees present.

Would _____ divisions be useful? Are _____ different forests different from _____ other in significant ways?

_____ you wandered through these _____ , you would indeed notice _____ differences between them. In _____ coniferous forests of the _____ , the pines or other _____ trees form a thick _____ overhead throughout the year. _____ of the light and _____ is intercepted by the _____ needles of the trees. _____ small trees or shrubs _____ in this forest. The _____ is covered with a _____ of fallen needles and

_____ debris from the trees. _____ and mosses and a _____ flowering plants are scattered _____ over the ground.

The _____ inside the forest is _____ warmer than in the _____ . Wind is almost entirely _____ by the coniferous forest. _____ may hear a gale _____ the tops of the _____ , but scarcely more than _____ breeze can be felt _____ the forest floor.

The _____ , or deciduous, forests are _____ different. Here a much _____ amount of light and _____ reaches the forest floor, particularly in the winter, when the leaves have fallen from the trees. Although the trees block the wind to a great extent, the wind within a hardwood forest is much stronger than the wind in the coniferous forests of the north.[1]

Answers to Sample Cloze Test

| | | |
|---|---|---|
| 1. forests | 18. these | 35. Ferns |
| 2. logging | 19. each | 36. few |
| 3. may | 20. As | 37. sparsely |
| 4. period | 21. forests | 38. temperature |
| 5. such | 22. great | 39. noticeably |
| 6. magnolia | 23. the | 40. clearings |
| 7. these | 24. north | 41. blocked |
| 8. be | 25. evergreen | 42. You |
| 9. between | 26. layer | 43. whipping |
| 10. There | 27. Most | 44. trees |
| 11. of | 28. rainfall | 45. a |
| 12. exist | 29. crowded | 46. on |
| 13. that | 30. Few | 47. hardwood |
| 14. to | 31. grow | 48. quite |
| 15. regions | 32. ground | 49. greater |
| 16. kinds | 33. layer | 50. rainfall |
| 17. such | 34. other | |

1. Lawrence W. McCombs and Nicholas Rosa, *What's Ecology?* (Menlo Park, Calif.: Addison-Wesley, 1978), pp. 14–16.

# Group Reading Inventories

In previous sections of this book the importance of the various organizational patterns was stressed as well as the need for students to develop certain study skills. Yet none of the evaluation instruments discussed thus far directly diagnose these skills. The best approach for completing such a diagnosis is to use what Shepherd (1978) calls *group reading inventories*. In this type of test teachers first analyze their textbooks to determine what skills are required to comprehend it. They then construct test items from textbook passages that measure student proficiency in these skills.

This approach resembles what testing expert Popham (1978) describes as *criterion-referenced tests,* tests that are used to determine a student's status with respect to a well-defined skill area. According to Hambleton and Eignor (1979), when a criterion-referenced test is developed, domain specifications (in this case, reading skills) are prepared and items are written to measure them. Those test items that are *reflective* of the domain are written and should serve as a representative set of test items defined by the domain specification. Hambleton and Eignor listed the three uses of criterion-referenced scores: "(1) to make descriptive statements about what examinees can do; (2) to make instructional decisions; (3) to evaluate programs and their effectiveness" (Hambleton and Eignor, 1979, p. 13).

Our major concern is with the first two uses of criterion-referenced tests, because these uses will help teachers identify groups of students relative to their mastery or nonmastery of skills as measured by the test. These data help teachers make instructional decisions. They help them decide how much assistance the class as a whole and individuals and subgroups within the class will need on the reading/study skills that are germane to the textbook(s) that will be used in that particular classroom.

## Developing Group Inventories for Content Areas

The steps that follow are designed to help teachers develop a group inventory for any content area.

The first step is to *determine reading/study skills objectives.* Completing this step does not have to be the painful exercise that is often associated with writing instructional objectives. However, it may be helpful at this point to review the different types of objectives teachers may consider using as they survey the book(s) they will use in their course.

Some of the objectives teachers select may lend themselves to description in *behavioral* terms. Popham (1978) and Mager (1962) are two advocates of behavioral objectives that state the *actual behavior* required of a student in order to demonstrate mastery of an objective, the *conditions* under which the behavior is observed, and the *standard* used to determine mastery. Here is an example of a behavioral objective.

> Given five passages from a ninth grade social studies textbook (conditions), the student will write the main idea of each passage (actual behavior) with 80% accuracy (standard).

Other objectives selected may lend themselves to just a *description*. With these types of objectives teachers describe what the students will do and then they examine outcomes as they emerge. According to Otto, Rude, and Spiegel (1979), descriptive objectives are used when no "right" response or behavior can be prescribed beforehand. These types of objectives are especially useful when teachers are interested in the skills associated with critical reading and divergent thinking. Here are two examples.

> The learner evaluates the supporting evidence presented by an author to support his opinion.

> The learner infers, through their actions, the motives and traits of characters.

Selecting reading and study skills objectives helps teachers identify precisely what competencies their students will have to possess in order to have success with the textbook used in their courses. Once the skills objectives have been identified, teachers have a blueprint to follow as they design their inventory. An elaborate objective need not be written for each skill. A form such as the one in the accompanying table will help teachers develop their blueprint.

| Skill Objectives | Mastery Level |
|---|---|
| 1. Has knowledge of technical vocabulary | 80% correct |
| 2. Perceives cause/effect relations | 80% correct |
| 3. Locates parts of the book | 80% correct |
| 4. Interprets graphs | 80% correct |
| 5. Compares two sources on the same subject | Subjective analysis of student's comparison |
| 6. Recognizes biased statements | Subjective analysis of student's written answer |

Obviously this table does not represent a complete blueprint, but it is apparent that the first four skills could be written in behavioral terms (but why bother?) and the fifth and sixth skills could be written as descriptive objectives. Regardless of the type of objective involved, the important reason for completing step 1 is to identify the skills students will need in order to use the textbook successfully.

It is impossible to include in the inventory *every* skill students will be required to use when reading and studying the textbook. As teachers carefully analyze the textbook, they should consider the following:

- The amount of technical vocabulary or common words used in an uncommon way. Perhaps every inventory should include a section on vocabulary, because student scores on this section may give an indication of the schema students already possess relative to the content area.
- The major organizational patterns used in the book.
- The major study skills needed to read the book.
- The need to read at flexible reading rates.

In short, the test should include the skills the students will *most often* have to use as they read the text.

The second step in designing a group inventory is to *prepare test items to measure objectives*. As teachers prepare items for their inventory, they will have to decide on the type of test item they wish to use: multiple-choice, true/false, matching, brief essay. The type of item used often depends on the skills to be measured and the way mastery will be determined. Most commercial criterion-referenced tests use multiple-choice items. But these are difficult to write and are inappropriate for measuring skills associated with divergent thinking. There are no hard and fast rules for determining test formats. Teachers should consider all possibilities.

How many test items should be written to measure each skill? This question raises a dilemma. If too few items are written, say 2 or 3, it is difficult to make an accurate judgment about the student relative to that skill. If too many items are written for each skill, say 15 or 20, the test becomes too long. Most teachers settle on 5 to 8 items for each skill that can be measured objectively. Two or three brief essay questions are usually sufficient for evaluating skills requiring divergent thinking.

If multiple-choice items are to be included in an inventory, Hambleton and Eignor (1979) suggest that test makers ask themselves the following questions about their multiple-choice items.

1. Is the item stem clearly written for the intended group of students? [An item stem is the statement or question preceding the answer choices.]
2. Is the item stem free of irrelevant material?
3. Is a single problem clearly defined in the item stem?

4. Are the answer choices clearly written for the intended group of students?
5. Are the answer choices free of irrelevant material?
6. Is there a correct answer or a *clearly* best answer?
7. Have words like "always," "none," or "all" been removed?
8. Are likely student mistakes used to prepare incorrect answers?
9. Is "all of the above" avoided as an answer choice?
10. Are the answer choices arranged in a logical sequence (if one exists)?
11. Was the correct answer randomly positioned among the available answer choices?
12. Are all repetitious words or expressions removed from the answer choices and included in the item stem?
13. Are all of the answer choices of approximately the same length?
14. Do the item stem and answer choices follow standard rules of punctuation and grammar?
15. Are all negatives underlined?
16. Are grammatical cues between the item stem and the answer choices, which might give the right answer away, removed?
17. Are letters used in front of possible answer choices to identify them?
18. Have expressions like "which of the following is *not*" been avoided?
19. Disregarding any technical flaws which may exist in the test item (addressed by the first 18 questions) how well do you think the content of the test item matches with some part of the content defined by the domain specification? (Remember the possible ratings: 1 = poor, 2 = fair, 3 = good, 4 = very good, 5 = excellent.)[2]

If your inventory is going to include essay questions, completion items, true/false items, or matching items, you may want to refer to the guidelines that follow.

1. Essay questions.
   (a) Use the essay question to measure objectives that cannot be measured as well with any other question types.
   (b) Limit and define the freedom of students' responses to essay questions.
   (c) Use several brief essays instead of one or two extended essays.
   (d) Indicate clearly in each question the desired extent and depth of each answer.

2. Reproduced, by permission, from Hambleton and Eignor (1979).

2. Completion items.

   (a) The test item should be concrete so that the students' answers will be limited to one or two specific words or phrases.

   (b) Limit any one item to one or two completions.

   (c) Place the blank near or at the end of the statement.

   (d) Avoid extraneous clues to the correct answer.

3. True/false items.

   (a) Write precise, unambiguous statements.

   (b) Base true/false items on statements that are absolutely true or false, without qualifications or exceptions.

   (c) Highlight the main point of the question by placing it in a prominent position in the statement.

   (d) Avoid partly true and partly false statements.

   (e) Avoid long, involved statements with many qualifying clauses and trick questions.

   (f) Avoid negative questions.

   (g) Avoid extraneous clues in the form of specific determiners.

4. Matching items.

   (a) Group only homogeneous premises and homogeneous responses in a singly matching item.

   (b) Keep the lists of premises and responses relatively short, and clearly arrange them.

   (c) Explain clearly in the directions the basis on which items are to be matched and the procedure to be followed.

   (d) Avoid extraneous clues.

   (e) Provide extra items to reduce guessing.

# Scoring Group Inventories

The next step in designing group inventories is to *develop criteria for scoring.* Once the test is completed, the main question to ask is, "How well do my students have to score on each skill to be considered proficient in that skill?" Teachers must set their own standards. No one answer is applicable to all skills in all content areas. (Determining a specific cutoff or passing score is vital in some situations, as in a district minimal-competency test. However, our purpose is not to identify failures but to identify what skills to stress with a particular individual or group of students in a content area class.) Because we are so conditioned to scores of 70% and higher as an indication of passing, 70% is often chosen as the score that indicates mastery of a particular skill. Teachers

# Figure 7.1 Test Results of Group Inventory

| Skills | Names | | | | | | |
|---|---|---|---|---|---|---|---|
| | Andrew | Carol | Christine | David | George | Harold | Joan |
| Reading rate (words per minute) | 280 | 195 | 310 | 525 | 307 | 210 | 220 |
| Parts of the book (%) | 80 | 100 | 80 | 80 | 80 | 80 | 70 |
| Vocabulary/context (%) | 100 | 90 | 40 | 60 | 80 | 80 | 40 |
| Main ideas (%) | 90 | 60 | 60 | 70 | 70 | 70 | 90 |
| Sequence (%) | 89 | 76 | 51 | 89 | 63 | 100 | 89 |
| Interpreting data (%) | 80 | 60 | 40 | 30 | 40 | 50 | 60 |
| Interpreting tables (%) | 100 | 90 | 60 | 40 | 100 | 80 | 80 |

may decide on a score that is either higher or lower; the criterion could even vary with each skill tested. On essay questions, subjective judgments of pass/fail will have to be made.

The last step in designing inventories is to *keep records*. A record of the test results of the group inventory should be kept on a profile sheet (see Fig. 7.1). This record will enable the teacher to identify quickly the skills needs of the students. The profile sheet should include the names of the students and the skills included in the inventory. If students have a skill deficiency, a slash can be marked by the skill and under their names. The profile sheet helps teachers decide what skills they will stress and what teaching techniques they will use with their classes.

Teachers may want to share the test results with their students. There is some research evidence that indicates that administering diagnostic pretests to students and sharing the results with them has a positive effect on subsequent learning (Hartley and Davies, 1976). The researchers believe this outcome happens because the "pretest directs the students' attention to what it is they do not know and [they] then pay particular attention to remedying these deficiencies during subsequent instruction" (Hartley and Davies, 1976, p. 248).

| Judy | Kathy | Leona | Louise | Paul | Romeo | Steven | Stuart | Sally | Tom | Terry | Walter | Wendy |
|---|---|---|---|---|---|---|---|---|---|---|---|---|
| 225 | 610 | 405 | 318 | 240 | 260 | 285 | 212 | 112 | 318 | 327 | 280 | 290 |
| 90 | 90 | 90 | 100 | 100 | 70 | 70 | 70 | 70 | 80 | 90 | 100 | 100 |
| 60 | 70 | 60 | 90 | 50 | 80 | 40 | 50 | 80 | 40 | 40 | 90 | 80 |
| 50 | 60 | 100 | 90 | 70 | 60 | 50 | 60 | 80 | 40 | 50 | 60 | 70 |
| 63 | 63 | 76 | 100 | 63 | 63 | 89 | 51 | 89 | 63 | 76 | 100 | 89 |
| 60 | 50 | 70 | 80 | 50 | 60 | 60 | 20 | 70 | 50 | 60 | 60 | 60 |
| 10 | 50 | 30 | 80 | 80 | 70 | 90 | 40 | 100 | 90 | 100 | 60 | 60 |

## Sample Group Inventory

As an illustration of the value of the group skills inventory, a sample inventory is given in Example 2. This test was administered to a group of students; the results of the test are included in Fig. 7.1. Review the test scores and then answer the questions that follow the test.

### Example 2   Group Inventory for Social Studies

*General Directions:* The purpose of this inventory is to determine how well you can read the textbook that has been chosen for this course. Your grade will not be affected by your performance on this inventory. Each section has a separate set of directions. Read each set of directions carefully before answering the questions on your answer sheet.

Section A: Parts of the Book

Use the appropriate sections of your textbook to answer the following ten questions.

1. How many *sections* are in this textbook?
2. How many *chapters* are in this textbook?
3. Who wrote the book? What qualifies them to write this book?
4. (a) In what year was the book published?

   (b) Why is this information important?
5. Read the preface. What hints do the authors give you on how to study this textbook?
6. On what page is a list of maps?
7. Look up the topic "Inflation" in the index. On what pages in the textbook can you find information on that topic?
8. Find the glossary; look up the definition of *economy* and write it on your answer sheet.
9. (a) Do the chapters contain either overviews at the beginning or summaries at the end?

   (b) How will this information help you?
10. What chapter discusses the three branches of government?

Section B: Reading Rate

Read pages 25 to 36. There are approximately 4000 words on these pages.[3] When you finish reading, look at the blackboard and write the figure you see there in the blank labeled "Time _____ ." Then answer the questions in Sections C, D, E, and F. You may refer back to the chapter when answering these questions.

Section C: Vocabulary/Context

The sentences below are taken from the pages you just read. Place a check before the best meaning of the underlined word.

1. Congress passed a law that would make it illegal to help any <u>fugitive</u> slave.
_____ (a) free
_____ (b) runaway
_____ (c) disobedient
_____ (d) helpful
2. The government, not pleased with the division, claimed that <u>secession</u> was unconstitutional.
_____ (a) friendship
_____ (b) war

3. Reading rate is determined by dividing the number of seconds it takes to read into the number of words read and multipling by 60 (words ÷ seconds × 60). The teacher should record a new time every 5 seconds.

_____ (c) withdrawal

_____ (d) disagreement

3. Southerners wanted to <u>distend</u> the area in which slavery was permitted.

_____ (a) reduce

_____ (b) contain

_____ (c) destroy

_____ (d) expand

4. John Brown and his group of followers <u>inflamed</u> the South by capturing the guns and supplies at Harper's Ferry, Virginia.

_____ (a) pleased

_____ (b) angered

_____ (c) concerned

_____ (d) joined

Section D: Main Ideas

Reread the passages noted below. In no more than one or two sentences, write the main idea for each.

1. Passage 1: page 25, column 1, paragraphs 2 and 3.
   The main idea is:

2. Passage 2: page 26, column 1, paragraph 5.
   The main idea is:

3. Passage 3: page 28, column 2, paragraphs 1 and 2.
   The main idea is:

4. Passage 4: page 33, column 2, paragraph 4.
   The main idea is:

5. Passage 5: page 36, column 2, paragraph 3.
   The main idea is:

Section E: Sequence

The historical events listed below were discussed in the section you read. Arrange them in the proper historical sequence by placing the letter of the event that happened first next to the 1, the event that happened second next to the 2, and so on.

(a) The Republican party was founded and opposed the spread of slavery into territories.

(b) John Brown tried to organize a slave rebellion.

(c) Lincoln became president.

(d) Henry Clay proposed the Compromise of 1850.

(e) The Kansas-Nebraska Act made use of the idea of popular sovereignty.

(f) The capture of Fort Sumter was the beginning of violence between North and South.

(g) The Dred Scott decision was cheered in the South.

(h) Many southern states seceded from the Union and formed the Confederacy.

1. ____        5. ____
2. ____        6. ____
3. ____        7. ____
4. ____        8. ____

Section F: Interpreting Data

In this section you read about (a) abolitionists, (b) secessionists; (c) Republicans, (d) Democrats, and (e) Southerners. Read the following ten statements. Place the letter (a), (b), (c), (d), or (e), corresponding to the person most likely to have spoken the words, in the blank preceding the statement. There may be more than one answer.

____    1. "They should hang John Brown and his followers."

____    2. "The South cannot survive within this Union."

____    3. "Let's free the slaves right now."

____    4. "Slavery should not be allowed to expand into the territories."

____    5. "We are friends, not enemies; we cannot be enemies."

____    6. "Free speech, free press, free soil, free men."

____    7. "The North has gained in population and economy."

____    8. "Cotton is King."

____    9. "No man has a right to wrong another human being."

____   10. "What the states have joined, they can unjoin."

Section G: Interpreting Maps

Use the map on page 34 to answer the following questions.

1. How many states were there in the Union in 1859?

2. How many states were there in the Union in April 1861?

3. (a) Which states have the design $\boxed{\text{XXXX}}$ ?

   (b) What can you infer about these states?

4. What does the dotted line represent?

5. What territories were opened to slavery north of the line?

The following questions concern the test results for the group reading inventory in Example 2. Review the results given in Fig. 7.1 on pages 286–287 and then answer the questions.

1. List the students who may take a long time to complete homework assignments involving reading. Is there any way you could help them?
2. What advice would you offer to Kathy and Sally?
3. Which students appear to be very poor readers? How can you help them?
4. What skill has been mastered by most or all of the students?
5. What skill will have to be emphasized with most or all of the students?
6. Which students appear to be unable to interpret maps? How will you help them?
7. Since several students are having difficulty picking out main ideas, you probably would want to provide them with some direct instruction on that skill. Would you include Andrew, Joan, Leona, and Sally as part of the instructional group for these lessons? If not, what would they do during the time you taught these lessons?
8. Who do you suspect are the best readers in the class? Would you differentiate their reading assignments? If so, how would you do it?
9. What conclusions can you draw about the class performance on the vocabulary test and the sequence test? What are the implications to you as the teacher?

# Informal Reading Inventory (IRI)

After reviewing the results of achievement tests, cloze tests, or group inventories, teachers may be particularly concerned or puzzled about a few of their students. Thus they may wish to get a more detailed picture of their reading performance. They can do so by constructing and administering individual assessment instruments such as content area informal reading inventories (IRI), individual diagnostic analyses (IDA), and miscue analyses (MA). In this section we will discuss the informal reading inventory; we will consider the IDA and the MA in succeeding sections.

Content-specific *informal reading inventories* consist of graded materials from a content area such as English or social studies. They are accompanied by comprehension questions reflecting the various categories or levels of comprehension. IRIs are designed to determine an individual student's independent, instructional, and frustration reading levels and to reveal certain skills weaknesses in oral reading and comprehension. Readers who function at the *independent level* are reading at a level where they recognize words instantly and comprehend without, or almost without, error. Those who function at the *instructional level* are reading words somewhat fluently and are comprehending well. If the readers are inept in recognizing words as well as in comprehending ideas, they are reading at the *frustration level.* Unfortunately, many textbooks assigned by teachers at the middle and high schools are written at the student's frustration level.

## Criteria for Determining Reading Levels

Many years ago Betts (1946) created the criteria for establishing the various reading levels. Over the years reading educators and practitioners have modified the criteria. The accompanying table gives a set of criteria appropriate for middle and high school students.

|  | Independent Level | Instructional Level | Frustration Level |
|---|---|---|---|
| Word recognition | 95%–100% accuracy | 90%–94% accuracy | 0%–89% accuracy |
| Comprehension | 90%–100% correct | 70%–89% correct | 0%–69% correct |

## Constructing the Inventory

Content area teachers should select passages from subject matter areas that are directly related to the topics they plan to cover in their classrooms. The passages must vary in reading level and come from a variety of sources, one of which should be the classroom textbook; but the passages should be ones that have not been read previously by the student.

The reading levels of the selections should be calculated by using one or more of the readability formulas discussed in Chapter 8. Do not rely on the publisher's estimate of the book's reading level.

The passages should range in difficulty from one or two grades above the chronological placement of the student(s) to be tested to several grade levels below. A ninth grade teacher, for example, may have passages ranging from grade 6 to grade 11. The lower-level passages may be taken from so-called high-interest–low-vocabulary materials that can be found in some secondary commercial reading programs or from high-quality children's books that are available in school and public libraries. When using the latter source, teachers should be sure to select passages that are mature in content. It may take some searching to find such passages, but they are available.

Two passages ranging from 200 to 300 words are selected for each grade level. One is for oral reading; the other is for silent reading. Both teacher and student must have copies of the passages. At least five and preferably ten questions are written for each passage. Questions should be based on the various levels and tasks outlined in Barrett's taxonomy of reading comprehension (see Chapters 3 and 5). The questions should be passage-dependent; that is, they should be questions that reflect new information that students gained from reading the passage as opposed to questions that reflect information gained from their general knowledge or experiences. Howard's advice about test questions is well taken: "We must devise clearly stated, direct questions which do not give the answers away, and which are not so obtuse or esoteric that they frustrate the reader because he cannot understand what you want . . . the questions we ask must not become part of the problem" (Howards, 1980, p. 82).

## Administering the Inventory

Administering the IRI is an individual enterprise. The teacher begins one or two grade levels below the level he or she feels the student is currently functioning at. In the case of learning-disabled youngsters, this initial level may be *several* grade levels below the student's chronological grade placement.

If the initial reading selection is at the student's independent reading level, the student reads the passages at increasing levels of difficulty until the frustration level is reached on both the oral and the silent reading level. At this point the teacher may exercise the option of reading the frustration-level passages *to* the student and continuing to do so on higher-level passages until the student's *potential reading level* is determined. [Spache (1980) believes that the level at which students can comprehend at least 70% of the material read to them constitutes their potential reading level.]

If the initial-level passage(s) read by students turn out to be at or above their instructional level, they read below and above this point until appropriate levels are determined.

Howards again offers some sound advice for preparing the student for the test.

Before launching the student into the actual oral reading of the graded materials, try a little casual, natural conversation to reduce normal nervousness connected with any kind of reading testing. Some students dread any kind of test no matter how well disguised. Make this [experience] an interview and as conversational as pos-

# Figure 7.2  Marking System for Oral Reading

| Error Type | Suggested Marking |
|---|---|
| Hesitations: Student hesitates at least 2 seconds before pronouncing the word[a] | Mark a check above the word(s) on which the hesitation occurs:<br><br>$\checkmark$<br>the pathetic person |
| Insertions: Words are added to the beginning, middle, or end of a sentence or phrase | Use a caret ($\wedge$) and write in the insertion(s):<br><br>then<br>Johnson $\wedge$ announced |
| Inversions: Word order of two or more words is changed | Use an inverted wavy arrow:<br><br>Johnson announced later |
| Mispronunciations: A whole word or part of a word is mispronounced | Cross out the mispronounced word and write the phonetic replacement:<br><br>dōcŭmants　　　santry<br>documents in the sanctuary |
| Omissions: Word parts, complete words, or groups of words are omitted | Encircle word(s) omitted:<br><br>Johnson later announced |

[a]Some examiners do not count these as errors because they are strategies (not errors) that students use to decode properly.

sible. Use your common sense, remembering that your objective is to get the *best* performance from this person. Try not to present the [experience] as another test or as some special hurdle to be cleared, but rather as reading and discussing what has been read. (Howards, 1980, p. 79)

As the student reads the selection, the teacher marks errors. These will give insight into word recognition difficulties. When the reading has been completed, the student, without referring back to the selection, answers the comprehension questions asked by the teacher. Then the student reads the silent reading passage at the same level and answers the teacher's questions based on the selection.

| Error Type | Suggested Marking |
|---|---|
| Punctuation ignored: Poor use of or failure to use punctuation markings | Encircle ignored markings. <br><br> to Brandeis◯Before leaving◯he said. |
| Repetitions: A whole or part of a word/phrase is repeated. | Draw a wavy line beneath the word(s) repeated: <br><br> to Brandeis. Before leaving, he said. |
| Self-correcting: Without prompting, an error is corrected[a] | Put parentheses around the word(s) and write "SC" over the word(s): <br><br> SC <br> (to Brandeis). Before leaving, |
| Substitutions: A sensible word or word part is substituted for the original[a] | Cross out the original word; write in the substitution: <br><br> going <br> to Brandeis. Before ~~leaving~~, |
| Words pronounced by examiner: After the subject hesitates for 5 seconds, the examiner says the word | Underline the word: <br><br> to Brandeis. Before leaving, |

## Marking Oral Reading Errors

A marking system for the oral reading errors appears in Fig. 7.2. Teachers can, of course, develop their own marking system. In any case, the purpose is to mark every deviation from the text so that the teacher can later peruse these errors and decide what kinds of problems in word recognition the student has. In addition to marking the passages, teachers can also note and record behavior characteristics of the examinee such as head movements, finger pointing, unusually high or low volume, and, for silent reading, lip movements and subvocalizations.

## Scoring and Interpretation

Performance on both the oral and the silent reading passages is considered when scoring the IRI. Sometimes teachers discover a discrepancy between performance on the two passages. When a discrepancy occurs, use the comprehension score on the silent reading passage as the final criterion. The reasons for doing so are that nervousness can cause oral reading errors, some of the oral reading errors do not affect the quality of the student's comprehension, and most reading in the middle and high schools is done silently.

This guideline does not mean, however, that the student's oral reading performance should be ignored. A careful analysis of that performance often generates valuable diagnostic information. Here are several observations that have been noted on secondary students' oral reading.

- The student gives up on proper nouns.
- The student cannot attack multisyllable words.
- The student reads fluently but comprehends poorly.
- The student uses context clues well.
- The student mixes up short and long vowel sounds.
- The student does not use grammatical clues to his or her advantage.
- The student fails to recognize root words.
- The student's tone indicates interest in the subject.
- The student confuses basic sight words like *saw* for *was* and *of* for *it.*

## In Summary

The steps for constructing, administering, and scoring content area IRIs are summarized below.

1. Passages from a content area are selected. The passages should range from one or two grades above the chronological placement of the student(s) to be tested to several grade levels below.

2. Two passages ranging from 200 to 300 words are selected for each grade level: one for oral reading, the other for silent reading.

3. At least five and preferably ten questions are developed for each passage.

4. The student reads and answers questions until his or her independent, instructional, frustrational, and if desired, potential reading levels are determined. This procedure is done for both the oral and the silent reading passages.

## Limitations and Advantages of IRIs

Like all testing devices, the IRI is far from perfect. There is no question that the teacher's ability to accurately and objectively record oral reading errors and score the test influences the results. Some critics dislike the rigid standards used to determine the students' reading levels and question the accuracy of the formulas used to determine the level of difficulty of the passages. Finally, constructing and administering an IRI takes a great deal of time.

On the other hand, the IRI gives content area teachers a good picture of a student's reading ability, one that is more complete than those provided by using other testing instruments. It gives teachers a criterion to use should they be inclined to assign alternative reading materials to certain members of the class. If they decide to tutor the child or arrange for tutoring, teachers are armed with a great deal of information from which a prescriptive program can be planned.

Two alternatives to the IRI testing device—which we mentioned earlier in this section—both involving oral reading and comprehension testing, are briefly discussed next.

# Individual Diagnostic Analysis (IDA)

An individual diagnostic analysis is constructed in the same way an IRI is. The administration of the IDA is less formal, though, because the examiner is encouraged to ask a number of follow-up and probing questions. Such questioning allows the examiner to make more inferences about the student's attitudes, beliefs, and knowledge, and it allows the examiner to uncover more clues to the way the student thinks, reasons, and uses vocabulary and logic. Because of the liberal use of probing questions, scoring is more subjective and less rigid than it is for the IRI. Howards says the purpose of the IDA is to "assess reading competencies in a natural contextual reading situation [and] to quickly measure the student's reading performance cognitively and affectively" (Howards, 1980, p. 61).

The information a teacher gains from administering an IDA is very similar to that gained from administering an IRI. Howards, however, believes that enough information is obtained from the IDA to document a complete diagnostic analysis, including the students' oral reading performance and all the skills of phonics, structural analysis, comprehension, and study skills. While this goal is a worthwhile one, some supplementary criterion-referenced tests would have to be administered in order to gather all this useful information.

A very appealing feature of the IDA is the use of probing and follow-up questions. While this questioning can be done when using IRIs, rarely, if ever, is it recommended in the literature.

> Good questioning provides essential diagnostic information on reading and language performance and it can also provide us with useful information on the student's thinking, concepts, feelings, background, and experience. Probing questions concerning the text and

related questions about attitudes, beliefs and knowledge add greatly to a teacher's reservoir of knowledge and understanding of the student. It provides a more comprehensive context within which to make better judgments about the person and his performance. (Howards, 1980, pp. 81–82)

In his discussion on the quality of student answers, Howards points out that the examiner can

get many clues as to how the student gets the answer (syntactically, semantically and emotionally) and we can search for more clues to the way he thinks as well as what he understands or misunderstands. Also we can continue to question the student if a response is not completely clear. We can detect his logic and reasoning, his vocabulary. . . . Simply, with good probing questions and an understanding of what the answer tells us about the skills he has and how he uses them in context, as well as how he thinks and reasons, we have the kind of diagnostic information we need in order to develop our effective program of correction. (Howards, 1980, p. 82)

Readers who are interested in examples of probing and follow-up questions are referred to Chapter 3 of Howard's (1980) text.

The IDA is a fine alternative for those teachers who dislike the rigid standards of the IRI. On the other hand, the IDA may be too open-ended for those who prefer more precise testing instruments.

## Miscue Analysis (MA) for Content Areas

*Miscue* refers to deviations from the text that occur during oral reading. In *miscue analysis* miscues like repetitions and substitutions are carefully studied to determine the extent to which they interfere with the reader's ability to gain meaning from a passage. The teacher's main interest when administering an MA is to analyze the reader's *strategy* for getting meaning as opposed to assessing skills that are commonly associated with the act of reading. The purpose of MA reflects a view of many psycholinguists such as Cooper and Petrosky (1976), Goodman (1969), Smith (1978), and Weaver (1980). Its potential as a valuable diagnostic instrument for learning-disabled adolescents has also been recognized (Brown, 1978).

Our suggested procedure for applying MA to a student's reading performance on middle and secondary textbook material is adapted from the work of Goodman and Burke (1972) and Weaver (1980). Readers should not infer, however, that these educators would necessarily agree with the procedure suggested here.

## Procedure

Teachers select content that is about one year *above* the estimated reading level of the student. In that way the material is difficult enough to cause the reader to make miscues without overly frustrating him. If expository material is used for testing, the selection should represent a *whole* section of text, one that has complete ideas and has clear meaning outside the context of the textbook chapter. If literature is used, there should be enough information so that characters, event, plot, and theme are discernible.

The tester must be able to collect at least 35 miscues. The only miscues to be considered are substitutions, omissions, insertions, reversals, and self-corrections. Most psycholinguists consider some of the errors listed in Fig. 7.2 to be *positive* reading strategies. They do not believe that *all* miscues are bad. For example, a good reader will regress and repeat words to correct any miscue that does not make sense in context. Should the material be too frustrating, a less difficult passage should be available; a more difficult one should be available in case the reader is not making enough miscues. It is recommended that the first 10 miscues be ignored because they may be symptoms of nervousness rather than real miscues.

As testers analyze and code the 25 miscues, they should keep the following in mind:

1. If the reader omits most or all of a line of text (or more), do not number the miscue for later analysis. But make note of such omissions if they occur at all frequently.

2. If a reader more than once makes the *same substitution* for a content word, number and analyze only the first occurrence.

3. If one particular miscue seems to have caused one or more others, it may be best to consider them together as a single miscue. Here is one such example.

Ain't ever heard anybody ∧ call her a beauty.
                    much about

Instead of three omissions and one insertion, what we seem to have is a longer substitution miscue: "much about her beauty," instead of "anybody call her a beauty." Regardless of how we first marked these miscues on the work sheet, it is probably best to number and analyze them as a single miscue (Weaver, 1980, p. 175).

## Analyzing the Miscues

Each miscue should be analyzed carefully to determine whether it was self-corrected by the examinee and whether it made sense within the context (e.g., substituting *toad* for *frogs*, *beach* for *ocean;* making a slight change in tense; replacing a preposition such as *in* for *at.*) If either of these conditions existed

## Figure 7.3  Miscue Analysis Chart

| Word in Text | Student Miscue | Self-corrects? | | Sense in Context? | |
|---|---|---|---|---|---|
| | | Yes | No | Yes | No |
| 1. Yelled | Shouted | — | — | X | |
| 2. Laborer | Labels | X | | — | — |
| 3. | | | | | |
| 4. | | | | | |

for 70% or more of the miscues, then the miscues are probably *not* seriously interfering with comprehension. If either of the conditions existed for less than 70% of the miscues, then the reader may be experiencing comprehension loss and need help with the use of grammatical and meaning clues. These types of miscues can be summarized on a chart such as the one in Fig. 7.3. Sample miscue analyses appear in items 1 and 2. This chart is a great simplification of both Weaver's (1980) and Goodman and Burke's (1972) procedures for ana-lyzing miscues. Teachers who are interested in completing a more detailed analysis of miscues should refer to their work.

## Analyzing Comprehension

After the student has read the selection, he or she is to tell the examiner as much as possible about what was read. During this period the examiner neither interrupts nor asks any questions. As the student retells the contents of the selection, the examiner compares the oral responses to the prepared summary of the content, which contains the main ideas and significant supporting details of the selection. If the retelling is sparse, then the examiner asks questions to help the reader expand on the retelling.

During the retelling the examiner can check items on the summary that have been mentioned and circle those that were not mentioned. Because of the nature of this approach to diagnosis, evaluating the retelling (and to some extent the oral miscues) is very subjective. Weaver (1980) suggests that the various parts of the retelling or the entire retelling be rated on a scale such as the one that follows.

| 1 | 2 | 3 | 4 | 5 | 6 | 7 |
|---|---|---|---|---|---|---|
| Poor | | Adequate | | Good | | Excellent |

## In Summary

The miscue analysis for content areas is a rather subjective analysis of strategies students use to gain meaning from text. The student is given an appropriate selection to read. As the selection is read orally, the examiner records the student's miscues. After the selection is read, the student retells the selection to the examiner, who compares the student's version with a prepared summary of the reading selection. The examiner then analyzes the student's miscues and retelling performance. From the analysis the examiner makes an assessment of how proficient the student is in using strategies for gaining meaning from the text.

## Learning Styles

Some educators believe that teachers can provide more productive learning experiences for their students by determining their *learning styles* (Canfield and Lafferty, 1970; Dunn, Dunn, and Price, 1975; Hunt, 1979; Renzulli, 1978). According to Gregorc: "Learning Style consists of distinctive behaviors which serve as indicators of how a person learns from and adapts to his environment. It also gives clues as to how a person's mind operates" (Gregorc, 1979, p. 234).

Dunn and Dunn (1979) believe they have accumulated enough research data to identify at least eighteen elements related to the learning style of individuals. Four of them, sound, light, temperature, and design, relate to environmental elements. Four others relate to emotional elements: motivation, persistence, responsibility, and need for structure. The sociological elements consider whether one prefers working alone, with a small group or team, with a few friends, with an adult, or in some such combination or variation. Finally, the physical elements refer to perceptual strengths (visual, tactual, kinesthetic, auditory), intake (the need for eating, drinking, chewing, nibbling while studying), time (desirable study time), and mobility (need for movement). Figure 7.4 summarizes and graphically displays the eighteen elements.

## Learning Style Inventories

Dunn, Dunn, and Price (1975) believe their *Learning Style Inventory* is a valid and reliable instrument for identifying the individual learning preferences of students in grades 3 to 12. The inventory includes 100 statements to which students answer either true or false. Two sample statements are "Noise bothers

# Figure 7.4  Diagnosing Learning Styles

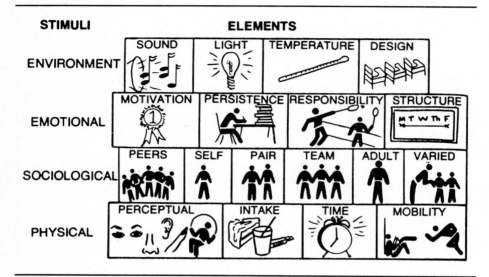

From Dunn and Dunn, *Teaching Students Through Their Individual Learning Styles: A Practical Approach*, 1978, p. 4. Reprinted with permission of Reston Publishing Co., a Prentice-Hall Co., 11480 Sunset Hills Rd., Reston, Va. 22090.

me when I am studying" and "I like to be told exactly what to do." All the statements are related to one of the eighteen elements discussed above.

Renzulli and Smith (1978) have also published a learning style inventory. Theirs is entitled *Learning Styles Inventory: A Measure of Student Preference for Instructional Techniques* and is designed to measure only student preferences for various instructional modes (projects, drill and recitation, peer teaching, discussion, teaching games, independent study, programmed instruction, lecture, and simulation). The inventory includes 65 statements about class activities that students rank as very pleasant, rather unpleasant, neither pleasant nor unpleasant. Two sample activity statements that students rank are "Reading a book in order to learn all about some topic" and "Working with a committee to prepare a lesson to present to the class."

Gregorc's (1982) approach to learning styles is to help individuals determine their "mediation abilities." His self-analysis tool, the *Gregorc Style Delineator,* helps individuals recognize and identify their most effective and efficient channels through which they perceive and express information. It is also designed to help people identify as many characteristics and behaviors as possible that are inherent in their style.

Individuals who complete the *Style Delineator* find out that their natural perceptions tend to lean more toward the abstract or the concrete and that their innate ordering qualities tend to be either linear (sequence) or nonlinear (random). They find that their personal orientation and capacity are such that they are "tipped" in one, two, or even three of the following styles: concrete/sequential (CS), abstract/sequential (AS), abstract/random (AR), and concrete/random (CR). According to Gregorc, all individuals possess all four qualities, but there is an inclination toward "tipping" that is natural and affects how individuals view themselves and how they are perceived by the world. The instrument, then, reveals the mediation abilities used by individuals to transact in and adapt to their environments, including the classroom and the home, and to conduct social interactions with others.

The *Style Delineator* consists primarily of descriptive words that the individual must rank-order. The words are equally strong as descriptors of preference and were selected to promote positive and negative psychological associations with the meaning of the word. The *Style Delineator* differs from most other learning style inventories in that it can reveal to individuals some learning styles that may not have been apparent to them or others. It also is not meant to be prescriptive in the sense that a match should be made between individuals' dominant styles and their environmental demands. Rather it is designed to help individuals understand their personal behavior, the behavior of others, and the demands placed on them by their environments.

Although learning style inventories appear to be useful instruments for identifying learning styles, Gregorc offers these caveats:

1. Instruments, by their very nature, are exclusive; that is, they focus on certain variables and therefore sacrifice other possibilities.

2. Some students wittingly or unwittingly lie on any type of self-reporting instrument. Others read elements into questions and statements that are simply not there.

3. Some students have used artificial means of adapting for so long that they report these as "preferred means of learning." By doing so they run the risk of receiving prescriptions that continue to reinforce artificiality rather than receiving means that would encourage and draw upon their natural abilities.

4. An educator's attitude (either positive or negative) toward a particular student or toward the concept of diagnosis/prescription itself can drastically influence both instrument interpretation and consequent prescription. (Gregorc, 1979, pp. 235–236)

Fischer and Fischer (1979) also are wary of questionnaires designed to identify learning styles and seem to prefer more research-oriented approaches such as the aptitude-treatment-interaction studies as advocated by Cronbach (1967).

# Figure 7.5 Model of Aptitude-Treatment-Interaction Study

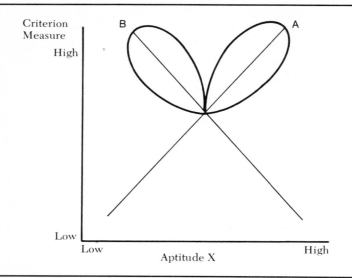

From Richard P. Santeusanio, "Do College Reading Programs Serve Their Purpose?" *Reading World* 13(1974):268. Reprinted by permission of the College Reading Association.

# Aptitude-Treatment-Interaction (ATI) Studies

The typical *aptitude-treatment-interaction study* is completed by selecting two modes of instruction (e.g., teacher-directed versus self-directed) that educators have reason to believe will interact differently with extremes of a measurable trait (e.g., introvert versus extrovert, high anxious versus low anxious). Students are randomly assigned to one of the two instructional modes. At the end of the instructional period the trait scores of the students are computed to see if they interact significantly with either of the modes of instruction. Regression lines are plotted, and if they intersect (see Fig. 7.5), a *disordinal interaction* has taken place, meaning that each instructional mode is better for certain types of students. For example, in one reading-related ATI study involving college freshmen enrolled in a reading improvement course, it was found that high-anxious students, students preferring a cognitive instructor, and those who viewed events in their lives as being externally controlled by others performed significantly better in a self-directed, individualized reading program (Santeusanio,

1972). In contrast, low-anxious students, students preferring an affective in-structor, and those who viewed events in their lives as being controlled internally by themselves performed significantly better in a teacher-directed group reading program.

According to Cronbach (1967), ATI research can help teachers assist *all* students in attaining the basic goals and objectives of various curricula. This goal is the same as that of *mastery learning*. While the proponents of mastery learning (Bloom, 1976) say this goal can be achieved by giving slower students more time to develop specific skills, Cronbach (1967) maintains that it can be done by differentially assigning students to appropriate treatments or instruc-tional modes.

## Teaching Styles

If teachers are interested enough to determine their students' learning styles or preferred modes of instruction, they should be prepared to vary their teaching style so that it is compatible with these styles or modes. Six styles of teaching are common (Fischer and Fischer, 1979). In the *task-oriented* style the teacher prescribes materials and demands specific performance; specified learnings may be individualized. In the *cooperative planner* style the teacher and student participate together in planning the student's programs of instruction. With the *child-centered* approach the student's interests and curiosity dictate the instruc-tional progam. In the *subject-centered* style organized content dictates the pro-gram, with little or no regard for individual differences. The *learning-centered* style is a combination of child-centered and subject-centered styles. Finally, the *emotionally exciting* style is a highly emotional, zealous approach to teaching.

Dunn and Dunn (1979) identify nine elements of teaching style. These elements include the teacher's instructional planning, student groupings, room design, teaching environment, personal characteristics, methodology, evalua-tion techniques, educational philosophy, and preference for students. They believe teachers can assess some of these elements in an instrument included in their faculty management and evaluation book (Dunn and Dunn, 1977).

Some research suggests that in certain situations student achievement can improve significantly when there is a match in learning and teaching styles (Domino, 1970; Farr, 1971; Rodriguez, 1978; Santeusanio, 1972). The im-plication of such research is that teachers need to vary their teaching styles because students have different styles of learning and different needs. Teachers must consider more than one way of approaching each of their lessons. The accompanying table (p. 306) lists some possible matches between student learning styles and an instructor's teaching style or an instructional technique.

At this point no research has been completed to support these suggested matches of learning style and teaching styles relative to content area reading

| Preferred Learning Style | Teaching Style or Instructional Technique |
| --- | --- |
| Lecture | Teacher-prepared structured overview |
| Independent study | Student-prepared structured overview |
| Small-group discussion | Small-group discussion of reading/study guide |
| Independent study | Individual response to adjunct questions |
| Little need for structure | Mapping note-taking system |
| Strong need for structure | Traditional note-taking system |
| Teaching games | Vocabulary reinforcement games |
| Drills and recitation | Direct teaching model |

instruction. Such research could contribute greatly to the improvement of teaching reading in the content areas. In the meantime, a point made by Dunn and her colleagues is well taken: "We can no longer assume that all students will learn through whichever strategy the teacher prefers to use" (Dunn et al., 1981, p. 372).

## Summary

Teachers can use different types of tests to determine the reading level and mastery of specific reading and study skills of their students. The major instruments are achievement tests, cloze tests, group reading inventories, and individual assessments.

Achievement tests are recommended for teachers who wish to determine the general reading ability of their students and how their students' achievement in reading compares to similar types of students in the country. Cloze tests are recommended for teachers who wish to determine the general ability of their students to read the specific book(s) chosen for use in their classroom. Group reading inventories are recommended for teachers who wish to determine the specific skills strengths and weaknesses of their students.

Individual assessments are recommended for teachers who want a detailed analysis of those students that concern and puzzle them. Content area informal reading inventories can help teachers determine an individual's independent, instructional, and frustrational reading levels. Fairly stringent criteria are used to determine these levels. A teacher can also determine these levels by administering an individual diagnostic analysis, but this instrument uses less formal criteria and, through the examiner's liberal use of probing questions, also provides inferences about a student's background, attitudes, and beliefs. Another type of individual assessment is the content area miscue analysis. This instrument is designed to analyze a reader's *strategy* for getting meaning as opposed to diagnosing specific skills or determining different reading levels.

# The Accident, Part II

Nora Ellsworth will be a substitute teacher for Nancy Andrews, who was involved in a serious bicycle accident. Nora is concerned about getting to know the strengths and weaknesses of the 125 students for whom she will be responsible during the next several months.

"Why don't you check with Nancy's friend Louie Caputo," Principal Keohane suggested. "He teaches right next door to her. I know Nancy keeps lots of records on her students. Lou probably will know where she keeps them."

"That's a good idea. When do you think I could chat with him?"

"Let me look up his program. Let's see. . . . It looks like he has a free period at eleven o'clock. I'll call on the intercom and tell him that you'll be up to see him at eleven."

"Fine."

As Nora strolled through Caputo's classroom door at eleven, he greeted her: "Good to see you again, Nora. It looks like we'll be seeing lots of each other."

"That's for sure!"

"Drew tells me you're interested in seeing Nancy's student records."

"That's right."

"Well, you're in luck. You probably already know how methodical Nancy is."

"Oh, yes!"

"I know she keeps her records in that file cabinet over there. I have a key to it because we exchange duplicate keys in case we forget or misplace them. Poor Nancy ends up opening my files almost every day! Anyhow, let's see what we can find for you."

As Caputo opened the file cabinet, he said, "I know Nancy gave her own reading tests to these rascals in September. She probably has them recorded some place. Let's see. . . . Here's her Period A class. Just as I thought—diagnostic tests on reading and study skills! You can see which students don't know how to find main ideas. Almost everybody in this class can pick out cause/effect relationships. Say, Nora, what's this 'cloze' score supposed to mean?"

Teachers may also be able to determine the learning styles of their students by administering learning style inventories. When there is a match between student learning styles and instructional teaching styles, students are apt to attain a higher level of achievement.

# Bibliography

## General

Armbruster, Bonnie B., Robert J. Stevens, and Barak Rosenshine. *Analyzing Content Coverage and Emphasis: A Study of Three Curricula and Two Tests.* Urbana: Center for the Study of Reading, University of Illinois, 1977.

Babcock, Natalie C. "Cloze Procedure and the Affective Domain." In *Proceedings of the Eighth Annual Conference of the Western College Reading Association,* edited by Roy Sugimoto. Santa Fe Springs, Calif., 1975.

Betts, Emmett. *Foundations of Reading Instruction.* New York: American Books, 1946.

Bloom, Benjamin S. *Human Characteristics and School Learning.* New York: McGraw-Hill, 1976.

Board of Directors of the International Reading Association. "Board Position, Misuse of Grade Equivalents." May 1980.

Bormuth, John R. "Comparable Cloze and Multiple-Choice Comprehension Test Scores." *Journal of Reading* 11(1967):291–299.

———. "Cloze Test Readability: Criterion Referenced Scores." *Journal of Educational Measurement* 5(1968):189–196.

Brown, Virginia. "Curriculum Development Resources." In *Teaching the Learning-Disabled Adolescent,* edited by Lester Mann, Libby Goodman, and J. Lee Wiederholt. Boston: Houghton Mifflin, 1978.

Buros, Oscar K., ed. *The Eighth Mental Measurements Yearbook.* 2 vols. Highland Park, N.J.: Gryphon Press, 1978.

Canfield, A. A., and J. C. Lafferty. *Learning Styles Inventory.* Detroit: Humanics Media, 1970.

Cooper, Charles R., and Anthony R. Petrosky. "A Psycholinguistic View of the Fluent Reading Process." *Journal of Reading* 20(1976):184–207.

Cronbach, Lee J. "The Two Disciplines of Scientific Psychology." *American Psychologist* 12(1967):671–681.

Domino, George. "Interactive Effects of Achievement Motivation and Teaching Style on Academic Achievement." *ACT Research Report* 39(1970):1–9.

Dunn, Rita S., Thomas DeBello, Patricia Brennan, Jeff Krimsky, and Peggy Murrain. "Learning Style Researchers Define Differences Differently." *Educational Leadership* 38(1981):372–375.

Dunn, Rita S., and Kenneth J. Dunn. *Administrator's Guide to New Programs for Faculty Management and Evaluation.* West Nyack, N.Y: Parker, 1977.

———. "Learning Styles/Teaching Styles: Should They . . . Can They . . . Be Matched?" *Educational Leadership* 36(1979):238–244.

Dunn, Rita S., Kenneth J. Dunn, and Gary E. Price. *Learning Style Inventory.* Lawrence, Kans.: Price Systems, 1975.

Farr, Beatrice J. *Individual Differences in Learning: Predicting One's More Effective Learning Modality.* Ann Arbor, Mich.: University Microfilms, July 1971, 1332.

Fischer, Barbara Bee, and Louis Fischer. "Styles in Teaching and Learning." *Educational Leadership* 36(1979):245–251.

Goodman, Kenneth S. "Analysis of Oral Reading Miscues: Applied Psycholinguistics." *Reading Research Quarterly* 5(1969):9–30.

Goodman, Yetta M., and Carolyn L. Burke. *Reading Miscue Inventory Manual.* New York: Macmillan, 1972.

Gregorc, Anthony F. "Learning/Teaching Styles: Potent Forces Behind Them." *Educational Leadership* 36 (1979):234–236.

————. *Gregorc Style Delineator.* Maynard, Mass.: Gabriel Systems, Inc., 1982.

Hambleton, Ronald K., and Daniel R. Eignor. "Introduction to Criterion Referenced Testing." In *Assessment of Minimum Competency in Basic Skills.* Princeton, N.J.: Educational Testing Service, 1979.

Hartley, James, and Ivor K. Davies. "Preinstructional Strategies: The Role of Pretests, Behavioral Objectives, Overviews and Advanced Organizers." *Review of Educational Research* 46(1976):239–265.

Howards, Melvin. *Reading Diagnosis and Instruction, An Integrated Approach.* Reston, Va.: Reston, 1980.

Hunt, David E. "Learning Styles and Students Needs: An Introduction to Conceptual Level." In *Student Learning Styles: Diagnosing and Prescribing Programs,* edited by James W. Keefe, pp. 27–38. Reston, Va.: National Association of Secondary School Principals, 1979.

Mager, Robert F. *Preparing Instructional Objectives.* Palo Alto, Calif.: Fearon, 1962.

Otto, Wayne, Robert Rude, and Dixie Lee Spiegel. *How to Teach Reading.* Reading, Mass.: Addison-Wesley, 1979.

Popham, W. James. *Criterion-Referenced Measurement.* Englewood Cliffs, N.J.: Prentice-Hall, 1978.

Pyrczak, Fred. "Definitions of Measurement Terms." In *Reading Tests and Teachers: A Practical Guide,* edited by Robert Schreiner. Newark, Del.: International Reading Association, 1979.

Rankin, Earl F., Jr. "The Cloze Procedure: Its Validity and Utility." In *Measurement and Evaluation of Reading,* edited by Roger Farr. New York: Harcourt, Brace & World, 1970.

Renzulli, Joseph S., and Linda H. Smith. *Learning Styles Inventory: A Measure of Student Preference for Instructional Techniques.* Mansfield Center, Conn.: Creative Learning Press, 1978.

Rodriquez, Joan H. "Abstract of Trait-Treatment Interaction Research: A Valuable Source for Individualizing Reading Instruction." *Reading World* 18(1978):148–155.

Royer, James M., and Donald J. Cunningham. *On the Theory and Measurement of Reading Comprehension,* Technical Report no. 91. Urbana: Center for the Study of Reading, University of Illinois, 1978.

Santeusanio, Richard P. *The Relationship of Individual Differences to Two Instructional Approaches in a College Reading Study Skills Course.* Ann Arbor, Mich.: University Microfilms, 1972, No. 73-14, 674.

Shepherd, David L. *Comprehensive High School Reading Methods.* 2nd ed. Columbus, Ohio: Merrill, 1978.

Smith, Frank. *Understanding Reading.* New York: Holt, Rinehart and Winston, 1978.

Spache, George D. *Diagnostic Reading Scales.* Monterey, Calif.: CTB/McGraw-Hill, 1980.

Taylor, W. "Cloze Procedure: A New Tool for Measuring Readability." *Journalism Quarterly* 40(1953):414–438.

Thelen, Judith. *Improving Reading in Science.* Newark, Del.: International Reading Association, 1976.

Viox, Ruth. *Evaluating Reading and Study Skills in the Secondary Classroom.* Newark, Del.: International Reading Association, 1968.

Weaver, Constance. *Psycholinguistics and Reading: From Process to Practice.* Cambridge, Mass.: Winthrop, 1980.

## Achievement Tests

*Basic Skills Assessment Test.* Grades 7 to adult. ETS/Addison-Wesley, 1979.

*California Achievement Test: Reading.* Grades 6–12, levels 16–19. CTB/McGraw-Hill, 1978.

*Comprehensive Assessment Program: Reading.* Grades 6–12. Scott, Foresman, 1979.

*Comprehensive Tests of Basic Skills.* Levels H, I, J. CTB/McGraw-Hill, 1981.

*Gates-MacGinitie Reading Test.* Levels E and F. Riverside Press, 1978.

*Iowa Silent Reading Test.* Grades 6–12, college. Psychological Corporation, 1978.

*Iowa Test of Basic Skills.* Levels 12–18. Riverside Press, 1978.

*McGraw-Hill Basic Skills Tests: Reading, Study Skills, Vocabulary.* College-bound juniors and seniors, college. McGraw-Hill, 1970.

*Metropolitan Achievement Test: Reading.* Grades 6–12, Psychological Corporation, 1978.

*Nelson-Denny Reading Test.* High school, college. Riverside Press, 1976.

*Nelson Reading Skills Test.* Grades 7–9 (level C). Riverside Press, 1977.

*Sequential Tests of Educational Progress: Reading.* Levels G–J. ETS/Addison-Wesley, 1978.

*SRA Achievement Series: Reading.* Levels F, G, H. Science Research Associates, 1978.

*Stanford Achievement Test: Reading.* Intermediate level II, advanced level. Psychological Corporation, 1973.

*Stanford Diagnostic Reading Test.* Brown and blue levels. Harcourt Brace Jovanovich, 1976.

*Publishers' addresses* for the tests listed above are as follows:

CTB/McGraw-Hill Division, Del Monte Research Park, Monterey, Calif. 93940.

ETS/Addison-Wesley, South Street, Reading, Mass. 01867.

Harcourt Brace Jovanovich, Inc., 757 Third Avenue, New York, N.Y. 10017.

McGraw-Hill Book Company, 1221 Avenue of the Americas, New York, N.Y. 10020.

The Psychological Corporation, 757 Third Avenue, New York, N.Y. 10017.
Riverside Press, Pennington-Hopewell Road, Hopewell, N.J. 08525.
Science Research Associates, Inc., 155 North Wacker Drive, Chicago, Ill. 60606.
Scott, Foresman and Company, 1900 East Lake Avenue, Glenview, Ill. 60025.

# Chapter 8
# Applying
# Readability Formulas

# The Rating Game, Part I

"I give it a nine," said Mrs. Grady.

"Put me down for an eleven," added Miss Dean.

"I say a ten in honor of Bo Derek," submitted Mr. Christensen.

"Do you really think it's a ten or are you playing your favorite role of male chauvenist?" Miss Dean asked.

"I'm serious about my ten—and I'm not a chauvenist!" replied Mr. Christensen.

"OK, calm down you two," said Mrs. Grady. "I have a nine, a ten, and an eleven. Where do we go from here? Does the publisher say anything about it?"

"I don't think so," Miss Dean answered. "I looked through the teacher's manual and couldn't find anything. Maybe they mention it in their advertising."

"Nope," offered Mr. Christensen. "I already checked it."

"OK," said Mrs. Grady. "We'll just have to go with our own guesses. Our guesses range from grade 9 to grade 11. Let's take a look at the next book."

Mrs. Grady, chairperson of the tenth grade social studies text selection committee, handed out another American history text to the other two members of the committee. They wanted to be sure that the new book

## Introduction

Procedures for determining the approximate grade level of written discourse have existed for several decades. Researchers devised these procedures because teachers, in addition to their subjective opinions, wanted some objective data to use in estimating the appropriateness of different textbooks for particular groups of students.

Many factors affect the readability of textbooks. Some of these factors, such as interest, appeal, the abstractness and density of concepts, and paragraph organization, are very difficult, if not impossible, to measure objectively. Two factors—word difficulty, as measured by word length or number of syllables, and sentence length—can be measured objectively. These factors, therefore, have been given primary importance by the creators of readability techniques.

Readability scores are not absolutes; they only provide an estimate of a book's difficulty level. Vaughan (1976) believes that a grade should be added and subtracted to the readability score attained from applying readability formulas. This technique will probably increase the validity of the reading-level they adopted for their course would be suitable for their students.

"Now this book has a companion volume that goes along with it. The publisher claims that the regular edition is written at the tenth grade level and the companion edition is written at the eighth grade level and you can use both books at the same time in one class."

"You mean one for the dummies and one for the not-so-dumb," Mr. Christensen commented sarcastically.

"Cut it out, Harry," cried Mrs. Grady. "Be serious. Didn't you use a program like this when you taught in another school?"

"Yes, I did. And seriously, folks, the students who used the companion volume were teased by the ones who used the regular edition. My recommendation is to use all regular editions in the class or all companion editions. Using both in one class just doesn't work out."

"Well, I'd like to keep this dual-book option open," said Miss Dean.

"Fine," said Mrs. Grady. "In any event, we at least got the reading levels from the publisher."

"Don't be so sure about what the publishers say. How do they know for sure? Their guess is as good as ours."

"They must have some way of knowing," said Mrs. Grady. "Do you think Mrs. Adams, our reading director, would know how they do it?"

At the end of the chapter you will find out how Mrs. Adams helped the social studies teachers.

estimates. For example, if a readability formula yields a grade score of 9, then a safe estimate of the readability range for the book is grade 8 to 10.

## Readability Procedures

Two readability procedures widely used by middle and secondary teachers have been developed by Fry (1968, 1977) and McLaughlin (1969). Both procedures are recognized for their brevity and simplicity. Another simple procedure was developed by Raygor (1977) and validated by Baldwin and Kaufman (1979). These three procedures are described in the following sections.

## Fry Procedure

When Edward Fry introduced his technique, he noted that few teachers, librarians, or publishers used the readability formulas that were then available because of the time it took to apply them. Without a doubt, Fry's simpler

# Figure 8.1 Fry Graph and Directions for Estimating Readability

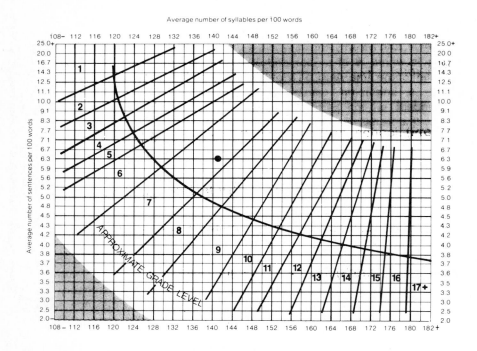

Average number of syllables per 100 words

approach has contributed to the current widespread use of readability measures. Fry has presented data on the validity of his procedure by completing correlation studies with the older, more complicated Dale-Chall and Spache readability formulas.

*Fry's procedure* involves selecting three or more 100-word passages, counting the number of syllables in the words in those passages, and determining the length of the sentences contained in the passages. The averages of the syllable counts and sentence lengths are plotted on a graph. Directions for using the Fry procedure appear in Fig. 8.1, along with Fry's readability graph.

## Raygor Procedure

Alton Raygor (1977) felt he could improve on Fry's procedure for determining the readability of books. In *Raygor's procedure* one counts words containing six or more letters instead of counting the number of syllables. This practice,

**Expanded Directions for Working Readability Graph**

1. Randomly select three (3) sample passages and count out exactly 100 words each, beginning with the beginning of a sentence. Do count proper nouns, initializations, and numerals.

2. Count the number of sentences in the hundred words, estimating length of the fraction of the last sentence to the nearest one-tenth.

3. Count the total number of syllables in the 100-word passage. If you don't have a hand counter available, an easy way is to simply put a mark above every syllable over one in each word, then when you get to the end of the passage, count the number of marks and add 100. Small calculators can also be used as counters by pushing numeral 1, then push the + sign for each word or syllable when counting.

4. Enter graph with *average* sentence length and *average* number of syllables; plot dot where the two lines intersect. Area where dot is plotted will give you the approximate grade level.

5. If a great deal of variability is found in syllable count or sentence count, putting more samples into the average is desirable.

6. A word is defined as a group of symbols with a space on either side; thus, *Joe, IRA, 1945,* and *&* are each one word.

7. A syllable is defined as a phonetic syllable. Generally, there are as many syllables as vowel sounds. For example, *stopped* is one syllable and *wanted* is two syllables. When counting syllables for numerals and initializations, count one syllable for each symbol. For example, *1945* is four syllables, *IRA* is three syllables, and *&* is one syllable.

---

From Edward Fry, "Fry's Readability Graph: Clarifications, Validity, and Extension to Level 17," *Journal of Reading* 21(1977):249.

he felt, would increase accuracy and decrease the time needed to complete readability studies.

Baldwin and Kaufman (1979) prefer the Raygor approach over Fry's because Raygor eliminates the need to count syllables. Thus he "has created a readability procedure which permits linguistic predictions in the absence of linguistic insights. Counting long words is a purely mathematical task; counting syllables requires a linguistic awareness which content area teachers, especially, may not have developed" (Baldwin and Kaufman, 1979, p. 152). In their study Baldwin and Kaufman found that 155 graduate and undergraduate students were able to apply the Raygor technique in 25% less time than the time they needed to use the Fry technique. Errors were noted when using both procedures. One type was in counting syllables (Fry); the other was in plotting scores

# Figure 8.2 The Raygor Readability Estimate

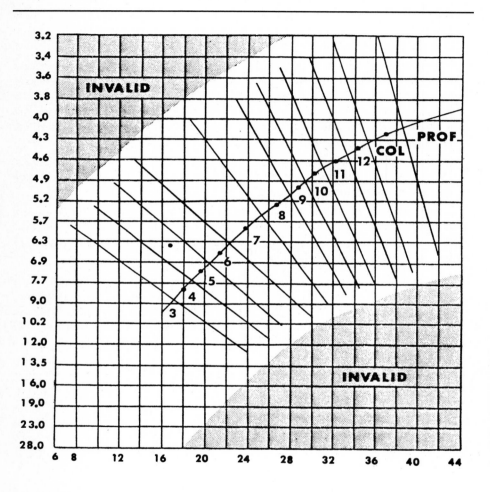

*Directions:* Count out three 100-word passages near the beginning, middle, and end of a selection or book. Count proper nouns, but not numerals.

1. Count sentences in each passage, estimating to nearest tenth.
2. Count words with six or more letters.
3. Average the sentence length and word length over the three samples and plot the average on the graph.

## Example

|  | **Sentences** | **6+ Words** |
|---|---|---|
| A | 6.0 | 15 |
| B | 6.8 | 19 |
| C | 6.4 | 17 |
| Total | 19.2 | 51 |
| Average | 6.4 | 17 |

Note mark on graph. Grade level is about 5.

on the graph (Raygor). Finally, the study demonstrated a high correlation between the Fry and Raygor techniques when they were applied to the same content.

Complete directions for using the Raygor procedure appear in Fig. 8.2.

# McLaughlin Procedure (SMOG)

The easiest readability technique to apply was developed by G. Harry Mc-Laughlin (1969). His "Simple Measure of Gobbledygook" (*SMOG*), like the techniques developed by Fry and Raygor, is based on both word length and sentence length. SMOG is a very quick predictor of readability because one counts only the polysyllabic (defined as having three or more syllables) words in three 10-sentence samples. Sentence length is a variable in this technique: if authors write long sentences, more polysyllabic words usually appear, resulting in higher readability levels. Conversely, if authors write short sentences, fewer polysyllabic words usually appear, resulting in lower readability levels.

The steps for completing a SMOG readability study follow.

1. Select 10 consecutive sentences near the beginning of the text, 10 in the middle, and 10 at the end, for a total of 30 sentences.

2. In the 30 selected sentences, count the words that contain three or more syllables. Any string of letters or numerals that contains three or more syllables when read aloud should be counted.

3. If polysyllabic words are repeated, count the repetitions.

4. Estimate the square root of the total number of polysyllabic words by taking the square root of the nearest perfect square. (For example, if the count is 85, the nearest perfect square is 81, which yields a square root of 9.)

5. If the total number of polysyllabic words falls roughly between two perfect squares, choose the lower number.

6. Add 3 to the approximate square root. This result gives the reading grade level that students must have if they are to understand the text completely.

For convenience, the accompanying table is provided for converting polysyllabic word counts to the nearest perfect square root.

| Polysyllabic Word Count | Nearest Perfect Square | +3 | Reading Level |
|:---:|:---:|:---:|:---:|
| 1–2 | 1 | +3 = | 4 |
| 3–6 | 2 | +3 = | 5 |
| 7–12 | 3 | +3 = | 6 |
| 13–21 | 4 | +3 = | 7 |
| 22–31 | 5 | +3 = | 8 |
| 32–43 | 6 | +3 = | 9 |
| 44–57 | 7 | +3 = | 10 |
| 58–73 | 8 | +3 = | 11 |
| 74–91 | 9 | +3 = | 12 |
| 92–111 | 10 | +3 = | 13 |
| 112–133 | 11 | +3 = | 14 |
| 134–157 | 12 | +3 = | 15 |
| 158–184 | 13 | +3 = | 16 |

Often when teachers apply the SMOG readability procedure and the Fry and Raygor procedures to the same material, they find that SMOG yields a higher readability level. This outcome happens because McLaughlin has attempted to identify a reading level required for *full* understanding of the text. The SMOG procedure predicts the reading ability level required for 90% to 100% comprehension (Estes and Vaughan, 1978). Students who have attained the reading level indicated by a SMOG readability study would need little or no guidance or assistance in order to understand the text. They could read the text independently.

The Fry and Raygor techniques, on the other hand, estimate the reading ability students need in order to understand the material with 50% to 75%

accuracy. Let us assume a Fry readability study yielded a grade-level score of 10. If a student's reading grade level was approximately at the tenth grade level, he could use this material but would need some instructional assistance from the teacher. He could not read the book independently.

# Limitations of Readability Procedures

Critics of readability procedures feel there is more to estimating the ease or difficulty of textboks than numbers or syllables per word and sentence length. Collins and his colleagues (1977), for example, mention "extra linguistic variables." These variables include illustrations, reader interest, reader knowledge, and writer's purpose and style.

In the past, few carefully controlled studies focused on the extent to which illustrations contribute to the readability of textbooks. However, recent research indicates that they probably do have a positive effect (Jenkins and Pany, 1981). Pictures and cartoons may help students recognize the author's intent. Graphs, charts, and maps may clarify information contained in the text.

Reader interest probably has a profound effect on readability. Unfortunately, the research in this area contains methodological problems (Collins *et al.* 1977). But common sense tells us that when students have an interest in an author's topic, they will more actively and readily seek that information and will find it more readable. That is, these students may find the reading easy. Unfortunately, many students do not have an interest in reading textbooks that they must read to fulfill various school assignments and requirements. In these cases the author's message is less readable, and students may find the material difficult.

The most important extra linguistic variable related to readability may be the student's knowledge of the assigned reading topic. It would appear that the more knowledge readers have concerning an author's topic, the more readable, or less difficult, the written material will be for them. If readers have little or no knowledge of the author's topic, the written material will be less readable, or more difficult to read.

The author's purpose in and style of writing may affect the readability of a text, but current readability techniques are unable to account for these variables. Many of us know how difficult it is to follow directions for assembling toys. How many of us find do-it-yourself manuals difficult to read? What about the subtleties of persuasive writing? How many of us lose interest and concentration when reading heavily detailed information? Many examples of prose and poetry contain simple words but complex ideas. Gordon (1980), for example, found that different readability formulas yielded scores ranging from fourth to tenth grade level when they were applied to Plato's *Parmenides*.

A readability formula could yield a deceptively low grade-level score because a writer uses simple language, but the text could, in fact, be very difficult because the writer did not live up to his or her contract (as discussed in Chapter 1). In other words, the text may be difficult to read because the author has been uninformative, irrelevant, or unclear. When authors display these characteristics, they have failed to write a "considerate" text (Armbruster and Anderson, 1981). Armbruster and Anderson have developed extensive guidelines designed to evaluate the considerateness of textbooks. These guidelines help teachers determine how considerate textbook authors are relative to the structure, coherence, unity, and audience-appropriateness of their text.

A *well-structured text* makes the author's topic, purpose or question, and writing pattern readily apparent to the reader. Titles, headings, and topic sentences, if the author uses them, match the author's purpose. The author uses a consistent structure when organizing his or her ideas.

A *coherent text* has its ideas woven together smoothly. The relationship among ideas is stated explicitly rather than inferentially. For example, cause/effect relationships are explicitly stated with the use of signal words. A coherent text also presents temporal sequences in the order that they actually occurred, and references to pronouns, qualifiers, noun phrases, and verb phrases are clear.

A *unified text* sticks to its purpose. The ideas contained in it contribute direcly to fulfilling the author's purpose. When adjunct aids are used, such as excerpts from diaries and human interest stories on personalities related to the content, they are in boxed-in areas and appendices.

An *audience-appropriate text* matches the readers' knowledge base. It contains ideas that take the readers' prior knowledge into account and defines technical terms and vocabulary when knowing their meaning is an intrinsic part of learning the content.

The legibility and visibility of a textbook also influence its readability. Dechant and Smith (1977) consider these factors to be major determinants of reading efficiency and ease. They believe factors such as line length, type size, style of typeface, space between lines and between letters, margins, and physical format are important (*legibility*). They also mention the textbook pages' color, finish, and print color (*visibility*). After reviewing the related research on legibility and visibility of textbooks, Dechant and Smith concluded that these variables "allow the sensory process to operate efficiently, and thus form a basis for the perceptual process of comprehensibility or readability" (Dechant and Smith, 1978, p. 305).

Many factors, then, must be considered when judging the suitability of textbooks for students. Jevitz and Meints (1979) have developed a comprehensive set of guidelines teachers can use when they are involved in the selection of text materials. Their guidelines are reproduced in Fig. 8.3.

# Figure 8.3  Guidelines for Textbook Evaluation

Name of textbook:                          Publisher:

Author:

Copyright date:                            Cost:

Evaluated by:

|  | Yes | No | Not Applicable |
|---|---|---|---|
| **A. Readability** | | | |
| 1. Readability of text. _____ | | | |
| 2. Formula used. _____ | | | |
| 3. Reading level is realistic for the students who will be using the text. | ___ | ___ | ___ |
| **B. Authority** | | | |
| 1. Author is a well-qualifed authority and reliable in this field. | ___ | ___ | ___ |
| 2. Author has certain biases or philosophies of which to be aware. | ___ | ___ | ___ |
| 3. Copyright date is recent enough to be up-to-date and reliable in the particular field. | ___ | ___ | ___ |
| 4. Publisher has a reputation for high quality and responsible publications. | ___ | ___ | ___ |
| 5. Publishing house is independently owned. | ___ | ___ | ___ |
| **C. Vocabulary** | | | |
| 1. Text identifies key words in each chapter or unit. | ___ | ___ | ___ |
| 2. Text presents vocabulary words which are most vital to the key concepts of the material. | ___ | ___ | ___ |
| 3. Key vocabulary words are printed in bold or italicized print and can be easily recognized. | ___ | ___ | ___ |

(continued)

# Figure 8.3 (continued)

|  | Yes | No | Not Applicable |
|---|---|---|---|
| 4. Key vocabulary words are listed either before or following the chapter. | ___ | ___ | ___ |
| 5. Words are defined either within the text or in a glossary. | ___ | ___ | ___ |
| 6. Definitions are readable, understandable, and clear. | ___ | ___ | ___ |
| 7. Students can be expected to learn these vocabulary words with a reasonable amount of preteaching and reinforcement on the part of the teacher. | ___ | ___ | ___ |

**D. Concepts**

| | Yes | No | Not Applicable |
|---|---|---|---|
| 1. Main concepts presented in the text are in keeping with the concepts the teacher expects students to learn. | ___ | ___ | ___ |
| 2. Main concepts presented are in accordance with the course of study prescribed by the school system. | ___ | ___ | ___ |
| 3. Main concepts are accurate and objective and fit into a well planned sequence of instruction. | ___ | ___ | ___ |
| 4. Main concepts are presented in an orderly and logical manner, and skills are sequenced properly. | ___ | ___ | ___ |
| 5. Main concepts and ideas are presented sequentially and one at a time, at a pace that is appropriate for the students. | ___ | ___ | ___ |
| 6. Format of the text separates main concepts visually, with headings or in sections. | ___ | ___ | ___ |
| 7. Concepts are presented in a concise format so that the text is not cluttered. | ___ | ___ | ___ |
| 8. Text is not so exhaustive that the teacher will have to omit much of the material. | ___ | ___ | ___ |
| 9. Concepts are at the level of the students who will be using the text—stimulating and challenging, yet not frustrating. | ___ | ___ | ___ |

|  | Yes | No | Not Applicable |
|---|---|---|---|
| 10. Text is not limited in scope and will not be inadequate or incomplete. | ____ | ____ | ____ |
| 11. Text fits into the multiplicity-of-text system in operation in the school. | ____ | ____ | ____ |
| 12. Concepts are stated in terms that will be understandable with adequate instruction. | ____ | ____ | ____ |
| 13. Study guide statements or questions accompany the text. | ____ | ____ | ____ |
| 14. Material and concepts are related to everyday life. | ____ | ____ | ____ |

**E. Presentation of Material**

1. The book covers the material:
   ____ chronologically
   ____ by unit
   ____ by category
   ____ by sequence
   ____ by topic

| | Yes | No | Not Applicable |
|---|---|---|---|
| 2. The above method is preferable in this content area. | ____ | ____ | ____ |
| 3. Bibliography of supplementary material is presented at the end of each chapter or unit, or at the end of the book. | ____ | ____ | ____ |
| 4. Material is related to other content areas and is interdisciplinary in nature. | ____ | ____ | ____ |

**F. Exercises or Accompanying Workbook**

| | Yes | No | Not Applicable |
|---|---|---|---|
| 1. Exercises are more than "busywork" and have definite value. | ____ | ____ | ____ |
| 2. Directions are clear and easy to follow. | ____ | ____ | ____ |
| 3. Exercises reinforce both vocabulary and concepts. | ____ | ____ | ____ |
| 4. Postreading questions and applications are challenging and stimulate thinking, rather than being all literal and mechanical. | ____ | ____ | ____ |
| 5. Practice exercises follow the sequence of skills and development. | ____ | ____ | ____ |
| 6. Practice exercises involve students' own experiences and everyday situations. | ____ | ____ | ____ |

(continued)

# Figure 8.3 (continued)

|  | Yes | No | Not Applicable |
|---|---|---|---|
| 7. Challenging and enriching materials are available for superior students. | ___ | ___ | ___ |
| 8. Appropriate materials are provided for the average or below average reader. | ___ | ___ | ___ |
| 9. Self-help materials are such that students can do them with a minimum of teacher guidance and help. | ___ | ___ | ___ |

**G. Visual Aids**

|  | Yes | No | Not Applicable |
|---|---|---|---|
| 1. There are sufficient illustrations, charts, graphs, maps, etc., to help reinforce students' understanding of materials. | ___ | ___ | ___ |
| 2. Illustrations, charts, maps, and graphs are clear and meaningful. | ___ | ___ | ___ |
| 3. Photographs or pictures illustrate the text. | ___ | ___ | ___ |
| 4. Photographs and pictures are clear, interesting, important, as well as accurate. | ___ | ___ | ___ |
| 5. Photographs and illustrations are colorful, of high artistic value, and appealing to readers. | ___ | ___ | ___ |
| 6. Illustrations help to motivate and stimulate class discussion. | ___ | ___ | ___ |
| 7. Illustrations aid students in thinking or problem solving. | ___ | ___ | ___ |
| 8. Text is generally attractive. | ___ | ___ | ___ |

**H. Freedom from Cultural and Sex Bias**

|  | Yes | No | Not Applicable |
|---|---|---|---|
| 1. Text presents minorities (races, religious groups, nationalities) without stereotype or bias. | ___ | ___ | ___ |
| 2. Ethnic groups are presented sensitively and with respect for individual and cultural differences. | ___ | ___ | ___ |
| 3. Materials portray racial, religious, and ethnic groups in such a way as to build mutual | | | |

|  | Yes | No | Not Applicable |
|---|---|---|---|
| understanding, appreciation, and acceptance. | ___ | ___ | ___ |
| 4. Status of women in society is presented without stereotype and bias. | ___ | ___ | ___ |
| 5. Role of women is portrayed as equal to and as important as the role of men in society—historically as well as in the present. | ___ | ___ | ___ |

**I. Parts of Text**

|  | Yes | No | Not Applicable |
|---|---|---|---|
| 1. Table of contents is usable and complete. | ___ | ___ | ___ |
| 2. Glossary definitions as well as the pronunciation key are simple, clear, and understandable. | ___ | ___ | ___ |
| 3. Index is complete. | ___ | ___ | ___ |
| 4. Appendices of charts, graphs, tables, and supplementary materials appear as necessary. | ___ | ___ | ___ |

**J. Teacher's Manual or Supplement**

|  | Yes | No | Not Applicable |
|---|---|---|---|
| 1. Manual, guidebook, or resource book is available. | ___ | ___ | ___ |
| 2. Answer key is available. | ___ | ___ | ___ |
| 3. Objectives and goals of the text are clearly stated in the manual. | ___ | ___ | ___ |
| 4. Concrete and practical suggestions are presented for the teacher. | ___ | ___ | ___ |
| 5. Alternative materials are listed for use with students. | ___ | ___ | ___ |

**K. Quality of Workmanship**

|  | Yes | No | Not Applicable |
|---|---|---|---|
| 1. Binding is of good quality and durable. | ___ | ___ | ___ |
| 2. Cover is durable and coated. | ___ | ___ | ___ |
| 3. Paper quality is good. | ___ | ___ | ___ |
| 4. Color of paper is not tiring to the eyes. | ___ | ___ | ___ |
| 5. Size of print is adequate. | ___ | ___ | ___ |
| 6. Print is clear and readable. | ___ | ___ | ___ |
| 7. Book is durable enough for the use and reuse that will be demanded of it. | ___ | ___ | ___ |

(continued)

---

# Figure 8.3 (concluded)

| | Yes | No | Not Applicable |
|---|---|---|---|
| **L. Cost** | | | |
| 1. Cost is realistic for the school and for the students who will be using it. | _____ | _____ | _____ |
| 2. Cost is worth the use that will be made of the text. | _____ | _____ | _____ |

---

From Lucille Jevitz and Donald W. Meints, "Be a Better Book Buyer: Guidelines for Textbook Evaluation," *Journal of Reading* 22(1979):734–738. Reprinted with permission of Lucille Jevitz, Donald W. Meints, and the International Reading Association.

## Applying the Formulas

Practice using the three formulas on the excerpts given in Examples 1–3; all are taken from an article that health teachers might consider using in their courses. The excerpts are reprinted from "The Theme of the Park Is Safety" by Virginia Reinhart (1975). The calculations for the first passage have been completed for you in Fig. 8.4. Record your data in Fig. 8.4. Then compare your readability levels with those discussed in the section titled "Interpretation of Readability Formulas."

### Example 1   Passages for Applying the Fry Formula

The number of syllables are placed above each word in Passage 1.

Passage 1

```
 1  1      3       1   1 1  2     3    1  2   2      4
In an amusement park, as in any industry, the finest safety engi-
        1      2      3    1 1   2   1  1 1   3
neering can't prevent accidents if the workers don't use it properly.
 1  1  1     2      1   2   1 1  1   2      1    2
At "The Old Country," the newest of the half dozen "Busch Gar-
      1     3       3      2   2  1  1    3    1
dens," in Williamsburg, Virginia, safety begins with the selection of
 1    2
the workers.
           1    1    1     1   1   1   1     1   1   1    1
           "We pick them more for their heads than for their hands,"
 1   1    2      3      3       3     1  2       3
says Tom Heilman, general services manager and safety director.
 1   1   2    2    1  1  2    2    1  1    3
"We want caring people, who like other people, who will remember
```

# Figure 8.4  Calculations from the Formulas

| Fry Technique | Number of Sentences | Number of Syllables |
| --- | --- | --- |
| Passage 1 | 4.1[a] | 154 |
| Passage 2 | | |
| Passage 3 | | |
| Average | | |
| Readability | | |

| Raygor Technique | Number of Sentences | Number of Words Containing Six or More Letters |
| --- | --- | --- |
| Passage 1 | 4.1[a] | 33 |
| Passage 2 | | |
| Passage 3 | | |
| Average | | |
| Readability | | |

| SMOG Technique | Number of Words Containing Three or More Syllables | | |
| --- | --- | --- | --- |
| Passage 1 | 31 | | |
| Passage 2 | | | |
| Passage 3 | | | |
| Total: | Square root: | +3 = Readability: | |

[a]To get 100 words, you must go 3 words into the last sentence, which has 20 words. Therefore these 3 words are 0.1 of the last sentence (3 divided by 20 = 0.15).

        1    2    1    1  1    1    1    2    1   1    2    1    3
    that older folks do not move as quickly and that children get excited
        1    1     2      1     1    1    1    2
    and don't always watch what they are doing.''
            1        3          1
        Each employee spent/more than 40 hours in training sessions

    before opening day; retraining courses are held throughout the sea-

    son.

(The 100th word in Passage 1 is *spent,* shown before the slash.)

Passage 2

Not all jobs can be rotated, of course. Cashiers do not change places with cooks at the food stands. But the cashiers do benefit from another safety device: Because a lot of money comes to them in a day's work, they conceivably could be robbed, a particularly unattractive job hazard. So the management installed a pneumatic system to carry off the money by tube to a central office, leaving only small sums in any ticket booth at any time.

A large crew starts work only after the park closes at 10 P.M. These workers lubricate and maintain all the/machinery.

(The slash marks the 100th word.)

Passage 3

On rides such as The Catapult, there's a double-check to see that customers are locked into their seats. Safety bars audibly snap into place, then an attendant checks to be sure. And with those rides that pass through darkened buildings, an attendant must signal that all safety bars are in place before the lights go out.

When push comes to shove, it shouldn't be in an amusement park. One of the most popular rides is an automobile racing course. To accommodate 1,200 passengers each hour, separate platforms were built for loading and unloading. This eliminates pushing and confusion, two natural/enemies of safety.

(The slash marks the 100th word.)

## Example 2  Passages for Applying the Raygor Formula

An X has been placed over the words containing six or more letters in Passage 1.

Passage 1

In an amusement park, as in any industry, the finest safety engineering can't prevent accidents if the workers don't use it properly.

At "The Old Country," the newest of the half dozen "Busch Gardens," in Williamsburg, Virginia, safety begins with the selection of the workers.

"We pick them more for their heads than for their hands," says Tom Heilman, general services manager and safety director. "We want caring people, who like other people, who will remember that older folks do not move as quickly and that children get excited and don't always watch what they are doing."

Each employee spent/more than 40 hours in training sessions before opening day; retraining courses are held throughout the season.

## Passage 2

Not all jobs can be rotated, of course. Cashiers do not change places with cooks at the food stands. But the cashiers do benefit from another safety device: Because a lot of money comes to them in a day's work, they conceivably could be robbed, a particularly unattractive job hazard. So the management installed a pneumatic system to carry off the money by tube to a central office, leaving only small sums in any ticket booth at any time.

A large crew starts work only after the park closes at 10 P.M. These workers lubricate and maintain all the/machinery.

## Passage 3

On rides such as The Catapult, there's a double-check to see that customers are locked into their seats. Safety bars audibly snap into place, then an attendant checks to be sure. And with those rides that pass through darkened buildings, an attendant must signal that all safety bars are in place before the lights go out.

When push comes to shove, it shouldn't be in an amusement park. One of the most popular rides is an automobile racing course. To accommodate 1,200 passengers each hour, separate platforms were built for loading and unloading. This eliminates pushing and confusion, two natural/enemies of safety.

## Example 3   Passages for Applying the SMOG Formula

A check has been placed over the words containing three or more syllables in Passage 1.

### Passage 1

In an amusement park, as in any industry, the finest safety engineering can't prevent accidents if the workers don't use it properly. At "The Old Country," the newest of the half dozen "Busch Gardens," in Williamsburg, Virginia, safety begins with the selection of the workers.

"We pick them more for their heads than for their hands," says Tom Heilman, general services manager and safety director. "We want caring people, who like other people, who will remember that older folks do not move as quickly and that children get excited and don't always watch what they are doing."

Each employee spent more than 40 hours in training sessions before opening day; retraining courses are held throughout the season.

The year-round employees tend to be highly skilled experts. The steam engine engineer, for example, has more than 20 years' experience. Often, year-round employees, totalling about 100, include mechanics, maintenance people, and the like, who handle repairs and installation of new attractions in the closed season, November to May.

But 10 times that many workers are seasonal. They do everything from sweeping the streets to acting in the bird show.

### Passage 2

Not all jobs can be rotated, of course. Cashiers do not change places with cooks at the food stands. But the cashiers do benefit from another safety device: Because a lot of money comes to them in a day's work, they conceivably could be robbed, a particularly unattractive job hazard. So the management installed a pneumatic system to carry off the money by tube to a central office, leaving only small sums in any ticket booth at any time.

A large crew starts work only after the park closes at 10 P.M. These workers lubricate and maintain all the machinery. The rides, in particular, have operated for 12 straight hours and need nightly attention. Before any ride opens in the morning, it must bear a tag showing the maintenance crew has checked it out and found it ready.

The morning crew runs the empty ride through its full cycle four or five times as a warm-up. Then the staff takes a test run as a final check before the customers are allowed to board.

Passage 3

On rides such as The Catapult, there's a double-check to see that customers are locked into their seats. Safety bars audibly snap into place, then an attendant checks to be sure. And with those rides that pass through darkened buildings, an attendant must signal that all safety bars are in place before the lights go out.

When push comes to shove, it shouldn't be in an amusement park. One of the most popular rides is an automobile racing course. To accommodate 1,200 passengers each hour, separate platforms were built for loading and unloading. This eliminates pushing and confusion, two natural enemies of safety. The cars, although they move only six miles an hour on their pre-set courses, have safety belts; and attendants enforce their use.

The Sky Ride has an additional safety factor. Two separate keys lock and unlock the safety bar for each car.

# Interpretation of Readability Formulas

Both the Fry and the Raygor formulas indicate a grade-level score of 9. Not surprisingly, the SMOG procedure indicates a grade-level score of 11. If you were considering using this article with your class, you probably would have to provide some instructional assistance for those students whose reading levels range from grade 8 to grade 10. Those who were reading at the eleventh grade level and higher could probably read the article independently with full comprehension. However, there are other factors that could make the selection either easier or more difficult for students. For example, the selection contains no illustrations. Would photos or figures help to convey the author's message?

What about student interest? Do students care about safety procedures used at theme parks? Are students interested in theme parks at all?

What do students already know about theme parks? Most have probably spent time at some type of theme or amusement park. Some may have ridden on malfuntioning amusement rides (and survived!). Some even may have worked at an amusement park. If students have knowledge about amusement parks, which is likely, the article may be easier for them to read. (They have a schema for amusement parks.)

Does the author's writing style help or hinder comprehension? Does the quoting of individuals add to or detract from interest in the article? Is the author's writing informative, relevant, and clear?

Finally, legibility and visibility factors should be considered. What effect does the type size, style of type, and so on have on the reader? Is the physical format attractive?

It should be clear that although objective readability data were obtained for this article, there are other important factors that the teacher must consider before deciding on the appropriateness of using this or any reading selection with particular groups of students.

## Summary

Readability techniques are far from perfect measures for estimating the reading levels of textbooks. However, they do provide teachers, with some objective data, which helps them in the following ways:

- To make choices for textbook selection and adoption.
- To make selections for supplementary reading.
- To determine which sections of textbooks are more difficult than others.
- To plan better reading assignments.

Teachers should also weigh the nonquantifiable and extralinguistic factors when completing readability studies. And they should note the following:

- Consider how the textbook will be used (e.g., apply the SMOG technique if students will use the text independently and use the Fry or the Raygor technique if they plan to assist students in comprehending the book).
- Realize that if polysyllabic words or proper nouns are repeated often, the readability level will be inflated.
- Avoid using readability procedures with poetry, because it does not conform to the basic characteristics of regular prose.
- Realize that the readability procedures are only estimates; adding and subtracting one year to the grade level suggested by the readability study increases the accuracy of the estimate.

# The Rating Game, Part II

Reading specialist Mrs. Adams is summarizing her explanation of readability to a group of teachers.

"So some of them do approach it scientifically, or pseudoscientifically, while some just report the author's opinion. But as you can see, with these techniques you can do your own readability studies. And don't forget to consider other factors," continued Mrs. Adams, "like the quality of the illustrations, graphs, and maps in the book."

"Oh yes," said Mrs. Grady, "we've got a little checklist to rate such things. We'll use both out lists and your readability techniques and then come to a decision."

"Do let me know how you make out," Mrs. Adams said.

"Thanks for your help," added Mrs. Grady.

"My pleasure."

## Bibliography

Armbruster, Bonnie B., and Thomas H. Anderson. *Content Area Textbooks,* Reading Education Report no. 23. Urbana: Center for the Study of Reading, University of Illinois, 1981.

Baldwin, R. Scott, and Rhonda K. Kaufman. "A Congruent Validity Study of the Raygor Readability Estimate." *Journal of Reading* 23(1979):148–153.

Collins, Allan M., Ann L. Brown, Jerry L. Morgan, and William F. Brewer. *The Analysis of Reading Tasks and Texts,* Technical Report no. 43. Urbana: Center for the Study of Reading, University of Illinois, 1977.

Dechant, Emerald V., and Henry P. Smith. *Psychology in Teaching Reading.* 2nd ed. Englewood Cliffs, N.J.: Prentice-Hall, 1977.

Estes, Thomas H., and Joseph L. Vaughan, Jr. *Reading and Learning in the Content Classroom.* Boston: Allyn & Bacon, 1978.

Fry, Edward B. "A Readability Graph That Saves Time." *Journal of Reading* 11(1968):513–516, 575–578.

———. "Fry's Readability Graph: Clarifications, Validity, and Extensions to Level 17." *Journal of Reading* 21(1977):242–252.

Gordon, Robert M. "The Readability of Unreadable Text." *English Journal* 69(1980):60–61.

Jenkins, Joseph R., and Darlene Pany. "Instructional Variables in Reading Comprehension." In *Comprehension and Teaching: Research Reviews,* edited by John T. Guthrie. Newark, Del.: International Reading Association, 1981.

Jevitz, Lucille, and Donald W. Meints. "Be a Better Book Buyer: Guidelines for Textbook Evaluation." *Journal of Reading* 22(1979):734–738.

McLaughlin, G. Harry. "SMOG Grading—A New Readability Formula." *Journal of Reading* 12(1969):639–646.

Raygor, Alton L. "The Raygor Readability Estimate: A Quick and Easy Way to Determine Difficulty." In *Reading: Theory, Research and Practice,* edited by P. David Pearson. Clemson, S.C.: National Reading Conference, 1977.

Reinhart, Virginia. "The Theme of the Park Is Safety." *Job Safety and Health* 3(1975):20–22.

Vaughan, Joseph L., Jr. "Interpreting Readability Assessments." *Journal of Reading* 20(1976):635–639.

# Chapter 9

# Accommodating Students with Special Needs

## Rita Replies, Part I

Living Pages

Every Thursday in the "Living Pages" the *Mirror's* Rita Ashley responds to your questions. Today's letters are from parents who are concerned with the educational progress of their children.

> Dear Rita:
>
> I've had it! When is my David going to learn how to read? Right from the first week of school (and he's going into grade eight now) there seemed to be a problem. I remember the first grade teacher told me he was one of the few in her class who couldn't read his name or recognize the letters of the alphabet. But I figured that he'd pick it up sooner or later.
>
> Well, that was just the beginning, Rita. Every year it was the same—low groups, special help, more testing—and still David struggles with his reading. Oh, he can cope. I usually read his homework to him and he does OK. But he's getting more and more homework and I just can't help him every night, especially now that I'm going to be working full time.
>
> It's not that the teachers aren't sympathetic. They all say he's a nice, bright boy, yet they feel he has this learning disability in reading and they can't figure him out. Maybe he's got dyslexia like Nelson Rockefeller and Albert Einstein did. A few teachers told me he could be dyslexic. He sure does have difficulty reading words. Yet when I read to him, he gets the ideas.

## Introduction

The vast majority of topics in this text relate primarily to instruction for the so-called typical students whose academic performance falls within the range of low-average, average, and high-average achievement. This chapter addresses those middle and high school students whose performance is at the two extremes of the continuum, or normal curve: students who are viewed as having special needs.

Special or exceptional students include those who are mentally retarded, emotionally disturbed, language-deficient, hearing- and/or visually impaired, physically handicapped, learning-disabled, and gifted. It is far beyond the scope of this chapter to consider the entire field of special education. Therefore it will focus on the two groups reading specialists and content area teachers are most likely to encounter in their classrooms, the learning-disabled and the gifted.

The schools have tried to help, but nothing seems to work. I hope it's not too late! Can you help? Please reply, Rita.

Yours truly,
Frustrated

Dear Rita:

I don't think the school system is meeting the needs of my daughter Sharon. She got practically all A's for the first nine years she was in school, but this last year her grades have begun to drop off. She says the work isn't hard, it's just boring. She gets B's and sometimes A's without any effort. She reads like crazy, but the books have little to do with her schoolwork. Lately she seems to be getting a little critical of her teachers and she sounds like she's becoming a bit of a skeptic. She complains about learning the same old things over and over again.

She's very independent, creative, and intelligent. But I fear she's losing interest in school fast. She seems more concerned with her flute lessons and about reading about how people behave. She's always reading biographies, autobiographies, and psychology books. She's very smart and sensitive. I feel, however, her talents are not recognized in the school. Could they be doing more for her?

Sincerely,
Wondering

At the end of the chapter you will find Rita's replies.

The major purposes of this chapter are to assist teachers in recognizing the characteristics of the learning-disabled and the gifted, identifying and diagnosing them, and providing programs for them primarily within the context of the regular classroom.

# The Learning-Disabled

## Characteristics

Learning disabilities is the newest recognized field in special education. Learning-disabled students have captured the interest of medical doctors, psychologists, social workers, and a variety of specialists in the field of education.

Recognizing that a diversity among professionals leads to a confusion of terminology and a possible conflict of ideas, Kirk, Kliebhan, and Lerner (1978) attempted to outline the characteristics typically used to describe learning-disabled students. According to these authors, learning-disabled students can exhibit weaknesses in one or in a combination of the following areas: motor development, perception, memory, language, cognition, attention, and maturational, emotional, and social characteristics. Savage and Mooney (1979) are concerned with learning disabilities that manifest themselves in an inability to read, and they say that the learning disabled are characterized by "any factor—physical, intellectual, or social emotional—within the mild-to-moderate range, that interferes with learning to read" (Savage and Mooney, 1979, p. 45). They also point out that it is important to remember that learning-disabled students show specific strengths as well as weaknesses.

Gleason and Haring (1974) claim that the learning-disabled have deficits in one or more of the channels (visual, auditory, kinesthetic) typically used to receive information in the classroom. Most students receive information by reading, listening, or discussing. They code, integrate, synthesize, and order this information in the brain. This process is a perceptual one: becoming aware of the environment through stimulation of the sensory modes and developing an integrated view of events in the environment. Perception leads to cognition and the development of learning abilities. While of average intelligence, a learning-disabled child often "has a dysfunction of the perceptual process that makes expected performance in the usual classroom curriculum difficult, if not impossible" (Gleason and Haring, 1974, p. 228).

While many lists are available that characterize the learning-disabled child in the elementary grades, few exist for the learning-disabled adolescent. One was compiled by Kahn (1980), who lists their general characteristics and their specific characteristcs in the areas of visual and auditory processing. As you read the lists that follow, keep in mind that that learning-disabled adolescent does not have *all* these characteristics.

### General

A. Behavioral characteristics
   1. Learning difficulty not attributable to impaired vision, hearing, intelligence, emotional or environmental well-being, plus underachievement in certain, but not all, academic subjects.
   2. Weak study habits
      a. inability to organize and budget time
      b. slow to start tasks
      c. difficulty completing tasks
      d. poor note taking and outlining skills
      e. struggles using reference materials

3. Discrepancy in quality of oral and written work
4. Poor attention span
    a. overactivity—constantly on the move
    b. underactivity
    c. distractibility
5. Language problems
    a. substituting easier words for complex words
    b. trouble verbalizing answers and speaking in whole sentences
    c. refraining from discussions or questions
    d. forgetting, confusing, or misarticulating words
    e. difficulty describing objects and defining simple vocabulary
6. Poor short- and long-term memory for information presented in class
7. Floundering when trying to follow oral or written directions
8. Disorganized thoughts
9. Lack of gestures when talking
10. Confusing left and right sides
11. Motor coordination problems
    a. unorganized
    b. sloppy
    c. clumsy—walking, running, holding pens and pencils
    d. failure to swing arms when walking or running

Visual

A. Behavioral characteristics to note
    1. Problems with visual tasks
        a. loses place easily
        b. becomes bored, restless, frustrated
        c. seems uncertain in recalling visually presented information
        d. shows signs of eye problems (rubbing, headaches)
    2. Mechanical problems taking examinations
        a. places answers in the wrong spots
        b. cannot draw lines on a matching test
        c. poorer performance when using a separate answer sheet
    3. Preference for auditory activities
        a. when shown a sound film, pays more attention to source of the sound than to the movie screen
        b. listens to lecture without making eye contact

4. Preference to avoid pictures and graphics
   a. difficulty interpreting
   b. slow rate of preception
   c. poor recall of information
   d. inattentiveness
5. Problems with oral and silent reading
   a. word-by-word or syllable-by-syllable reading
   b. excessive lip movement or vocalizing in silent reading
   c. body motion while reading
   d. numerous oral reading errors: mispronunciation (both gross and minor), omissions, substitutions (meaningful and non-sense), hesitations, short eye-voice span, regressions
   e. poor comprehension
   f. slow reading pace
   g. substandard reading level
   h. mistaking words that look similar
   i. using finger to keep place
   j. failure to recognize a word when it reappears
   k. easy eye fatigue
   l. participation better with materials presented in class (as opposed to read for class)
6. Oral spelling better than written spelling, or often words written phonetically
7. Visual-motor problems when printing, writing, copying, and drawing
   a. reverses letters, words, phrases
   b. seems sloppy and careless
   c. constantly refers to the visual model
   d. spaces poorly
   e. unorganized
8. Notices visual stimuli usually unnoticed by other students (marks on blackboard, etc.)
9. Seems more confused if visual material is crammed together (difficulty using a map, dictionary)
10. Responds better to verbal directions
11. Difficulty focusing and following print when going from far-to-near or near-to-far vision (looking from the blackboard to the textbook)

Auditory

A. Behavioral characteristics
   1. Seems to hear but not to listen
      a. makes inappropriate responses
      b. hesitates before responding to oral questions
      c. ignores, confuses, and forgets verbal directions
      d. often seems to misunderstand
   2. Has problems of articulation, enunciation, grammar, limited vocabulary, speech pace
   3. Has trouble blending syllables or pronounces words as they physically appear
   4. Has difficulty understanding and paying attention (day dreaming, hyperactive, blank expression on face) to oral activities and presentations
   5. Seems perplexed when trying to understand people who speak quickly or quietly, as well as those who move while talking
   6. Has problems with academic subjects taught orally
   7. Spells poorly
   8. Easily distracted by noises inside and outside classroom (noises unnoticed by other students)
   9. Frequently asks what just has been said (What?, Huh?)
   10. Substitutes gestures for words
   11. Watches the speaker's lips
   12. Often looks at others before following directions[1]

# Definition of the Learning-Disabled

The United States Congress created an official definition of children with learning disabilities in 1969. The definition was later included in Public Law 94–142, entitled the Education of All Handicapped Children Act of 1975. It reads:

> The term "Children with specific learning disabilities" means those children who have a disorder in one or more of the basic psychological processes involved with understanding or in using language,

---

1. Michael S. Kahn, "Learning Problems of the Secondary and Junior College Learning Disabled Student: Suggested Remedies," *Journal of Learning Disabilities* 13(1980):40–41. Reprinted by permission of the Professional Press, Inc., 101 East Ontario St., Chicago, Ill. 60611.

spoken or written, which may manifest itself in imperfect ability to listen, think, speak, read, write, spell, or do mathematical calculations. Such disorders include such conditions as perceptual handicaps, brain injury, minimal brain damage, dyslexia, and developmental aphasia. Such a term does not include children who have learning problems which are primarily a result of visual, hearing, or motor handicaps, of mental ratardation, of emotional disturbance, or of environmental disadvantage. (Public Law 94–142, Section 5(b)(4), 1975)

# Individualized Education Plans (IEPs)

The purpose of PL 94–142 is to provide adequate and appropriate special education and related services to all handicapped children. These children are to have *individualized education plans* (IEPs) that specify the student's annual goals, instructional objectives, a description of educational services to be provided, date for initiation of the program, duration of the program, and criteria for evaluating the IEP.

IEPs of learning-disabled students usually state that they will be *mainstreamed*, that is, they will be integrated into regular education classrooms. Mainstreaming also "recognizes the need for a broad range of services and encourages the assignment of a child to the 'least restrictive' program. The least restrictive program means the one that is closest to the regular education program but still allows the child all the [special] help he/she needs" (Savage and Mooney, 1979, p. 47). Therefore most secondary school teachers will have at least a few students in their regular classes each year who have been identified as learning-disabled.

# Diagnosing the Learning-Disabled

The learning-disabled are often identified and diagnosed through the use of achievement tests, group inventories, and informal individual assessments like those described in Chapter 7. Some specialists in the field of learning disabilities also use process tests. *Processing* refers to "what takes place after an individual has perceived something by means of his senses—how he interprets or puts it into meaningful use intellectually" (Hallahan and Kauffman, 1978, p. 130). Two popular process tests are the *Illinois Test of Psycholinguistic Abilities* (Kirk, McCarthy, and Kirk, 1961, 1968) and the *Marianne Frostig Developmental Test of Visual Perception* (Frostig, Lefever, and Whittlesey, 1964). A student's IEP is sometimes partly based on the results of these tests.

Readers interested in these and other specialized approaches to diagnosing the learning disabled can find more information in textbooks on special education, such as ones by Hallahan and Kauffman (1978) and Blake (1981), or books that are totally devoted to teaching the learning-disabled, such as ones by Mann, Goodman, and Wiederholt (1978) and Bryan and Bryan (1978).

# Differentiating Instruction for the Learning-Disabled

Although there are several ways to diagnose the learning-disabled middle or high school student, few corrective models for teaching those who have reading and learning problems have been substantiated through research. After reviewing the literature in this field, Lindsay and Kerlin concluded that there are "limited hard data to draw conclusions about the reading problems of learning disabled adolescents and educational programming to meet these problems" (Lindsay and Kerlin, 1979, p. 55).

Given this unfortunate situation, we are forced to appeal to our common sense in making instructional adjustments for these students. Kahn (1980, pp. 40–44) does just this when he lists some general suggestions and some specific suggestions for students who have visual or auditory problems. Those suggestions, many of which are applicable to all students, are listed below. In some cases Kahn's wording has been changed slightly.

Kahn's general suggestions are as follows:

1. Before beginning each class, review material previously taught.
2. Preview material to be presented. (See Chapter 2, "Developing Readiness for Reading Assignments.")
3. After presenting information, help students summarize it.
4. Eliminate classroom distractions such as excessive noise, physical motion, flickering lights, shiny jewelry, and loud ticking clocks.
5. If the student's work is incomplete or incorrect and he or she is frustrated, give a related, alternative assignment.
6. Notice and respond to nonverbal and verbal signs of anxiety and frustration.
7. Ask a student's "buddy" to help him or her with assignments.
8. Before moving on to new or more complex material, be sure the student understands what you have said, done, or demonstrated.
9. When appropriate, suggest mnemonics for recalling content.
10. Encourage the student to proofread assignments and tests. Perhaps the "buddy" can read the student's work back until the student is capable of proofreading.

11. When presenting information to the class, proceed as follows:
    (a) Talk distinctly and not too fast.
    (b) Present the information in an orderly fashion.
    (c) Stop periodically and encourage questions.
    (d) Highlight and repeat important information.
    (e) Reinforce information presented orally with visuals such as blackboard, overhead projectors, and dittos.
    (f) Help students to summarize the information.
    (g) If you required notes to be taken, give students time to edit them and ask questions.
12. Encourage students to reflect on a task before starting it.
13. Capture student attention before beginning class.
14. Emphasize meaningful associations, be organized, and relate material to be taught to student experiences.
15. Whenever possible, have individual conferences to guide students and monitor understanding of assignments and course content.
16. Review material and check understanding of it frequently.
17. When giving directions, proceed as follows:[2]
    (a) Take your time and be relaxed and positive.
    (b) Be sure you have the student's attention before starting, and encourage questions.
    (c) Keep directions simple and concise.
    (d) Point out sequential steps.
    (e) Be sure written ones are legible.
    (f) Tell students what materials are needed and where they can be found.
    (g) Present directions both orally and in writing.
    (h) When appropriate, demonstrate them.
    (i) Complete an example together.
    (j) Display a completed project.
    (k) Monitor students once they begin the activity.
    (l) Ask for periodic status reports with long-term assignments.
18. Encourage students to keep only the materials needed for class on their desks.
19. Be sure students understand time limits for classroon activities.
20. Help students budget their time when taking tests. (See Chapter 6.)

2. For more suggestions on helping students with this skill, see Joynes, McCormick, and Heward (1980), Kahn (1978), and McCullough and Towery (1976).

21. Help students get themselves organized by doing the following:
    (a) Posting a weekly schedule of class and study times.
    (b) Listing materials needed for class.
    (c) Posting the deadline when assignments are due.
22. Teach students the parts of a book. (See Chapter 2.)
23. Provide for small-group or independent projects.
24. If possible, have students work in study carrels.
25. Give several short classroom activities instead of one long activity.
26. Make furniture arrangements easy to maneuver around. (Kahn, 1980)

Kahn's suggestions for the student with *visual perception problems* follow [visual perception is "the ability to differentiate, organize, and interpret information received through the eye" (Savage and Mooney, 1979, p. 9)].

1. Tell students to read orally when studying.
2. Tape-record some classes.
3. Provide more auditory presentations of information.
4. Write legibly. (Printing is preferable.) Do not clutter blackboard information and information on ditto sheets.
5. Have a consistent format for papers and assignments.
6. Consider using materials paralleling the textbook but written at a lower reading level.
7. Tell the student to use a ruler or a blank white index card to hold reading place and to avoid confusion where a figure ground problem exists. (Figure ground refers to the ability to attend to one portion of a visual stimulus while perceiving it in relation to the rest of the stimulus.)
8. Make tapes of the textbook chapters and have the student listen to them as she or he reads the material silently.
9. If visual-motor problems exist, lower standards of acceptable writing, allow more time for writing, and encourage the student to use a typewriter.
10. Minimize visual stimuli by providing study carrels.
11. If possible, reinforce blackboard work (far vision) with ditto papers (near vision). (Kahn, 1980)

Kahn's suggestions for the student with *auditory perception problems* follow [auditory perception is "the ability to differentiate, organize, and interpret information received through the ear" (Savage and Mooney, 1979, p. 3)].

1. Use short one-concept statements.
2. Encourage the student to tape lecture classes.

3. Talk at a slower rate.

4. Do not penalize for incorrect spelling, but do correct it.

5. Seat the student away from auditory disturbances.

6. Encourage the student to visualize material that has been orally presented.

7. Provide a brief written outline of material to be presented orally.

8. Instruct students to repeat your questions before answering.

9. Reinforce oral directions with written ones or with other visual clues. (Kahn, 1980)

# Helping the Learning-Disabled

## In Comprehension

Given the fact that comprehension difficulties affect more secondary learning-disabled students than any other type of disability (Lerner, 1976; Lindsey and Kerlin, 1979), it behooves teachers to consider ways of assisting these students in this area. They may have to make *extra* efforts in preparing the readiness activities discussed in this text as well as in carefully developing direct teaching lessons, adjunct questions, and reading guides. If these approaches do not work, they can consider using a more individualized technique such as Manzo's (1969) ReQuest procedure.

When using the *ReQuest procedure* with a learning-disabled student, the teacher must match the student with a special tutor, a classroom teacher, or a "buddy." The goal is to improve the student's comprehension through the use of teacher-student reciprocal questioning of the text. By presenting himself as a model of good questioning behavior, the teacher assists the student in modifying her own questions and helping her to set a purpose for reading.

Here is how the procedure works.

1. The student and teacher/special tutor/buddy each has a copy of the assigned reading.

2. Each silently reads the first sentence.

3. The student asks any and as many questions as she wants while the teacher closes his book. The student is encouraged to ask teacher types of questions.

4. The teacher attempts to answer the questions as completely as possible without faking and sometimes by referring to the text for justification.

5. Whenever there is uncertainty about the correctness of the answer, it is checked against the text.

6. When the student is finished with her questions, roles are reversed and the teacher asks the questions.

7. Steps 1 through 6 are repeated until the student can provide a reasonable response to the question, "What do you think is going to happen in the rest of the selection? Why?" Then the teacher instructs the student to read to see if she was correct.

8. Reciprocal questioning usually does not go beyond the first three paragraphs. At this point, "Any of the traditional follow-up activities may be used: e.g., consulting an additional reference for an elaboration or verification of what had been read; vocabulary related exercises; tasks requiring the application of newly acquired information, etc." (Manzo, 1969, p. 125).

The teacher should always serve as a model of good questioning behavior by asking relevant literal questions and by moving toward interpretive, critical, and applied questions.

## In Test Taking

Chapter 6 included the section "Test-taking Tips." These tips should be reviewed very carefully with learning-disabled students.

Kathy Amico, teacher of the learning-disabled at Danvers (Massachusetts) High School, has offered some cogent suggestions to content area teachers regarding the testing of learning-disabled students. She suggests ways of preparing them for teacher-made tests and techniques for developing and administering the tests. These suggestions are listed below.

When preparing students for the test, teachers should follow these steps:

1. Prepare review sheets listing important terms to be learned.

2. Preview the essay questions that will be on the test.

3. Give students an opportunity to practice answering the essay question with a resource person or buddy before the test situation.

4. Discuss the format of the test (objective, essay, etc.) with students during the review period.

When developing and administering the test, teachers should follow these steps:

1. Keep the directions simple.

2. Read the directions orally to students and *repeat* them.

3. If essay questions will be included on the test, carefully *list* the exact type of response you expect. For example:

    (a) What is the Declaration of Independence?

    (b) Name three parts.

(c) Discuss each part.

(d) Tell why you feel the Declaration was so important.

4. Check to see whether students have begun working on the test after directions have been explained. Some students may still be confused about directions but are too embarrassed to ask about them.

5. Allow students ample space for writing their answers. Their writing is often large and awkward and may not fit in the space you have provided.

6. If many multiple-choice questions are included on the test, divide them into small sections containing four or five questions each.

7. Allow students to cross out questions they have completed. This step decreases the visual field, thus making the test format less complicated.

8. Avoid multiple-choice questions that have tricky choices, such as these:

(a) Rain.

(b) Heat.

(c) Both (a) and (b) are correct.

(d) Neither (a) nor (b) is correct.

9. If possible, avoid using separate answer sheets that require transferring answers, especially those that must be placed in small circles or small spaces.

10. Let students know the relative importance of the test with respect to their final grade.

11. Select tests that accompany textbooks judiciously. They often do not represent the important points of a chapter or what you have stressed in class.

12. Use daily or weekly quizzes, which are preferable to unit tests, especially for those who have memory problems.

13. Allow students to read over class notes or review sheets for a few minutes before taking a test.

## Closing Remarks

The frustrations learning-disabled students experience are many. There is no question that, especially at the secondary level, we can do more for these students than we have in the past. Perhaps we can be guided in our efforts by listening to the students themselves. For example, we are provided with some clues from some learning-disabled elementary and high school students and young adults who completed a questionnaire designed and administered by Lindsey (1981).

The purpose of the study was to elicit from learning-disabled students their perception of learning at school, interpersonal relationships, and other situations. The study generated the following moving, sobering conclusions:

> The answers to the questions in these three groups reveal a number of commonalities of experience. As a group, these people have reported their happiest moments to be equated with success and their saddest moments with failure. They seemed to enjoy doing things: engaging in sports and physical activities, working with their hands, doing experiments and going on field trips. It is only when they sat down to read and study that they experienced frustration and unhappiness. The subjects of this study were nearly unanimous in considering reading to be extremely difficult, whether for its own sake or as a study strategy. On the whole, films, field trips and oral and written drills were the favored means of learning. Still, time spent in school was never pleasant for these children; they lived for recess, Friday nights and graduation (a paradox?). Those who had less endurance merely dropped out. As a group, these people are very specific about what could have made a difference in their learning experiences; teachers with patience and understanding of their problems, teachers with time to explain things as many times and in as many ways as necessary, teachers with a pleasant attitude, and no frightening pressure. (Lindsey, 1981, p. 8)

The group that participated in this study named teachers as the most significant others in their lives in terms of the difference they could have made. Yet teachers were not named as most influential. Perhaps if we will listen to what our learning-disabled children are saying about their experiences and needs, then we will have a chance to become an important positive influence in the lives our our students.

Lindsey's conclusions are not surprising when one considers Good's (1981) review of the research on teacher expectations and student perceptions. He found that teacher behavior toward low-achieving students (many of whom are undoubtedly learning-disabled) varies from their behavior toward high achieving students. Specifically, low-achieving students are seated farther from the teacher, given less positive reinforcement, called on less often, given less time to answer questions, rarely provided with probing questions upon initial failure, criticized more frequently, praised less frequently after achieving success, praised more frequently for marginal or inadequate responses, given less accurate and detailed feedback and less demanding work, and interrupted more frequently during their oral recitations.

It is hoped that classroom teachers will become more sensitive to the needs of the learning-disabled by modifying the type of behavior described by

Good. It is clear that learning-disabled adolescents must be treated by their teachers with more compassion and understanding.

Learning-disabled adolescents have some characteristics that differentiate them from their peers. Before appropriate instruction can be planned for them, they should be evaluated by a learning disabilities or reading specialist. Content area teachers who have the time, interest, and ingenuity can also evaluate their learning-disabled students by constructing and administering tests such as informal reading inventories. However, content area teachers should keep in mind that they are usually not qualified to determine whether a student does or does not have a learning disability. They can and should refer students to the appropriate specialists for a formal evaluation.

On the basis of the information gained from these evaluations, teachers can make adjustments and differentiate their instruction for these students who, without the support of sympathetic and understanding teachers, are doomed to academic failure.

# The Gifted

## Characteristics

Other special students likely to be found in some content area classes are gifted adolescents. Their needs are vastly different from those of the learning-disabled; thus classroom adjustments designed to meet their needs are different. However, before teachers attempt to make such adjustments, they should be familiar with the characteristics of gifted students and ways of identifying them.

During the fifties and early sixties the major characteristic that was said to differentiate the gifted from the regular student was high intelligence or IQ scores above 130 (Tuttle, 1978). Then Guilford's (1967) structure-of-the-intellect model sensitized educators to other characteristics associated with gifted students, such as creativity. According to Torrance (1962), important aspects of creativity are *fluency*, the ability to produce many ideas given a specific stimulus; *flexibility*, the ability to produce different types of ideas; *originality*, the ability to produce unique ideas; *elaboration*, the ability to contribute details to an idea; *synthesis*, the ability to fuse two or more figures into a related whole; and *closure*, the ability to postpone completion of a task to allow for the intellectual inspiration necessary for the creation of original ideas.

In 1970 a fact-finding status report of education for the gifted and talented was mandated by Congress. Former Commissioner of Education Sidney Marland (1972) presented a report to the Subcommittee on Education. While this report includes intelligence and creativity as characteristics of the gifted, it also cites specific academic aptitude, ability in the visual and performing arts, leadership ability, and psychomotor ability. [The Council for Basic Education has taken issue with the federal definition for the inclusion of leadership and psychomotor abilities. Psychomotor ability was dropped recently from the federal definition because it was believed these students get recognition in other programs.] The gifted student may demonstrate achievement or potential ability in these areas either singly or in combination.

Tuttle and Becker (1980) list 12 characteristics that they say typify the many lists that currently are disseminated across the country. The first 3 characteristics relate to personal qualities, 4 through 7 relate to interpersonal qualities, and 8 through 12 relate to information processing. Tuttle and Becker warn us that their list, like others, only gives tentative, general characteristics, and particular gifted and talented students may not possess all of them. The list follows.

A gifted individual—

1. is curious.
2. is persistent in pursuit of interests and questions.
3. is perceptive of the environment.
4. is critical of self and others.
5. has a highly developed sense of humor, often a verbal orientation.
6. is sensitive to injustices on personal and worldwide levels.
7. is a leader in various areas.
8. is not willing to accept superficial statements, responses, or evaluations.
9. understands general principles easily.
10. often responds to the environment through media and means other than print and writing.
11. sees relationships among seemingly diverse ideas.
12. generates many ideas for a specific stimulus. (Tuttle and Becker, 1980, p. 13)

# Renzulli's Cluster

Renzulli (1977) is another educator who does not believe that any one ability or aptitude characterizes the gifted. After reviewing and synthesizing the research related to creative and gifted adults, he concluded that there was no single criterion that could be used to determine giftedness. However, he did discover that those adults who had achieved reputations of eminence did have an identifiable cluster of three traits: (1) above-average intelligence (not necessarily exceptional), (2) task commitment or intrinsic motivation to perform in an area of chosen interest, and (3) creativity. Renzulli further emphasized that there exists an interaction among these traits and it is this interaction that results

# Figure 9.1 The Ingredients of Giftedness

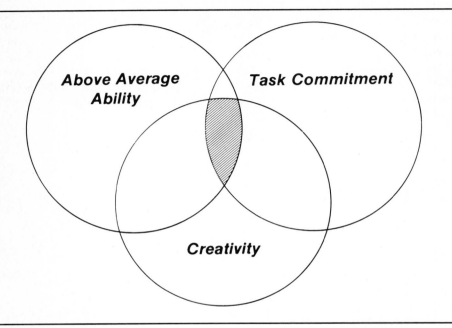

From Joseph S. Renzulli and Linda H. Smith, "An Alternative Approach to Identifying and Programming for Gifted and Talented Students," *G/C/T* 3(1980):5. Reprinted with permission: *G/C/T* Magazine, P.O. Box 66654, Mobile, Ala. 36660.

in superior performance. Figure 9.1 depicts the interaction of the traits. Those students who manifest or are capable of developing an interaction among the three traits will probably require educational opportunities and services that are not ordinarily provided in the typical classroom.

## Giftedness in the Content Areas

Feldhusen and Kolloff (1978) feel that some students are gifted in certain traditional academic areas (mathematics, science, language arts, or social studies) and display their giftedness by scoring at or above the 90th percentile on achievement tests in one or more of these academic areas. If this high achievement is supported with IQ scores above 140, they recommend advanced-placement acceleration programs.

Feldhusen and Kolloff also acknowledge a need for programs for special or gifted students who display creative or expressive talents. If these talents are supported with IQ scores within the range of 110–140, they recommend establishing enrichment programs for them. Some writers have suggested some characteristics of gifted students in specific content areas (Plowman, 1980; Romney, 1980; West, 1980). In the *social studies* class, for example, Plowman says that gifted students "are those who seem to have a natural inclination toward and interest in other human beings, in ideas about them, and in the relationships among people and their social, political, and economic institutions" (Plowman, 1980, pp. 11–12). They also want to investigate cause/effect relationships and understand the underlying reasons behind laws, theoretical principles, and events.

Gifted social studies students may exhibit the following behavior:

- They read extensively in the social studies.
- They show an unusual interest in economics.
- They reveal a concern about foreign people, the environment, and human relations.
- They interrelate the various areas of the social studies.
- They want to demonstrate their understanding of the social studies through creative activities such as role playing, slide presentations, skits, and so on. (Plowman, 1980)

Romney (1980) suggests that characterizing gifted *science* students is very difficult, but he still offers some clues. He believes gifted science students display specific behavior characteristics such as taking risks, making intuitive leaps, keeping careful records, displaying curiosity, recognizing the interconnectedness of events, and showing a strong sense of purpose.

West (1980) notes behavior characteristics of gifted *English* students such as reading avidly; writing fluently, frequently, and for their own pleasure; participating in oral activities; and producing and perceiving humorous language. He also outlines an extensive list of questions teachers can consider as they try to identify giftedness relative to the various language arts: language, literature, composition, reading, and speaking. The questions related to reading are the following:

1. Is the student confident of word analysis, phonics, vocabulary from context, and other skills?
2. Does the student have listening, reading, writing, and speaking vocabularies beyond those of his peers?
3. Does the student possess abilities in comprehension, interpretation, evaluation, and rate beyond those of peers?
4. Does the student have independent study, library, dictionary, and research skills? (West, 1980, p. 13)

## Identification Procedures

Most specialists in teaching the gifted and talented recommend that procedures for identifying these students should begin as early as possible. However, it is advisable to search for the gifted and talented on all grade levels in order to find the late bloomers.

Procedures for identifying gifted students should be effective and efficient. When the identification procedures do in fact find the gifted students, the techniques are *effective*. When a high proportion of students selected by the identification procedures eventually turn out to be gifted, the techniques are *efficient* (Hallahan and Kauffman, 1978). For example, if 100 students were identified as being potentially gifted and 80 turned out to be truly gifted, the identification procedure would be 80% efficient.

Group-administered achievement and intelligence tests can be used as initial screening devices for identifying the gifted. For students who may have ability as creative and divergent thinkers, individual IQ tests and tests of creativity are appropriate. Other approaches to identification include rating scales, interest inventories, and parent and peer referral.

## Differentiating Instruction for the Gifted

What can classroom teachers do to meet the special needs of gifted students? Most models for education programs for the gifted assume that there is somebody in the school system responsible for directing programs for the gifted. When this is the case, classroom teachers can cooperate with this person in developing appropriate programs for these students. However, many school systems do not employ a coordinator of programs for the gifted; even when they do, their programs often focus primarily on elementary schoolchildren.

Still, middle and high school classroom teachers can learn and adapt from some of the instructional models discussed in the literature. Most of these models suggest that students be involved in creative and problem-solving activities as well as independent research projects. It is possible for classroom teachers to plan and monitor such activities within the regular classroom. As you review the models that follow, keep in mind that while you may not be able to follow them precisely, you can adapt and modify them in order to meet some of the needs of the gifted and talented students in your classroom.

## Self-Directed Learner Model

Developing self-directed learners is, as its name implies, the major priority of the *self-directed learner model* for the gifted and talented (Treffinger, 1975). The basic goals of self-directed learning are to function effectively in one's total environment; to make choices and decisions and to assume responsibility for choices and decisions; to define problems and determine solutions; and to evaluate one's own work (Treffinger and Barton, 1979).

The four basic components of the self-directed learner model are identifying goals and objectives, assessing entering behavior, planning and implementing instruction, and assessing performance. In the first step, gifted students gradually move from meeting the teacher's instructional goals and objectives to developing their own. The purpose of the second step, assessing entering behavior, is to determine whether or not students have already met the planned objectives. The teacher completes the diagnosis at first, but it soon becomes a team effort, and, finally, "assessment of the possible goals and objectives, the necessary background or prerequisites, and the available resources, are made by the learner" (Treffinger, 1975, p. 56).

When planning and implementing instruction, step 3, teachers help students move toward self-direction by increasing the nature and number of alternatives for learners to follow. Thus many resources must be available. Ultimately the learners select their own projects that are designed to meet self-declared goals and objectives.

In the final step, assessment of performance, the teacher helps students identify alternative ways of evaluating whether or not the objectives have been met. This process may involve teacher-student conferences and peer evaluation.

Treffinger, then, feels that students should be provided with experience involving increasing degrees and kinds of self-management. It is clear that if this goal is to be met, teachers of the gifted would have to become far less directive in their teaching and move more toward the role of a resource person who assists students in planning and developing projects, locating and using resources, and finding appropriate audiences or outlets for products.

# Cumulative Learning Effect Model

Datnow's (1980) *cumulative learning effect model* recommends the grouping of students in advanced courses for various content areas. Special activities are designed so that they meld with what is being studied in the classroom.

First the coordinator of the program (assuming there is one) meets with the content area teachers of each advanced class. They decide on the main areas of study (see column 1 of Fig. 9.2), including the goals of the program, student activities, and content. Note taking, research, and advanced reading skills are required of students.

Extensions of this first step are completed in the exploration and in-depth investigation steps. The goals, activities, and content associated with these steps are clearly outlined in Fig. 9.2. Notice that these steps require the assistance of a resource person, supervisor, or mentor (a highly qualified adult who works

# Figure 9.2 Datnow's Cumulative Learning Effect Model

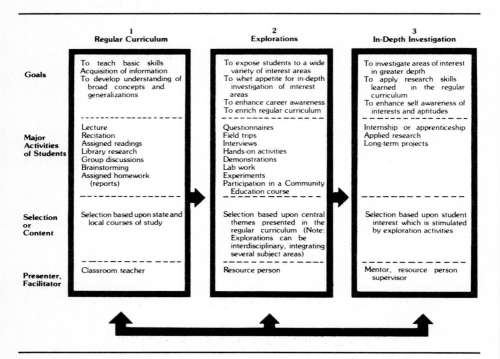

From Claire Datnow, "The Cumulative Learning Effect: A Model for Coordinating Educational Opportunities for Gifted Students," *G/C/T* 3(1980):55. Reprinted with permission: *G/C/T* Magazine, P.O. Box 66654, Mobile, Ala. 36660.

with students in particular areas of interest). As mentioned above, these activities are to be closely related to the regular classroom activities.

## The Enrichment Triad Model

Three interrelated types of enrichment activities characterize Renzulli's (1977) *enrichment triad model*. All learners, says Renzulli, should be exposed to the first two types: general exploratory activities and group training activities. The third type of activity, individual and small-group investigations of real problems, is generally reserved for the gifted and talented students.

The general exploratory activities (type I) give learners an opportunity to study topics of interest to them. Renzulli's three guidelines for these activities are as follows:

1. Activities and experiences are to be explored with a purpose, and their self-analysis of them should lead to alternative suggestions for further study.
2. Interest centers should be developed to provoke interest in subjects and should include descriptive information about fields of knowledge.
3. Teachers should be prepared to assist students with a variety of exploratory activities, depending on the nature of the topic being explored.

The group training activities (type II) are designed "to develop in the learner the processes or operations (the 'power of mind') that enable him or her to deal more effectively with content" (Renzulli, 1977, pp. 24–25). The training activities are to stimulate open-ended responses that enable learners to become more fluent, flexible, and original thinkers and problem solvers. They often include games and simulation exercises. Since all students can profit from increasing their creative abilities, awareness of feelings, and problem-solving abilities, type II activities can be used with all children.

The real focus of Renzulli's model is the small-group investigation of real problems, type III enrichment. Renzulli and Smith describe these activities.

> In these types of activities, the student emulates the practicing profes-
> sional within given fields of endeavor and hopefully becomes a first-
> hand inquirer him or herself. Although students doing this type of
> advanced work may draw upon existing knowledge, their purpose
> in doing so is not simply to rewrite or summarize information that
> is already known. Rather, their primary goal is to solve an existing
> problem, to add to present bodies of knowledge, or to create an
> artistic product that is relatively new to a given field. These contri-
> butions, in turn, are shared with well-defined target audiences which
> can give meaningful and productive feedback to the young scientist,
> author or artist. (Renzulli and Smith, 1980, p. 7)

Figure 9.3 illustrates the enrichment triad model and shows how the three types of activities mutually influence one another.

The regular curriculum, the general environment, type I activities, and type II activities all provide stimulation for type III real life investigations. Teachers of the gifted, says Renzulli (1977), must help these students translate and focus a general concern into a solvable problem; must provide students with the tools and methods necessary to solve the problem (e.g., reference books, journals, indexes, etc.); and must help students communicate their findings to appropriate audiences.

## Figure 9.3  The Enrichment Triad Model

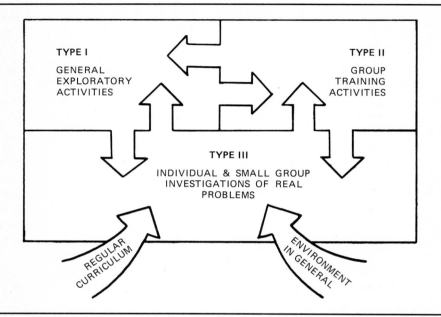

From Renzulli, J. S., *The Enrichment Triad Model: A Guide for Developing Defensible Programs for the Gifted and Talented* (Mansfield Center, Conn.: Creative Learning Press, 1977), p. 14. Reprinted by permission.

## The Enrichment Triad in a Developmental Reading Course

Noyce (1981) recently suggested that reading instructors consider using Renzulli's enrichment triad in reading classes. The following examples of its application to a reading class are adapted from her article.

### Example 1   Type I Enrichment: General Exploratory

Mr. Jones, a middle school reading teacher, plans to assign a brief selection on careers. As an extension of this lesson he has decided to establish a Career Interest Center. This center contains books, magazines, pamphlets, filmstrips, and videotapes related to careers. In addition to the information on the various careers, the center also includes biographies of successful people in different careers and how-to-do-it books related to careers.

Mr. Jones encourages students to add their own materials to the interest center. Mr. Jones also plans to have guest speakers, including parents, talk to the class about their careers. The class will take some field trips to observe people at their jobs. The loci of the field trips will be determined, in part, by the results of an interest inventory students completed at home and brainstorming sessions they had in class.

## Example 2    Type II Enrichment: Group Training Activities

Now that his students have had the opportunity to explore careers, Mr. Jones conducts group activities. In these activities the students do the following:

- Discuss what they have learned.
- Compare/contrast different types of careers.
- Evaluate the quality of the published information on careers.
- Reveal careers of particular interest to them.
- Relate personal values to career interests.
- Categorize/classify careers.
- Reveal new appreciations for different careers.
- Hypothesize about careers that do not presently exist.

## Example 3    Type III Enrichment: Investigate Real Problems

At this point some of Mr. Jones's students decided that the school library could use a career center so that other students would have access to what they learned about careers. Those students who revealed a sincere interest in this project took on the responsibility of acquiring more raw data from books, pamphlets, interviews, surveys, and observations. From this data they produced their own career center that was the result of firsthand inquiries, designed for a real audience, and the result of their own techniques and methods for gathering information.

These examples illustrate how students moved from exploring a topic on a general basis, to participating in group training activities related to that topic, and, finally, for some students, to producing, as firsthand inquirers, a product related to that topic. Resourceful content area teachers can provide similar types of enrichment activities in their own classes.

## Rita Replies, Part II

Below are columnist Rita Ashley's suggestions to parents of special students.

Dear Frustrated,

If you have not already done so, you should immediately have a full assessment completed of Daniel's needs. You are entitled to this under Public Law 94–142. I realize you said he's been tested a great deal, but you have a right to demand a complete educational and, if necessary, psychological assessment of your child. An individualized educational plan (IEP) for Daniel, which will outline a specialized program for him, will then be written.

Perhaps your child is dyslexic. It doesn't matter what you call it. The fact is that you want to get some intensified assistance for Daniel. Call the school immediately and tell them you want an evaluation and an individualized educational plan.

You should also contact these agencies for help: The Association of Children with Learning Disabilities (ACLD), 5225 Grace Street, Pittsburgh, Pa. 15236; The Orton Society, 8415 Belonia Lane, Towson, Md. 21204; The International Reading Association, 800 Barksdale Road, Newark, Del. 19711; and The Council for Exceptional Children, 1920 Association Drive, Reston, Va. 22091.

Daniel is not alone with his problems. Keep trying. He'll make it!

Rita

## Conclusion

It is clear that for students to carry out the activities described in these different models, their reading comprehension and study skills would have to be highly developed, and teachers would have to emphasize reading at the higher levels of comprehension. For example, gifted students would probably be more involved with the tasks associated with Barrett's inference and evaluation levels of comprehension and with the activities associated with Herber's applied level of comprehension. Gifted students would also have to be highly competent in the self-directed study skills discussed in Chapter 6.

Dear Wondering,

You have good reason to wonder. I'm wondering, too, . . . wondering that you may have a gifted and talented child who is not being challenged in school. Make an appointment to see Sharon's guidance counselor and principal. Tell them about your concerns and ask them how they might be able to establish a more challenging program for Sharon. Find out if your school system has a special program for the gifted and talented student.

Perhaps the school has an advanced placement or accelerated program or special tutoring. But it will first be important to identify Sharon's particular gifts and talents and her social maturity.

If the school system has no program for the gifted and talented, lobby for one. Find parents of other gifted and talented students and present your case to the school board. They'll listen, and chances are that they'll support a program. I also suggest you get information from organizations such as these: The American Association for Gifted Children (AAGC), 15 Gramercy Park, New York, N.Y. 10003; The Gifted Child Society, Inc., 59 Glen Gray Road, Oakland, N. J. 07436; U.S. Office of Education, The Office of Gifted and Talented, Donohue Building, Room 3835, 400 Maryland Avenue, S.W., Washington, D.C. 20202; and Parents for the Advancement of Gifted Education, 5015 Glenwood Avenue, Raleigh, N.C. 27612.

Good Luck!

Rita

## Summary

Two special populations that are included in the classrooms of many content area and reading specialists are the learning-disabled and the gifted and talented. The learning-disabled often exhibit weaknesses in processing information through visual and auditory modalities. They are easily confused and often delayed in their language development. The vast majority of learning-disabled students are placed in special programs as outlined in their individualized education plans. Most are also integrated with regular education classes.

Teachers can differentiate programs for the learning-disabled by carefully monitoring their work, helping them to compensate for their visual and auditory problems, and developing their comprehension and test-taking skills. Teachers must become more sensitive to the needs of the learning-disabled students. Otherwise many of these students will find their school experiences confusing and frustrating.

Gifted and talented adolescents have some characteristics that differentiate them from their peers. Unfortunately, the needs of gifted students often are not met because some parents and teachers do not place any particular value on their special abilities. Regular classroom teachers can help gifted students attain their potential by first identifying them and then adjusting their curriculum and instruction to meet their needs.

Before appropriate instruction can be planned for the gifted, they must be identified through the use of IQ and achievement tests, creativity tests, rating scales, and parent/peer and self-identification procedures. Teachers can differentiate instruction for their gifted students by adopting, adapting, or modifying different models that have been developed for gifted and talented students. This activity should be a high priority for all educators, for the gifted are a precious, natural resource of society.

# Bibliography

Blake, Kathryn A. *Educating Exceptional Pupils.* Reading, Mass.: Addison-Wesley, 1981.

Bryan, Tanis H., and James H. Bryan. *Understanding Learning Disabilities.* 2nd ed. Sherman Oaks, Calif.: Alfred Publishing, 1978.

Datnow, Claire. "The Cumulative Learning Effect: A Model for Coordinating Educational Opportunities for Gifted Students." *G/C/T* 3(1980):54–57.

Feldhusen, John F., and Margaret B. Kolloff. "A Three Stage Model for Gifted Education." *G/C/T* 1(1978):3–5,53–58.

Frostig, Marianne, D. W. Lefever, and J. R. B. Whittlesey. *The Marianne Frostig Developmental Test of Visual Perception.* Palo Alto, Calif.: Consulting Psychology Press, 1964.

Gleason, George, and Norris Haring. "Learning Disabilities." In *Behavior of Exceptional Children, An Introduction to Special Education,* edited by Norris G. Haring. Columbus, Ohio: Merrill, 1974.

Good, Thomas L. "Teacher Expectations and Student Perceptions: A Decade of Research." *Educational Leadership* 38(1981):415–422.

Guilford, J. B. *The Nature of Human Intelligence.* New York: McGraw-Hill, 1967.

Hallahan, Daniel P., and James H. Kauffman. *Exceptional Children, Introduction to Special Education.* Englewood Cliffs, N.J.: Prentice-Hall, 1978.

Joynes, Yvonne, Sandra McCormick, and William E. Heward. "Teaching Reading Disabled Students to Read and Complete Employment Applications." *Journal of Reading* 23(1980):709–714.

Kahn, Michael S. "The Answer to 'What Did You Say.' " *New England Reading Association Journal* 13(1978):33–35.

————. "Learning Problems of the Secondary and Junior College Learning Disabled Student: Suggested Remedies." *Journal of Learning Disabilities* 13(1980):40–44.

Kirk, Samuel A., Sister Joanne Marie Kliebhan, and Janet W. Lerner. *Teaching Reading to Slow and Disabled Learners.* Boston: Houghton Mifflin, 1978.

Kirk, Samuel A., J. J. McCarthy, and W. D. Kirk. *Illinois Test of Psycholinguistic Abilities.* Urbana: University of Illinois Press, 1961, 1968.

Lerner, Janet W. *Children with Learning Disabilities.* 2nd ed. Boston: Houghton Mifflin, 1976.

Lindsey, Jimmy D. "The Experience of Learning Disability: A Qualitative Time Series Study." Unpublished manuscript, Louisiana State University, 1981.

Lindsey, Jimmy D., and Marcella A. Kerlin. "Learning Disabilities and Reading Disorders: A Brief Reveiw of the Secondary Level Literature." *Journal of Learning Disabilities* 12(1979):55–61.

McCullough, Barbara, and Gene Towery. "Your Horoscope Predicts: You Can Teach Students to Follow Directions." *Journal of Reading* 19(1976):653–659.

Mann, Lester, Libby Goodman, and J. Lee Wiederholt. *Teaching the Learning Disabled Adolescent.* Boston: Houghton Mifflin, 1978.

Manzo, Anthony V. "The Request Procedure." *Journal of Reading* 13(1969):123–126, 163.

Marland, Sidney. *Education of the Gifted and Talented: Report to the Congress of the United States by the U.S. Commissioner of Education and Background Papers Submitted to the U.S. Office of Education.* Washington, D.C.: Government Printing Office, 1972.

Noyce, Ruth M. "Try the Enrichment Triad in Reading Class." *Journal of Reading* 24(1981):326–330.

Plowman, Paul D. *Teaching the Gifted and Talented in the Social Studies Classroom.* Washington, D.C.: National Education Association, 1980.

Renzulli, Joseph S. *The Enrichment Triad Model: A Guide for Developing Defensible Programs for the Gifted and Talented.* Mansfield Center, Conn.: Creative Learning Press, 1977.

Renzulli, Joseph S., and Linda H. Smith. "An Alternative Approach to Identifying and Programming for Gifted and Talented Students." *G/C/T* 3(1980):4–11.

Romney, William D. *Teaching the Gifted and Talented in the Science Classroom.* Washington, D.C.: National Education Association, 1980.

Santeusanio, Richard P., and Alphonse Tatarunis. "Reading for the Gifted." Paper presented at the Twelfth Annual Conference of the Massachusetts Reading Association, April 10, 1981, Worcester, Mass.

Savage, John F., and Jean F. Mooney. *Teaching Reading to Children with Special Needs.* Boston: Allyn & Bacon, 1979.

Torrance, E. Paul. *Guiding Creative Talent.* Englewood Cliffs, N.J.: Prentice-Hall, 1962.

Treffinger, Donald J. "Teaching for Self-Directed Learning: A Priority for the Gifted and Talented." *Gifted Child Quarterly* 19(1975):46–59.

Treffinger, Donald J., and Betty L. Barton. "Fostering Independent Learning." *G/C/T* 2(1979):3–6,54.

Tuttle, Frederick B., Jr. *Gifted and Talented Students.* Washington, D.C.: National Education Association; 1978.

Tuttle, Frederick B., Jr., and Laurence A. Becker. *Characteristics and Identification of Gifted and Talented Students.* Washington, D.C.: National Education Association, 1980.

West, William W. *Teaching the Gifted and Talented in the English Classroom.* Washington, D.C.: National Education Association, 1980.

# Chapter 10

# Summing Up

# Introduction

Both content area teachers and reading specialists have the responsibility of helping their students master the content of their textbooks. Students must be guided in techniques of how to read and study the books assigned to them.

As teachers provide this guidance, they should keep in mind that reading is an active thinking process involving the interaction of readers and writers. The major task of their students is to reconstruct, critically analyze, and remember the ideas that authors have put into writing. There are many practical ways teachers can help their students remember what they have read. Furthermore, teachers can provide assistance before, during, and after their students read the assignments.

# Providing Assistance

## Before Reading

Prior to asking students to complete the reading of a new assignment, teachers can prepare them for that reading. Many students need to experience some readiness activities in order to successfully acquire the information and ideas contained in the reading assignment. Readiness activities include previewing and reinforcing vocabulary words contained in the reading assignment, preparing structured overviews, writing advanced organizers, surveying chapters, sharing instructional objectives related to the assignment, and implementing the prereading plan (PReP).

Teachers can utilize one and possibly two of these activities for each new reading assignment. They can vary the activities from assignment to assignment. Or if they find that one or two are particularly successful, they can use them fairly consistently.

## During and After Reading

As students delve into the reading of their assignment, they will comprehend it better if they have an awareness of its organizational pattern and are provided with some assistance in reconstructing the ideas contained in the assignment. Teachers can help students by providing them with direct instruction and by preparing reading guides and adjunct questions.

It is important for students to learn how to generate main ideas from what they read and to see how details support main ideas. The main idea/details pattern provides the foundation for all the other organizational patterns, including the data, sequence, cause/effect, problem/solution, and persuasive patterns.

Students can learn how to retain the information gained from their reading by developing self-directed study skills. Teachers can introduce and teach students study skills such as the SQ3R and OK5R study systems, note taking, underlining and outlining, mapping, test taking, and flexibility of reading rates.

When teachers have prepared students for their reading assignment, assisted them with comprehending the information contained in the reading, and demonstrated ways they can retain that information, they have contributed greatly to their students' success in mastering the content of their reading assignments. The steps leading to mastery are outlined in Fig. 10.1.

While appropriate for the majority of their students, some of these procedures may be inappropriate for those with special needs, such as the learning-disabled and the gifted. For these students, teachers will have to adopt a more flexible teaching style, vary the nature of their assignments, and adjust their expectations.

Teachers can be better prepared to meet the needs of *all* their students if they take the time to identify their instructional needs and learning styles near the beginning of the year. They can do so by administering evaluation instruments such as achievement tests, cloze tests, group inventories, individual assessments, and learning style inventories. Teachers can also make better decisions about new textbook adoptions if they first apply readability formulas to them and evaluate them with respect to their authorship, vocabulary, concepts, content presentation, and so on.

The topics reviewed thus far in this chapter are included in some content area reading programs. However, a variety of approaches are used to implement content area reading programs. These approaches are described in the following section.

# Approaches to Implementing Content Area Reading Programs

## Functional Approach and Consulting Teachers

When content area programs are approached in a *functional way,* the teaching of reading skills is left up to the content area teachers. The skills are taught according to the nature of the teacher's assignment (Herber, 1978). If, for example, the assignment calls for cause/effect reasoning, then that skill is taught

# Figure 10.1  Steps Leading to Mastery of Reading Assignments

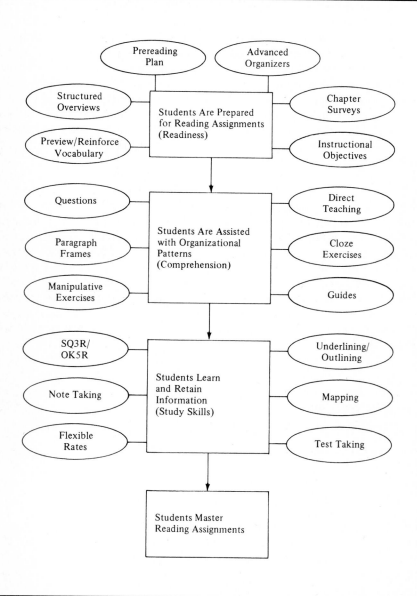

in the context of the reading assignment. This practice reinforces the idea to students that reading is a process, not a subject. But regardless of their good intentions and the fine pre- and in-service training they may have received, content teachers may still neglect to integrate the teaching of reading skills with the teaching of content.

However, when a *consulting reading teacher* is available to work hand in hand with the content teacher, school systems are "likely to end up with a content teacher who knows *how* to teach and *is* teaching students how to read and learn from text." (Singer and Donlan, 1980, p. 475). This outcome results because the consulting reading teacher has worked so closely with both the content teachers *and* their students. (There are many variations of this role of the reading specialist as a consulting teacher of reading. In Reading, Massachusetts, for example, the reading specialists assist content teachers to a large extent with their research paper assignments because this activity involves the use of so many reading and study skills.)

How do consulting reading teachers organize their programs? First they identify a content teacher who is interested in receiving assistance. This step can be done effectively through informal conversation in places like the teachers' lounge. The content teacher and the reading specialist then have a planning session. Together they construct lesson plans and decide on which of the reading/study skills to stress with the particular lesson to be presented. The first few classes are presented by the reading specialist. The next few are team-taught. Finally, the content teacher presents the lesson alone. This gradual phasing in and phasing out on the part of the reading specialist takes place for a period of three to four weeks. Then the cycle begins again with a new content area teacher.

When working with content teachers, wise reading specialists keep in mind some of the caveats offered by Devan (1977) and Readence, Baldwin, and Dishner (1980). They keep their lessons and recommendations reasonably simple and use workable, realistic techniques. For example, rather than suggest that teachers write advanced organizers, they demonstrate a lesson on chapter surveys. Rather than ask teachers to complete an individual reading inventory on each student, they suggest using the group cloze procedure for classroom diagnosis.

Sensible reading specialists do not claim they will achieve instant success and they do not pretend to have all the answers to every problem. They do not ignore department chairpersons; in fact, they explain their role and offer their services at department meetings. As Readance, Baldwin, and Dishner (1980) put it, reading specialists should try to "hook" the department heads.

It should be remembered that despite good intentions and careful attempts at cultivating teachers and administrators, not all are willing to entertain the idea of having outside visitors in their departments and classes. It is, of course, expensive and time-consuming to develop a content area reading program with the consulting teacher as its core.

## Direct Skills Approach

When the *direct skills approach* is used, most content reading instruction is provided by the reading specialists. The specialists focus on a skill, teach it by using original and commercially prepared materials, and then use relevant textbook passages or chapters to help students apply the skill to content areas. This approach is given great emphasis in some school systems and sometimes involves both the reading specialists and the content teacher in the direct teaching of skills.

For example, in one school system all teachers of academic subjects literally become teachers of reading. In this program students attend a reading class daily, which is taught by either a reading specialist or content area teachers who have received in-service training. Students proceed through a sequence of different reading and study skills, each of which is taught for about two weeks. At the end of this time students are exposed to a different teacher and a different skill.

Content teachers in this program become specialists in the teaching of at least two skills. They may, for example, specialize in main idea and note taking, or in sequence and graphs. The instructors become familiar with commercial materials that stress the skills for which they are responsible, teach with these materials, and then help students apply the skills to subject matter textbooks. Reading specialists teach longer units on "Reading the Newspaper" and "Speed Reading." A unit on library skills is taught by the librarian/media specialist. There is also a supervised unit on independent or sustained silent reading.

Another school system implemented the direct skills approach by organizing the reading classes around the skills most germane to various content areas. The reading curriculum is divided into four quarter-long units. Students rotate each semester; by the end of the year they have completed units on "Reading in Science," "Reading in Mathematics," "Reading in English," and "Reading in Social Studies." Each of these units is taught by the content area teachers who received in-service training. Students attend their classes on a six-day cycle; teachers devote two of these periods exclusively to teaching reading skills that are particularly important to their content area. For instance, the mathematics teacher might focus on reading and interpreting problems, tables, charts, and graphs. The social studies teacher might focus on critical reading and organizational patterns. The English teacher might focus on pleasure reading and research skills, and, finally, the science teacher might focus on following directions, root words, and affixes. Both commercial skills materials and the regular textbooks are used to teach the skills.

Since students rotate each quarter in this program, content teachers only have to prepare one quarter-long reading skills unit. Because students receive their content instruction from the same teachers who teach reading instruction, the likelihood of applying reading skills to specific content areas is enhanced.

In this program reading specialists primarily teach the remedial students. They also serve as a resource to the content area teachers and sometimes team-teach with them during skills lessons.

The direct skills approach has the disadvantage of reinforcing the idea that reading is a subject rather than a process. However, this approach ensures that all students will receive at least *some* content area reading instruction, and they may begin to independently apply the skills to their textbooks.

## Support Services Approach

In a *support services approach* reading specialists or Title I teachers become responsible, on a limited basis, for teaching specific subject matter to students who are poor readers. For one or two periods a week students report to the specialist instead of the content teacher. A social studies teacher, for example, gives the assigned pages to the Title I teacher but leaves the method of study to the discretion of the specialist. After analyzing the assignment, the specialist emphasizes the skills needed to master the content of the assignment and then teaches those skills by using the textbook as the content of the lesson.

Content teachers sometimes agree to give extra credit to students who complete special projects in the reading class. One such extra-credit project is constructing original crossword puzzles of selected vocabulary words from the reading assignments. Often the content teacher uses these puzzles with the entire class as a review exercise. When teachers use this approach, they tend to increase the remedial student's sense of self-esteem.

When support services are the only type of content area reading services available in a school system, only a few students benefit from them. But the small-group instruction is likely to significantly help remedial students cope with their content assignments.

## Separate Developmental Reading Course

Cooper and Petrosky (1976) believe it is unlikely that content area teachers will, on a large scale, accept the responsibility for teaching their students the reading/study skills they need to master subject matter areas. They therefore recommend that all students be required to complete a one-semester developmental reading course in the first semester of grade 7 and in the first semester of either grade 9 or grade 10.

This *reading strategies course* is based on a psycholinguistic–information-processing model of the fluent reading process. The premise of the model is that fluent readers are language users who respond to the written page and work at "reconstructing a message encoded in the graphic display by the writer"

(Goodman, 1969, p. 11). Readers select productive cues from the graphic display in order to produce guesses about the writer's meaning. Reader anticipation is important in this "psycholinguistic guessing game" (Goodman, 1967). Readers draw on previous life experience (schema theory), and their experiences with and knowledge of language help them make logical predictions or guesses at words and meanings they encounter in print.

Students are exposed to four basic activities in this course: sustained silent reading, content area reading, sentence manipulation games, and rapid reading exercises. In sustained silent reading (SSR), students freely select books, which are read for two or three of the days the class meets each week. Students periodically confer with their instructor (who also reads when she is not conferring) and keep an informal log of their reactions to their reading. The purpose of SSR days is to give students the opportunity to "get continuous quantity practice in the reading strategies natural to the reading process" (Cooper and Petrosky, 1976, p. 200).

On days when content area reading activities are taught, students learn study skill techniques like PQ4R and mapping. They also study vocabulary from their textbooks and become acquainted with the various organizational patterns.

Some time is also spent on sentence manipulation games and cloze passages. The purpose of these activities is to increase "students' insightfulness about redundancy in printed text" (Cooper and Petrosky, 1976, p. 203). Finally, students participate in an informal speed reading program designed to sensitize students to flexible reading rates.

The only instructional materials for this course are trade books and textbooks. There are no machines, boxes of cards, or commercial workbooks, because such materials do not enhance the strategies natural to the reading process.

To summarize, the separate developmental reading course stresses increasing students' facility as users of language. Students participate in sustained silent reading, content reading activities, sentence manipulation games, and rapid reading instruction. Trade books and textbooks are used exclusively for instructional material. Despite this positive feature, and the fact that practically all students participate in the program, this approach still has the disadvantage of leaving all the responsibility for improving content reading in the hands of the reading teacher.

# A Comprehensive Secondary Reading Program

Ultimately all school systems may want to strive to develop the type of comprehensive secondary reading program described by Peters (1977). The *comprehensive program* has as its focal point the *content teacher*, who interacts

## Figure 10.2  Model for a Comprehensive Reading Program at the Secondary Level

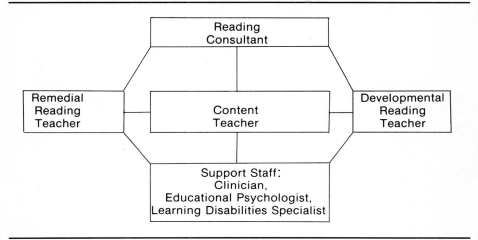

From Charles W. Peters, "How to Get More Comprehensive Reading Programs at the Secondary Level," *Journal of Reading* 20(1979):516. Reprinted with permission of Charles W. Peters and the International Reading Association.

and cooperates with the reading consultant, developmental reading teacher, remedial reading or Title I teacher, and the support staff. See Fig. 10.2.

The *reading consultant* is an administrator who works with teachers, support staff, and building administrators in developing content area reading programs and in establishing and maintaining communication between other elements of the program. The *developmental reading teacher* teaches reading courses to all but the disabled reader and tries to work closely with the content teacher in order to reinforce mutually taught skills. The *remedial reading specialist* works with the disabled readers and also communicates with the content teachers with respect to the educational needs of the disabled readers. The *support staff* consists of psychologists or counselors, the learning disabilities specialists, and administrators. They work with all others in providing ancillary services that contribute to the success of the program.

While this approach may appear to represent an ideal model, it is one worth emulating. Without the ideal model, there is nothing to strive for—reality is built on dreams.

# Bibliography

Cooper, Charles R., and Anthony R. Petrosky. "A Psycholinguistic View of the Fluent Reading Process." *Journal of Reading* 20(1976):184–207.

Devan, Steven. "Strategies for Resource Teachers in the High School." *Journal of Reading* 21(1977):131–133

Goodman, Kenneth S. "Reading: A Psycholinguistic Guessing Game." *Journal of the Reading Specialist* 4(1967):126–135.

―――. "Analysis of Oral Reading Miscues: Applied Psycholinguistics." *Reading Research Quarterly* 5(1969):9–30.

Herber, Harold L. *Teaching Reading in Content Areas.* 2nd ed. Englewood Cliffs, N.J.: Prentice-Hall, 1978.

Peters, Charles W. "How to Get More Comprehensive Reading Programs at the Secondary Level." *Journal of Reading* 20(1977):513–519

Readance, John E., R. Scott Baldwin, and Ernest K. Dishner. "Establishing Content Reading Programs in Secondary Schools." *Journal of Reading* 23(1980):522–526.

Singer, Harry, and Dan Donlan. *Reading and Learning from Text.* Boston: Little, Brown, 1980.

# Index

## Names

# Subject